Asian American Comparative Collection Research Reports
Series editor, Priscilla Wegars

No. 1, 2005

Asian Americans and the Military's Academic Training Programs (ASTP, ASTRP) at the University of Idaho and Elsewhere during World War II
by Charles M. Rice

No. 2, 2007

Chinese Servants in the West: Florence Baillie-Grohman's "The Yellow and White Agony"
Edited, and with an introduction, by Terry Abraham

No. 3, 2010

Imprisoned in Paradise: Japanese Internee Road Workers at the World War II Kooskia Internment Camp
by Priscilla Wegars

Also by Priscilla Wegars

Uncovering a Chinese Legacy: Historical Archaeology at Centerville, Idaho, Once the "Handsomest Town in the Basin" (2001).

Golden State Meets Gem State: Californians at Idaho's Kooskia Internment Camp, 1943-1945 (2002).

Polly Bemis: A Chinese American Pioneer (2003*).*

As Editor or Co-Editor

Hidden Heritage: Historical Archaeology of the Overseas Chinese (1993).

Chinese American Death Rituals: Respecting the Ancestors, with Sue Fawn Chung (2005).

Major Articles

"Entrepreneurs and 'Wage Slaves': Their Relationship to Anti-Chinese Racism in Northern Idaho's Mining Labor Market, 1880-1910." In *Racism and the Labour Market: Historical Studies*, ed. Marcel van der Linden and Jan Lucassen (1995).

"Japanese and Japanese Latin Americans at Idaho's Kooskia Internment Camp." In *Guilt by Association: Essays on Japanese Settlement, Internment, and Relocation in the Rocky Mountain West*, ed. Mike Mackey (2001).

"From Old Gold Mountain to New Gold Mountain: Chinese Archaeological Sites, Artefact Repositories, and Archives in Western North America and Australasia." In *Australasian Historical Archaeology* (2003).

"Polly Bemis: Lurid Life or Literary Legend?" In *Wild Women of the Old West*, ed. Glenda Riley and Richard W. Etulain (2003).

"World War II Kooskia Internment Camp." In *Idaho Yesterdays* (2005).

"The Asian American Comparative Collection: A Unique Resource for Archaeologists and Historians." In *Historical Archaeology* (2008).

IMPRISONED IN PARADISE:
Japanese Internee Road Workers at the World War II Kooskia Internment Camp

Author **Priscilla Wegars** is the volunteer curator of the University of Idaho's Asian American Comparative Collection (AACC), a resource center of artifacts, images, and bibliographical materials that help a wide range of individuals better understand the history, culture, and archaeology of Asian Americans in the West. She has a Ph.D. in history from the University of Idaho, Moscow, and is also an independent editor, historian, historical archaeologist, and artifact analyst. Her earlier research focused on Chinese immigrants in the West, and her book, *Polly Bemis: A Chinese American Pioneer* (Cambridge, ID: Backeddy Books, 2003), received an Honorable Mention as the Idaho Book of the Year from the Idaho Library Association.

Foreword author **Michiko Midge Ayukawa** is a well-known historian of, and consultant on, the Japanese Canadian experience before, during, and after World War II. She holds a Ph.D. from the University of Victoria, British Columbia, and has published and lectured widely on Japanese Canadian history. Her most recent book is *Hiroshima Immigrants in Canada 1891-1941* (Vancouver: University of British Columbia, 2007).

Kooskia Internment Camp sign. Courtesy Kooskia Internment Camp Scrapbook, Historical Photograph Collection, University of Idaho Library (henceforth, Scrapbook), PG 103-03-1.

IMPRISONED IN PARADISE:
Japanese Internee Road Workers at the World War II Kooskia Internment Camp

Priscilla Wegars

With a Foreword by
Michiko Midge Ayukawa

*Best wishes,
Priscilla Wegars*

Asian American Comparative Collection
University of Idaho, Moscow, Idaho
2010

Asian American Comparative Collection Research Report, No. 3

ISBN 978-0-89301-550-3

All author's royalties from the sale of this book benefit the
Asian American Comparative Collection
Laboratory of Anthropology
Department of Sociology/Anthropology
University of Idaho
P. O. Box 441111
Moscow, Idaho 83844-1111
http://www.uiweb.uidaho.edu/LS/AACC/

Dedication

To the memory of Kooskia internees James Isao Yano and Koshio Henry Shima, in gratitude for their willingness to share their personal experiences with me, and to the memory of all other Kooskia internees, especially Hozen Seki.

To the memory of Kooskia employees Cecil Boller and Amelia Jacks, with grateful thanks for all their help, and to the memory of all other Kooskia employees.

To my wonderful husband, Terry Abraham: computer wizard, eagle-eyed editor, and hardy survivor of innumerable Kooskia-related adventures and futile photo replication forays.

Contents

List of Illustrations

Foreword

Although the Kooskia Internment Camp was the only one like it in the U.S. during World War II, Canada had four road projects with over thirty individual road construction camps for Japanese Canadian internees. Japanese road workers at the World War II Kooskia Internment Camp may have been "Imprisoned in Paradise" but I have never heard the term applied to any of the road camps in Canada.

Three of the road projects were in British Columbia. They held men segregated according to their citizenship status.[1] The Issei (first generation, born in Japan) were sent to the Yellowhead-Blue River project; the "naturalized Japanese-born" and many Nisei (second generation, born in Canada) went to the other two – the Hope-Princeton and the Sicamous-Revelstoke projects. Young, single, able-bodied Nisei were sent to the Schreiber road project in northern Ontario.

The Issei, termed "enemy aliens," were "evacuated" as early as late February 1942 to the Yellowhead-Blue River project. The authorities took great pains to avoid calling it an "internment camp," because otherwise they would incur greatly increased costs from the necessity of complying with the rules of the Geneva Convention, a 1929 international agreement specifying appropriate treatment for prisoners of war, later extended to internees. Although it was still winter, the men slept in tents and railway boxcars until they themselves built log houses using the nearby trees. The foremen and overseers were all Caucasians and their actions often led to grievances. The Issei had no recourse but to "sit down" or "slow down." Stronger acts of protest would have caused them to be sent to the Angler Internment Camp in northern Ontario where hundreds of protesters were imprisoned. The internees in Angler included a number of Nisei who had demanded, unsuccessfully, that they be evacuated together with their young families and elderly parents.

In all the camps, the men labored with pick and shovel but they found ways of bringing some joy to their everyday existence. They formed baseball teams and played against other camps. Some created vegetable gardens to supplement their diet and others, beautiful Japanese gardens to feed their souls.

The Canadian Japanese internees were paid $50 a month. Unlike the U.S. internees, who could keep all their wages, the Canadians had $20 deducted for their families and another $22.50 subtracted for their room and board. This left very little, just $7.50 per month, for their own use. Moreover, office and postal delays often left their families destitute, giving the internees yet another reason to protest.

Meanwhile, families from coastal towns were gathered into the live-stock barns at the site of the Pacific National Exhibition, Hastings Park, in Vancouver, British Columbia. It was soon obvious that this could only be a temporary solution. Old, empty buildings near abandoned mine sites in the interior of British Columbia were prepared for the families. Needing still more family housing, the British Columbia Security Commission rented ranchland from local farmers and built shacks with green lumber. Men in the road camps agitated to be sent to help build the houses. As a result, some were labeled "troublemakers" and were sent to the Angler Internment Camp.

My father, Kenji Ishii, an Issei carpenter, was given twenty-four hours' notice in mid-March 1942 to go to Thunder River, one of the work camps on the Yellowhead-Blue River Road project. I have photos of him sitting on the roof of one of the log houses the carpenter crew built, another image of the mess hall table and benches, and one of the crew posing in front of a bridge that they had built across the Thunder River.

In the 1990s a friend and I drove along the Yellowhead Highway from Jasper to Kamloops in search of the camp at Thunder River. We managed to find the site. There were few traces of the camp except a log, ten to twelve feet long, cut in half longitudinally (it could have been one of the benches in the mess hall), and the base of the bridge across the Thunder River.

Papa had always been "mad about baseball," as a spectator. It seems that he was finally able to now play, although he was forty-seven years old. One day in May 1942, a Japanese man who had been at the same camp returned to Vancouver to join his family (I don't know the details of how he managed this). He visited my mother and told her my father had been injured playing ball. She was horrified and expressed her disgust!

Later, when my mother heard that men were being sent to the Slocan Val-ley to build houses for the families, she went to some office in Japantown and told them her husband was a professional carpenter and surely he should be transferred to help out there. My father did return for several days to Vancouver in May or June. (I am not certain as to when but I was still going to school.) He was then sent to Slocan where my elder brother had been sent earlier. We followed in September.

The road camps were gradually closed as the men were reunited with their families. By March 1946 there were still ninety-five single men at the Yellowhead-Blue River camps. They had signed to be repatriated to Japan but twenty-four reconsidered and did not go there; the rest presumably did return to Japan to rejoin their families.

A roadside sign with a map showing the location of the camps has been erected on a pullout at Lucerne Lake on the present-day Highway 16, the Yellowhead Highway. It was erected by the Province of British Columbia following a crusade by Frank Kiyooka and the Japanese Canadian Redress Foundation.

Michiko Midge Ayukawa

Preface

The text of the ... [Geneva C]onvention ... shall be posted, wherever possible in the native language of the prisoners of war, in places where it may be consulted by all the prisoners.
Geneva Convention, Article 84.

Following a lecture on the World War II internment and incarceration of Japanese Americans, a fellow audience member asked the visiting professor, "Can you tell us about the Japanese at the Kooskia Internment Camp? In 1943, when I was in high school, we went down to the train station at Kooskia and saw them get off the train."[1] Just over fifty years later, Idaho's Kooskia Internment Camp was so obscure that the noted expert had "never heard of it."[2]

Background

From the early 1930s through the mid-1940s, hundreds of men, from all over the United States and from several foreign countries, ventured to the remote Idaho wilderness for employment with the Civilian Conservation Corps (CCC) or incarceration by the Bureau of Prisons (BP) and the Immigration and Naturalization Service (INS).[3] All had volunteered for their jobs, but on arrival most were not free to leave.

Of the work camps associated with these groups, the most significant, and least known, is the INS's Kooskia (pronounced KOOS-key) Internment Camp, a virtually forgotten World War II detention facility that the INS operated for the Justice Department between late May 1943 and early May 1945 in a remote area of north central Idaho.[4] This unique wartime experiment was a road building project employing Japanese alien internee volunteers.

Housing the Kooskia Internment Camp in this pristine wilderness presented a paradox between the spectacular beauty of the surroundings and the injustice of the Japanese aliens' incarceration. Tommy Yoshito Kadotani called it "… a paradise in mountains!," saying, "It reminds me so much of Yosemite National Park."[5] Since Kadotani, a landscape gardener from California, came to the Kooskia camp from the Santa Fe Internment Camp, in the New Mexico desert, the Kooskia camp site must have seemed like "paradise" in comparison. By early July, the internees realized, instead, that they were actually "shut off from the rest of world and living in the 'Noman [no man's] land.'"[6]

Prior to the Kooskia camp's establishment, the location formerly housed a CCC camp, from mid-June to mid-October 1933, and subsequently the BP's Canyon Creek Prison Camp, from late August 1935 to late May 1943.[7] Legacies of the two groups, expressed in buildings and activities, determined the placement of the later Kooskia Internment Camp at that exact location, as well as the work that the internees performed while there. Also in Idaho, but unrelated to the Kooskia Internment Camp, was the Minidoka "relocation" camp in southern Idaho, near Hunt. This much larger War Relocation Authority (WRA) incarceration camp housed West Coast families of Japanese descent, mainly from Alaska, Oregon, and Washington. Some of the Kooskia internees had family members confined at Minidoka.

Over time, the Kooskia camp's Japanese internees eventually numbered about 265 men, all so-called "enemy aliens" who were previously detained in other INS camps.[8] They volunteered to become road workers in Idaho and received wages for their labor. However, this is far from being just an "Idaho story." The Kooskia internees came from numerous states, from the then-territories of Alaska and Hawai'i; from Mexico, and were even kidnapped from Panama and Peru. Depending upon their origins and education, they spoke Japanese, English, and/or Spanish. The camp's civilian employees, including several women, numbered about twenty-five. During the second year of operation, a Japanese American man joined the staff as interpreter, translator, and censor. Two successive internee doctors, an Italian and a German, provided medical services to the internees and employees. With its national, international, and polyglot component of internees, shunted from camp to camp in the early years of the war, the Kooskia camp became a microcosm of the wider internment camp experience. Perhaps more so than at any other internment or incarceration camp, the Kooskia internees had interconnections with many other Japanese American World War II confinement sites, e.g., Camp Livingston, Louisiana; Crystal City, Texas; Kenedy, Texas; Fort Lincoln, Nebraska; Fort Meade, Maryland; Fort Missoula, Montana; Fort Richardson, Alaska; Lordsburg, New Mexico; Manzanar, California; Moab,

Utah; Minidoka, Idaho; Puyallup, Washington; Sand Island, Hawai'i; Santa Fe, New Mexico; Seattle, Washington; Seagoville, Texas; Sharp Park, California; Topaz, Utah; Tuna Canyon, California; and certainly others.[9]

Site History

While some of the internees held camp jobs, most of them were construction workers for the Lewis-Clark Highway, now U.S. Highway 12. Paralleling the path of the explorers for whom it was named, this road runs beside the wild and scenic Lochsa River and traverses the mountains between Lewiston, Idaho, and Missoula, Montana.

Centuries ago, the Nez Perce and other Native Americans established ridgetop trails through this wilderness, for use during their seasonal migrations. Subsequently, when the 1805-1806 Lewis and Clark Expedition belatedly learned that the rivers were not navigable; they, too, utilized the Nez Perce/Lolo Trail, as did subsequent adventurers.[10] General William Tecumseh Sherman, of Civil War fame, reportedly called the Lolo Trail "one of the worst trails for man and beast on the North American continent."[11]

From 1921 on, the Lewis-Clark Highway Association schemed on the local, state, and national level to get a road built between Idaho and Montana through the rugged Bitterroot Mountains.[12] In 1935, negotiations with the Bureau of Prisons resulted in the transfer of federal prisoners from the Leavenworth, Kansas, penitentiary to the vacant CCC camp at Canyon Creek. There they engaged in heavy-duty road work in exchange for shortened sentences. In later years, construction superintendent M. D. Bradshaw refuted public perceptions that the Canyon Creek Prison Camp was "a chain gang in the sense of armed guards or a brutal regimen." However, he recalled that the work "wasn't any job for pantywaists," adding, "It didn't take long to separate the men from the boys."[13]

The "politics of the road" involved machinations to enlist support from those in high places, even President Franklin D. Roosevelt (FDR). First approached in 1937, he subsequently "expressed familiarity with the project and made suggestions for construction work."[14] When the federal government increased support for the Canyon Creek Prison Camp, inmate numbers rose to two hundred. As the road steadily advanced, convict Ludwig (Lud) Freier, a member of the jackhammer crew, declared that the granite they sometimes encountered was "as hard as a district attorney's heart."[15] By early 1943, expenses related to U.S. involvement in World War II resulted in lessened appropriations for the prison system, so the Canyon Creek Prison Camp closed, making way for the Kooskia Internment Camp.

Although the Kooskia camp was the only one of its kind in the United States, there were similar facilities in western Canada and Ontario during

World War II.[16] That country also interned her Japanese aliens and removed her Japanese Canadian citizens inland from their coastal homes.[17] Since the Canadian road camps had no connection with, or influence on, the Kooskia Internment Camp, a detailed comparison of them with the Kooskia camp is beyond the scope of this book. Still, occasional mentions are made of activities or customs that the various camps had in common.

Research Materials

Documentary research in the National Archives and elsewhere located INS, U.S. Forest Service, and U.S. Border Patrol photographs and other records, as well as a photograph album owned by former Kooskia camp guard E. D. Moshier.[18] Individual internees' Closed Legal Case Files were especially helpful.[19] These, combined with internee and employee oral and written interviews, as well as one internee diary and a later reminiscence, illuminate the internees' experiences, emphasizing the perspectives of the men detained at the Kooskia camp.

Much additional information came from local newspapers. While they were very useful for depicting life at the Kooskia camp, sensitive readers may well cringe when reading certain contemporary newspaper articles. These often include the words "Japs" or the "Jap camp." Such terms were highly offensive to Japanese Americans then, and are even more so today, when many other members of the general public also perceive them as racist. Rather than change them to the awkward "Jap[ane]s[e]" or "Jap[anese] camp," however, they are left as they occur, with this writer's sincere apologies for the pain that will be caused by reading such hurtful words.

Terminology

Controversy has long surrounded the World War II "evacuation" and "relocation" of over one hundred twenty thousand Japanese Americans and Japanese permanent resident aliens. Although most people now recognize that such terms are euphemisms for what actually were horrendous violations of civil and human rights, others disagree. This dispute escalated in the 1980s, during debate on the U.S. government's apology, and redress payment, to survivors. Whereas certain writers contend that internment and incarceration were "justified by military necessity,"[20] the present author is firmly on the side of those who consider the event to be an egregious example of "racial profiling" before that term was coined.

In rejecting the euphemistic language of "evacuation" and "relocation" usually used to describe this shameful episode, scholars and survivors alike have introduced more appropriate, but still controversial, terminology to express the Japanese "internment" experience.[21] That word itself is the source of much misunderstanding. "Internment" is most accurately used to describe the detention of so-called "enemy aliens" in facilities such as the Kooskia Internment Camp. Run by the INS for the Justice Department, internment camps held Japanese, German, Italian, and other aliens, primarily men, whom the FBI had identified as "potentially dangerous" to national security during a declared state of war with their countries of citizenship.

Confusion exists because the term "internment camp" is often incorrectly used for the ten WRA camps that held mostly Japanese American citizens, together with many permanent resident aliens deemed not dangerous. Because these installations primarily confined U.S.-born Japanese Americans, they should more accurately be called concentration camps. The latter phrase was even used by FDR, in connection with Japanese Americans, as early as 1936.[22]

In October 1940, in a memo to FDR, Secretary of the Navy Frank Knox proposed fifteen ways in which the U.S. could impress Japan with our readiness for war. Number 12 directed the War and Justice departments, specifically the U.S. Army and the INS, to "Prepare plans for concentration camps."[23] Once work on the camps began, "the WRA and the army agreed … to explicitly forbid the use of the term 'concentration camps' as too negative and coercive."[24] As late as 1944 FDR belatedly recognized the possible unconstitutionality of incarcerating Japanese Americans in concentration camps.[25]

Although it is accurate to describe the WRA camps as prisons or concentration camps, the term "concentration camp" has come to typify Nazi Germany's horrific death and extermination camps.[26] Therefore, many people reject that designation as too severe to use in describing the WRA camps.[27] For example, before his death in 2003, a landowner bordering Idaho's Minidoka WRA camp "had threatened to place a large sign on his … property reading 'Remember Pearl Harbor' if the Park Service portrayed Minidoka as a concentration camp."[28]

Abandoning "concentration camp" to describe the WRA camps has, however, led to another terminological difficulty, wherein people now combine the contrasting WRA and INS installations under the common denominator of "internment camp," which is strictly accurate only for the INS camps. In order to distinguish between the two very different types of camps, the solution consists of choosing another word to describe the WRA facilities. The Densho Project, a group that exists "to preserve the testimonies of Japanese Americans who were unjustly incarcerated during World War II," suggests that the term "incarceration camp" is a better choice for the WRA camps because it more accurately describes them.[29] "Internment camp" can then be reserved for the INS camps.

The circumstances under which Japanese Americans were imprisoned provide further justification for the changed terminology. Even though the WRA detainees were not there to be murdered, their own government had forcibly assembled them, denied them the due process guaranteed by the U.S. Constitution, and confined them behind barbed wire. There they languished beneath guard towers containing sentries whose rifles pointed inward. Inadequate medical care and nervous, trigger-happy guards meant that some died as a result of their confinement. These facts, combined with the inmates' unjust and demeaning experience, fully qualify the term "incarceration camps" to be used when referring to the WRA installations.

Dawning awareness of the difference between INS internment camps for Japanese aliens and WRA incarceration camps for Japanese American citizens is leading to calls for changes in other terminology. For example, in mid-2006 the National Park Service, manager of the Minidoka Internment National Monument in Idaho, a former WRA facility, requested that Congress vote to drop "internment" from the name of the monument. The new name became Minidoka National Historic Site, in common with that for the Manzanar National Historic Site in California. While some people, including the present author, would prefer that the Minidoka camp be called "Minidoka Incarceration Camp National Historic Site," removing "internment" from the name at least recognizes the difference between the WRA camps and the INS camps.[30]

Former incarceree James Azumano has commented,

It is a real dilemma and a constant challenge: How politically correct do you want to be over what at the time was a civil rights atrocity? It's a struggle with terminology that continues today. What are you going to call Guantánamo 50 years from now?[31]

Significance of the Kooskia Internment Camp

The ultimate significance of the Kooskia Internment Camp, and what differentiates it from the other internment or incarceration camps, lies in the internees' awareness and exploitation of the rights and privileges guaranteed to them by the Geneva Convention, a 1929 document specifying conditions for holding prisoners of war (POWs) that was later extended to internees. Treatment the INS detainees received contrasted sharply with that accorded their relatives and friends in the WRA incarceration camps, who had no such principles governing the conditions under which they were incarcerated. The Kooskia internees' knowledge of the Geneva Convention and its provisions empowered them in establishing a symbiotic relationship between themselves and the Kooskia camp administration. Since the road building project could not function without the internees, their refusal to accept substandard living and working conditions was crucial in compelling the INS to agree to their demands. After being deprived of both liberty and property without the due process of law supposedly guaranteed by the Fifth Amendment to the U.S. Constitution, the Geneva Convention became their "safety net."

Furthermore, the Kooskia camp is unique not only because it was the sole work camp for Japanese internees in the U.S. but also because the internees achieved an admirable amount of control over their own lives. First, they volunteered to leave other INS camps to go there to work; second, they received wages of $55 to $65 per month; and third, they courageously petitioned INS authorities to mitigate unacceptable living and working conditions, even achieving replacement of the camp superintendent.[32]

Author's Statement

Readers may rightly wonder how someone not of Japanese descent could be so passionate about investigating the history of this obscure World War II Japanese internment camp. Besides a sincere admiration for the accomplishments of the Kooskia internees, several personal experiences come to mind. In one, as a child in our family's new, $10,000 tract house in postwar California, I listened as a real estate agent asked my father if he would "mind" if a Japanese American family moved into our neighborhood. Although Dad replied, "I don't care," the suggested family never appeared, so plenty of people must have cared too much to allow it to happen in those days of racist restrictive covenants. The significance of that conversation, of course, did not become apparent to me until many years later.

In the late 1950s, while attending the University of California, Berkeley, I lived in a University Students' Cooperative Association dorm, the least expensive type of housing for students on a budget. Nearly one-quarter of my housemates were young Japanese American women. One day I overheard Chiyo and Akemi talking about being "in camp" together. The phrase had an ominous sound, and as they conversed, I soon realized they were not talking about being "at" Girl Scout camp. Some probing on my part elicited the true and horrible nature of these camps, which had been absent, or euphemized, in my high school history book. To my great amazement, these young women and their families were not bitter about their mistreatment.

Subsequently, as a junior high school librarian in California, I obtained, for the school library, the few books appropriate to those grade levels that were then available on the Japanese American incarceration camp experience. Students thus learned about Executive Order 9066, the mandate that ultimately "justified" the forced removal of thousands of Japanese American citizens and permanent resident aliens from the West Coast into inland incarceration camps.

During the height of the Black Power movement in the late 1960s and early 1970s, frightened Caucasians resurrected the idea of applying EO9066 to African-American activists, suggesting they should be put into concentration camps. That directive, never revoked, would have facilitated such unjust actions. EO9066 thus became of great interest to concerned students, mostly black, at the school where I worked; they feared that it might be used against their friends and relatives. We rejoiced together when President Gerald R. Ford rescinded EO9066 on February 19, 1976, its thirty-fourth anniversary.[33]

Two years in the Peace Corps, in Thailand, and independent travel in Southeast Asia and the Far East, gave me an appreciation of Asian cultures. This culminated in founding the University of Idaho's Asian American Comparative Collection (AACC), a repository of artifacts, images, and documentary materials essential for understanding Asian American archaeological sites, economic contributions, and cultural history.[34]

As an historian and historical archaeologist, who has written extensively on Chinese American history and archaeology since the 1980s,[35] I have often come too late to a project to be able to interview its main participants - everyone involved has died.[36] For the Kooskia Internment Camp, that was almost the case, but not quite. During the past decade it has been my great pleasure and privilege to meet and/or interview two former internees and two former employees, as well as many descendants of deceased internees and employees. Many Japanese Americans who suffered the indignities of internment and incarceration want to put it all behind them and move on. Others feel that their stories must be told so that future generations remember, and do not repeat, or perpetuate, past injustices.

The few surviving internees and employees gave life to the abundant archival documents, and I resolved to tell their stories in a scholarly, but approachable, way, so that their experiences would become meaningful to, and remembered by, future generations. This mutual information-sharing experience has been of immense benefit to all of us as we strive to finally tell the complete story of the Kooskia Internment Camp.

While participating in the Idaho Humanities Council's former Scholars-in-the-Schools program, I took the story of the World War II Japanese internment and incarceration camps to junior high and high school students in many Idaho communities. At the end of my presentation, I always asked them, "This happened over sixty years ago, so why are we talking about it now?" Although they gave many answers, the one that I always looked for, and always eventually received, was, "So it will never happen again."[37]

Sadly, the threat is still present. Immediately following the ghastly terrorist attacks on September 11, 2001, the U.S. government detained more than twelve hundred people.[38] Many were arrested in secret, without charge, and some of those in custody were badly beaten. Although there were over five thousand arrests within two years, of which "hundreds were tried in closed hearings," not one person was convicted of terrorism.[39] With the pain of their own unjust imprisonment never far from their minds, Japanese Americans immediately became a significant, vocal, force protesting against the unfair detention of Muslims and Arabs.[40]

Racial profiling has since directly affected millions of Americans, particularly, but not limited to, those of African, Asian, Hispanic, Middle Eastern, and Native American descent. One study found that "racial profiling occurs in almost every context of people's lives," particularly while walking, driving, and shopping, and at home, at airports, and at places of worship. Incidents have occurred in urban, suburban, and rural areas, and victims include men and women of all ages, as well as children, from all income groups.[41] No matter how much we hope that an unjust mass incarceration will indeed never happen again, "the same dark impulses present in 1941 are still with us today."[42]

Acknowledgments

The Kooskia Internment Camp project would not have been possible without financial assistance from the Civil Liberties Public Education Fund (CLPEF), an Idaho Humanities Council Research Fellowship (IHCRF), and the California Civil Liberties Public Education Program (CCLPEP). I very much appreciate the support and encouragement of Hiroko Kowta, James Migaki, Dale Shimasaki, and Robert Sims; they believed in this project enough to write letters of recommendation to the granting agencies on my behalf. Many thanks to Anna Rendish, whose question about the Kooskia camp sparked this project; to Lee Sappington, for getting me started with some newspaper articles that he found on the Kooskia Internment Camp and on the prior Canyon Creek Prison Camp; and to the late Joan Abrams, who called a *Lewiston Tribune* article on the Kooskia camp to my attention. Special thanks to Jane Pritchett and Alison T. Stenger, whose generous support of the University of Idaho's Asian American Comparative Collection (AACC) helped underwrite the printing of this book.

My deepest gratitude is reserved for the late Koshio Henry Shima, formerly Koshio Shimabukuro, and the late James I. Yano, formerly Isao Yano, the only two surviving Kooskia internees whom I was able to locate. Shima was quite helpful, despite his time at Kooskia being of very short duration; I appreciate Grace Shimizu of the Japanese Peruvian Oral History Project for putting me in touch with him and for her help with information about Japanese Latin Americans at the Kooskia camp. Yano was there much longer, and over a period of several months he graciously responded to my questions and provided first-hand information obtainable in no other way. I am indebted to his wife, Chiyoko, for bringing his name to my attention, and for facilitating his replies. Through him I learned of Kooskia internee Toraichi Kono, former employee of Charlie Chaplin; subsequently, Philip Chung, Kono researcher and filmmaker, kindly provided copies of Kono's FBI file.

Grateful thanks also to Amelia Jacks and Cecil Boller, both Kooskia Internment Camp employees, now deceased, who provided invaluable assistance with details about staffing, camp buildings, and administrative activities. Ken Jacks forwarded his mother's replies to questions via e-mail; Amelia's daughter, DeAnn (Jacks) Scrabeck, provided family photographs and information about internee crafts; and DeAnn's daughter, Joan Pills, furnished photographs and measurements of two internee-made chests. Cecil Boller and his wife, Verna, graciously consented to be interviewed, and also provided photographs, two of which were facilitated by Cheryl Tousley and Bruce Wassmuth, Kooskia High School. Family members of deceased Kooskia camp employees who assisted with this project were Jan Boyer, daughter of guard Henry F. Boyer; Pauline DeHart and Virginia Tomita, daughter and sister of translator Paul Kashino; Carol Williams, daughter of guard Alfred Keehr; and Micheal Moshier and Betty Uebel, son and daughter of guard E. D. (Ed) Moshier. Special thanks to Micheal for taking such excellent care of his father's photograph album of Kooskia camp scenes, now at the University of Idaho Library Special Collections, and to Brenda Mitchell for putting us in contact with one another.

Relatives of deceased Kooskia internees generously shared important information, crucial documents, and/or treasured photographs with me, and I greatly value their contributions. Some of these family members are, unfortunately, now deceased themselves. Internee relatives who participated include Betty Okamura, daughter, and Ted Arase, son, of internee Shohei Arase; Yoshi Mamiya, daughter, and Pauline Asaba, daughter-in-law, of internee Kinzo Asaba; Edna Matsubu, daughter of Hamao Hirabayashi; Gary Imanishi, grandson of internee Umajiro Imanishi; Rikito Momii and Takeshi Momii, sons, Rick Momii, grandson, and Molly Momii and Yasu Momii, daughters-in-law, of internee Kizaemon Ikken Momii; Thomas Okazaki and Theresa Walker, grandchildren of internee Takeshi Okazaki; Kay Endo, nephew of internee Kyutaro Nakamura; Masako Hachisuka (Paris Mako Hachiska), granddaughter of internee Haruyuki Nagamine, and her cousin, Noriko Iwamoto; Carol Inouye-Matthews, great-niece of internee Kiichi Sanematsu; Tad Sato, son of internee Kosaku Sato; Hoshin Seki, son of internee Hozen Seki; Mariagnes Medrud, daughter of internee Joseph Kozo Uenishi; Kim Nakamura, daughter of internee Yoshitaka Watanabe; Jim and Kiyoshi Yoshinaka, sons, and Robin Payne, granddaughter, of internee Sei-ichi Yoshinaka; and Mary Ann Yakabi, daughter of Kooskia internee Arthur Shinei Yakabi. Special thanks to Hoshin Seki for so kindly providing a copy of his father's diary.

U.S. Bureau of Public Roads (USBPR) employee family members also helped in many ways. They include Milton (Mickey) Barton, son of USBPR employee Milt Barton; Nedra Hall, Lawrence Mack Hall, and Sharon Hall, wife, son, and daughter-in-law of USBPR employee Lawrence Hall; G. Arthur Misner, Marvin (Mike) Misner, and Marilyn Rea, nephew, son, and daughter of USBPR employee Bill Misner; and Don and Gwen Weseman, nephew and niece-in-law, and Steve and Leslie Weseman, grandnephew and grandniece-in-law of USBPR employee Ralph Willhite. Special appreciation to Mike Misner for donating an internee-made pillow and two mats to the AACC.

Thanks very much to Mae Betty Rainville, formerly Piersol, who provided wonderful details about her memories of interactions with the Kooskia internees whom she met while a student nurse at St. Joseph's Hospital in Lewiston, ID. Thanks to Carl Sasaki for providing me with a copy of the letter Mae Betty wrote to Sakaye Ed Yoshimura after his discharge from the hospital, and to everyone who helped me find her, including the *Adams County Record*, Marge Angelo, Ruth Bird, Peggy Chetwood, Gayle Dixon, Dick Fike, Betty Greenwell, the *Lewiston Tribune*, Ann Mattoon, Jami Steele, and St. Joseph Regional Medical Center.

Research for this project has taken more than ten years. During that time, many individuals, from various archives, historical societies, and government entities, helped me track down, and facilitate access to and use of, relevant documents and photographs. Although some of these people are now retired, employed elsewhere, or even, unfortunately, deceased, I gratefully acknowledge their assistance. They include Terry Abraham, Nathan Bender, Anar Imin, and Marilyn Sandmeyer, Archives and Special Collections, University of Idaho Library, Moscow, ID; Jason Bain, Robert Brown, L. J. Richards, and Diane Sands, Historical Museum at Fort Missoula, Missoula, MT; Pat Bower, Douglas Carr, Mark Hill, Chris Jenkins, and Linnea Keating, Clearwater National Forest, Kooskia and Orofino, ID; Carolyn Bowler, Mary Anne Davis, Kathy Hodges, and Linda Morton-Keithley, Idaho State Historical Society, Boise; Mary Beth Donelan and Shaun O'L. Higgins, *Spokesman-Review*, Spokane, WA; William R. Ellis, Jr., Eugene Morris, Richard Peuser, Fred Romanski, and Donald L. Singer, National Archives and Records Administration, Washington, DC, and College Place, MD; Lora Feucht and Mary White Romero, Nez Perce County Historical Society, Lewiston, ID; John Fitzgerald and Kris Kinsey, National Archives and Records Administration, Pacific Alaska Region, Seattle; David M. Hardy, Federal Bureau of Investigation, Washington, DC; Debbie Henderson, Karin Higa, Marie Masumoto, and Jane Nakasako, Japanese American National Museum, Los Angeles; Keith Harrison, Federal Highway Administration, San Francisco; Alice Ito, Densho Digital Archive, Seattle; Michael Kirkwood and Brenda Tisdale, National Border Patrol Museum, El Paso, TX; Mike

Maller and Jeff Stratten, Idaho Transportation Department, Boise; Karl Matsushita, Japanese American National Library, San Francisco; Elaine Miller and Ed Nolan, Washington State Historical Society, Tacoma; Jennifer O'Laughlin and the staff of the Interlibrary Loan Department, University of Idaho Library, Moscow, ID; Bernice Pullen, Clearwater Historical Museum, Orofino, ID; Rick Romagosa, *San Francisco Chronicle*; June Schumann, Oregon Nikkei Endowment, Portland; Marian L. Smith, Historian, U.S. Immigration and Naturalization Service, Washington, DC; Lily Wai and the staff of the Documents Department, University of Idaho Library, Moscow, ID; Lyle Wirtanen, The Historical Museum at St. Gertrude's, Cottonwood, ID; Shirley B. Witcher, U.S. Census Bureau, Washington, DC; and Terry Zontek, Bureau of Reclamation, Billings, MT.

Several people provided assistance with translation of Japanese terms or characters, or assisted with identification and interpretation of Japanese culture and customs. I am indebted for this help to Tomomi Kamiya, Janet and Seiichi Murai, Noriko Iwamoto, Charlotte Omoto, Rod N. Omoto, Yosh Shimoi, Ikuyo Suzuki, Yukio Tatsumi, Masumi Yagi, and Akiko Yamazaki. Thanks to Tim Taira for providing a Kooskia internee's letter in Japanese, and to June Taira for translating it. Special appreciation to Yosh Shimoi for his encouragement throughout the project, and for providing some crucial documents.

During the course of this research many, many other people helped me in various ways, and I am sincerely grateful to them all. Examples of such contributions include granting interviews; publicizing the project; writing letters or contacting others on my behalf; taking, digitizing, enhancing, or permitting use of photographs; providing copies of primary or secondary source materials that mentioned the Kooskia camp; directing me to relatives of former Kooskia internees, employees, or others with helpful information; or proposing additional research avenues, even though time often did not permit following up on them. Space limitations do not permit listing everyone's name here; many more names, of contributors to earlier phases of this project, are acknowledged in "'A Real He-Man's Job': Japanese Internees and the Kooskia Internment Camp, Idaho, 1943-1945," prepared for the CLPEF (1998); in "Japanese Internees and Idaho's Kooskia Internment Camp, 1943-1945," prepared for the IHCRF (2000); and in *Golden State Meets Gem State: Californians at Idaho's Kooskia Internment Camp, 1943-1945*, prepared for the CCLPEP (2002). Additional contributors, who provided information relevant to the Civilian Conservation Corps camp at Canyon Creek, or to the Canyon Creek Prison Camp, or to Germans and Italian internees in the vicinity, will be acknowledged in subsequent publications. For this one, I recognize, with appreciation, the contributions of Steve

Armstrong; Melba and Robert Ashburn; David Bearman; Frank Bowles; Sue Boydstun; Greg Captain and Lee Heydolph, Imaging Center, *New Yorker*; Louis Fiset; Janie Fluharty; Marilyn George; Richard Gilman; Karl Gurcke, Ladd Hamilton; Al Hayward; Ronald R. Helm, MD; Carol Hennessey; Vera M. Hewitt; Jan Higashi; Larry Hogan; Harry K. Honda; Rich Iwasaki; Eric Jensen; Irving Kalinoski; Mike Lawler; Maya Hata Lemmon; Bill London; Lubomyr Luciuk; Diane Matsuda, former director of the California Civil Liberties Public Education Program; Don McPherson; Judy Fike Mercer; Gail Miyasaki, *Rafu Shimpo*; Hiroyuki Ono, Chaplin Society of Japan; Dick Riggs; Diane Ronayne; Herman Ronnenberg; A. James Sather; Darby Stapp; Joseph Svinth; Helen Thiessen; Tom Trail; Irene Trenary; Thomas Uyehara; Carol Van Valkenburg; Kathleen Warnick; and K. Stanley Yamashita. I am particularly grateful to Harry K. Honda for suggesting that Michiko Midge Ayukawa write the foreword to *Imprisoned in Paradise*, and to Midge for her splendid contribution.

My husband, Terry Abraham, financed my first visit to the National Archives in Washington, DC, and solves my computer-related problems with patience and humor and without making me feel stupid. Terry, who willingly read several earlier, and much longer, versions of this manuscript, made numerous excellent suggestions for its improvement. Roger Daniels' and Stan Flewelling's rigorous reading of Chapter 1 pointed out some errors and clarified my thinking, as did Grace Shimuzu's for Chapters 1, 8, and 10. I am grateful to all of them for their guidance. While I hope no errors remain, I regret any that do, and take full responsibility for them.

During the book production process, several people shared their advice and expertise with me or helped me in other ways. Many thanks to Dennis Baird, Patty Carscallen, Cort Conley, Scott Gipson, Bob Greene, Ivar Nelson, and Delora Shoop. Special appreciation to Melissa Rockwood for her book designing skills and for her sympathetic understanding of my desire for (obsession with) perfection.

Sincere apologies to anyone who provided assistance but whose name was inadvertently omitted, and to anyone whose information was unintentionally misinterpreted. I would greatly appreciate receiving any additions or corrections to the information presented in *Imprisoned in Paradise*, and will happily continue to share internee documents with family members. All research materials collected as a result of this project will be housed at the Asian American Comparative Collection, University of Idaho, Moscow.

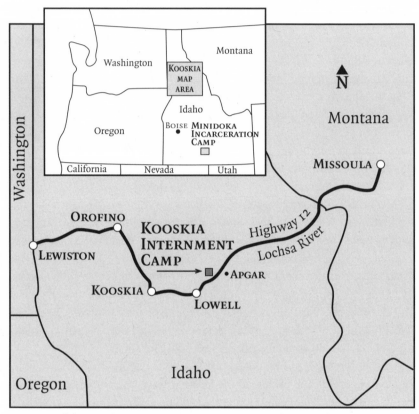

Location of the Kooskia Internment Camp on U.S. Highway 12 between Lewiston, Idaho, and Missoula, Montana, in the vicinity of Milepost 104.

Chapter One
Anti-Japanese Attitudes:
Foreshadowing Japanese American Internment and Incarceration

No person shall ... be deprived of life, liberty, or property,

without due process of law ... .

Fifth Amendment to the Bill of Rights, the first
ten amendments to the U.S. Constitution.

Idaho's Kooskia Internment Camp, the subject of this book, succeeded the Canyon Creek Prison Camp, a road-building camp for federal prisoners from Leavenworth, Kansas, that operated from 1935 to 1943. Declining prison appropriations during wartime caused the U.S. Bureau of Prisons to cease operating their satellite camps. However, because the U.S. War Department had designated the route as a "First Priority Military Highway" in 1940,[1] strategic concerns dictated that the road building must continue, this time using Japanese internees to perform the work.

Incarceration of Japanese aliens at the Kooskia Internment Camp from May 1943 to May 1945 resulted from a complex series of events that began in the closing decades of the nineteenth century. Immigrants from Japan were first welcomed for their labor, later resented for their agricultural independence and commercial acumen, and finally despised as "the enemy."

Prior to World War II, the U.S. denied naturalization to people of Asian ancestry.[2] Nevertheless, Japanese immigrants sought to improve their financial circumstances, most through hard manual labor, productive farming, or small business establishments. However, anti-Japanese agitation and legislation, fueled by racist jealousy, thwarted their ambitions. By 1924, federal

1

laws curtailed new Asian immigration to the U.S., and state laws on the West Coast prohibited both land ownership and leasing by immigrant residents from Asia.[3] In the late 1930s, as World War II loomed, the U.S. government prepared to arrest certain Japanese, German, and Italian aliens, primarily men. The Federal Bureau of Investigation (FBI) compiled dossiers on individuals it considered "potentially dangerous"; Japanese teachers, clergymen, and journalists were special targets.

The U.S. entered World War II in response to Japan's bombing of Pearl Harbor, Hawai'i, on December 7, 1941. Immediately following that tragic event, the FBI began arresting and interning the previously targeted aliens; the Japanese were mostly taken to Fort Missoula, in Montana, and to Fort Lincoln, at Bismarck, in North Dakota. These camps already held, respectively, Italian and German merchant seamen.[4]

Unfortunately, status as U.S. citizens did not save West Coast residents of Japanese descent from being incarcerated also. On February 19, 1942, President Franklin D. Roosevelt (FDR) issued Executive Order 9066 authorizing the Secretary of War to establish "military areas" from which "any or all persons" could be excluded.[5] Although that document did not specifically mention people of Japanese ancestry, subsequent government actions clearly show that its intent was to justify their removal.[6]

FDR's Executive Order 9102, issued March 18, 1942, created the War Relocation Authority (WRA).[7] This agency had the task of "evacuating" the remaining people of Japanese ancestry from the now-forbidden "military areas" No. 1 and No. 2, encompassing all, or parts of, Washington, Oregon, California, and Arizona.[8] No longer could Japanese American residents "voluntarily relocate" to inland areas from "military," "restricted," or "prohibited" areas, a practice that the government had earlier encouraged.[9]

Incarceration of Japanese American Citizens

The U.S. government eventually excluded all persons of Japanese ancestry from the western half of Washington and Oregon, the southern half of Arizona, all of the Territory of Alaska, and all of California; people who earlier had moved to the eastern half of California hoping to escape incarceration were, instead, compelled to experience it. "Exclusion" meant, for example, that people of Japanese descent living in Seattle, Washington, were placed into WRA camps, but those living in Spokane, Washington, were not. Similarly, Japanese American residents of Colorado, Idaho, Montana, Nevada, Utah, and other inland states were not removed to WRA facilities.

Of the more than one hundred twenty thousand people placed into WRA incarceration camps,[10] two-thirds were American citizens, or "non-aliens," the government euphemism for citizens, while only one-third of them were aliens.[11] These aliens escaped internment because there were no, or too few, "suspicious" circumstances in their backgrounds. Although Japanese Americans comprised less than one-tenth of one percent of the total U.S. population, the anti-Japanese hysteria directed at them was vastly out of proportion to their numbers.[12]

The "relocatees" or "evacuees" were first incarcerated in one of sixteen "assembly centers," a euphemistic term for temporary detention facilities. Most were racetracks or fairgrounds, with horse stalls converted into housing; hasty whitewashing could cover the dirt but did nothing to hide the smell.[13] Poet James Mitsui eloquently captured their atmosphere in the ending of his poem, "Holding Center, Tanforan Race Track, Spring 1942":

> *Hay, horse hair & manure*
> *are whitewashed to the boards.*
> *In the corner*
> *a white spider is suspended*
> *in the shadow of a white spider web.*[14]

The inmates remained in the temporary detention centers for up to six months while the government hastily constructed more permanent accommodations intended to confine them for the duration of the war. These inland "relocation centers" comprised ten enormous WRA installations that hastily mushroomed in inhospitable locations within seven states. Ironically, five of these camps were in states whose own Japanese American residents were not incarcerated. One was Minidoka, at Hunt, in the southern Idaho desert; some of the Kooskia internees had family members confined there.[15] Although the U.S. was also at war with Germany and Italy, U.S. citizens of German and Italian ancestry rarely suffered similar violations of their constitutional rights.[16]

Internment of Aliens during Wartime

Historian Roger Daniels reminds us that "'internment' is a well-defined legal process by which enemy nationals are placed in confinement in time of war."[17] As early as 1798, in the event of war between the U.S. and any other nation, the Alien Enemies Act provided for the arrest of male aliens fourteen and up.[18] During World War I, the Act was amended to include females.[19]

By late 1939 the prospect of global conflict loomed menacingly. Because any resident non-citizen would automatically become an "enemy alien" if the United States warred with his or her native land, the U.S. government, through the FBI, began to compile lists of potential enemy aliens.[20] During their investigations, the FBI placed each person into one of three categories on so-called, informally known, "ABC lists," [also A, B, C lists] according to each alien's perceived subversive potential.[21] The "A" list contained names of "aliens who led cultural or assistance organizations"; "B" listed "slightly less suspicious aliens"; and "C" was for "members of, or those who donated to, ethnic groups, [and for] Japanese language teachers and Buddhist clergy."[22] Following compilation of the lists, the FBI filed them with the Justice Department.[23] Historian Greg Robinson describes the ABC lists as "secret,"[24] which may explain why they have so far been unobtainable.[25]

As war drew inevitably nearer, Congress passed the Alien Registration Act, or Smith Act, in June 1940, the same month that the Justice Department took over the Immigration and Naturalization Service (INS), formerly in the Labor Department. The Smith Act required all aliens over fourteen, of every nationality, to register, to be fingerprinted, and to receive a number.[26] Between late August and late December 1940, more than five million did so, providing the government with yet another means of keeping track of them.[27]

Even before the U.S. entered World War II, the INS was prepared to assume responsibility for "temporary detention of alien enemies." In late November 1941 Lemuel B. Schofield, Special Assistant to the U.S. Attorney General, wrote a "<u>PERSONAL AND CONFIDENTIAL</u>" letter to the INS's district director in Spokane, Washington, and probably to other directors elsewhere, seeking "quarters suitable for detention stations … throughout the country." The FBI would make most of the arrests and take the detainees first to county jails.[28]

Following the Pearl Harbor atrocity, the United States declared war on Japan. That day and the next, FDR issued proclamations 2525, 2526, and 2527, making it possible to arrest and detain Japanese, German, and Italian aliens.[29] The main difference among these three groups, besides nationality, was that that the Germans and Italians were eligible to become naturalized American citizens if they chose to exercise that privilege, but the Japanese were not. Because of their birth in Japan, they remained permanent resident aliens with no hope of ever becoming naturalized, even though they often had American-born wives and children.

On the evening of Sunday, December 7, using the "ABC lists" compiled previously, FBI director J. Edgar Hoover directed his agents to:

Immediately take into custody all Japanese who have been classified in A, B, and C categories in material previously transmitted to you. Take immediate action and advise Bureau frequently by teletype as to exact identity of persons arrested. Persons taken into custody should be turned over to nearest representative of Immigration and Naturalization Service.[30]

Oddly, the arrests of the Japanese on the FBI's "ABC lists" were not done in order of perceived dangerousness of the individuals apprehended.[31]

Overwhelmingly, the arrested Japanese aliens were community organization officials, language teachers, ministers, newspaper reporters and editors, business owners, and other community leaders. Historian Greg Robinson describes these prominent Japanese individuals as essentially hostages; holding them would "assure community good behavior."[32]

The "ministers" were usually Buddhist clergy, often called priests, and were seen as "more marginalized than Protestants." The larger society perceived them "as 'foreign' and more closely tied to Japan"; besides, "Buddhism was often confused with state Shintoism that was used by the Japanese government to instill nationalism in its citizens during the 1930s."[33]

Arrest and subsequent incarceration followed a carefully orchestrated government plan. Briefly, the Justice Department had established the Alien Enemy Control Unit (AECU), under which were over one hundred Alien Enemy Hearing Boards (AEHBs), each within a federal judicial district. To start the process, an FBI field office submitted, to the U.S. attorney, its file on a particular person. If the attorney agreed with the FBI's findings, he requested that the AECU ask the attorney general for a "presidential warrant of apprehension." Following the issuance of a warrant, the FBI made the arrest.[34] Reports of such arrests often appear in the Kooskia internees' files (Fig. 1).

Those detained were first jailed locally. The next stop for them was usually an internment camp. Often, this was Fort Missoula, in Montana. There, the alien would have a hearing before an AEHB. Each AEHB was composed of three civilians, including one attorney, appointed from the district where the detainee had lived. Representatives of the FBI, the INS, and the U.S. attorney for that district also attended. Although an arrested alien could present affidavits testifying to his character and loyalty, and could invite an "advisor" (usually a family member) to accompany and support him at his hearing, he could not retain a lawyer to represent him, making it difficult to dispute the government's "evidence" against him. Such draconian measures were intentionally planned to avoid slow and expensive court formalities.

Following the hearing, AEHB members rendered their recommendation for release, parole, or continued internment and forwarded it to the AECU to review. If the AECU agreed that internment was necessary, they drew up an order so stating, obtained the attorney general's signature, and had the alien transported to an internment camp run by the U.S. Army.[35]

By mid-December 1941, FBI Director J. Edgar Hoover could boast that 1,291 Japanese aliens had been arrested, 367 in Hawaii and 924 in the continental U.S. By mid-February 1942 the Justice Department had interned 2,192 Japanese, as well as 1,393 Germans and 264 Italians.[36] Although fewer than fifty thousand of the U.S.'s five million resident aliens were of Japanese

JOHN EDGAR HOOVER
DIRECTOR

CONFIDENTIAL

Federal Bureau of Investigation
United States Department of Justice
Washington, D. C.

September 28, 1942

CLASSIFICATION CANCELLED
Per letter May 18, 1942
Chief, Administrative Serv..., ... O.S.
Date OCT 1 1942 By ...

Brigadier General Hayes A. Kroner
General Staff
Chief, Military Intelligence Service
War Department
Washington, D. C.

Dear General Kroner:

This is to advise that information has been received that on July 20, 1942, the Attorney General ordered the internment of Inao Minato who was previously apprehended by the San Francisco Field Division of this Bureau as an alien enemy of Japanese nationality.

Sincerely yours,

J. E. Hoover

John Edgar Hoover
Director

FILE
PMGO
Date OCT 1 1942
Initials

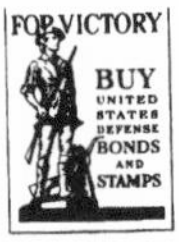
FOR VICTORY
BUY
UNITED STATES DEFENSE
BONDS
AND
STAMPS

CONFIDENTIAL

Fig. 1. Letter from John Edgar Hoover, Director, Federal Bureau of Investigation, reporting on the arrest and internment of future Kooskia internee Inao Minato, July 20, 1942; E466F, Minato, Inao; OPMG, RG389, NARA II.

descent, they were detained well out of proportion to their total in the population.

The Justice Department practiced a policy of "selective internment," driven by concerns of prominent U.S. alien refugees and anti-Nazis such as Albert Einstein,[37] by then a U.S. citizen. Although actual numbers may never be known, what historian Tetsuden Kashima believes are the "most accurate" statistics come from W. F. Kelly of the U.S. government's Alien Enemy Control Program. Just over three percent (31,899) of the U.S.'s resident aliens were ever interned, including 17,477 Japanese, 11,507 Germans, and lesser numbers of Italians (2,730) and other nationalities (185).[38] In a subsequent memoir, Jerre Mangione, the INS's former public relations director, stated that the "selective internment policy" practiced by the Justice Department "was not nearly as selective as it might have been." During a two-month tour of the INS internment camps, Mangione discovered that "many of their occupants represented no threat to the national security; had they been accorded due process of law, they would probably never have been interned."[39]

Hindsight suggests that Mangione's statement was all too true. Journalist Bill Hosokawa has written, "The record shows that arrests of Japanese aliens after Pearl Harbor were on the basis of suspicion and potential danger rather than for the commission of any specific subversive acts."[40] Hosokawa also observed that "when the United States became a belligerent, it was an altogether new ball game with new rules for everyone but the Japanese Americans. They continued to be judged by the old rules."[41] In other words, a double standard applied to them. If aliens of Japanese ancestry had shown any support of Japan whatsoever prior to declared war, these actions were held against them as signs of disloyalty to the U.S. no matter what their behavior once war broke out. Similar pre-war actions by German and Italian aliens did not, for the most part, give rise to later accusations of disloyalty.

Alien Arrests Divide Families

Mere numbers cannot even hint at the poignancy of the alien arrests, with their accompanying loss of occupations or businesses and the consequent disruption and impoverishment of families. A few personal accounts provide glimpses into the federal government's unjust actions against innocent aliens.

Shohei Arase

Future Kooskia internee Shohei Arase lived in Seattle with his wife and six children (Fig. 2), and was a driver for a dry cleaning business.[42] On February 21, 1942, FBI agent Hamilton C. Dowell, accompanied by two members of the Seattle police, arrested Arase at his home in the presence of his wife and youngest daughter, Betty.[43] "Evidence" the FBI seized from Arase's residence included numerous copies of the *Wall Street Journal* and other investment publications, cards denoting membership in the Seattle Japanese Chamber of Commerce, and receipts for his children's tuition at a Japanese language school.[44]

Fig. 2. Shohei Arase family, June 30, 1937, taken in their living room at 1643 South King Street, Seattle. Shohei Arase, age 44, is third from left. Others in the photo are, from left, wife Misao, age 36; daughters Betty Fumiko, age 3; Violet Sumiko, age 12; Margaret Mutsuko, age 17; son Tetsuo, age 10; daughter Hanako, age 14; Misao's sister, Sayo Obayashi, age 39; and Arase daughter Frances Yukiko, age 8. Courtesy Betty Arase Okamura.

Although Betty was only seven years old at the time, years later she still had a "vivid memory" of the terrifying events of that day. She remembered "the FBI first calling our house to see if my father was home. When my mother told them that he was at work, they … went there to pick him up. They brought him home and searched our house before taking him to the INS."

> I don't know why he was considered an 'enemy alien' other than because he was not allowed to become a U.S. citizen, and was of the same race as the enemy. He was a very sociable person and belonged to many Japanese community organizations. Because of this, the FBI may have considered him to be one of the leaders of the Japanese community, even though he was not politically inclined.[45]

In mid-March 1942 the INS shipped Arase to their Fort Missoula facility.[46] Subsequently, his wife and children were removed to the WRA's Minidoka incarceration camp in southern Idaho. Arase arrived at the Kooskia camp in September 1943; relatives believe he volunteered for that assignment to be closer to his family.[47]

The FBI's "Confidential Informants"

FBI reports on Arase and other Kooskia internees contain incriminating information about their memberships in various "subversive" organizations as well as other "questionable activities." The FBI received assistance in identifying these from certain "Confidential Informants" referred to only with initials. In Arase's case, these people were probably informers from the Japanese American community, possibly living in Seattle ("SE-1") and Tacoma ("T-1"). The latter person told the FBI "that the subject and his family live above the ordinary means of Japanese families and that Japanese people have been unable to understand how the subject and his family lived upon his earnings as a truck driver on a laundry route."[48] Unknown to the informant, who was possibly motivated by jealousy, Arase's prosperity was probably related to successful investments in the stock market.

The FBI had collected information from such "Confidential Informants" since at least mid-January 1941.[49] Both SE-1 and T-1 had intimate knowledge of Arase's memberships, and must have been close friends, business associates, or even members of the same groups themselves. Today, it is particularly maddening to family members to know that, in incarcerating Shohei Arase, the FBI relied upon damaging information about him from unidentified informants whom he was never able to confront in person. It is especially infuriating to know that Arase's descendants cannot learn the names of people who said that he "definitely expressed himself as pro-Japanese" or, if true, the context in which he made that statement.[50]

One researcher, who claims to know the names of some "Confidential Informants," feels that it would serve no good purpose to let the families of those they informed on know the identities of their accusers, even if the informants themselves are no longer living. Some of the deceased informants have surviving adult children who would be badly disillusioned to learn that their respected parent had informed on fellow Japanese Americans.[51] To this day, members of the Japanese American community's Nisei generation vividly recall the epithet *inu* (dog), as well as the accompanying ostracism, that applied to perceived informers and their family members.[52]

Why Japanese aliens, Issei, or American citizens, Nisei, would inform on fellow Japanese is deplorable, but some certainly did so. Historian Tetsuden Kashima reported that Japanese American Citizens League (JACL) leaders, including Mike Masaoka, "passed on 'facts or rumors relating to [various people's] ostensible business and sympathies, family relationships, and organization ties.'"[53] Kashima suggests a complex set of motives, including fear, patriotism, or offers of money. Some informants may have felt flattered, because the FBI seemed to value their knowledge and expertise, whereas others perhaps sought revenge against people they felt had slighted them in past dealings.[54] Too, informants who believed they were under suspicion themselves might have wanted to improve their own position with the FBI.

Kizaemon Ikken Momii (Fig. 3)

The arrest of future Kooskia internee Kizaemon Ikken Momii, editor and publisher of the *Nanka Times*, occurred in San Francisco on Christmas Eve 1941.[55] "Confidential Informant SF-9" must have known him very well indeed. That person collaborated with the FBI beginning in early April 1941, and provided them with additional information about Momii on three occasions between mid-November and early December 1941.[56]

Fig. 3. Kizaemon Ikken Momii in his newspaper office. The Japanese calligraphy at left is a motto or resolution for living one's life. Courtesy Molly Momii and Rick Momii.

Momii arrived at Fort Missoula by the end of December,[57] and by mid-October 1942 he was at Camp Livingston, Louisiana.[58] In the meantime, his family, consisting of his wife, Matsuko (Matsu), and their four sons, Rikito (Rick), Takeshi (Tak), Manabu (Jamo), and Tonomo (Toa/Vincent), ages about 23 to 17 (Fig. 4), had been removed to the Topaz incarceration camp in Utah. In early January 1943 Ikken Momii received the devastating news that his wife had died from complications following an operation in the Topaz camp hospital.[59] Camp Livingston authorities allowed Momii to attend her funeral (Fig. 5), but required him to pay his own expenses as well as those of the Army men who escorted him there and back. On June 7, 1943, Momii transferred to the Kooskia Internment Camp, perhaps to be closer to his sons in Utah.[60]

Fig. 4. Kizaemon Ikken Momii and his family, San Francisco, 1937. Seated, Ikken and wife Matsuko (Matsu) Ikeda Momii. Standing, left to right, their sons, Manabu (Jamo), Rikito (Rick), Takeshi (Tak), and Tonomo (Toa/Vincent). Courtesy Molly Momii and Rick Momii.

Fig. 5. Funeral of Matsuko (Matsu) Ikeda Momii, wife of Kooskia internee Kizaemon Ikken Momii, Topaz incarceration camp, Utah, January 1943. The six men directly behind the casket are, from left to right, Ikken Momii's brother, Kiyoshi; son Tonomo (Toa/Vincent); Rikito (Rick); Ikken; Takeshi (Tak); and Manabu (Jamo). Courtesy Molly Momii and Rick Momii.

*Fig. 6. Sokichi Harry
Hashimoto at the
Kooskia Internment
Camp, May 1944.
Courtesy Mickey
Barton.*

"Manzanar Riot" Internees Sokichi Harry Hashimoto (Fig. 6) and Genji George Yamaguchi

Sokichi Harry Hashimoto and Genji George Yamaguchi escaped the earlier alien roundup but later were forced into Manzanar, the WRA incarceration camp in southern California. In early December 1942 that facility witnessed the so-called "Manzanar Riot," a confrontation between the military police and a throng of Manzanar inmates.[61] Hashimoto and Yamaguchi were two of the five committee members who tried to calm the mob, but they could not get it to disperse.[62] After the police fired into the crowd, two young men died. Ten other people were wounded, including one military police corporal.[63] Instead of being praised for their attempts to reason with the mob, the committee members, who spoke to the crowd in Japanese, were arrested on suspicion of having incited the riot. Although Hashimoto and Yamaguchi declared that they were "absolutely 100% innocent,"[64] authorities sent them to the Fort Missoula Internment Camp.[65]

In early December 1943, following their hearings at that facility, officer in charge Bert Fraser commented that the two men were among Fort Missoula's "hardest workers." Hashimoto, in particular, took over the gardening project there, and "did a wonderful job." Fraser could not understand why the two men were supposedly "such dangerous troublemakers at Manzanar" but were "model internees at Fort Missoula."[66] Subsequently, Hashimoto and Yamaguchi both volunteered for work at the Kooskia Internment Camp. Yamaguchi transferred there in August 1943 and Hashimoto arrived in March 1944.[67]

Hozen Seki

Today it is scarcely believable that the late Reverend Hozen Seki, founder and minister of the New York Buddhist Church (NYBC) in New York City, was once a Kooskia internee. Seki arrived in the U.S. as a Buddhist missionary in 1930 and moved to New York City in late 1936, where he founded the NYBC.[68] A photograph of the congregation showed that in 1938 it had some two dozen adult members, with about the same number of children (Fig. 7).

Fig. 7. Members of the New York Buddhist Church, 1938. Center left, Hozen Seki; center right, Satomi Seki with eldest son, Hoken Seki. Courtesy Hoshin Seki, with retouching by Greg Captain and Lee Heydolph, Imaging Center, New Yorker.

Seki, too, was the victim of FBI "Confidential Informants." "T-1" stated that Seki's church disseminated militant Japanese propaganda, mostly motion pictures. "T-2" told the FBI that Seki was closely connected with Hokoku Dan, "a Japanese militaristic organization."[69] After gathering this and other incriminating information, the FBI finally interviewed Seki himself in early May 1942 and again the following September. Seki reiterated that he had never "engaged in any activities inimical to the welfare of the United States," and provided plausible explanations for other accusations.[70] The FBI was not convinced, and arrested him on September 23.[71] None of the collected testimony provided any evidence for pro-Japanese activity after Japan's attack on Pearl Harbor. Rather, the Seki family's purchase of U.S. National Defense Bonds totaling $1,550 held in the names of all four family members is certainly, given their limited family income, a measure of extreme pro-American patriotism.[72]

Obviously, the authorities misconstrued the activities that took place at Seki's church between 1939 and early 1941. Even if certain speakers or films spoke well of Japan, it is only natural that they might have, given the fact that Seki himself, and presumably many church members, were, in legal language, "aliens ineligible for citizenship" because of racist U.S. laws forbidding their naturalization. Prior to Japan's bombing of Pearl Harbor, being "pro-Japanese" was not a crime for citizens of that country who were living in the U.S. Nevertheless, it was grossly unfair of U.S. authorities to judge the post-attack loyalty of Seki and his congregation with reference to the NYBC's pre-war speakers, films, and activities. Following Pearl Harbor, Seki and his congregation performed only innocent and humanitarian acts that the FBI completely misinterpreted.

Seki's captors delivered him to Ellis Island in care of the INS.[73] He remained there until mid-December when he was transferred to Fort George G. Meade, Maryland, near Washington, DC. That facility then held some three hundred inmates, two hundred Japanese and one hundred Italians and Germans, under the jurisdiction of the U.S. Army.[74] Because of his command of the English language, and his respected ministerial position, Seki's fellow Japanese internees elected him as their spokesman to represent them in dealings with the administration.[75] He transferred to Fort Missoula in late May 1943 and to the Kooskia camp in mid-June.[76]

Internees from Alaska

During World War II, the U.S. government removed and interned ninety-four men of Japanese descent who resided in the territory of Alaska.[77] Of these, twenty-eight were at the Kooskia Internment Camp for some part of their detention. The experiences of one of them, Tom Kito, illustrate what happened to most Japanese aliens in Alaska once the U.S. entered World War II. Arrested in early January 1942, Tom and his brother Sam were first taken to the Petersburg, Alaska, jail.[78] In mid-February the brothers were transferred to Fort Richardson, at Anchorage, where they joined other Japanese from all over Alaska. There they were forced to wear prisoner-of-war (POW) shirts, an experience that Tom found especially humiliating.[79] Even worse, Tom's wife, a Tlingit Indian, and their four children, were left penniless by his removal.

From Alaska the brothers were sent to Lordsburg, New Mexico (Fig. 8), and in mid-June 1943 they arrived at the Santa Fe, New Mexico, internment camp.[80] There the authorities asked for volunteer road workers for the Kooskia camp. The reason Tom decided to go to the Kooskia Internment Camp was probably the same one he gave for a later job, on the Anderson Ranch Dam, near Boise; he wanted to work outside, in the fresh air.[81]

Internees from Hawai'i

On December 9, 1941, military officials herded the first Japanese alien arrestees from Hawai'i onto a barge and took them to the deserted Sand Island, a ten-acre, part manmade island adjacent to the Honolulu Harbor entrance and formerly used as a quarantine station.[82] Learning that they would all be

Fig. 8. Left to right, Tom and Sam Kito at the Lordsburg, New Mexico, internment camp, 1942 or 1943. Courtesy Marilyn George.

treated equally was a shock for some who were used to their respected positions and eminent titles; setting up four-man tents, and cots for sleeping, proved daunting for those who had always had others to perform manual labor for them.[83]

In mid-February 1942 the Army issued each man an overcoat and a pair of shoes and told them they would be going to a cold climate on the Mainland. They could take only what they could fit into one duffel bag. On February 20 the group departed in heavily guarded trucks that took them to the pier where they boarded the *U.S.S. Ulysses Grant*, part of a convoy shepherded by two destroyers. Nobody had informed their families, so no one witnessed their departure.[84]

The men, including future Kooskia internees Yoshio Hino and Sokan Ueoka, both Buddhist priests, endured miserable conditions during their voyage to the Mainland.[85] In early March 1942 the Hawaiians reached snowy Camp McCoy, Wisconsin. At first, even their government-issue overcoats, over flimsy tropical garments, were no match for the penetrating cold, but three blankets each, and humane treatment, helped them survive what remained of winter.[86] After an interim stay at Camp Forrest, near Tullahoma, Tennessee, they were moved to a longer-term facility at Camp Livingston, Louisiana.[87] This camp was so unpleasantly hot that the men had to cool themselves by resting in holes they dug in the sandy soil under the barracks.[88]

15

After enduring Camp Livingston for about a year, seventeen of the Hawaiian Japanese internees volunteered for the Kooskia Internment Camp.[89]

Japanese Latin Americans

Few people realize that during World War II the United States colluded with a number of Latin American countries to expel over two thousand people of Japanese descent.[90] The nations that ousted Japanese residents succumbed to existing anti-Japanese hostility, together with unsupported fears that those kidnapped might otherwise commit sabotage in their home countries. A contributing paranoia, particularly for Japanese from Panama, was the unfounded suspicion that they would conspire to blow up the Panama Canal.[91]

Historian C. Harvey Gardiner described Peru as the major offender, and documented that country's expulsion of 1,771 Japanese.[92] American ships and planes brought the Japanese Latin Americans, and other Axis nationals, to the United States.[93] Once outside the jurisdiction of the originating country, U.S. officials confiscated all kidnappees' passports and even their drivers' licenses.[94] In addition, acting under instructions from Washington, the American consul in Peru did not issue them visas.[95] These actions meant that the prisoners became illegal immigrants once they reached the U.S., and the U.S. thus became complicit in war crimes.

The U.S. intended to use the Latin American Japanese in a "repatriation" scheme, i.e., as unwilling pawns in prisoner exchanges for U.S. citizens held captive in Japan.[96] Eventually, at least nine hundred Japanese Latin Americans, including both citizens and permanent resident aliens, were flagrantly exploited in this way,[97] but a full discussion of U.S. war crimes is beyond the scope of this book. The Japanese Latin Americans who were not sent to Japan for exchange languished in various INS internment camps.[98]

Arturo Shinei Yakabi (Fig. 9), born in Peru, was arrested after his Japanese alien employer bribed officials to take Yakabi in his stead.[99] Once in the U.S. Yakabi somehow avoided the forced repatriation. He arrived at the Kooskia Internment Camp in mid-June 1944 and was one of twenty-seven Japanese Peruvians who eventually worked there. Other Japanese Latin Americans at the Kooskia camp included two men from Panama and eleven from Mexico.[100]

Justice Department (INS) and War Department (U.S. Army) Jurisdiction over Aliens

U.S. internment camps, run by the INS, initially held German and Italian merchant seamen and cruise ship crew members who were stranded in U.S. ports beginning in late 1939 with the outbreak of war in Europe.[101] Responsibility for constructing facilities to contain these people fell upon the INS,

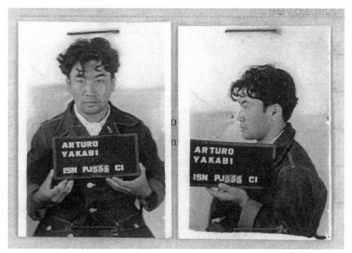

Fig. 9. Arturo Shinei Yakabi, from his "Basic Personnel Record (Alien Enemy or Prisoner of War)" card, March 5, 1943, 1; E466F, Yakabi, Arturo; OPMG, RG389, NARA II. On the sign he is holding, "ISN" means Internee Serial Number, "PJ" stands for Peruvian Japanese, and "CI" is Civilian Internee.

a branch of the Justice Department, under Commissioner Earl G. Harrison, a Roosevelt appointee and "Progressive Republican." Harrison delegated the running and staffing of the camps to an INS agency, the Border Patrol, under its then-supervisor Willard F. Kelly.[102]

Various sources list at least two dozen INS-run, Justice Department, permanent and temporary detention stations, and the War Department had a similar number of Army-run temporary and permanent internment camps.[103] Most of these facilities contained only men. Some held just one or two nationalities, whereas others incarcerated Japanese, German, and Italian aliens, and occasionally aliens of other ethnicities. Seagoville, in Texas, held mostly women, plus a few of their husbands, whereas Crystal City, also in Texas, housed aliens together with their families. Again, all were internment camps, and thus were unrelated, administratively, to the ten WRA incarceration camps mentioned earlier.

The first one built, about January 1941, was the Fort Stanton Internment Camp in New Mexico,[104] followed by another at Fort Missoula, Montana, in April.[105] In July 1941, anticipating U.S. involvement in World War II, the Justice Department and the War Department collaborated on eventual jurisdiction over internment of enemy aliens. The Justice Department agreed to take responsibility for the apprehension and subsequent hearings of those aliens listed as "potentially dangerous." The FBI would arrest them and place them in INS custody. In that capacity they would have "detainee" status, a temporary holding classification.[106] Following a hearing at the INS camps (but not for Japanese Latin Americans), detainees would either be released or interned. If interned, jurisdiction over them passed to the War Department, which then transferred the detainees from Justice Department camps administered by the INS, to War Department camps administered by the U.S. Army.[107] The Army would not take responsibility for arrested females, children under fourteen, or married couples; they remained under the control of the INS, first at Seagoville and later at Crystal City.[108]

The Justice Department established their own alien internment camps as demand required. Actual numbers of these camps are elusive, partly because of a media conspiracy of silence, fostered by the Department itself. That agency requested "that as little as possible be said about the arrest and detention of alien enemies" in part because the Geneva Convention, an international agreement dating to 1929 that specified how POWs should be treated, required that POWs, and by agreement, alien internees, "be ... protected ... against acts of violence, insults, and public curiosity."[109] This proved to be a wise policy. The INS's Jerre Mangione recalled that in early 1942, a heavily armed "mob of angry New Mexicans ... marched on the Santa Fe internment camp with the intent of murdering all of its two thousand Japanese occupants" after learning that the New Mexico National Guard had suffered severe casualties in the Philippines. The camp commander deflected the massacre by convincing the rabble that harming Japanese internees would encourage the Japanese to reciprocate against American POWs.[110]

When the U.S. entered World War II, Fort Missoula already housed about one thousand blockaded Axis seamen, mostly Italians and a few Germans.[111] In late 1941 and early 1942 the camp expanded by an additional one thousand men, all Japanese.[112] Fort Lincoln, near Bismarck, North Dakota, was organized at the same time and in the same way as Fort Missoula, and both camps were set up to house two thousand people.[113]

The Santa Fe Internment Camp in New Mexico was established in 1942.[114] As World War II progressed, the War Department anticipated receiving additional POWs from Europe. In order to take on this increased responsibility, that agency needed to relinquish control over civilian alien internees. The Justice Department agreed to accept jurisdiction over them, so the U.S. Army returned thousands of internees to Justice Department camps administered by the INS, including Santa Fe.[115] In May 1943 Santa Fe thus became the point of origin for the first 104 Kooskia internees.

Justice Department Internees Compared with War Relocation Authority Inmates

The Justice Department program that interned the Kooskia detainees and the WRA program that incarcerated their families were two very different entities, but are frequently confused. People are often surprised to learn, as Roger Daniels has recognized, the alien Issei (first generation) internees, "although separated from their families, [were] given better treatment than were most incarcerated Japanese Americans." Even more importantly, "once they [the alien internees] were locked up, there was a kind of due process as each internee was entitled to an individual hearing. In short, however unjust, the internment of these enemy aliens did follow the forms of law and did conform, generally, to the terms of the Geneva Convention."[116]

Although the Geneva Convention initially applied only to POWs, it was later extended to govern treatment of alien detainees. Some of the major provisions in its ninety-seven sections, or articles, that affected the Kooskia and other Japanese alien internees include Article 10, "Prisoners ... shall be lodged in buildings or in barracks affording all possible guarantees of hygiene and healthfulness ... the conditions shall be the same as for the troops at base camps of the detaining Power"; Article 11, "The food ration of prisoners ... shall be equal in quantity and quality to that of troops at base camps"; Article 13, "It shall be possible for them [prisoners] to take physical exercise and enjoy the open air"; and Article 34, "Prisoners utilized for other work shall be entitled to wages ... in accordance with the rates in force for soldiers of the national army doing the same work ... ."[117]

Japan did not ratify the Geneva Convention, but pledged, through the Swiss government, one of the neutral nations that represented Japanese interests with Japan's enemies, "de facto compliance regarding prisoners of war and also agreed to apply the convention to noncombatant enemy aliens ... subject to reciprocity, and on the condition that the belligerent nations did not subject Japanese noncombatant internees to manual labor against their will."[118] Despite both countries' declared good intentions, mistreatment of Japanese aliens did occur in U.S. internment camps, although to a much lesser extent than mistreatment of POWs and civilian internees occurred in Japan and in countries under wartime Japanese occupation.[119]

In early May 1942, for example, Fort Lincoln witnessed the abusive beating of an internee from Terminal Island, California, an event called "the most severe recorded at a wartime enemy alien internment camp."[120] The thirty-three-year-old victim, Otosaburo Sumi (Fig. 10), who later volunteered for the Kooskia Internment Camp, had several teeth knocked out by blows from two immigration officers and two Korean interpreters. During Sumi's fifth interrogation, he tried to express, in his imperfect English, that

19

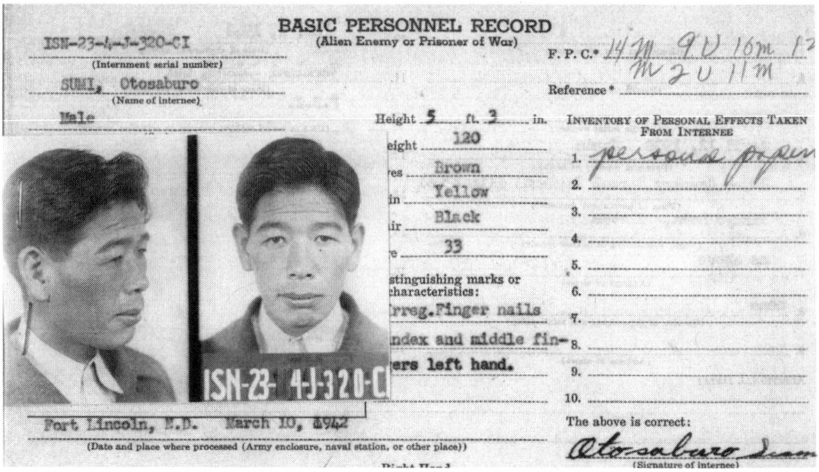
BASIC PERSONNEL RECORD
(Alien Enemy or Prisoner of War)

ISN-23-4-J-320-CI
(Internment serial number)
SUMI, Otosaburo
(Name of internee)
Male

F. P. C.*
Reference *

Height 5 ft. 3 in.
eight 120
es Brown
in Yellow
ir Black
e 33
stinguishing marks or characteristics:
rreg. Finger nails
ndex and middle fin-
ers left hand.

INVENTORY OF PERSONAL EFFECTS TAKEN FROM INTERNEE
1. personal paper
2.
3.
4.
5.
6.
7.
8.
9.
10.
The above is correct:
Otosaburo Sumi
(Signature of internee)

ISN-23-4J-320-CI

Fort Lincoln, N.D. March 10, 1942
(Date and place where processed (Army enclosure, naval station, or other place))

Fig. 10. Otosaburo Sumi, from his "Basic Personnel Record (Alien Enemy or Prisoner of War)" card, March 10, 1942, 1; E466F, Sumi, Otosaburo; OPMG, RG389, NARA II. His brutal beating occurred two months later.

he was fed up with being questioned yet again. He wanted the interpreter to help explain in Japanese, but when he said "Come on," meaning, "Come on and help me," the four men interpreted it as an invitation to fight.[121] An investigation of this and other incidents, some at Fort Missoula, led to the dismissal of the four perpetrators.[122]

Ironically, adherence to the principles of the Geneva Convention for the Japanese alien internees meant that they received better treatment than did the incarcerated U.S. citizens. Food quality at the "assembly centers" and at the later WRA facilities was notoriously poor in comparison to the ample and varied menus at the INS camps. In mid-May 1942 Teruko Teddy Ogami, incarcerated at "Camp Harmony," the Puyallup, Washington, "assembly center," wrote his father interned at Fort Missoula, "All we eat here it seems is watery food … which we had practically every meal since we came and if we have it again, I'm going to scream."[123] Accommodations at the poorly built WRA camps were extremely substandard, with crowded conditions and lack of privacy the chief complaints. In contrast, the Kooskia Internment Camp provided steam-heated barracks and private lockers, and the many windows furnished "plenty of light and ventilation."[124]

Chapter Two
Anticipating Internee Arrival:
Establishing the Kooskia Internment Camp

The Power detaining prisoners of war is bound to provide

for their maintenance.

Geneva Convention, Article 4.

On the morning of May 27, 1943, a "curious crowd" assembled at the Lewiston, Idaho, Union Pacific train depot. They had come to observe the arrival of what the *Lewiston Morning Tribune*, using the racist terminology characteristic of the times, blatantly called the "Jap special," a regularly scheduled train whose three extra cars carried 104 Japanese internees. Supervising them were an Immigration and Naturalization Service (INS) inspector and "six husky, armed members of the border patrol." Although the Japanese "looked clean, relaxed and content," they were obviously not free to leave.[1]

In the midst of World War II and only a year after the infamous Bataan Death March, several reasons explain why the crowd was "curious" rather than antagonistic at the presence of so many Japanese aliens. First, the newcomers had a certain "novelty value"; very few individuals of Japanese descent lived in the Lewiston area. Second, the Minidoka incarceration camp in southern Idaho, run by the War Relocation Authority (WRA), then housed thousands of people of Japanese ancestry, but it was several hundred miles away. Finally, the intense interest in completing the Lewis-Clark Highway between Idaho and Montana meant that local residents wanted to glimpse the new arrivals who would do the work.

It had taken just three months to establish the Kooskia Internment Camp as a unique road construction facility housing Japanese alien internees, mainly because the INS was able to acquire the buildings and infrastructure of the Canyon Creek Prison Camp. Once that was accomplished, the INS hired administrators and staff, sorted out various bureaucratic details, and obtained commitments to volunteer from interested internees.

INS Acquisition of the Canyon Creek Prison Camp

In February 1943 W. F. Kelly,[2] assistant commissioner for alien control at the INS's Philadelphia headquarters, directed Bert Fraser (Fig. 11), the officer in charge of the INS's alien detention station at Fort Missoula, Montana, to inspect the Canyon Creek Prison Camp to determine its suitability as an internment camp "for troublesome internees."[3] At the time of Fraser's visit, it housed just seventy-nine prisoners, and was preparing to close as a prison camp because of the need for the prison system to conserve funds by consolidating operations, thereby assisting the war effort.

Fig. 11. Bert Fraser (second from left, with cigar), officer in charge, Fort Missoula, Montana, Internment Camp. Courtesy Vera M. Hewitt and The Historical Museum at Fort Missoula from the Clarence Hewitt Collection.

Following his inspection tour, Fraser sent Kelly a written report describing the camp's facilities and location, in "a wild and undeveloped country." The camp's buildings (Fig. 12) included an administration headquarters, with offices, and lodging for single officers; a utility building, housing a laundry, a power house, and a repair garage; a storehouse with a large diesel refrigerator; a kitchen and mess hall; a dormitory, whose four 25 x 125 ft. wings could house sixty men each, in double-decked beds; a central bathroom block; and a crafts building. Housing for the married employees was located one-half mile away, at Apgar Creek, and consisted of twelve, four-room homes and one, five-room home, all "attractive and in good condition" (Fig. 13, Fig. 14).[4]

The camp's utilities included heating, lighting, water, fuel, and sewer systems.[5] A central power plant, with two boilers, warmed the entire facility; for fuel, it burned Pres-to-logs, a commercial product made from compressed wood chips, shavings, and sawdust.[6] A diesel engine generated power for lighting, all buildings obtained water from the adjacent Canyon Creek, and three septic tanks contained the camp's sewage.[7]

Fig. 12. Prison camp, later internment camp, 1930s. Photograph by Don McCombs. Courtesy Clearwater National Forest, Lochsa District, Kooskia Ranger Station.

Under operations, Fraser discussed supplies, medical facilities, communications, transportation, recreation, and work projects. All supplies came from Kooskia, thirty miles away, population three hundred, or from Lewiston, "a progressive city" one hundred miles distant, population twenty

Fig. 13. Lewis-Clark Highway at Apgar Creek, showing employee housing on both sides of road, for prison camp, later internment camp, 1941. Photograph by J. W. Gillmore. Courtesy Idaho State Historical Society, MS 281, Box 9, Folder 9, District File No. 15532.

Fig. 14. Employee cottage at Apgar Creek for prison camp, later internment camp, showing terrace and lawn, 1930s. Photograph by Don McCombs. Courtesy Clearwater National Forest, Lochsa District, Kooskia Ranger Station.

thousand. A one-car passenger train served Kooskia daily, and a freight train arrived twice weekly. Medical facilities at the prison camp consisted of a well-equipped emergency medical room and ample dental equipment; a local dentist visited weekly. The camp had telephone service and a small shoe repair shop. Vehicles included twelve trucks of various sizes and one automobile.[8] Recreational opportunities comprised a motion picture projector, a classroom, and a one-thousand-book library. Severe winters limited leisure activities, but in summer the men were permitted to swim in the river and they also had a small baseball diamond and a handball court.[9]

The prison camp personnel typically numbered twenty-four employees, mostly men. Superintendent Deane A. Remer had been there for eight years and seemed to be "a very capable man." Others included clerks, guards, a medical technical assistant, and a junior steward, who was filling the vacant position of chief cook. In Fraser's opinion, the current staff would be sufficient to manage an internee camp of at least 225 men.[10]

To Fraser's surprise, the prison camp was unfenced, despite nearly twenty prisoner escapes in eight years,[11] but he correctly assumed that potential Japanese internees were not flight risks. Since most local residents owned hunting rifles, a Japanese escapee would likely be vulnerable to the adage, "shoot first and ask questions later." Fraser observed that fencing the camp would be difficult and expensive, requiring not only some two thousand feet of fence, but also numerous postholes. These would cost an exorbitant $3 apiece, a price dictated by the need to drill or blast them into the solid rock comprising the canyon floor.[12]

By late March, Kelly, in Philadelphia, concurred that the potential fencing difficulties would make the prison camp unsuitable for troublesome internees. Instead, it could house internee laborers. Such a camp could then operate under Fraser's jurisdiction as a satellite to the INS's Fort Missoula detention station.[13]

In early April 1943 Fraser met in Ogden, Utah, with U.S. Bureau of Public Roads (USBPR) employees B. J. Finch, district engineer; R. R. Mitchell, senior highway engineer; and H. K. Bishop, chief, division of construction.[14] The four men agreed on the running of the camp and on the organization of the road work. The INS would operate and maintain the camp, furnish and feed the Japanese internee workers, and transport them to their work sites. The USBPR would employ the men, paying them $55 per month.[15] The choice of Japanese aliens as road workers was not random. Bishop preferred to have Japanese labor on this type of work because he had used men of Japanese descent successfully on similar projects in the Hawaiian Islands.[16]

Fraser's subsequent report to Kelly detailed additional agreements resulting from the meeting. Some 200 Japanese internees would be necessary, with 175 needed for road work and 25 for camp maintenance. The $55 per month might include a deduction for special clothing and other necessary items. Since aliens could not receive wages for maintenance of the camps where they were incarcerated, salaries for those workers would have to come from contributions made by the road gang. The Japanese were neither expected nor allowed to handle "powder" [explosives] nor to do any work that might be regarded as dangerous. The prison camp's Superintendent Remer would be retained in the same capacity for the Kooskia camp.[17]

In closing his report on the meeting, Fraser made a number of specific suggestions. He recommended that the INS take over the facilities as soon as possible, and that the entire prison camp, including equipment and supplies, be left intact. He suggested that (1) the Japanese selected should be willing and capable of doing road construction work; (2) no fences were needed; (3) the Japanese were not to do dangerous work; (4) they would receive $55 per month plus room and board; (5) a responsible Japanese or Korean censor should be employed; and (6) an INS employee needed to familiarize prison camp staff with Geneva Convention requirements.[18] The latter point would ultimately prove to be the most difficult to implement.

Application of Geneva Convention Directives

Since the USBPR was to supervise the construction work, their foremen also needed to learn how to deal with alien enemies under the Geneva Convention.[19] The INS had facilitated this requirement by creating, for their Santa Fe Internment Camp, a list of over seventy detailed rules regarding U.S. treatment of alien internees.[20] They then condensed these down to twenty-three important provisions relating to the minimum standards of detainee custody and sent the instructions to the other INS camps, clearly stating that "reciprocity" was the underlying motivation for the care of internees. If an alien were to complain of poor treatment, it would provide the enemy with an excuse for retaliating by treating American detainees in a harsh and cruel manner.[21]

The "rules to be observed" were minimum standards, and could be exceeded at the discretion of the officers in charge of the detention camps. The detainees were entitled to humane treatment, and must not be subjected to "violence, insults, and public curiosity," nor could they be humiliated or degraded. No "physical coercion" was allowed, and INS employees were not permitted to "invade the person of any detainee" unless in self-defense or to prevent escape.[22]

Additional specific requirements covered living and working conditions, recreational pursuits, and other topics. Subsequent chapters will discuss these, as well as the failure of some INS employees to observe the Geneva Convention requirements.

Administering and Staffing the Kooskia Internment Camp

The Kooskia camp's first superintendent was Deane A. Remer (Fig. 15).[23] As the former prison camp administrator, he was thoroughly experienced in the operation of such a facility, and in the supervision of its employees. Some of the prison employees joined the INS, retaining their former positions, while others, who wanted to transfer to prisons elsewhere, were replaced.

At the time, two INS employees, Dave Aldridge and Walter C. Wood, were on assignment to Fort Missoula from the Sharp Park Detention Camp in California. In early June, Fraser sent Aldridge to the Kooskia camp, to help Remer make the transition from prison camp to internment camp. At first, Aldridge was the assistant officer in charge of alien detentions.[24] Shortly thereafter, presumably to better introduce Remer to INS procedures, Fraser switched Remer's and Aldridge's positions. Aldridge became

Fig. 15. D. A. Remer, prison camp superintendent and first officer in charge of the Kooskia Internment Camp, 1943. Courtesy Nez Perce County Historical Society Inc., Lewiston, Idaho, from Tish Erb, "Jap Internees Work Hard, Well Treated, at Kooskia Road Camp," Lewiston Morning Tribune, September 26, 1943, sec. 2, p, 1.

the officer in charge, with Remer as his assistant. This change would remain in effect "until such time as the camp has been placed on a full Immigration Detention Station basis." Since Aldridge was "experienced ... in handling aliens under the terms of the Geneva Convention," he would remain in charge until Remer and the other Kooskia staff "have been fully indoctrinated in such methods and procedure."[25] This comment only hints at what will later become a enormous dilemma for the INS and for the Kooskia Internment Camp's Japanese internees, namely, Remer's difficulty in adjusting to internment camp management from prison camp administration. Compounding his unhappiness and humiliation was his knowledge that the internees believed him to have "lost face" through his temporary demotion.

Besides the superintendent, also known as the officer in charge, the initial Kooskia Internment Camp staff included an assistant officer in charge, a surveillance-liaison chief, nine immigration guards, eight custodial officers, a chief supply officer, a clerk, a steward, and an assistant supply officer who also served as warehouseman and general maintenance man.[26]

Aldridge observed the former prison camp employees for two weeks. Then, after consulting with them as to their wishes, he made recommendations regarding nine men he felt should be transferred from the Bureau of Prisons (BP) to the INS.[27]

Information about wages is available for some of the Kooskia camp employees, whose salaries were the same as those paid by the BP. Remer's pay remained at $3,500 per year, senior guards received $2,200, junior guards got $2,040, and the chief clerk received $2,600.[28] Salaries for other positions included assistant officer in charge, $3,200; financial clerk, $1,800; two clerks "s & t" [shorthand and typing], $1,620; a junior steward/storekeeper, $2,300; and a Japanese American interpreter/translator, $2,000.[29] Other guards received a base salary of $1,860 per year, plus overtime.[30] Some of the recruiting for those positions was quite casual. Former guard Alfred Keehr (Fig. 16) recalled that he was employed at a store in the town of Kooskia when Deane Remer "came down and got seven of us to sign up" to work at the Kooskia Internment Camp.[31]

Employees who required meals and housing had those amounts deducted from their salaries. One meal a day for employees, in the officers' mess, cost $5 per month, and three meals daily were $15 per month.[32] Men who lived in the administration building's "bachelor quarters" paid just $1.50 per month for housing. The employees living in the four-room cottages at Apgar Creek paid $7.50 per month, and Remer's five-room dwelling cost him $10 per month.[33]

Once the internees arrived, the new administration required additional secretarial assistance. In early June 1943 Aldridge sent Fraser a draft of an

Fig. 16. Guard Alfred "Al" Keehr with his baby daughter, Carol, 1943. Courtesy Carol Keehr Williams.

agreement between the INS, represented by Fraser, and the USBPR, represented by Finch. Aldridge asked if Fraser could get it typed at Fort Missoula, since "we're short of clerical help, as a matter of fact have no clerk, only a supply man, and I'm doing all my own typing."[34]

A week later Aldridge wrote again, specifically requesting, "if the services can be spared," that "a qualified typist, with some knowledge of the Missoula file system" be detailed to the Kooskia camp for two weeks to help reorganize the office. He explained that the BP clerk was taking care of administrative details related to the closing of the prison camp, while the other clerk was acting as supply officer. Fort Missoula granted Aldridge's request; a handwritten notation on the file copy of the letter reads, "Virginia Blackwood sent 6-15-43."[35]

Recollections of several former employees are important in understanding the day-to-day workings of the Kooskia camp. The guards, especially, performed many tasks. Some supervised the road workers during the day, while others were on duty at night. Alfred Keehr's own work day began at 4 p.m. One of his hourly responsibilities was to check the electric pump that provided water from Canyon Creek. He also made the rounds of the camp to see if there were any problems needing his attention. After his helper came on at midnight, they visited the barracks with a flashlight, counting the men to be sure they were in their beds. Empty bunks usually indicated that their occupants were socializing with the kitchen crew, whose quarters were near their workplace.[36]

Guard Cecil Boller (Fig. 17) helped with the bed check at midnight. He also drove the outgoing mail to Kooskia and collected the incoming mail, milk, and daily groceries.[37]

Amelia Jacks (Fig. 18) was a secretary at first,[38] and later became the camp's financial officer with complete responsibility for preparation and disbursement of the payroll. Because she paid the internees and employees, and

Fig. 17. Kooskia Internment Camp
guard Cecil Boller in his official
uniform. Courtesy Cecil Boller, with
assistance from Cheryl J. Tousley and
Bruce Wassmuth.

Fig. 18. Financial officer Amelia Jacks,
1943. Courtesy DeAnn Jacks Scrabeck.

disbursed cash, she was designated a deputy U.S. Marshal, and had to be bonded in the amount of $5,000.[39] In a telephone interview, she stated that the timekeeper, a man she remembered as "Taki," gave her the men's hours, and she figured out the amount due them. Once a month, she drove to Lewiston and obtained cash to pay the internees. They were only authorized to have $10 in their possession at any one time, but could draw up to $30 a month. The remainder of their pay was banked for them in Lewiston.[40]

Amelia's husband, Ed Jacks (Fig. 19), also worked at the Kooskia camp. First employed as a guard, he later became the chief steward in charge of alien mess adminis-tration. In the latter capacity, he administered the internees' food program. He had the responsibility for obtaining groceries, distributing them to the internee kitchen crew, and seeing that the meals met dietary standards.[41] Large shipments, of rice and other bulk food supplies, came twice weekly by train, so Jacks ar-ranged for a big truck to get those.[42] He also calculated the average daily food allowance per internee.[43] After finding that office work did not ap-peal to him, he returned to his guard duties, worked with the camp's team of horses, and sometimes provided the camp with wild game.[44] He also monitored the camp's water delivery and sewage disposal systems, and repaired them when necessary.[45]

Fig. 19. Guard and later chief steward Edwin "Ed" Jacks, left, and chief clerk Albert Stark, right, at Apgar housing area with camp horses, about 1943. Courtesy Janie Fluharty.

Alien Internees Agree to Volunteer for Road Construction

Communications from Fort Missoula officials to other alien detention stations revealed that a number of detainees were interested in the opportunity of working at the Kooskia Internment Camp. By late April 1943 some 116 internees at the Santa Fe, New Mexico, INS detention center had indicated their willingness to volunteer for the road construction project, as had an initial 17 of 79 internees at Fort George G. Meade, Maryland.[46] The officer in charge of the Santa Fe camp must have relayed some of the prospective internees' questions and concerns to W. F. Kelly in Philadelphia, since a reply from him provided a detailed description of the conditions that would prevail at the Kooskia camp.

Kelly stated that it was quite isolated and would be guarded by INS officers, so internees were in no danger of molestation by outsiders during the several years that the project would last. There were facilities for medical and dental care, internees could take their personal property with them, and their income would not be subject to tax. The barracks were well constructed and in excellent condition, and were well-lighted and well-heated. Recreational facilities included a small baseball diamond and a handball court, as well as a motion picture projector, a classroom, and a library; internees could also go swimming in the river. The workweek would be eight hours a day, six days a week, with pay at $45 per month, not the $55 that was previously suggested.[47] In his letter, Kelly expressed concern that no one had volunteered for the camp operation and maintenance positions. He stressed that the camp could not function without twenty-five such persons, but they would only receive eighty cents per day.[48]

By early May one hundred Japanese internees from the Santa Fe camp had definitely committed to the Kooskia camp and had solved the camp operation problem. They agreed to provide twenty-five kitchen, laundry, and other camp workers from among their number. Although pay for the camp workers was just ten cents per hour, the road workers agreed to contribute from their wages so all would receive the same amount.[49] The following day, an additional four names were added to the list. In all, 104 men comprised the initial group that would relocate from Santa Fe to the Kooskia Internment Camp.[50]

From Prison to Internment Camp

Once the Santa Fe and Fort Meade contingents had agreed to go to the Kooskia camp, arrangements were made to remove the Canyon Creek federal prisoners to another location, keeping on a few men to maintain the camp until the Japanese arrived.[51] The BP agreed to leave most of the equipment and supplies for the INS. The few exceptions were items that the BP needed elsewhere in the prison system, ones they thought the INS would not want.[52] Nevertheless, misunderstandings occurred. For example, until he was stopped, the BP supervisor of prison camps, detailed to the Kooskia camp to arrange the transfer, intended to move the laundry and power plant to another prison facility.[53]

The Canyon Creek Prison Camp thus became the Kooskia Internment Camp, utilizing virtually the same plant that had housed federal prisoners since autumn 1935.[54] With an administrator and a minimal staff in place, the camp was ready to welcome its first contingent of internee workers. The last of the federal prisoners departed on May 22, 1943.[55] Less than a week later, on May 27, Japanese alien internees began arriving to replace them.[56]

Japanese Internees Reach the Kooskia Camp

According to the terms of the Geneva Convention, internees could not be conscripted for this kind of work; therefore, they were all volunteers. Most of the men who came to the Kooskia camp were permanent residents of the United States, but their alien status subjected them to detention in internment camps for the duration of World War II. Newspaper accounts;[57] numerous government documents; and statements from two former Kooskia internees, James I. Yano and Koshio Henry Shima, all confirm that the men volunteered for assignment to help build the Lewis-Clark Highway and that they received wages for their labor.

The men who lived and worked at the Kooskia camp for the two years it was open, from late May 1943 until early May 1945, were all Japanese males ranging in age from the low twenties to the mid-sixties (Appendix). During that time, some 265 of them lived there, not all simultaneously. They came from both coasts, from a variety of states, and from the then-territories of Alaska and Hawai'i. Some were from Mexico, and others had even been kidnapped from Panama and Peru.

The first three groups of internees arrived from Santa Fe, New Mexico; Fort Meade, Maryland; and Camp Livingston, Louisiana. Their comments on their journeys, and on the meals supplied to them upon arrival in Lewiston, indicate that their treatment was far better in comparison to the well-known, unpleasant experiences of Japanese Americans sent to WRA incarceration camps.

The First Group

Upon leaving Santa Fe the evening of May 24, the 104 internees in the first group traveled via Colorado, Wyoming, and Oregon.[58] While they were stopped in Lewiston, one Japanese man came to the doorway of the train and stood briefly on the step (Fig. 20), just long enough for his image to be captured by local press photographer Eddie Webster. The photo appeared in the local paper the following day.[59]

At Lewiston the internees ate at the depot before continuing on their journey. A lengthy newspaper article reported on the men, their stopover, and their meal, which was lunch prepared by a nearby restaurant, the White Front Cafe, located next to the courthouse and across the street from the train station. Because the cafe could only seat about thirty-five people, the meal was instead set up on the lawn west of the depot. Plans originally called for serving the food, picnic-style, to the aliens, and numerous local residents had turned up hoping to get a good look at the Japanese. Disappointingly for them, but a relief to the Japanese who would not have enjoyed being ogled, security concerns necessitated a change in arrangements. Instead, everything was dished up and carried to the train. There the guards received the plates and distributed them to the internees. The lunch was ample, and "consisted of baked ham, beans, potato salad, deviled eggs, bread and butter sandwiches, milk and coffee."[60] This was a splendid feast, and even included some rationed items, such as ham and butter. In contrast, Japanese Ameri-

Peep At A Camera-Shy Jap

—Eddie Webster photo.
The only Japanese who emerged from the privacy of the railroad coaches bringing the first contingent of internees and aliens through Lewiston Thursday enroute to the Lochsa federal camp to work on the Lewis & Clark highway is shown in the photograph above. He retreated into the train when he saw the press photographer, explaining that Japs are "superstitious" about being photographed. At the left is a member of the border patrol which guarded the contingent and, in the center with his back to the camera, the supervising inspector of the federal bureau of immigration and naturalization.

Fig. 20. Japanese internee from first group, aboard train at meal stop in Lewiston. Eddie Webster photo. Courtesy Nez Perce County Historical Society Inc., Lewiston, Idaho, from "Peep at a Camera-Shy Jap," Lewiston Morning Tribune, May 29, 1943, 10.

cans in the WRA incarceration camps seldom, if ever, ate so well during their confinement.

Irving Kalinoski remembers the meal clearly. His widowed mother, Helen Kalinoski, ran the cafe, and Irving, age fourteen, helped carry the meals to the men aboard the train. He recalled that a white-haired Japanese man tipped him twenty-five cents. The internee handed the money to the guard and then "looked out to see that the kid got it." The guards also counted the silverware as it went into the train, and again when the empty plates came back out.[61]

Helen Kalinoski, later Helen Thiessen, age ninety-four when interviewed, recalled many details about feeding the first group of internees. She and her son loaded the food onto several carts brought from the depot, took it over to the station, and arranged it on tables set up on the lawn. When the guards would not let the internees off the train, she fixed two or three plates to show what the amounts should look like, and then had the guards help her dish it all up.[62]

Besides the food mentioned in the newspaper account, Thiessen remembered that she also provided fresh fruit and cookies. Although coffee was available, the internees mostly chose tea. Because Thiessen did not know when the train would arrive, she had to prepare something that would do for breakfast, lunch, or dinner. She thought she received $1 or $1.25 per person, since the meal was comparable to what she served her customers for Sunday dinner, and that cost $1.[63]

Following the lunch stop at Lewiston, the train continued for another seventy or so miles up the Clearwater River to the town of Kooskia. The group disembarked and boarded trucks for the rest of the journey to the internment camp, thirty miles away (Fig. 21). At the hamlet of Lowell, two rivers, the Selway and the Lochsa, come together and flow into the Clearwater. From Lowell, the trucks followed the wild and scenic Lochsa River for seven miles until they reached the Kooskia Internment Camp. Once there, these 104 internees, and others yet to arrive, would spend up to two years working on construction of the Lewis-Clark Highway, a portion of the present U.S. Highway 12.[64]

A week after his arrival, internee Sakaye Ed Yoshimura, a photographer from California (Fig. 22), described the journey in a letter to relatives confined at the Poston, Arizona, WRA incarceration camp. During the three days and nights they spent on the train, the men played poker, slept, and enjoyed the scenery.[65] The fact that the men could enjoy the landscape means that they were not required to keep the shades drawn in the train, in contrast to their relatives' experience in their forced journeys to the WRA incarceration camps.

Fig. 21. Trucks brought the internees from the train station to the Kooskia Internment Camp, and later took them to their daily work assignments along the road. Courtesy Scrapbook, PG 103-38-2.

The Second Group

The next contingent, comprised of fifteen internees from Fort George G. Meade, Maryland, reached Kooskia the following day, on May 28.[66] The early hour of their arrival at Lewiston, 2:35 a.m., meant that the previous crowds

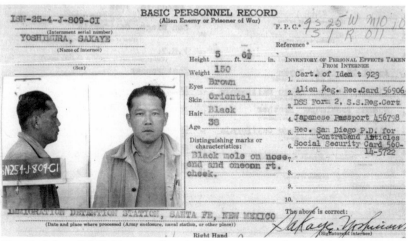

Fig. 22. Sakaye Ed Yoshimura, from his "Basic Personnel Record (Alien Enemy or Prisoner of War)" card, undated [1942], 1; E466F, Yoshimura, Sakaye; OPMG, RG389, NARA II.

were absent, so the prisoners were allowed off the train for their meal. Once again, the White Front Cafe provided it, and served them "prunes, ham and eggs, toast and coffee."[67] Irving Kalinoski recalled that when smaller detainee groups came through Lewiston and ate in the restaurant, the internees were ushered in, the doors were locked, and a guard with a Thompson submachine gun stationed himself at the back door of the restaurant.[68]

The Third Group

An additional fourteen internees arrived on June 7 from Camp Livingston, Louisiana.[69] As with the two previous groups, their train stopped at Lewiston so the internees could eat breakfast at the White Front Cafe. This time, the meal consisted of oatmeal, scrambled eggs, potatoes, hot biscuits, and coffee.[70]

Instructions to Internees on Arrival

Once the men reached the Kooskia Internment Camp, Walter C. Wood, sent from Fort Missoula to be the assistant officer in charge, welcomed them and issued instructions for their conduct while at the Kooskia camp. He suggested they should "feel a considerable degree of satisfaction" for being selected for this "honor camp," which he described as "a small community of workmen designed to give you the opportunity to lead a normal life while here." Wood admonished them "to govern your conduct so that the common welfare of the entire camp will be promoted and insured," and warned them of certain rule infractions for which they would be disciplined.[71]

Wood listed the offenses, including

insubordination toward officers, camp authorities or duly elected camp leaders of their own nationality; refusal to perform work; escape or attempted escape; conduct tending to disrupt the harmony of the camp or facility; malicious destruction of property and kindred offenses; and serious infractions of the rules of conduct established for the camp.[72]

Wood even provided detailed instructions on bedmaking:

In making your bed, you should tuck the edges of the blanket neatly under the mattress. The top sheet should be folded back from the head of the bed so that 10 inches of the sheet is showing. All extra blankets are to be neatly folded and placed on the foot of the bed.[73]

Reasons for Volunteering

What brought these Japanese internees to such a rugged area of Idaho, to contend with boot-camp bedmaking lessons and transgressions they were not likely to commit? The long-forgotten answers lay in crumbling documents at the National Archives in Washington, DC, and in the recorded memories of the internees and their family members.

As a group, the Kooskia internees had a wide variety of reasons compelling them to volunteer for road work in this isolated region. Where their explanations are known, most fall into several distinct categories. Mainly, some of the internees wished to leave an unpleasant physical or psychological environment; others desired to be closer to relatives; and many wanted, or needed, to earn money. Some individuals hoped to help their adopted country; others simply wished to escape the enforced boredom at other INS camps.

Physical and Psychological Concerns

James I. Yano (Fig. 23), a former internee spokesman, gave several reasons for going to the Kooskia camp. Mainly, he wanted to get away from the dusty, dry climate of the Santa Fe Internment Camp.[74] Yasuo Suga, a fisherman from Mexico, wrote a detailed account of why he and others transferred from Santa Fe. Unfortunately, very little of what he said passed the censor, who translated and excerpted Suga's letter and underlined passages to be deleted from it before sending it on to the intended recipient. At first, Suga and his companions thought Santa Fe

> … was really a good place with the mild weather and also very nice views like resort. <u>But the building where we lived was very old</u> … . <u>[T]he worst of all was that they didn't get along well in camp</u>. <u>I felt unhappy why they couldn't enjoy happier camp life</u>. Anyway bachelors impressed me as if they were <u>stubborn</u>. Furthermore, <u>foods were not satisfactory</u>. To tell you the truth, when they asked for volunteers, I thought it was a good chance, and <u>got out of there</u>.[75]

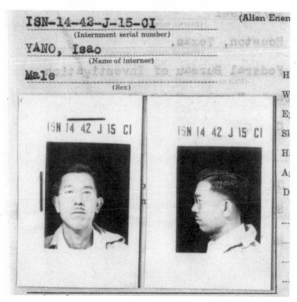

Fig. 23. James Isao Yano, from his "Basic Personnel Record (Alien Enemy or Prisoner of War)" card, January 19, 1942, 1; E466F, Yano, Isao; OPMG, RG389, NARA II.

Family Considerations

Kinzo Asaba and Shohei Arase both volunteered for the Kooskia camp because they wanted to be closer to family members who were imprisoned at the WRA's Minidoka incarceration camp in southern Idaho.[76] Even though the Minidoka camp was some four hundred miles away from the Kooskia camp, at least they would all be in the same state.

Financial Motives

Kosaku Sato was the owner of a store selling second-hand goods in Seattle. When interned, he shut up the store with everything in it. He volunteered for the Kooskia camp in order to earn money to pay rent for the store. Doing so would free his son from that obligation, thus enabling Tad to join the U.S. Army.[77]

Other Reasons

James I. Yano also appreciated the opportunity to do road construction work during wartime; that way he could "do something for my adopted country."[78] Kidnapped Japanese Peruvian internees Taro Shimabukuro and his son Koshio [later Koshio Henry Shima] volunteered for the Kooskia camp because there was nothing to do at Kenedy, Texas, their previous location. Shima stated that "it was better to work - the time goes fast."[79]

Internee Cohesiveness

Despite their diverse backgrounds, different languages, and varied occupations, wartime anti-Japanese hysteria had brought all these men together. At Idaho's Kooskia Internment Camp they formed into a unified crew that ultimately defied racist stereotyping to win praise and admiration for their work ethic and their successful achievements. On arrival at the Kooskia camp, the internees first concerned themselves with ensuring that their living conditions were satisfactory, and as promised.

Chapter Three
No Barbed Wire:
Living Conditions at the
Kooskia Internment Camp

The quarters must be fully protected from dampness, sufficiently heated and lighted. ... The food ration of prisoners shall be equal in quantity and quality to that of troops at base camps.
Geneva Convention, Articles 10 and 11.

The internees at the Kooskia camp and elsewhere were fortunate to be covered by Geneva Convention requirements specifying the sort of accommodations they would be provided. These were in marked contrast to the treatment their relatives received, first at the temporary detention centers and later at the War Relocation Authority (WRA) incarceration camps. Ironically, as mentioned, the interned Japanese non-citizens received better treatment than their incarcerated American citizen relatives, whose only crime was having Japanese ancestry.

As a teenager, Sakiko Nakashima was imprisoned at the euphemistically named "Camp Harmony," the former Puyallup, Washington, fairgrounds. In May 1942 she wrote her father, Kintaro, "We made mattresses out of straw. The room smells like an elephant's pen."[1] Kintaro, later a Kooskia internee, was a so-called "alien enemy" detained at Fort Missoula, Montana, an Immigration and Naturalization Service (INS) internment camp. There, and at other INS camps, conditions were far superior to those endured by his daughter and the rest of his family, but the Kooskia camp was unique in the U.S. for being an internee work camp.

Once the Japanese internees had arrived at the Kooskia camp, they took a keen interest in their living conditions. This is evident from messages they sent to friends and relatives, announcing their transfer to Idaho. The Kooskia camp compared very favorably with previous INS camps where they had stayed.

Some of the Kooskia internees wrote letters and cards in English, others corresponded in Japanese, and later arrivals from Latin America wrote in Spanish. According to articles 36 to 38 and 40 of the Geneva Convention discussing censorship of internee mail, regulations allowed internees to send and receive letters, postcards, and telegrams; their outgoing and incoming correspondence was all read and censored. Internees could receive parcels containing food and clothing, and these were opened and inspected before being given to the addressee.[2] Where forbidden statements were deleted from their outgoing correspondence, officials made copies of certain letters for government files.

Mail and Censorship

As Louis Fiset has explained in greater detail than is possible here, both incoming and outgoing alien enemy mail was subject to censorship during World War II.[3] Generally, each Kooskia internee could write one letter and one postcard daily; postage was free.[4] No restrictions governed the number of packages, telegrams, or telephone messages they could send.[5] International mail to countries at war with the U.S. had to be written on a special Red Cross form (Fig. 24).[6] Messages that contained "prohibited or objectionable matter" were returned to the detainee who was asked to rewrite the letter, except in cases where the letter was confiscated in its entirety. Any deleted matter "should be cut out from the letter rather than obliterated with ink."[7] Prior to the assignment of a censor at the Kooskia camp, the internees' outgoing mail, whether in Japanese or English, was forwarded, unsealed, to the INS interpreters at Fort Missoula. Some were Korean, and one, Paul Kashino, was a Japanese American. Evidently, only Kashino censored the Kooskia correspondence since all the available copies bear his name rather than those of the Koreans.[8]

The Kooskia internees' earliest communications are dated May 28, 1943, the day after the first group arrived. All bore the return address, "Kooskia Camp, Box 1539, Missoula, Montana," an indication that the men were complying with a directive stating that Fort Missoula would handle the Kooskia camp's mail under the specified address.[9]

The men soon learned that non-compliance with the rules meant return of their mail. When that happened, a form attached to each envelope explained the reason. Detainees were admonished to "write on one side of the

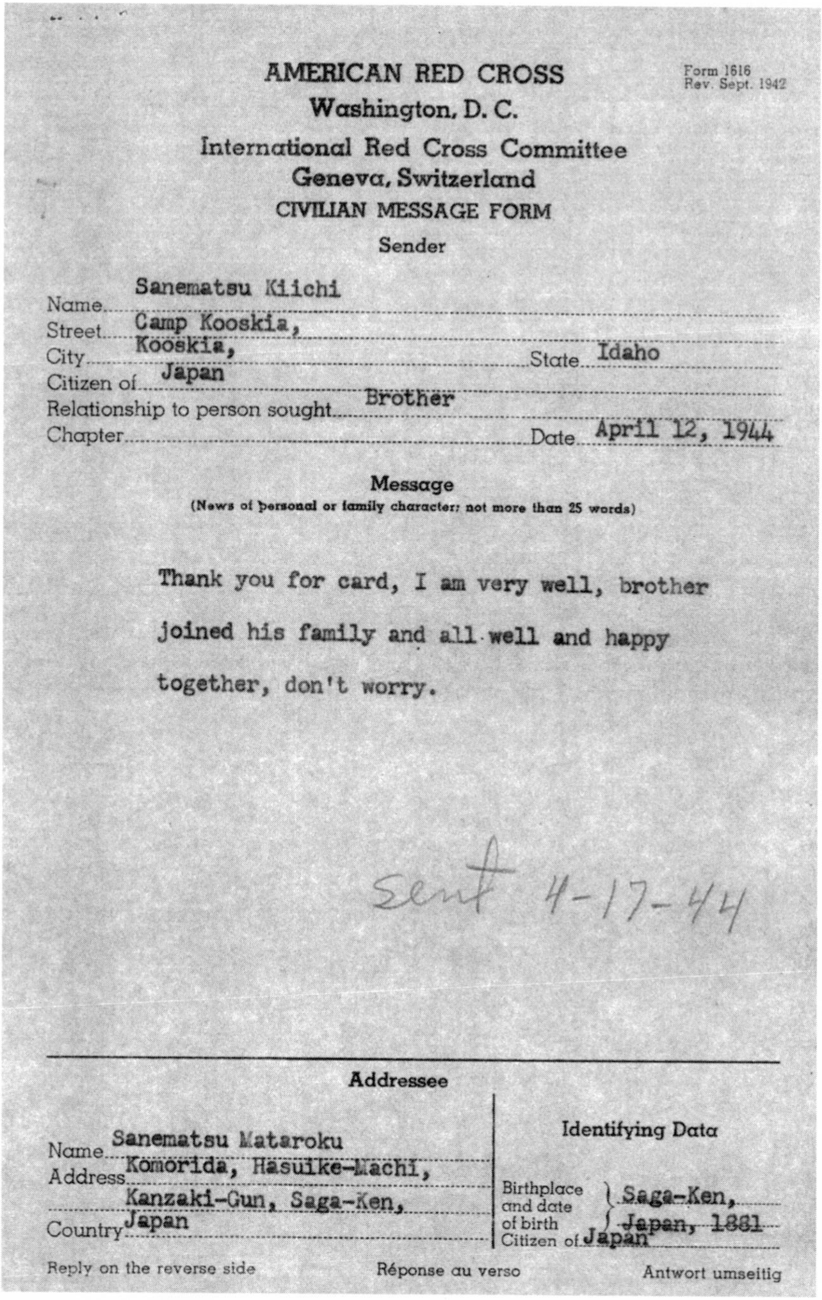

AMERICAN RED CROSS
Washington, D. C.

Form 1616
Rev. Sept. 1942

International Red Cross Committee
Geneva, Switzerland
CIVILIAN MESSAGE FORM

Sender

Name... Sanematsu Kiichi
Street... Camp Kooskia,
City... Kooskia,   State... Idaho
Citizen of... Japan
Relationship to person sought... Brother
Chapter...   Date... April 12, 1944

Message
(News of personal or family character; not more than 25 words)

Thank you for card, I am very well, brother

joined his family and all well and happy

together, don't worry.

sent 4-17-44

Addressee

Name... Sanematsu Mataroku
Address... Komorida, Hasuike-Machi,
Kanzaki-Gun, Saga-Ken,
Country... Japan

Identifying Data

Birthplace } Saga-Ken,
and date } Japan, 1881
of birth }
Citizen of Japan

Reply on the reverse side   Réponse au verso   Antwort umseitig

Fig. 24. Message from Kooskia internee Kiichi Sanematsu, a gardener from Riverside, California, to his brother in Japan. Because normal postal service was suspended during wartime, the Red Cross forwarded such brief communications, maximum 25 words and printed on bright pink paper, as a humanitarian gesture. From E466F, Sanematsu, Kiichi, OPMG, RG389, NARA II.

paper only," letters could not be more than twenty-five lines, and postcards were limited to seven lines.[10] Fort Missoula returned some mail because the men had failed to write the correct return address on the envelope, or had enclosed cash rather than a personal check or money order.[11]

The censor was instructed to delete from the Kooskia men's writings any complaints they expressed. Sometimes these mentioned the food, but more often they were passages that told how many men were in the camp and where the camp was located. In late May Yoshie Charles Yoshikawa, a cook from Vermilion, Ohio, wrote a friend, "<u>Yesterday small number companions from East and I understand we will have some more be here sometime today which will fill up this camp</u>."[12] Inao Minato's letter mentioned "<u>only 35 miles from the railroad</u>."[13] Although the underlined passages were censored from the men's outgoing letters, they were preserved in copies retained in the Kooskia camp files, now at the National Archives in Washington, DC.

The addition of Kooskia camp correspondence, to the already-heavy volume of mail to and from Fort Missoula detainees, must have overwhelmed the censors at Fort Missoula.[14] Soon, letters in English to and from the Kooskia internees began to be censored locally. In early July Bert Fraser, officer in charge at Fort Missoula, so notified the INS central office and requested a "Censor Stamp" for the Kooskia camp (Fig. 25).[15] Officer in charge Deane Remer and clerk Albert Stark received individual "censorship numbers" to enter on the stamped mail, logged all incoming and outgoing messages, and forwarded letters not in English to Fort Missoula.[16] Because Japanese-language letters from the Kooskia camp bear Missoula postmarks, Louis Fiset deduced that such mail must have been "forwarded outside the postal system, probably by commuters between the two camps."[17]

Fig. 25. Censor stamp, actual size. The blank line is for the number of the person who censored the document, and "U. S. I. & N. S." stands for U. S. Immigration and Naturalization Service. From ACAC, by AcACAC, to Superintendent, KIC, July 14, [19]43; E291, 1000/K(1), RG85, NARA I.

Once Remer and Stark had censored the outgoing English-language mail, the post office in the town of Kooskia postmarked it and sent it onward. Confirming data came from family members of Kizaemon Ikken Momii; they kindly provided a photocopy of an English-language letter Momii wrote to his son Rikito. The postmark on the envelope is "Kooskia Idaho Jul. 29, 1943" (Fig. 26).

Fig. 26. Envelope addressed to Rikito Momii at the Topaz incarceration camp, Utah, from his father, Kizaemon Ikken Momii, at the Kooskia Internment Camp. The postmark is Kooskia, Idaho. Courtesy Rick and Yasu Momii.

Besides being subject to censorship, the Kooskia internees' incoming and outgoing communications were freely shared with other INS employees, sometimes because they included positive statements, and at other times for negative, censored ones. Where comments were deleted, the censor typed up excerpts from the letters. If the original was in Japanese, Paul Kashino translated the selection into English and underlined anything he had censored from the original. Copies of his typed extracts were routinely sent to six different offices within the INS system.[18]

Certain internees' mail received special attention, probably because the authorities somehow perceived these men as being more "dangerous" than others. One such person was Reverend Hozen Seki, founder of the New York Buddhist Church. The Kooskia administration complied with a "request for copies of all [Seki's] correspondence," and made duplicates for higher authorities of all his outgoing mail, even a postcard he sent to a fellow minister.[19]

Despite censorship, the Kooskia internees enjoyed being able to communicate with relatives and friends. As can be seen from their surviving correspondence, most initially were quite satisfied with their living arrangements. In their letters and postcards, they described how pleased they were with their new location, especially the scenic surroundings and the absence of the barbed wire fence common to other INS internment camps. Nearly all reported favorably on the barracks accommodations, but the men had mixed feelings at first regarding the food.

Scenic Surroundings

The internees' correspondence revealed a deep appreciation for the natural scenic beauty of the Kooskia Internment Camp's location (Fig. 27). Several, such as Minoru Jo Wazumi, a clerk from Stamford, Connecticut, appreciated that there was "no barbed wire around here."[20] Hisahiko Teraoka and his father, Takehiko Teraoka, fishermen from Ensenada, Mexico, were both at the Kooskia camp. Shortly after their arrival, Hisahiko wrote to a friend still interned at the Santa Fe Detention Station: "What a wonderful place! We certainly love it."[21]

The Kooskia Internment Camp's setting, in the Bitterroot Mountains, was indeed idyllic. A turning off the main road led past single-file administrative

Fig. 27. Five internees atop rock pinnacle, Kooskia Internment Camp vicinity. Courtesy Scrapbook, PG 103-35-1.

buildings that hugged the hillside, beyond which was a wider area containing the dormitories. Then as now, Canyon Creek flows through the camp
and under the road into the adjacent Lochsa River.

Tommy Yoshito Kadotani, a landscape gardener from Santa Cruz, California, enthusiastically endorsed the Kooskia Internment Camp to friends
still interned at Santa Fe:

> In its vicinity greenish trees, firs and cedars, and common brakes
> [ferns] grow thick and rank, and freshness of the air is unsurpassed.
> Of course, there isn't that unpleasant fence. Really it's a paradise in
> mountains! It reminds me so much of Yosemite National Park ... I
> recommend that if any one of you wishes, he should come here.[22]

Sakaye Ed Yoshimura, a photographer from San Diego, particularly
enjoyed the "wild flowers, birds, water-falls" and observed that "even the
deers and the bears are roaming all over the place."[23] In another letter he
commented, "we are very fortunate to be in such a well equipped camp with
a group of nice officers in charge of us."[24]

Accommodations, Camp Layout, and Facilities

The Geneva Convention's Articles 9 and 10, reflected in the INS's "Instructions concerning the treatment of alien enemy detainees," specified
certain details about appropriate living quarters that were applicable to the
Kooskia Internment Camp. Detainees were entitled to "the same amount of
space as is the standard for United States troops at base camps," meaning
sixty square feet [six by ten feet] of floor space, with enough ceiling height to
provide the required seven hundred and twenty cubic feet of air space. "All
quarters must be properly heated, lighted, and well ventilated. They must be
kept clean and sanitary at all times."[25]

In their letters, those men who related their perceptions of the
Kooskia camp's accommodations spoke of them with approval. Teraoka
commented,

> Rooms are heated with steam. Each one is provided with a private
> locker, a table and chair are shared by two a[nd] the beds are double
> decked. The floors are painted brown, the walls varnished and the
> ceilings are white plaster boards. There are many windows which
> give us plenty of light and ventilation.[26]

Kadotani added, "The automatic electric fan with steam heat a[d]justs con-
veniently and cleanly temperature of room. We are all thankful. Our mess-hall
is clean, and there are wa[sh]ing room and clinic ... ."[27] Kuromitsu Banba, a
waiter from Honolulu, wrote a friend, "The accommodations is far better than
your place [Santa Fe Internment Camp] and the atmosphere is something like
the one of the hot-spring resort in Shin-Etsu district in Japan."[28]

Several photographs show the camp buildings and their relationship to one another. Former Kooskia guard Cecil Boller's identifications of them correlate well with a sketch map of the camp drawn about 1982 (Fig. 28).[29] Closest to the road there was a parking area next to a generator/shop building; it also housed the boiler room. The next building housed the warehouse and laundry. Then came the administration building, which had offices for the superintendent, the secretaries, and later the Japanese American censor; a lounge; and two bedrooms for guards. The next building housed the kitchen and dining hall. Beyond the mess hall was a five-building cluster containing a bathroom barracks and four sleeping barracks, one of which had an eight-bed infirmary. A bridge across Canyon Creek led to a canteen building/recreation room. On a hill above the camp there was a round wooden water tank about ten feet in diameter and ten feet high, as well as a cement slab used as a tennis or handball court.[30]

Heating the Barracks

Huge boilers, fed with Pres-to-logs, generated steam for heating the camp. To procure the fuel, the camp clerk contacted potential suppliers and also posted bids at four post offices. In 1943 and 1944 the only bidder was Potlatch Forests, Inc., of Lewiston. The first year the price was $6.90 per ton[31] and the second year it was $6.94 per ton.[32] Consumption in summer was two tons per day, rising to four tons per day in winter.[33]

When guard Cecil Boller made his daily trip to Kooskia, internees seldom came with him. However, when a rail car of Pres-to-logs arrived in town, usually in winter, he took some internees in a larger truck to help load the fuel. It often took a couple of days and two or three trucks to get all the logs loaded. Even the guards helped by joining the line that passed the logs two at a time until they were all loaded up.[34]

Photographs show the Pres-to-logs in use (Fig. 29), and Hozen Seki, who kept a diary in English for part of the time he was at the Kooskia camp, mentions his involvement with some of the journeys to get them. In late August 1944 he wrote, "I expected to go [to] Kooskia for pressed-wood but it was too late to catch the car."[35] In September, Seki "prepared four truck[s] for tomorrow because they will carry the press-wood."[36] He also helped unload Pres-to-logs. It was heavy work for him but he found it "not so bad."[37] For the internees, going into town for the Pres-to-logs, hard work as it was, must have been a welcome break.

Food Services, Rationing, and Allowances

Although the Kooskia road building camp was the only one of its kind in the U.S., there were a number of them in western Canada. One former Japanese Canadian internee recalled that "the good food ... did much psy-

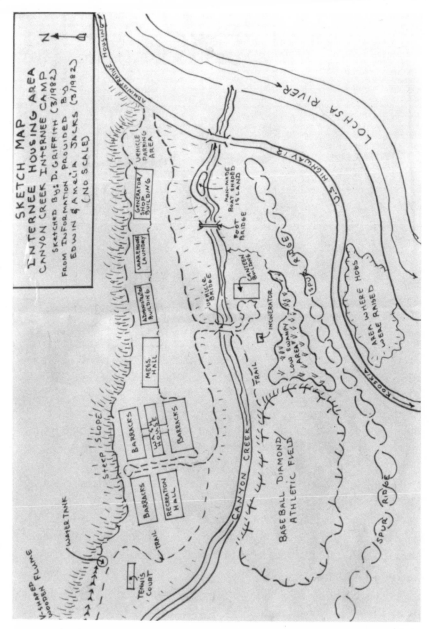

Fig. 28. Sketch map of the Kooskia Internment Camp, not to scale. Drawn by
Dennis Griffith in 1982 from information provided by Edwin and Amelia Jacks.
Courtesy Lochsa District Kooskia Ranger Station, Kooskia, ID.

Fig. 29. Building interior, probably the recreation room, with unknown internees gathered around the stove and others playing a game on a table in the background. Note Pres-to-logs stacked in back, on right; stove wood stacked on left; a large kettle for tea water on stove, and a non-government-issue teapot, left. Courtesy Scrapbook, PG 103-19-3.

chologically to alleviate the emotional hardship of the time."[38] This statement was equally true for the Kooskia Internment Camp.

Article 11 of the Geneva Convention provided specific instructions regarding the food ration for prisoners of war.[39] When the INS applied those guidelines to their camps, the restated regulation read that internees' food had to be "equal in quantity and quality to that of United States troops at base camps."[40] However, if items were rationed to the civilian population, then the same ration allowance would apply to detainees.

Food Rationing

During wartime, certain food items were in short supply. To allow an equal distribution of them, and to prevent hoarding and subsequent profiteering, a rationing system was imposed on the entire country. People were issued ration books containing coupons, or "points," that allowed them to purchase rationed items not to exceed a designated limit per month, and institutions took over this function for individuals in their care.[41] Calculation of ration points was very complex, because different foods "cost" different numbers of points, and the point values of rationed foods increased over time. Processed foods, sugar, coffee, and meat required ration points, but fresh fish and poultry were not rationed.[42] Fort Missoula even detailed one employee to assist at the Kooskia camp for at least a month, to "establish mess analysis controls and rationing accounting" as practiced at Fort Missoula.[43]

Food Allowances

Each internee was entitled to receive an average of five pounds of food per person per day, divided among specific items.[44] As the war progressed, the INS modified the amounts of various foods to reflect "local procurement conditions," namely, whether fresh fruits and vegetables were plentiful (A-1) or not (A-2).[45] Where necessary, the camp doctor could prescribe special diets. Certain hospital patients, for example, received the A-1 diet, except that they got more eggs and milk, less meat and fish, and fewer potatoes and other root vegetables, but the total amount of food was higher, nearly 5.8 pounds of food per patient per day.[46]

Food at Temporary Detention Centers Compared with Internment Camp Food

Thanks to the Geneva Convention requirements, food provided to detainees at the INS internment camps constituted an ample and varied diet, in contrast to that provided the men's family members at the temporary detention centers and, later, the WRA incarceration camps. Just as they had complained to their fathers about the substandard accommodations, internees' children complained to their fathers about the food.

In May 1942 Ruth Hoshimiya, at the Santa Anita, California, racetrack "Assembly Center," wrote to her father, Toske Hoshimiya, at the Santa Fe Detention Center:

> Lots of children and adults [are] always vomiting this food. I even do. Always stew and 'Brides Rice.' You know what I mean, hard rice that's burnt. … The coffee here is terrible. One cook tells me that they make it out of yesterday[']s old coffee. Lots of men have come back from Montana [Fort Missoula Internment Camp] and they live near our room. They tell me that they got good food, especially coffee. They want to go back to Montana again - just for the food.[47]

Kooskia Internees Comment on the Kooskia Camp Food

When the Kooskia Internment Camp first opened, the food served was similar to what had been fed to the prison camp inmates. INS employees, who were used to better rations, quickly protested, and the standard improved. The internees varied in their assessment of the quality of the meals. Their appraisals were probably influenced by personal taste as well as by their experiences with the food served to them at previous internment camps. In late May 1943 Hisahiko Teraoka praised the food quite highly in a letter to a friend, writing, "… every day we get something new from the oven, such as buns, cinnamon rolls, biscuits, cookies or doughnuts." He thought everything tasted "mighty good."[48] Other detainees disagreed with Teraoka's assessment. In late May, Kuromitsu Banba wrote a friend, "<u>But foods is not so good, so we are floored.</u>"[49] The censor deleted the underlined statement from Banba's letter.

The food improved noticeably in the next couple of weeks. In early June, Dave Aldridge, the Kooskia camp's acting officer in charge, wrote, "There has been a marked improvement of the quality and quantity of food as served now compared with the food served to the institution under the Bureau of Prisons."[50]

In mid-June 1943 Fort Missoula medical officer Frank V. Brown, together with Dr. Francis G. Reineke, conducted a "Sanitary Survey" of the Kooskia Internment Camp.[51] The two men paid special attention to the kitchen (Fig. 30), and pronounced the meals to be "adequate, nutritious, and well prepared." Brown and Reineke questioned the men individually and learned "they were all well satisfied with the food and its preparation. Almost all the internees agreed that 'The food is much better than it was.'"[52] Bimonthly reports that the camp's mess officer submitted to the officer in charge support the doctors' observations. They demonstrate an increase in the quantity of food provided to the internees.[53]

A newspaper article reported that "the cost of sustenance for the internees ranged from 46 to 50 cents per day."[54] To supplement the food provided, the Kooskia internees had a garden as well as some fruit trees.[55] Apple, cherry, and plum trees all remain at the Kooskia camp site, although the previous Canyon Creek Prison Camp inmates probably planted most of them.

Meals at Fort Missoula and the Kooskia Internment Camp

Purchase orders and contracts show that the Kooskia camp obtained food items both locally and regionally. Fort Missoula's warehouse was another source of supply. Although menus for Kooskia were not located, except for one day as reported by a visiting journalist, a few menus from the Fort Missoula Japanese mess survive.[56] Meals served to the Japanese at the Kooskia camp would have been comparable to those available at Fort Missoula.

The meals were sufficient and varied, but the items offered to the Japanese internees would have had very little appeal for men accustomed to eating Japanese food prior to their incarceration. Breakfasts over the ten-day period included dry cereal, cream of wheat, oatmeal, and boiled eggs. There was no meat at breakfast, perhaps because of rationing constraints, but milk was usually available. Fruit appeared daily, often as jam and other times as apple slices, applesauce, stewed prunes, stewed apricots, or stewed figs. "Butter,"

Fig. 30. Kooskia Internment Camp kitchen. Note large kettles on left, probably for cooking rice. Courtesy Scrapbook, PG 103-14-1.

coffee (but no tea), cream, and sugar were always supplied at breakfast, and toast was usually available.[57]

Dinner, the main meal, was served at noon. Entrees included baked fish, boiled fish in tomato sauce, beef stew, boiled beef with Spanish sauce, beef stew, roast beef and dressing, roast pork, chop suey, and tripe Spanish style. Rice was always available, mostly as steamed rice but sometimes as curried rice. Side dishes included vegetable soup, green or cabbage salad, spinach, stewed tomatoes, string beans, peas, and carrots. Desserts, when occasionally provided, were bread pudding and chocolate pudding. The men could have bread, tea, and sugar with their dinner, but butter was available at dinner only on Sundays.[58]

Supper, the evening meal, was served daily except Sunday. It was lighter, but still ample and changing. During a ten-day period the main dishes were corned beef hash, cold cuts, pork and beans, boiled salt mackerel, pork sausage, Japanese noodles, frankfurters, and hamburger with or in tomato sauce. Side dishes comprised vegetables, soup, salad, and pickles. The vegetables offered were string beans, lima beans, steamed rice with radishes, boiled or mashed potatoes, sauerkraut, and creamed macaroni. The one soup was "soyu" (i.e., flavored with soy sauce, *shoyu*) and the salads were vegetable, potato, green, and coleslaw. Pickles included sweet pickles, pickled beets, and white radishes, probably daikon. Fruit and desserts included stewed prunes, canned peaches, fresh apples, Jell-O, and cornstarch pudding. Bread, "butter," and tea were served at every supper and sugar was usually available.[59]

Only one day's menu is known from the Kooskia Internment Camp. Breakfast, on the day *Lewiston Morning Tribune* reporter Tish Erb visited, consisted of "stewed figs, fried eggs, toast, butter, bran flakes, [and] coffee." Dinner was "meatballs with Creole sauce, julienne potatoes, creamed new turnips, turnip-carrot salad, fruit Jell-O, milk and coffee." Supper included "egg fouyoung [*sic*] with steamed rice, army fried potatoes, head lettuce, apple, [and] milk or coffee." Erb observed that the Japanese were "light eaters" who did not take advantage of their rights under the Geneva Convention to eat what a U.S. soldier would receive. In June the men ate so little meat that the unused ration points "would have purchased another 900 pounds" of it.[60]

Despite the internees' preference for fish and rice,[61] fish became "too much of a good thing." In mid-1944 Spanish delegate Captain Antonio R. Martin, together with State Department representative Charles C. Eberhardt, visited the Kooskia camp.[62] They interviewed the internees to learn how they were treated, and recorded a few criticisms. Afterwards, officer in charge Merrill H. Scott prepared a report to W. F. Kelly, the INS's assistant commissioner for alien control, based in Philadelphia, responding to the charges, which included a complaint about too much fish. At first, the men had requested more fish, so it was served three times a week. After they began supplementing their diet with fish they caught in the Lochsa River (Fig. 31), however, they were "getting just a little bit too much fish. It is rather amusing to think that they did request that the fish be reduced."[63] Scott, unlike Remer, his predecessor, was much more responsive to internees' concerns. He immediately ordered that the kitchen serve fish only twice a week, stating, "Their wishes in the matter had not been made known to me before."[64]

Much later, in 1981, T. Mitsu Shiotani testified before the Commission on Wartime Relocation and Internment of Civilians about his experiences at the Kooskia Internment Camp. He testified that " ... the food was very bad."[65] If a man were used to a diet of Japanese food, the meals would have seemed very unappetizing indeed. The meal components heavily favored Caucasian American dishes, with minimal effort made to cater to Japanese tastes.

Non-Asian Food Available at the Kooskia Internment Camp

Because of the Kooskia Internment Camp's isolation and small size, food was frequently difficult to obtain at a reasonable price. Fort Missoula often furnished the Kooskia camp with items from their stock, including "A-Co-

Fig. 31. Unidentified internee fishes from raft in the Lochsa River. Courtesy Scrapbook, PG 103-21-2.

Lene" [lard], "Double XX Seasoning sauce," and other items that did not require ration points.[66] The Montana camp also provided peanut butter,[67] and attempted to find "sandwich spread cheese";[68] ultimately, Fort Missoula did supply the Kooskia internees with three boxes of it.[69] At times of food shortages at Kooskia, the Montana camp sent other items from their stock. These included twenty-four cases of string beans and ten cases of carrots, each containing six, No. 10 [106 ounce] cans of the vegetables.[70] Another time, they sent thirty-six dressed chickens.[71]

In mid-June 1943 Fraser gave Aldridge permission to spend up to $50 at a time for purchases made locally, without advance authorization.[72] Some of the items that could readily be obtained in the vicinity included eggs, milk, flour, fresh produce, and perhaps meat.[73] T. G. Gilroy and Company of Kooskia delivered fresh eggs weekly. A month's order was 480 dozen at thirty-five cents per dozen.[74] Huggins Dairy Products of Lewiston supplied fresh milk and butter. During July 1943 they furnished 360 gallons of Grade A pasteurized milk at forty cents per gallon, and sixteen pounds of butter at forty-four cents per pound.[75]

The Mason Ehrman Company of Lewiston had a contract to supply white beans, No. 10 cans of corn, Rice Krispies, curry powder, and salt.[76] Lewiston's Prairie Flour Mill won the bid to provide flour, one thousand pounds for $37.15. They declined to bid on beet sugar, dried fruit (raisins, figs, and currants), syrup, and evaporated milk; the provider of those necessities is unknown.[77] The Pacific Fruit and Produce Company in Lewiston supplied grapefruit, lemons, oranges, beets ("with tops"), cabbage ("fresh new crop"), carrots, celery, green onions, lettuce, onions, radishes, spinach, and turnips.[78]

The Kooskia camp had to pay for some of the packaging supplied with the food. Pacific Fruit and Produce charged the INS for one hundred "egg cases with fillers" at twenty-six cents each, and forty burlap bags for coffee, beans, potatoes, and vegetables, at ten cents each.[79] The Lewiston Grocery Company similarly furnished two types of gallon glass jugs, at seven cents each; forty white muslin rice sacks, ten cents each; and fifteen coarse woven red sacks for onions, ten cents each.[80] Charging for the containers ensured return of the empties for reuse.

Although meat was reportedly obtainable locally, the actual contract was let to Carstens Packing Company of Spokane, Washington, who provided large amounts of meat to the Kooskia camp. One purchase order, in May 1943, specified delivery, each week, of twenty pounds of smoked bacon; two quarters of beef; and forty pounds each of beef liver, bologna, and frankfurters.[81] Other meats the same firm supplied later included ham, oxtail, pickled pigs' feet, pork shoulder, and pork loin.[82]

Some food items traveled a much greater distance. Fresh fish came from the Portland Fish Company of Portland, Oregon, and during June 1943 that firm sent one hundred pounds each of red snapper, salmon, and ling cod alternately at weekly intervals, always on a Tuesday. Then, as now, salmon was the most expensive, at fifty cents per pound, while the red snapper and ling cod were eighteen and fourteen cents per pound respectively.[83]

Before Fort Missoula closed on July 1, 1944,[84] officials there sent a number of food items to the Kooskia camp in late March and early April. The non-Asian ones included multiple cases of cherries, applesauce, dried apples, canned milk, grapefruit juice, and margarine. The Montana camp also supplied the Kooskia Internment Camp with hundreds of pounds of cheese, onions, spaghetti, and macaroni, as well as sacks of coffee and potatoes.[85] In early May 1944 Fort Missoula sent the Kooskia camp another shipment of canned food, including carrots, beets, green beans, corn, peas, spinach, catsup, tomato paste, grapefruit, figs, raspberries, strawberries, youngberries, blackberries, and loganberries. These were worth a total of 4,186 Processed Food Points, which Kooskia forwarded to Fort Missoula.[86] Other foods that Fort Missoula provided before that facility closed in 1944 included powdered sugar, Argo cornstarch, honey, olive oil,[87] and margarine.[88]

Asian Food Provided at the Kooskia Internment Camp

Rice was an essential food item for the Japanese internees, and the camp received thousands of pounds of it. Kooskia Internment Camp files contain two contracts for rice. One was with the Mason Ehrman Company of Lewiston, for seventy-eight hundred pounds of rice,[89] and the other was with the Pacific Fruit and Produce Company, also of Lewiston, for twenty-two hundred pounds of it, for a total of ten thousand pounds.[90] In addition, Fort Missoula might have been able to negotiate a lower price with their suppliers, and include the Kooskia camp's needs, since they purchased rice in even larger quantities. The Red Cross also furnished a large amount of rice to the internment camps, and Kooskia received some at least once.[91] When meals at the Kooskia camp included rice, the cooks prepared a hundred pounds of it each time. Former guard Alfred Keehr remarked colloquially, "They were heck for rice."[92]

By early June 1943 the Kooskia camp administration had made an effort to obtain, from Fort Missoula, groceries "peculiar to Japanese needs." [93] These included seaweed, dried shrimp, and minced clams.[94] Following their success in obtaining those items, the Japanese internees at the Kooskia camp convinced then-superintendent Remer to request that Fort Missoula send other foods important in Japanese cuisine. Remer asked for rice flour; canned bamboo shoots; dried mushrooms; "Kon-nyaku powder," a vegetable root product; "'Ita Kobu' - seaweed in large ribbon"; "'Kan pyo' - gourd flesh cut in long ribbon and dried, to be cooked with other things"; and "'Udon' - noodle."[95]

Fort Missoula obligingly offered to transfer some canned bamboo shoots and some dried seaweed, although they did not know if the latter was the exact kind requested. They also provided the names of three firms that could supply "Oriental items." These were J. T. Iwanaga & Company, Salt Lake City; Mountain and Plain Jobbing Company, Denver; and Jensen-McLean Company, Seattle.[96]

Items that the Kooskia internees desired on a regular basis included "miso sauce, soy sauce, bean sprouts, rice, et cetera." The Kooskia camp administration asked Fort Missoula to include these foods in their bids, in order to obtain better prices. Isolated as the camp was, Kooskia personnel felt they might have trouble obtaining these items at all, especially if they were only ordering small quantities.[97] Fort Missoula helped out when they could; on one occasion they did not have any Chinese noodles, but did send some soy sauce and some *miso* paste [fermented soybeans, often with rice or barley].[98] Another time they offered to send Kooskia ten tubs of *shoyu* (soy sauce), part of a shipment they had received from the Red Cross.[99]

The Kooskia camp also needed tea; when this item was available, they bought large quantities of it. In early June 1943 an INS order for the Kooskia camp included 122 pounds of black tea.[100] By September, however, tea had become difficult to obtain, and the men were "using substitutes most of the time." Albert Stark, chief clerk at the Kooskia camp, wrote Fort Missoula requesting fifty or one hundred pounds of tea from their stocks.[101] In early October, Fort Missoula telegraphed, "Green tea has been ordered and will be shipped to you as soon as received."[102] The Kooskia camp also received a "box," perhaps a case, of tea from the Red Cross in March 1944.[103]

In late March and early April 1944, with Fort Missoula's closing imminent, that camp divested their stores of surplus food items and delivered them to the Kooskia Internment Camp. Asian food items they released included dried seaweed, *goma* (sesame seed), soy sauce, "Mu-gi-cha" [*mugi-cha*, roasted barley tea, a traditional Japanese beverage], dried squid, dried shrimp, canned salmon, rice, noodles, and soybeans, totaling hundreds of cases and several thousand pounds.[104] Three additional foods, in numerous small jars, were all listed as *tsukudani*, a Japanese condiment made by boiling various food items in soy sauce and *mirin* [sweet Japanese wine]. Fort Missoula transferred nearly 150 jars of shrimp, seaweed, and "Fillet" [probably meat or fish] *tsukudani* to the Kooskia camp.[105] In mid-April 1944 another food shipment went to the Kooskia camp, in two trucks. One truck carried fifty, one-hundred-pound sacks of second-grade rice and thirty-two pounds of fresh ginger root. The other truck held another ten sacks of rice; over one thousand pounds of *azuki* beans, in sacks; and a case of canned mandarin oranges.[106]

Garbage and Sanitation

In an interview, former employees Amelia and Ed Jacks stated that paper garbage was burned at the Kooskia Internment Camp, but wet garbage was hauled away to Kooskia, in cans. Sewage flowed into a log crib septic tank that was under the road in front of the administration building.[107]

The Geneva Convention's Article 13 discussed sanitation requirements. The INS's "Instructions concerning the treatment of alien enemy detainees" required that the Kooskia internees must always have access to clean "sanitary installations" with "daily access ... to shower baths." Enough soap and hot and cold water "must be furnished in sufficient quantities to insure bodily cleanliness."[108]

The internees had the use of twelve showers and twelve toilets, as well as four, ten-foot-long urinals. The showers provided both hot and cold running water.[109] Surprisingly, there is as yet no confirmation that the Kooskia internees constructed a Japanese-style bath as was done by Japanese internees at

Fort Missoula and at road camps in Canada. At Fort Missoula the Japanese obtained two-inch-wide boards, built tubs, and sealed the joints with tar. They elevated the tubs, built fires under them, and bathed after work.[110]

Several accounts describe Japanese baths at Canadian road camps.[111] If one existed at the Kooskia camp, it would likely have resembled Canadian internee Takeo Nakano's wooden tub, five by five feet square, about three feet deep, filled nearly to the top with water. The tub sat on a brick base, below which a wood fire burned constantly. Cold water could be added to adjust the temperature. Outside the tub there was a wooden platform where the men first soaped themselves and rinsed off before getting into the tub for a hot soak.[112]

The only clue that there might have been a Japanese-style bath at the Kooskia Internment Camp comes from Hozen Seki's diary. During a visit by his wife and two sons in early April 1945, Seki wrote, "I took Hoken, Hoshin to the bath in camp,"[113] thus hinting that the men might have built a Japanese-style bath at the Kooskia camp to augment the provided showers.

In general, the internees found that, on the whole, they were pleased with their living conditions at the Kooskia Internment Camp. They could send and receive mail; they lived amid scenic surroundings, with no barbed wire fence; the barrack accommodation was improved over that of their previous detention camps; the meals were ample and varied, and even included a few Japanese foods; and the sanitary facilities were adequate. With those basic necessities in place, the men were ready to begin work.

Chapter Four
"A Real He-Man's Job":
Work Assignments and Working Conditions

*Work done for the State shall be paid for in accordance with
the rates in force for soldiers of the national army
doing the same work ... .*
Geneva Convention, Article 34.

Although the amenities were important in contributing to morale, the Kooskia internees were there primarily to work. They looked forward to beginning their tasks. On May 28, 1943, the same day he arrived at the Kooskia camp, Minoru Jo Wazumi, a clerk from Connecticut, wrote to Elizabeth Nesbitt in Philadelphia, "There are ... many boys here who are quite willing for Uncle Sam. We expect to go to work probably soon."[1]

A notice to internees about their work assignments probably reflected a directive in use at the prison camp. It encouraged the men to view this as an

> opportunity to gain the work habit. The first step in vocational self-improvement is to get out of the idleness habit if you have ever had it. Good wholesome hard work within your physical capacity never hurt anyone. You will not be called upon to do anything which you are not physically able to do.[2]

Although these instructions may appear more appropriate for the federal prisoners than for the Japanese internees, former guard Cecil Boller recalled that the Japanese were "the same as Americans - some were hard working and some would 'goof off.'"[3]

The Road Work Begins

The men's first workday was June 1. That evening, Sakaye Ed Yoshimura described it in a letter to his relatives at the Poston War Relocation Authority (WRA) incarceration camp:

This wa[s] the first day on my new job since we came out here and it's not merely a job but a real he-man's job -- I drive a dumping truck and you ought to see the size of the truck; a great big monster as big as locomotive and as husky as war-tank and I am not exaggerating either (Fig. 32). Now I know that I am going to be a regular rough-neck. ... We are sort of selected group volunteered to get out of the wired fence and work so that we allow no chis[e]lers and strictly co-operative. We are much happier now and that's exactly how I wanted to get by in this circumstances [*sic*] we are in.[4]

Yoshimura's positive attitude did not hint at certain difficulties needing to be overcome. These mainly concerned the internees' treatment in accordance with Geneva Convention requirements. Once work began, it must have become immediately apparent that the former prison guards were not sufficiently acquainted with Immigration and Naturalization Service (INS) procedures. On June 5, after the detainees had been working less than a

Fig. 32. One of the project's dump trucks. Internee Sakaye Ed Yoshimura described it as "a great big monster as big as locomotive and as husky as war-tank." Courtesy Scrapbook, PG 103-41-3.

week, assistant officer in charge Dave Aldridge directed all personnel in charge of work crews to "immediately familiarize themselves" with certain Geneva Convention articles governing treatment of internees, specifically, Article 2 which protected the internees "against acts of violence, insults and public curiosity." Detainees also could not be interviewed or photographed except by permission of the officer in charge.[5]

After two weeks on the job, Yoshimura did not mention any problems when writing to a friend detained at Santa Fe. Despite suffering from "stiff necks and sore legs," the men were "all very happy and much delighted" with their "wonderful surroundings."[6]

Road Workers and Their Duties

Intense public curiosity accompanied the project. To help satisfy it, a *Lewiston Morning Tribune* reporter visited the camp in mid-1943 to observe the men's daily activities.[7] After assembling at 7:25 a.m., the internees boarded trucks and were driven to various places along the Lochsa River (Fig. 33). Pick and shovel crews cleared brush and debris or removed rockslides, while additional groups manned air hammers or jackhammers, drilling holes in rock outcrops to receive dynamite for blasting (Fig. 34).[8] Other work opportunities included tree cutting (Fig. 35);[9] driving large dump trucks; running compressors and rock crushers; helping with shop mechanics;[10] welding, both electric and acetylene; driving, and repair of, motor vehicles; and operating tractors, bulldozers, rollers, road graders, and diesel engines.[11]

Fig. 33. Boarding the trucks for work on a cool, foggy morning. Courtesy Scrapbook, PG 103-31-1.

Fig. 34. Unidentified internee and crew, drilling with an air hammer. Courtesy Scrapbook, PG 103-35-3.

Fig. 35. Crew cutting timber with a crosscut saw and splitting the logs. Courtesy Scrapbook, PG 103-17-1.

Mickey Barton, son of Milt Barton, a U.S. Bureau of Public Roads (USBPR) employee for the Kooskia project, dispelled a myth that has arisen regarding the nature of the work, namely, that most of the construction work was done by hand. While many men did labor with pick and shovel, Mickey Barton recalled that the equipment was new and of the latest design for that era, in particular "a very large power shovel" which was the most important single piece of equipment on the project.[12]

Dump Truck Drivers

In a 1982 interview, former Kooskia Internment Camp employees Amelia and Ed Jacks recalled that there were four road crews, with one truck for each group,[13] and each dump truck had two drivers assigned to it.[14] The power shovel loaded the trucks with dirt and rock from the dynamite blasts, and this material was used "to fill road cuts, and to build up the road slope to the Lochsa River."[15] James I. Yano, one of the dump truck drivers, remembered that the dump trucks could carry up to twelve tons of rock. To dump the load, he had to back up to the river bank while being careful not to back into the river.[16]

Jackhammer Operators (Fig. 36)

Men who could operate the jackhammers were in particular demand, but few internees wanted to do such heavy work. Resident engineer J. W. Gillmore complained to the USBPR's district engineer B. J. Finch that in order to make any progress on the road he needed twenty-five jackhammer operators to drill the immense amount of rock so it could be blasted. Finch seconded the urgency of this request, suggesting that such skilled workers might be obtained from the "main detention

Fig. 36. Jackhammer crew at work. Courtesy Scrapbook, PG 103-36-1.

centers," perhaps meaning the WRA incarceration camps. He lamented that somehow, potential workers had gotten the impression "that only pick and shovel workers" were needed for the project.[17]

Only four Japanese at the Kooskia camp initially volunteered to be jackhammer operators.[18] Minoru Jo Wazumi was one of them. In mid-June he wrote to Ruth Miller in New York City:

> Though it is a quite hard job, I think I can take it and like it. ... [A]fter being idle more than one year I am certainly happy about the opportunity Uncle Sam has given to me. Here are about <u>100</u> [underlined number censored] boys who volunteered their service. They came from all over the states. I am so glad that I came here. ... Here are all boys and no girls. So you can imagine that due to the nature of our work, our feelings get quite rough.[19]

Bert Fraser, officer in charge at the Fort Missoula, Montana, internment camp, tried to get more jackhammer workers from the other INS camps. He emphasized the "very strenuous" nature of the work, and stated, "only young, physically fit aliens will be able to perform such duties."[20]

Each jackhammer eventually had five Japanese internees assigned to it. Although the USBPR would have preferred just two men to a drill,[21] guard Alfred Keehr once saw three men who appeared to weigh only eighty to ninety pounds apiece trying to hold the machine while drilling.[22] Arturo Shinei Yakabi, a Japanese Peruvian on a drilling crew, recalled that they drilled holes fifteen feet deep, three feet per man.[23] Some particularly difficult sections were accomplished only by tying a rope around the waist of a jackhammer operator and lowering him down the slope.[24]

Laborers

The older men made up the three pick and shovel crews (Fig. 37).[25] After fifteen days of work, T. Mitsu Shiotani described how they cleared the way for the steam shovel by cutting brush and trees from the mountainsides and then burning everything. He commented, "I could have had a kitchen or other inside work but it pay less and beside I wanted to work on a outside work. ... It is not too easy for me but I think I can keep it up."[26]

Safety Concerns and Accidents

After meeting the newly arrived internees, officer in charge Dave Aldridge was concerned that some were too old or physically incapable of performing such hard work. He recommended that no additional volunteers be sent to the Kooskia camp unless they were "capable of performing arduous outdoor duty during the ... summer months."[27] This was important because Article 29 of the Geneva Convention stated, "No prisoner of war may be employed at labors for which he is physically unfit."[28] Aldridge stressed that internees

Fig. 37. Pick and shovel crew clearing brush from hillside. Courtesy Scrapbook, PG 103-36-3.

could not be forced to perform any "dangerous or unhealthful" duties, and that they were forbidden to handle any form of explosives or even to be in the vicinity of explosives that had been placed but had failed to detonate.[29]

Explosives (Fig. 38)

In April 1943, before the camp opened, authorities discussed the issue of whether or not the internees would be permitted to handle explosives. D. A. Remer, then superintendent of the prison camp, reported to Fraser that he and engineer Gillmore had received a visit from a Mr. Bentley of the U.S. Bureau of Mines. Bentley advised Remer "of certain restrictions relative to the handling of explosives by Japanese aliens" and provided Remer with a copy of the restrictions from the Federal Register: "Persons of Japanese ancestry, whether they are aliens or American citizens, are forbidden to use or have possession of explosives or component parts thereof, anywhere in the eight Western States … ." Although the restrictions only applied to individuals, they were interpreted as also being applicable to persons of Japanese ancestry who worked for any organization that might use explosives in their work, in this case, the USBPR.[30]

The INS continued to follow up on the internees' access to explosives, but whether in response to Geneva Convention directives or to security concerns is not clear. In mid-June, W. F. Kelly, INS assistant commissioner for alien control, wrote Fraser asking for a report on how explosives were

Fig. 38. Blasting the rocky canyon. Courtesy Scrapbook, PG 103-37-2.

handled at the Kooskia camp, "and whether or not detainees have access to such explosives."[31] Remer assured Kelly that only USBPR employees had handled any explosives, and that these were "used several miles from any Japanese internees."[32]

Once the jackhammer crews had drilled the fifteen-foot-deep holes to receive the dynamite, Bailey Rice, a USBPR employee called the "powder monkey," placed dynamite charges into them. Japanese internees assisted him,[33] and one Japanese man even worked on the blasting crew.[34] Clearly, contrary to regulations, the Japanese did handle explosives at the Kooskia camp.

Safety Equipment

As part of their "Sanitary Survey" of the Kooskia camp in mid-June 1943, Drs. Frank Brown and Francis Reineke observed the internees at work. After learning that one Japanese worker "had his ear nearly severed" by a falling rock, Brown interviewed Gillmore regarding the available safety equipment. In response, Gillmore "very brusquely informed me that he had nothing to do with that." When Brown asked Gillmore about safety-related articles such as helmets, boots, belts, and goggles, Gillmore responded that he considered such items to be clothing rather than equipment, and the INS "was supposed to furnish the clothes." Therefore, Gillmore "would not give the Japanese … any safety equipment whatever."[35]

Physical Examinations

Besides his distress over Gillmore's inattention to safety, Brown also determined that the internees had had no physical examinations and had worked for nearly three weeks without them. He observed that the Japanese at the Kooskia camp were there without any consideration for "their age, state of health, or physical ability and strength," and that many of them were too old and infirm for such hard work. Several men had hernias and at least one was a diabetic.[36] Brown recommended that all the internees receive physical examinations; that their abilities, and the work, be classified as arduous, moderate, or light physical labor; and that safety precautions be instituted.[37] On June 21, Brown performed the examinations himself. He certified that ninety-nine men were "all physically capable of performing arduous physical labor." Eight other men "should be permitted to do only light duty," and one man, who was blind in one eye, "should not be allowed to handle any dangerous equipment whatsoever."[38]

Accidents and Other Dangers

T. Mitsu Shiotani described one near miss on the job: "One ... fellow almo[st] went over into the river with his big dumping truck but he managed to jump off just in time. ... It is not so dangerous as one [is] inclined to think of ... road building, providing one takes reasonable precaution."[39] Mickey Barton disagreed. He described the dump truck work as "all very dangerous," adding, "More than one piece of equipment ended up in the river."[40]

Some accidents occurred when internees on kitchen duty requested a transfer to the road work. This could be exceedingly hazardous for a man not well-trained for his new job. Guard Al Keehr described one such incident in which an older internee decided he wanted to abandon his kitchen tasks, so was assigned to Keehr's tree-cutting crew instead. Keehr instructed him where to stand, first when the tree fell and later when removing the limbs. As Keehr recalled, the man did "just the opposite" of what he was told. The tree rolled over him and a broken branch gouged a big wound behind his ear. Keehr took the man to the camp doctor who "fixed him up." Several days later Keehr asked him, "You going back out on the road again?" "No," he said, "I'm going to stay in the kitchen."[41]

Camp Workers and Their Duties

Camp workers were essential to the project, because without them the road work could not take place. By July 21, there were 132 internees at the Kooskia camp. Of that number, 29 performed camp jobs.[42] These included barber, boiler room operators, canteen clerk, dormitory orderlies, garage men, kitchen workers, laundrymen, shoe repairman, tailor, and, later, miscellaneous other jobs such as carpenter, plumber, and painter. Some of the camp workers also received assignments to the fire brigade, in addition to their other duties.

Barber

Several documents mention a barber and a barbershop at the Kooskia camp (Fig. 39). James Denkichi Urabe, a chef from Pennsylvania prior to internment, worked as the camp's first internee barber.[43] Following stays at

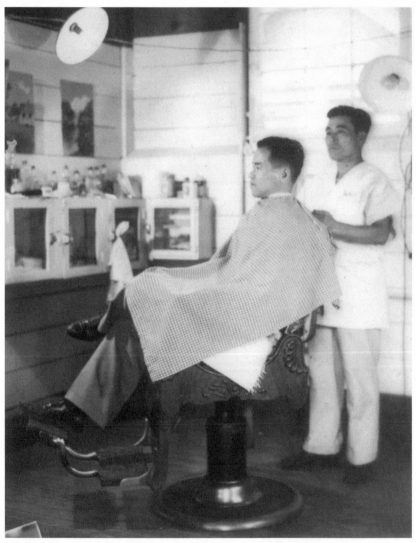

Fig. 39. Unidentified internees in barbershop. The camp's only known barber, James D. Urabe, had achieved parole before this photograph was taken. Courtesy Scrapbook, PG 103-28-2.

several detention stations, Urabe was interned at Fort George G. Meade, Maryland, in mid-March 1942.[44] Urabe's file provides no clues to his knowledge of the barber's trade. Perhaps he had previous experience, or learned it from another detainee. Nevertheless, through his demonstrated loyalty to the U.S., the Fort Meade authorities allowed him to buy a pair of barber's scissors in July 1942.[45] Urabe, who had a "colored" wife, Hattie,[46] received a long letter from her describing her ill health and her impoverished condition. Hattie wrote, "... a little bit would help me. Dont want to beg dont want no charity dont want no relief and I dont have quite enough to eat could somebody someplace some where show me how to get a little food with out begging. ... I am 57 years old. I have been very sick need some help."[47] The news that his wife was destitute surely devastated Urabe. He keenly felt his responsibility to provide for her, and, at twelve years younger, he would be fully able to do so if only he could be released from his unjustified internment.

Urabe's barbering skills during detention allowed him to earn money that he regularly sent to Hattie. Before coming to the Kooskia camp, Urabe wrote to Fort Meade's commanding officer asking for advice regarding $40 in "canteen tickets" he had saved up from giving haircuts to fellow internees. He hoped to exchange it for money to help his wife and to pay his property taxes.[48] For Urabe, the chance to get paid for work at a road camp in Idaho was the answer to his financial difficulties.

Boiler Room Operators

The boilers were used to heat the sleeping quarters, so at least one internee needed to be on duty in the boiler room all night, to stoke the fires with Pres-to-logs. Sometimes, when former guard Boller helped with the nightly bed check, not all the internees were present. If the men were not in the kitchen, the guards checked the boiler room and often found the missing persons "sittin' down there reading or something."[49] To internees from California, Hawai'i, and other warm climates, the boiler room provided a welcome respite from an Idaho winter.

Canteen Clerk (Fig. 40)

A document describing the organization of the camp's fire brigade mentions the job of canteen clerk.[50] Gitaro Kozima held that position until at least March 1945, and was by then the internee spokesman as well. Prior to internment he had been a merchant in the Los Angeles area, so was a logical choice to manage the canteen.[51]

Dormitory Orderlies (Fig. 41)

The fire brigade document also names three men who worked as dormitory orderlies. Urabe was one; others were Yoshito Kadotani, a gardener

Fig. 40. *Unidentified internees in canteen. Courtesy Scrapbook, PG 103-20-1.*

Fig. 41. *Unidentified camp worker with broom and dustpan. Courtesy Scrapbook, PG 103-04-3.*

from California, and Kiyusaburo Higashi, a hotel owner from Oregon. They probably cleaned the toilet and sink areas also, since no documents mention any separate latrine orderlies.[52]

Garage Mechanics (Fig. 42)

The Kooskia camp needed a garage for changing tires and for minor repairs on INS vehicles, and two Japanese worked there.[53] Hozen Seki, a Buddhist minister from New York, described in his diary what he had accomplished each day. During a one-week period in April 1944 he "washed two car[s]," "repaired chains," "changed the hose clamps," "repaired the tail box" [back end of a vehicle transmission], "repaired the spring of truck," "repaired windshield of truck," and even "repaired the garden plough."[54] On one occasion, Seki's work clothes were "so dirty that officer complains." Seki agreed, writing, "It was reasonable."[55] In winter, the mechanic's duties included making sure the water supply did not freeze.[56]

Fig. 42. Unidentified mechanic. Courtesy Scrapbook, PG 103-28-5.

Vehicles

The INS received fourteen vehicles from the prison camp. These included a Pontiac four-door sedan; two, one-quarter-ton Chevrolet pickups; three, one-and-a-half-ton GMC trucks; one, one-and-a-half-ton International truck; six, one-and-a-half-ton Ford stake trucks;[57] and one, one-and-a-half-ton Ford panel truck. Gasoline for the vehicles cost twelve and a half cents per gallon, and oil was eight cents a quart.[58]

Because it was wartime, parts for vehicles were difficult to get. Even though the Pontiac was a 1942 model, its front shock absorbers were already worn out. In a letter justifying his request for new ones, Fraser wrote that replacement was necessary because the vehicle traveled "more than two hundred miles nearly every day over a road which is only 40% completed and which is very rough."[59]

Kitchen Crew (Fig. 43)

Twelve internees made up the kitchen crew, which included a chief cook, three assistant cooks, one steward, one baker, three waiters, and three dishwashers.[60] Guard Al Keehr recalled that "there was one little building for the internees who worked in the kitchen [be]cause they had to get up earlier." Two or three internees slept there in order not to disturb the others when they arose.[61]

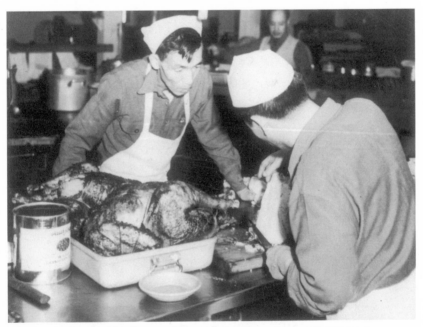

Fig. 43. Unidentified kitchen workers. Courtesy Scrapbook, PG 103-08-2.

Laundry Workers (Fig. 44)

Although no specific Article in the Geneva Convention refers to a laundry as such, an INS directive stipulated certain requirements. The internees' blankets "shall be laundered as required and should not be reissued without laundering"; pillow cases and sheets were changed at least once a week. Detainees also received "a bath-size Turkish towel which shall be changed

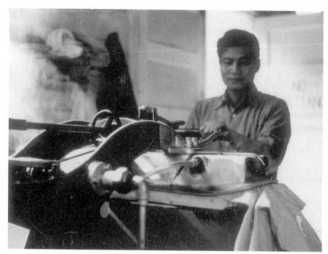

Fig. 44. Unidentified laundry worker, ironing. Courtesy Scrapbook, PG 103-28-3.

three times weekly."[62] The Kooskia camp must have begun operations with towels retained from the prison camp, but by mid-January 1944 these needed replacing. Fort Missoula provided four hundred bath towels and an equal number of hand towels.[63]

Depending on the detainee population, two to four Japanese internees worked in the laundry.[64] During his "Sanitary Survey" of the camp, Dr. Brown found the laundry "in very good running order and perfectly satisfactory."[65] Camp employees could also pay to have their laundry done there; that money was credited to the internee welfare fund.[66]

Shoe Repair Man

The rough usage given the road workers' footwear probably necessitated a full-time shoe repair person, and this individual made himself useful in other ways. Hozen Seki once commented, "In the shoe shop, they made the drum which was taking the deer skin."[67]

Shoes

Some footwear became available from Fort Missoula in June 1943. The sixty-five pairs of shoes included brown, "work-type" oxfords; "regular type" work shoes; and "composition sole type" work shoes.[68] The following month the Kooskia camp received an offer for "1300 pairs of Army shoes, unused, 1917 model" for fifty cents per pair, then stored at Albuquerque, New Mexico. The proposal noted, "The low price may be due to deterioration and dry rot."[69] Shortly afterwards, Loyd Jensen, officer in charge at the Santa Fe Detention Station, inspected the shoes and found them to be "of doubtful quality, in that the leather was stiff, dry and lifeless."[70] In early August, Remer refused the shoes, writing, "Much climbing over rocky cliffs is done by the majority of the Alien workmen on this road project. Shoes of questionable quality would be of little value to us … ."[71]

Tailor

Road work was also hard on the men's clothing, necessitating a tailor shop for mending garments. In the fall of 1943 Fort Missoula sent the Kooskia camp four sewing machine bobbins for a Singer sewing machine.[72]

Clothing

Keehr recalled that for work, the men wore "blue jeans and … faded out overall jackets."[73] In early June 1943 the Kooskia camp obtained a large shipment of work clothing from Fort Missoula's extra stock. They received hundreds of blue chambray work shirts, blue and white work trousers, "inmate" caps, work gloves, socks, and dark blue wool trousers.[74] Straw hats were also available.[75] Because federal prison inmates made work gloves, mittens, wooden furniture, and other items, federal law required that the INS and other agencies purchase those items through the Federal Prison Industries catalogue.[76]

When winter drew near, the road workers needed warmer clothing. In mid-November 1943 Fort Missoula sent the Kooskia camp a shipment of winter caps, denim work pants, heavy work pants, denim work coats, sweat-shirts ("in lieu of balance of work coats"), heavy overcoats, windbreakers ("in lieu of balance of work coats"), and part wool heavy socks.[77] Remer later requested two hundred scarves and four hundred mittens.[78] The Montana camp sent these in late November,[79] and in mid-December they arranged for the Kooskia camp to receive some hip boots and some "arctics" [waterproof overshoes], "ex U. S. Army."[80] In late January Fort Missoula provided a ship-ment of coveralls, "used, laundered"; raincoats, "salvage"; and gaiters,[81] and in mid-March they sent some "Navy Type Coats."[82]

Miscellaneous Camp Jobs

In mid-June 1943 Fort Missoula's Fraser asked the INS's head office in Philadelphia for permission to employ two temporary carpenters at the Kooskia camp. They would "make certain improvements and alterations" and build "additional facilities."[83] Other essential camp jobs, some of which were eventually filled by more internees from Santa Fe, included an electrician, a plumber, two painters, four carpenters, three clerks, two hospital attendants, and three teachers "capable of teaching language and music."[84]

U.S. Bureau of Public Roads Caucasian and Japanese Employees

The USBPR engineered and managed the Lewis-Clark Highway project through their division headquartered in Ogden, Utah. They provided the equipment, the payroll services, and the supervisory personnel for the Japanese internees. The USBPR employees, together with their families, lived in various locations as the work progressed. At the time of the Kooskia Internment Camp, some families were based in Lowell, six miles down river from the camp, and others lived at the mouth of Pete King Creek, two miles upriver from Lowell. The children were all bussed to school at Kooskia, some twenty-five miles away.[85]

Caucasian USBPR Employees (Fig. 45)

The skilled USBPR construction personnel varied over the years. Employees typically included the head project engineer and overall manager; one or more engineers/surveyors; a construction foreman; an operator for the large power shovel; a "cat skinner" [bulldozer operator]; a head mechanic;

Fig. 45. U.S. Bureau of Public Roads clerk Wally Williams, right, with unknown coworker, in front of the USBPR project office at Pete King Creek. Courtesy Scrapbook, PG 103-44-2.

an assistant mechanic; a road foreman; a "powder monkey," in charge of explosives; and one or more office clerks.[86]

Japanese USBPR Employees

The USBPR also hired up to ten Japanese detainees to perform additional duties, other than road work, that they considered essential to the project. These jobs included drivers who transported road workers; a first aid assistant; "shop men," meaning vehicle mechanics; and a timekeeper.[87]

Drivers

The drivers had the responsibility of taking the internees and their guards to the various places on the road where the different crews were stationed. They made two round trips per day, out in the morning and back at noon for "dinner," then out again after that meal and back to camp at the end of the eight-hour day. Once at the work site, the drivers had other duties, such as helping with the road work.

First Aid Assistant

At the time the volunteers were being recruited for the Kooskia camp, one man at the Santa Fe Detention Camp was an ideal candidate for the first aid assistant position because he was a registered pharmacist. After volunteering, he withdrew his name after the INS erroneously offered him only eighty cents per day.[88] Instead, other Kooskia internees filled the position.

"Shop Men"

Head mechanic Ralph Willhite was responsible for maintaining and repairing all the construction equipment. Willhite "had a large shop [at the USBPR yard], and was assisted by several Japanese, some of whom were also learning the Mechanic's trade."[89]

Timekeeper (Fig. 46)

The Japanese timekeeper prepared the internees' daily time sheets, showing their duties and hours worked.[90] Amelia Jacks recalled that the timekeeper's name was similar to "Taki."[91] In comparing that name with the names of the known Kooskia internees, a number of men had "Take" [pronunciation approximates "Taki"] as part of either their first name or their surname. Where their former occupations are known, they ranged from cook, gardener, laundryman, farmer, and fisherman, to "money collector" and importer.[92] Although the latter two occupations seem equally likely for the Kooskia timekeeper, he was probably Takeshi Okazaki, the importer, who also knew English.

Work Schedule

Plans originally called for a forty-eight hour week of six, eight-hour days, with overtime beyond that paid at forty cents per hour. Travel time to and from the work site was included in the eight hours. Injured workers who

Fig. 46. Schedule board with probable timekeeper. Courtesy Scrapbook, PG 103-30-4.

were absent from work would continue to be paid, but men absent from work because of misconduct would not.[93] Sunday was their day off.[94]

The work week may have changed over time, or perhaps just in the winter. Former internee spokesman James I. Yano recalled, "We worked 5 days a week. Saturdays and Sundays off." Although winters were very cold, it was not too windy, and Yano could not remember any day when bad weather made work impossible.[95]

Internees' Pay and Other Benefits

Three agencies coordinated efforts to accommodate an unusual situation, and all tried very hard to accomplish what must have been a bureaucratic ordeal. Because the road was on U.S. Forest Service (USFS) land, that agency was responsible for funding the wages of those internees, whereas the INS paid the camp workers' earnings. The USBPR paid the salaries of their workers and the internees they hired for specialist jobs.

The original salary offered to potential internee road workers was $45 per month, plus $10 for extra clothing, but it effectively became $55 per month, including the $10 clothing allowance. At first, $10 was supposed to be deducted from the $55 and given to the INS who in turn would furnish "extra clothing and other items of necessity." However, the INS soon determined that they could only charge the internees the actual cost of any special clothing provided.[96]

The internees did not receive their entire wages in cash. Once a month they got a $10 allowance for necessities, and the rest of their money was taken to a Lewiston bank and put into an account that had been established for each of them when they arrived. When they left, they could draw on that money,[97] or have it sent to a bank in their new location.

The detainees' $55 per month, $660 per year, was comparable to the $50 per month salary earned in 1944 by a "buck private," or new recruit in the U.S. Army.[98] In comparison, monthly wages earned by cooks and chauffeurs were at least $160.[99] Insurance company employees, public utility workers, and real estate agents made about $1,800 per year on average.[100] The lowest salary paid to a Caucasian Kooskia camp clerk, who knew typing and shorthand, was $1,620.[101]

In contrast, those working at camp duties were paid only eighty cents per day, or about $20 per month. Although those doing road work were willing to contribute to equalizing the difference in income between themselves and the camp workers, they would only consider it for those working in the kitchen, the laundry, or the boiler room, i.e., for the men doing jobs that directly supported the road workers, and not for those doing unspecified "other camp activities."[102] Even so, guard Al Keehr recalled, "there was a little friction there" because the kitchen workers had to arise an hour or two earlier than the road workers and work up to two hours later in the evening.[103]

In response to a proposal to recruit twenty-five to thirty more skilled laborers, and to bring the camp up to two hundred men,[104] Remer suggested that before filling those positions, another twenty men should be recruited for camp jobs at eighty cents per day. Then another forty-eight or fifty men could be recruited for the skilled road work.[105]

Pay Increases Lure More Workers

In mid-June 1943 officer in charge Dave Aldridge suggested that Fraser investigate the possibility of paying the skilled workers $65 per month. Besides jackhammer operator, these would include timekeeper; steam shovel, dump truck, and tractor operators; garage and boiler room men; and medical assistants. Not only might the extra money induce more men to volunteer for the skilled work, but there was an existing precedent for it, since some Italian internees working for the Forest Service earned that much.[106] .

W. F. Kelly, INS assistant commissioner for alien control, in Philadelphia, even suggested that it might be necessary to recruit German internees if enough Japanese volunteers could not be found, and reiterated that a higher wage might produce capable volunteers from even the Kooskia camp itself, and also from Santa Fe, where a number of additional internees had expressed interest in the road building project.[107]

Early July brought continued trouble finding enough jackhammer operators, and H. K. Bishop, head of the Division of Construction for the USBPR, also suggested hiring Italian detainees, "provided they are suitable to work with the Japanese."[108] In order to obtain sufficient skilled workers, the USBPR and the INS agreed to offer them more money. In mid-July Finch and Fraser modified the portion of the Memorandum of Agreement (MOA) that governed salary. Unskilled laborers would continue to receive $55 per month, but skilled workers, including "Pneumatic Drill Operators, Heavy Duty Truck Operators[,] and Spokesman Foremen" would receive $55 per month plus forty cents per day. For a six-day week, that effectively meant a raise of about $10 per month.[109] The raise also covered a blacksmith, a signal man, two mechanics, and a first-aid person.[110] The internee spokesman, James I. Yano, also a dump truck driver, "specifically stated that he did not desire to receive the skilled classification because of the effect it might have on the other internees."[111]

The "Spokesman Foremen" were very important to the project. They needed to speak both English and Japanese so they could relay instructions to the crews. Gillmore thought they were quite necessary, and cited one instance where the lack of them meant "work ordered had been skipped." In his example, two men on a certain crew could speak English, but neither one had been designated as spokesman, so "they would not pass on the information from the guard to the other men without such designation."[112]

Besides Yano, a few other internees had multiple work assignments, including some with two positions at different rates of pay.[113] These men alternated between the two jobs, sometimes doing both in a single day. The timekeeper kept track of how many hours they had worked at $55 a month and how many at $65 per month, but the USBPR, which had the responsibility for checking the payroll against the time sheets, found this system to be a bookkeeping ordeal. In a report to Fraser, Finch complained that checking for June 1943 took one week of auditor time and two and one-half days of clerical assistance. If such checking had to be continued, "it will constitute a serious problem in this office." Finch then prepared a sample form demonstrating a more efficient way to report payroll information.[114]

Prior to some of these improvements in salaries and recordkeeping, conditions for the internees had begun to deteriorate at an alarming rate, and even their spirits, originally high, were in decline. On July 7, Torajiro Imahashi (Fig. 47), a fisherman from Mexico, sent a postcard to Tosuke Sukegawa at the Santa Fe Detention Station, replying to his friend's letter.

Imahashi reassured Sukegawa, writing, "I am the same old husky, so don't worry about me," but continued, "Well, the camp here is not so bad but lately there have been some things we don't particularly like so we are morally wounded [experiencing poor morale]. We hope things will improve soon."[115] That very day, however, other internees believed conditions at the Kooskia Internment Camp had deteriorated so badly that their only recourse was to petition Fort Missoula for help.

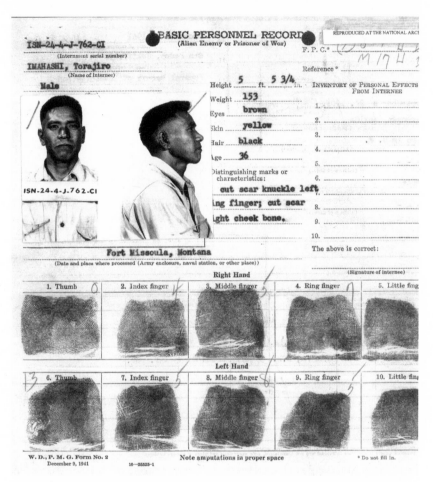

Fig. 47. "Basic Personnel Record (Alien Enemy or Prisoner of War)" card for Torajiro Imahashi, undated [1942], 1; Entry 466F, Imahashi, Torajiro; OPMG, RG389, NARA II.

Chapter Five
A Powerful Petition:
Internees Protest Deteriorating Conditions
at the Kooskia Camp

Prisoners of war shall have the right to inform the ... authorities in
whose power they are of their requests with regard to the conditions
of captivity to which they are subjected.
Geneva Convention, Article 42.

Despite the mitigating presence at the Kooskia camp of Immigration and Naturalization Service (INS) employees Dave Aldridge and Walter C. Wood, on temporary duty from California's Sharp Park Detention Camp, the Kooskia internees' initial euphoria soon gave way to unhappiness. This was almost entirely due to the managerial style of the Kooskia camp's officer in charge, Deane A. Remer, formerly superintendent of the Canyon Creek Prison Camp. In early June 1943 Bert Fraser, officer in charge at the Fort Missoula, Montana, INS detention station, wrote Remer, prophetically, "It is realized that we will encounter many difficulties because of transfer of one government agency to another."[1]

Administrative Confusion and Managerial Dilemmas

Fraser had earlier detailed Aldridge and Wood to the Kooskia camp to help Remer make the transition from prison camp to internment camp. At first, Aldridge was the assistant officer in charge, but Fraser soon had Aldridge and Remer exchange positions so that Aldridge could better show Remer how to implement INS procedures.[2] Perhaps resentful of their role reversal, Remer proved recalcitrant. On June 9, in a letter to Fraser, Aldridge recommended that Remer not be retained as officer in charge at the Kooskia camp.[3]

With his return to California imminent, Aldridge realized that the camp, under Remer, would depart from effective administration of INS policies, especially adherence to the Geneva Convention. Consequently, Aldridge's apprehension fueled a plan of action, culminating in the suggestion that Wood be considered for a permanent appointment as the Kooskia camp's assistant officer in charge.[4] Fraser, understanding the complexity, and delicacy, of the situation, forwarded Aldridge's suggestion to W. F. Kelly, the INS's assistant commissioner for alien control.

Kelly, based in distant Philadelphia, had never been to the Kooskia camp, thus he had difficulty appreciating the problems the INS faced there. In his reply to Fraser, Kelly questioned whether it was really necessary to create another position. He thought that "after a period of proper instruction" regarding INS procedures for supervising internees, together with continuing oversight from Fort Missoula, Remer should be able to run the camp satisfactorily without needing any more help than he had had while supervising prison camp inmates.[5] Nevertheless, Aldridge continued to have reservations about Remer's suitability for INS employment, and recommended that he not be transferred to the INS. In addition, Aldridge also had a poor opinion of J. W. Gillmore, resident engineer for the U.S. Bureau of Public Roads (USBPR).

Deane A. Remer, Superintendent

In Aldridge's view, Remer was completely unfit for INS employment because, after thirteen years' experience with hardened felons, he resisted changing his approach. Aldridge found him intolerant, inconsiderate, uncooperative, condescending, barely friendly, openly opposed to the liberal treatment of internees, and given to passive resistance when faced with suggested reforms. The INS preferred to deal with internees on a "self-governing, cooperative" basis, but Remer, an advocate of harsh discipline, called this approach "mollycoddling."[6]

In a report to Fraser, Aldridge commented that many of his suggestions to Remer were "not too politely glossed over and later ignored," and that Remer had "intimated to certain cronies an intention to pursue his own policies later." Aldridge knew "positively" that Remer, "instead of setting an example to his subordinates, ridiculed the efforts of myself and my assistants." Although Aldridge had "leaned backwards in an effort to establish friendship" and hoped to achieve compliance "through mutual cooperation," his efforts had failed. Instead, as acting officer in charge, he "instituted the necessary changes" himself. In summary, Aldridge felt that Remer was "an excellent prison executive, but certainly if his reaction during my period of observation is to be taken as a criterion of the future, I cannot but recommend that he not be retained."[7] On June 16, Remer himself indicated to Aldridge that he wanted to transfer from Kooskia because he was "not satisfied with [the] immigration setup." Aldridge immediately telegraphed this information to Fraser.[8]

Another INS employee had also observed problems with the camp administration. Joel Koppang, financial officer from Fort Missoula, had an unpleasant experience on June 21 when he visited the Kooskia camp to pay the men's salaries and help with their "financial problems." Remer met Koppang's train at Lewiston, but the train was late and the banks were closed, so Koppang could not cash a $4,250 check to pay the internees. Remer did not cooperate in seeking out an official of one of the closed banks, saying that the Orofino bank could cash the check the next day. However, when Koppang tried to do so, the bank did not have sufficient money, and he had to revisit Lewiston to get it, a two-hundred-mile round trip. On returning to the Kooskia camp, Koppang suggested to Remer that the men needed a one-time infusion of extra cash to buy work clothing, set up a commissary, and pay for purchases already made. However, Remer refused to let Koppang disburse more than $10 per person, saying, "Frankly, I don't give a damn about their commissary, or how many debts they owe."[9]

Remer's strict adherence to limiting the internees to $10 was in accord with the Geneva Convention's Articles 6 and 24 governing detainees' finances, supplemented by the INS's interpretation of it. The latter document clearly specified regulations governing detainees' money, including limiting an internee to no more than $10 in his possession.[10] Koppang's point, however, was that the internees had not had any money for some time, and that an exception needed to be made to get them back on track. Here, as elsewhere, Remer did not take a benevolent attitude towards the internees under his supervision. After making his arbitrary ruling, Remer "disappeared from Camp and was not thereafter available to the Camp spokesman who desired to appeal the decision."[11]

One document in the Kooskia camp files at the National Archives in Washington, DC, provides damning evidence for Remer's uncooperative attitude during late June and early July 1943. Although it is unsigned, Wood and Aldridge probably collaborated in its authorship. On June 23, for example, Wood suggested to Remer that a speed limit of ten miles per hour be established in areas where Japanese crews were working. Remer said "such orders were posted in trucks," but the notice in the trucks was for a thirty-five-mile-per-hour limit. Remer also had not reported an accident where a Japanese road worker was hit by a government truck.[12]

On July 1, one crew of twenty men was working about two miles from camp. Covered transportation was supposed to be furnished to transport them to and from work, "as storms are frequent and sudden." When a heavy hailstorm arose, "thus leaving the men out in same with no protection," Wood so informed Remer, but "the latter merely laughed the matter off. Thus a situation was created that threatened to develop into a strike upon the part of the Japanese. Mr. Wood then made trips back and forth with the passenger car bringing the men into camp."[13]

Another grievance concerned the Japanese internees who manned the boiler room twenty-four hours per day. On July 2 the Japanese Board, a group of elected internee representatives, applied to Remer on behalf of the boiler room workers to stagger the shifts so that the same man did not always have the midnight to 8:00 a.m. shift. After Remer "arbitrarily vetoed" this suggestion, the Internee Board members "expressed to Mr. Wood their dissatisfaction with the attitude of Mr. Remer towards their problems in the camp."[14]

Other unhappiness related to earlier difficulties in obtaining beer for the internees' consumption. Using policies at the Fort Meade, Maryland, detention camp as precedent, where detainees could purchase one bottle of 3.2 beer per day, the Kooskia internees requested similar permission to sell beer in their canteen.[15] Fraser offered no objections to the plan as proposed, and suggested that Aldridge should decide what method to use to control the sales to individuals.[16]

Although the internees were thus entitled to obtain beer for their canteen, Remer proved uncooperative in helping them obtain it. In early July the local District Attorney suggested that Remer obtain a distributor's license on behalf of the canteen. He declined to do so, "giving the spurious reason that 'his lodge prohibited it,'" but other members stated that there was "no such restriction."[17] Wood, then the acting assistant officer in charge, obtained the necessary permits, thus sidestepping Remer's refusal to cooperate in getting the beer.[18] Once the beer became available, each internee would receive a ration card to facilitate his purchase of it. Remer was supposed to sign each card and put some beer in the refrigerator, but "failed to do any of this."[19]

On July 4, traditionally a day of celebration, Aldridge arrived back at camp and confronted the beer distribution problem directly. Learning from the canteen manager that "Remer ... stated that he had nothing to do with beer," Aldridge signed all the beer ration cards, placed one bottle of beer per person in the canteen refrigerator, and distributed it a few hours later, after it had cooled sufficiently (Fig. 48).[20]

The letter concludes, ominously,

One thing is so obvious that it is quite outstanding: all those immigration procedures to which he is opposed ... will either die a natural death later through his refusal to cooperate in maintaining them or will be summarily discontinued by him. The Canteen is provided by [the Geneva Convention] Treaty; yet he is bitterly opposed to it, and if he cannot discontinue it, at least upon the departure of Mr. Aldridge he can jeopardize its existence by his failure to cooperate ... .[21]

Fig. 48. Kooskia internees enjoying a hard-earned beer. Courtesy Scrapbook, PG 103-20-3.

Shortly before Aldridge finished his temporary assignment and left the Kooskia Internment Camp, he sent a report to N. D. Collaer, then head of the deportation and detention section of the INS at Philadelphia.[22] Collaer had visited the Kooskia camp the previous month and requested that Aldridge provide him with an update on conditions there before returning to California. Aldridge did so, but commented that he disliked having to make such a report, stating, "If I feel Remer is not going to make a success of this thing, it will do me no good to say so since he is already on the job; and if he is not going to make a success of it, the future will tell its own story." Aldridge also mentioned that Remer had informed Wood "that he is not to take seriously the possible title of Assistant Officer in Charge at the Kooskia Camp ... . They say that coming events cast their shadows, and I believe that Wood interprets this warning in that light."[23]

J. W. Gillmore, Engineer

J. W. Gillmore of the USBPR, the resident engineer and supervising manager for the Lewis-Clark Highway project, had previously worked with the prison camp inmates. Like Remer, he showed little sympathy for, or understanding of, the internees and their rights. On June 3, in a letter to Fraser, Aldridge commented on Gillmore's expressed hostility, complaining that he was "belligerent, tactless," and stubborn, and that he was "temperamentally unfit to be supervising the Japanese internees." Aldridge feared that Gillmore would eventually "antagonize a group of [internees] to the extent that it will disrupt the project entirely."[24]

Aldridge raised another point concerning Gillmore's inattention to safety. At the two men's first meeting, Gillmore asked if internees would be allowed to handle "powder" [explosives]. When Aldridge referred him to an exchange of telegrams on the subject, namely, that internees were not to touch explosives, Gillmore himself exploded:

> Whereupon in abusive language he wanted to know why we hadn't informed him; I informed him that we had notified his superior officer. Again, just today, he appeared before the Officer in Charge [Remer] and stated that regardless of the instructions to the contrary contained in the above-mentioned telegrams, he intends soon to use the Japanese to handle powder, at which time the officer in charge could have the opportunity to see what he could do to prevent him.[25]

In closing, Aldridge stated, "I cite these for your information in the event opportunity should arise to discreetly bring them to the attention of District Engineer Finch [Gillmore's superior] with a view to replacing Mr. Gillmore."[26] His comments must have had some effect because on June 24 and 25, R. R. Mitchell, senior highway engineer, inspected the project "for the purpose of determining the underlying causes for certain telephone calls and letters which have been received from various sources ... ." In his report to Finch dated July 6, Mitchell said that both Presidential Proclamation No. 2525 and Western Defense Command Public Proclamation No. 3 prohibited the use of explosives by people of Japanese ancestry. Gillmore

> was instructed to arrange for employment of such men as might be needed to handle the explosives. Since the Japanese arrived on the project all explosives used have been handled by our own personnel and no Japanese have been permitted to touch them nor is any such action contemplated.[27]

In fairness to Gillmore, Mitchell observed that Aldridge was not present during his inspection, had not been at the camp since June 21 "and possibly would not return at all." With regard to Aldridge's assessment of Gillmore as "noncooperative" and "belligerent," Mitchell ascertained that Aldridge in fact had spent no time with Gillmore, and that "Aldridge's criticism seems to be somewhat unwarranted and overdrawn, if not an absolute falsehood, as he has apparently arrived at his findings from reports from others and not from actual contact" with Gillmore. Mitchell himself found Gillmore to be a person who speaks "rather bluntly" and who makes "rather pointed personal remarks which do not tend to promote harmony in his dealings with other persons." Gillmore "doubted if he could change his way of speaking at his age."[28]

Mitchell made several recommendations, some of which referred to Gillmore. He mentioned the need for cooperation between the INS and the USBPR, stressing that in order for the project to be successful:

> ... there must be complete understanding and equality between these agencies and their representatives on the project. This is particularly important because of the use of Japanese labor and the emphasis placed on 'face' by the Oriental mind. From my experience in the Orient and my observations on the project I am of the opinion that the project has already started on the wrong foot and unless this false start can be corrected it will be better for all concerned to abandon the project.[29]

According to Mitchell, Aldridge pursued a "policy of completely ignoring" Gillmore. Mitchell also observed,

> Regardless of any personal faults which may be attributed to Mr. Gillmore, I believe it cannot be truthfully said that he has been given the proper opportunity to cooperate. We assign a Resident Engineer to a project with the expectation that he will be available on the project or at his office at all hours during the working day. We have a right to expect the Immigration service to assign a resident Officer in Charge on the same basis. These two men should be of equal standing and capable of conferring together without friction to handle the routine problems of the work. ... If there is any assumption of superiority by any one in authority the Japanese will be the first to sense it and will act accordingly. At the time of my inspection there seemed to be considerable doubt on both sides as to whether there was an officer in charge.[30]

Mitchell noted that the agreement between the INS and the USBPR required the USBPR to replace any unsatisfactory employee but there was no similar requirement for the INS. He commented, "This clause should apply equally to both agencies."[31]

In comparing Remer and Gillmore, the first man did not last long at the Kooskia camp, but Gillmore remained until it closed in mid-1945. Although both seemed to be prejudiced against the Japanese internees, had worked within the prison system, and were inclined to treat the Japanese as prisoners rather than internees, they differed in that Remer had no defenders, whereas Gillmore had the weight of the USBPR behind him. Gillmore was very competent at his job; was willing to work in this remote location; and was too valuable, or impossible, to replace. Complaints against him could be rationalized away by indicting Aldridge's character and by accepting Gillmore's self-assessment that he was too old to change.

Internee Complaints and Petition

Caught amidst the bureaucratic wrangling, the internees soon realized that all was not as had been promised. During his June inspection visit, Dr. Frank Brown spoke privately with some of them. Although hesitant to discuss any problems, they seemed "dissatisfied," "suspicious of the guards," and "generally depressed with their conditions." Brown reported to Fraser that the guards were unsympathetic and had "the wrong mental attitude" towards the internees.[32]

The detainees' disgruntlement stemmed from an awareness of their rights under the terms of the Geneva Convention, as supplemented by an INS directive. The text of the Geneva Convention had to be posted where they could consult it and it must be interpreted to them orally if they could not read or understand it. The INS then believed that, besides the "safekeeping" of internees, it was equally important "to treat them fairly and humanely in accordance with the principles of treatment to which the United States Government is committed."[33]

As the Kooskia internees began to sense the dichotomy between assurances and actuality, censorship prevented their dissatisfaction from reaching the outside world. In early July internee Tommy Yoshito Kadotani, a gardener from California (Fig. 49), wrote to Miss M. Kadotani, at Poston [underlined sentences censored]:

> As a result of recent shift of officers, majority of them has been changed, but it has been decided that Mr. Remer, former Officer in Charge, will remain in office. This fellow is not in the least cooperative and does not give us convenience, so we are all really disappointed, and some of us is insisting to change our residences.[34]

Once Aldridge left for California on July 7,[35] conditions worsened rapidly. With Aldridge gone, and Wood clearly subordinate to Remer, the INS no longer had an effective administrative presence at the Kooskia camp, a deficiency that had immediate, and severe, consequences for internee morale. That very day the disgruntled internees prepared a lengthy petition, in Japanese, detailing their complaints and sent it to Fraser at Fort Missoula. Only the English translation survives.[36] The men appealed to Fraser, Collaer, and Kelly for an amicable and early settlement of the charges set forth in their petition:[37]

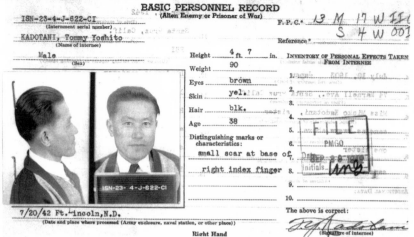

Fig. 49. Tommy Yoshito Kadotani, from his "Basic Personnel Record (Alien Enemy or Prisoner of War)" card, July 20, 1942, 1; E466F, Kadotani, Tommy Yoshito; OPMG, RG389, NARA II.

Although more than one month has elapsed since our transfer here … our desire has not as yet materialized but also the facilities for our sanitation and recreation has not [been] set up yet, and further more there have been many cases that the harmonious relationship and understanding between officers in charge of this station and ourselves has been disturbed. And we can not bear it any longer, so we have to request your settlement today.

THE REASONS OF THIS PETITION

1. In spite of the fact that we are engaging in co[n]siderably dangerous constru[c]tion, proper measures has not as yet set up for the emergency. The medical officer who [w]as once stationed here has been transferred to somewhere else and there is not even [a] single medical officer to look after lives of 130 persons. … Thus, those fellows engaging in dangerous works seem to have become reluctant to do such works.

2. … necessary accommodation for first aid should be established in or around the working place … .

3. More than half of us need treatment of teeth … .

4. … many tens of us need eye glasses … .

5. … there are people working without proper clothings … .

6. … the recent indication that suspension from works on account of wound, sickness, weather condition[,] and other reason which is beyond our controls, will be deducted from our wages same as in the

case when such suspension is made by own personal reason. If it is to be true, it is against the original contract.

7. ... Our pay day and amount of wage has not been cleared yet to us. It is our deep regret that we would be treated with the least s[ym]pathy.

8. This matter may be our prejudice but for us who respect other's character, it is unbearable to have learned by Mr. Remer's words and attitude as if he desires to treat us cruelly like prisoners on account of his habitual or traditional ideas as officer who has been in the past in charge of convicts. In order to make our living happier and also to have us more cooperative to the authority, it is our desire that offici[al]s in charge of this station should correct their habitual ideas.

9. On last July 1, the unusually heavy hail storm att[a]cked this district. In spite of the fact that this unfavorable weather could predict beforehand, Mr. Remer, Officer in Charge, has not even tried to provide us, labor[er]s, trucks for the return trip. Disregarding that he was on the way [to] his home, Mr. Wood, Assistant Office[r] in charge, made three trips in order to rescue about 16 persons. The rest of people were soaked wet under the heavy hails, rains[,] and winds, and returned by trucks which arrive quite late. But there were some who had to walk back 4½ miles under such conditions and it was almost unbearable for those persons who has warm heart, to watch this miserable scene. It is not merely due to carelessness of Officer in Charge but it really proved his mental attitude toward us. And our disappointment is much stronger than our physical sufferings.

10. As to transportation to work or from work, lack of his consideration is obvious. There is some of us who had to return to the camp on foot on account of delayed arrival of trucks, and there is still some more who are doing it after being ordered to walk back to the camp.

11. Lack of understanding as [to] our recreation is the most regrettable for us. Although there is tendency that we become quite sentimental due to being shut off from the rest of world and living in the "Noman [no man's] land" and engaging with the unaccustomed nature of work ... , there isn't any recreation facilities for us, so we feel quite loneliness. In order to make our life happier and brighter, we demand proper recreation facilities ... . Mr. Aldri[dge], Officer of Immigration and Naturalization Service, and Mr. Wood understand it and promised us to improve it, but only Mr. Remer, Officer in Charge, has not agreed with our desire. Thus ordering sport goods and movie machine has not materialized.[38] Furthermore, sales of

beers in our canteen has been fortunately materialized by kind assistances of Mr. Wood, and Mr. Aldri[dge], but Mr. Remer, Officer in Charge, was, one reason or another, so reluctant that he has once even opposed to send trucks [to get beer].

12. According to one of terms which was promised before our departure, it was our understanding that guard would be sent only for our protection. But there is one fact that one of guards has fired against us, labo[re]rs.[39]

Regardless whether we are internees or detainees, our status were gu[a]ranteed that we are still same as internees. We, therefore, demand the proper treatment accordingly and we are not engaging in this work to serve our crimi[n]al terms.

By telling you our gr[ie]vances, we desire your kind and sympathetic settlement of this matters ... .

It is our deep regret that such appeal to you ... was [necessary] for us on account of the misunderstanding and in consideration of officer in charge, especial[l]y when we realized that we came here bravely disregarding some of oppos[it]ion made by some of people who feared such conditions as described as above.

This appeal was not made merely because we desire to make trouble, but it was made by our sincere desire to continue our first purpose to live here happily for the duration with kind understanding of officials of this station by calling their attention for the above facts and also by proper arbitration. We still have this desire now but since it has become unbearable for us any longer, we are compelled to make this petition.

In the case our desires does not meet with your approval, we wish that we will be transferred to Missoula Dete[n]tion Station, as we can not bear to cause further trouble to you.[40]

Internees Prevail in Their Demands

Of all the aliens detained by the INS who were subject to the humane provisions of the Geneva Convention, the Kooskia internees were one of only two groups to use that document to its greatest effect. Earlier, in June 1942, internees at the U.S. Army-run Lordsburg, New Mexico, internment camp called a strike to protest being made to work outside the camp area, which the Geneva Convention prohibited.[41] Since some of the Kooskia internees had previously been at Lordsburg, they surely brought that knowledge with them.

The internees' petition clearly implies that they understood and invoked the rights guaranteed to them by the Geneva Convention, and that the provisions of the "original contract" which brought them to Idaho were not being followed. In addition, the petition carried extra weight because the road work was a national military priority that would probably be abandoned without their wholehearted cooperation.

The INS moved quickly to begin addressing the internees' complaints, and the next few months saw a number of changes at Kooskia in response to the detainees' appeal. These involved attention to medical care and dental care, improvements in procedures and recreation, and changes in administrative staffing.

Medical Care Improvements

On July 8, the day after the internees submitted their petition, a radiogram from Fort Lincoln, North Dakota, to Fort Missoula, stated,

KELLY INSTRUCTS TO ARRANGE WITH YOU TO EFFECT TRANSFER DOCTOR BOROVICKA TO CAMP KOOSKIA TO SERVE AS INTERNEE DOCTOR STOP WILL PERSONALLY ACCOMPANY TO MISSOULA OR PERHAPS KOOSKIA IF YOU SO DESIRE STOP CALL ME ON RADIO YOUR CONVENIENCE [SIGNED] MCCOY.[42]

Since the internees' petition was dated only the previous day, it is hard to believe that they got such quick action from a federal bureaucracy. However, while the assignment of Dr. Borovicka may just have been coincidental, the urgency of the radiogram argues otherwise. By mid-July 1943 Italian internee Dr. Ludwig R. Borovicka (Fig. 50) was on duty at the Kooskia camp.[43]

Dental Care Improvements

Concurrently with Borovicka's arrival, Fraser wrote to the INS's Central Office detailing some of the problems with the dental care at Kooskia, and mentioning that Fort Missoula's dentist, Dr. Francis G. Reineke, offered to cover the Kooskia camp in addition to his other duties.[44] Once Borovicka had arrived to attend to the internees' medical needs he also began supervising their dental care. Internee Keiji Kijima, a "dental mechanic" [dental technician], from New York, could manufacture dentures and also did

Fig. 50. Dr. Ludwig Borovicka at the time of his arrest. CLCF, Ludwig Borovicka; General Records, DJ, RG60, AN085-53, NARA II. Scanned image courtesy Louis Fiset.

basic dental examinations. Borovicka observed, "Several of these men need quite extensive work, due to their advanced age and the generally known caries among this race, if they should be kept in good shape, to carry on with their hard work on the road."[45]

Procedural and Recreational Changes

Fraser was well aware of Remer's recalcitrant and unreasonable attitude towards providing any amenities, including beer and movies, to the Japanese internees. This was a serious matter because they had threatened to transfer en masse to Fort Missoula where such conveniences were provided without question.[46]

On July 8, Francis Burns, assistant officer in charge at Fort Missoula, telephoned Kelly in Philadelphia suggesting Wood be appointed as the Kooskia camp's assistant officer in charge. On gaining approval, Burns requested Wood to write a letter stating that he would accept that appointment.[47] Wood's subsequent letter surely stunned and disappointed its recipients. After thanking INS administrators for offering him the position, Wood respectfully declined it, stating, prophetically, "I feel that the atmosphere is charged with undesirable possibilities, and … have had ample proof thereof within the past few days,"[48] meaning, following Aldridge's departure. Wood nevertheless remained on detail at the Kooskia camp.

In mid-July Fraser appointed Wood as the Kooskia camp's acting officer in charge.[49] Remer was then absent, in part to consult with INS officials in Philadelphia. Wood "finally took the matter into his own hands,"[50] and seized the opportunity to effect some procedural and recreational changes that Remer had opposed.

Two months later the INS recalled Wood to Sharp Park, California.[51] Before Remer returned, Wood wrote him a memo containing numerous suggestions "For continued harmony between the Officer in Charge and Detainees." This served as Wood's final effort to encourage Remer to conform to INS requirements. Wood advised that movies should be shown on Wednesdays and Saturdays and new films should be ordered on a timely basis, hospital orderlies should be paid for a seven-day week, detainees should be able to get more than $10 at a time if necessary, and clothing already requested should be obtained.[52] As might be expected, Remer ignored Wood's recommendations.

Before leaving, Wood also wrote a memo to the internees:

TO: ALL DETAINEES, CAMP KOOSKIA:

This camp is now one of the model camps of the Immigration and Naturalization Service. Your close cooperation with Mr. Remer will help it to remain as such. The principle [sic] reason for the camp being here is to establish a road between Kooskia and Missoula--a very essential road--and if this camp works out, I believe Japanese people on the whole, will benefit by it. So, please, do not take any steps that might prove to be a detriment to the completion of the road and to those Japanese that wish to be placed in this camp in the future.

I, also, wish to state that there will be a reflection on the work that I have done if there is [*sic*] any thoughts on the part of the Detainees to transfer to Missoula after I am gone.

I wish to take this opportunity to assure the Detainees at Camp Kooskia, that Mr. Remer will do everything in his power to keep the moral [*sic*, for morale] privileges that have been granted to you at its [*sic*] high level.

Also, I wish to thank one and all of you for the splendid coopera-tion that you have given me and request that you continue to give the same to Mr. Remer.[53]

Just before Wood's departure, Borovicka sent Fraser a "Personal letter" detailing Wood's relationship with the Japanese internees at the Kooskia camp:

I also want to inform you confidentially, that all the Japanese will be very upset, if Mr. Wood should leave his position, as I think, he might want to; because he is just as essential for the smooth run-ning of this Camp, as I imagine you must be for yours in Missoula. I can only say, what I have witnessed, and that is, that he has saved many times the day by his tactful and very intelligent and efficient interventions, and that the Japanese are willing to do anything just for him alone.[54]

Administrative Changes

Shortly after Wood left for California, Remer arrived back at the Kooskia camp where he resumed his duties as superintendent.[55] Although Remer had transferred into the INS, he still regarded the internees as prisoners, and treated them accordingly. With Wood gone, the INS's contrasting philosophy of internee treatment was no longer represented at the Kooskia camp.[56]

Remer himself remained for only a few more weeks. In mid-November he wrote Kelly requesting his release from the INS. In his four-page letter, Remer detailed a number of reasons for his "feeling of dissatisfaction." In particular, these included complaints about Aldridge and Wood, both of whom "came from San Francisco." Remer accused them of wearing out tires and equipment by commuting between the camp and Orofino, denying him the use of the camp's government car, having a clerk transferred, and try-ing to intercept his telephone calls and telegrams. Remer also claimed that the internees were "being continuously advised that [he] intended to treat them as prisoners, and that [he] could not do that." In self-defense, Remer reported that the internee spokesman had called on him, saying that the internees recognized that his "ideas on operating the Camp were different than Mr. Aldridge's" but that they were prepared to cooperate with him.[57]

Kelly responded to Remer, accepting his resignation.[58] Kelly then sent a copy to Fraser, asking him to comment on Remer's allegations.[59] In his five-page reply, Fraser rebutted Remer's charges, and vigorously defended Aldridge's and Wood's actions. Fraser also stated, "I advised both Aldridge and Wood to do everything possible to cooperate with Remer and warned them that from remarks I had heard Remer make we must expect some difficulty in persuading Remer to see our way of running such a camp as compared with that of a criminal institution ... ."[60]

By early December 1943 Kelly had named Merrill H. Scott (Fig. 51) as Remer's replacement.[61] Scott was a career INS officer who was then working at the Santa Fe, New Mexico, Detention Station. Previously, he was the superintendent for the Tuna Canyon Detention Station at Tujunga, California.[62] There, his "thoughtfulness and democratic spirit" and his "kindly and considerate treatment" inspired the Japanese detainees in his care to write several testimonial letters on his behalf.[63] Remer presumably returned to the

Fig. 51. Merrill Scott, the Kooskia Internment Camp's second officer in charge, at the officers' table in the camp mess hall, 1944. Courtesy Scrapbook, PG 103-14-4.

Bureau of Prisons; a newspaper account of his departure from the Kooskia camp said only that he "will be transferred to another assignment within the next two weeks."[64]

Internees Become Empowered

The Geneva Convention enabled the Kooskia internees to regain some control over their lives. Once they submitted a petition detailing their complaints, conditions began to improve for them. The change that affected them the most was the resignation of Remer, who had treated the internees like prisoners. Scott, his replacement, had extensive experience with the INS and enjoyed good rapport with the Japanese internees. Scott's sympathy for their plight, combined with the obligations for their care as detailed in INS regulations based on Geneva Convention requirements, ensured that the Kooskia internees would finally be treated in a dignified and respectful manner. A few difficulties still remained to be corrected, but with the major irritant in their lives removed, the men's patience and cooperative attitude allowed time for other problems to be addressed and solved, particularly opportunities for recreation.

Chapter Six
Finding Freedom in Leisure:
Recreation at the Kooskia Internment Camp

... belligerents shall encourage intellectual diversions
and sports organized by prisoners of war.
Geneva Convention, Article 17.

While incarcerated, detainees require activities that will both boost their morale and maintain their physique. It is crucial to keep them from sinking into depression over their fate, thus averting possible suicide and the attendant unpleasant publicity. A variety of intellectual and physical recreation opportunities eventually became available to the Kooskia internees, and they gladly filled their leisure hours with enjoyable pursuits.

Intellectual Activities

Shortly after their arrival at the Kooskia camp in late May 1943, and even before they began working, the men started to participate in mind-building recreational opportunities. At first, they could only enjoy those that had earlier been available to the convicts. Tommy Yoshito Kadotani, a landscape gardener from California, described some of them in a letter to a friend: "In recreation room, there is a piano and we can study and read books as we please."[1] Besides a classroom and a library, the camp also had a movie projector.[2]

In accordance with Articles 17 and 39 of the Geneva Convention, as interpreted by the Immigration and Naturalization Service (INS) in their "Instruction No. 58" dated April 28, 1942, detainees were entitled to both physical recreation and mental pursuits.[3] By mid-July 1944 a commodious recreation room neared completion;[4] it would house the camp library, the schoolroom, movies, religious services, and various sports and games.[5]

97

Diversions available to the Kooskia internees included arts and crafts; a canteen; dance, drama, and music; food gathering and cooking; games and gambling; gardening and landscaping; movies and radio; pets; reading, studying, and writing; religion; and receiving visitors.

Arts and Crafts

People of Japanese ancestry confined in U.S. internment and incarceration camps during World War II beautified their surroundings and made gifts for friends and relatives through a great variety of arts and crafts.[6] At the Kooskia camp, such activities included drawing and painting, weaving, metalworking, plastic carving, stonecrafting, and woodworking.

Two drawings and one painting, created by Kooskia internees, survive in public and private collections. Toshio Sumida, a student from Los Angeles, drew two pencil sketches of camp scenes, both highlighted with some color (Fig. 52, Fig. 53).[7] The Japanese timekeeper created an oil painting of the Kooskia camp and gave it to employee Amelia Jacks (Fig. 54).[8]

Weaving occupied other men, one of whom made an elaborate pillow cover and several mats (Fig. 55); he gave them as gifts to U.S. Bureau of Public Roads (USBPR) employees.[9] Their creator may have been the camp dentist, Hiromi Tojo; in early December 1944 internee Hozen Seki, a Bud-

Fig. 52. Drawing by Toshio Sumida depicting camp canteen or recreation building, with bridge leading to it. Courtesy Scrapbook, PG 103-27.

Fig. 53. Drawing by Toshio [Sumida] depicting camp buildings with cleared hillside beyond. Courtesy Scrapbook, PG 103-09.

dhist minister from New York, wrote in his diary, "Aoyagi Co. sent the yarns to [me] for Dr. Tojyo [Tojo]."[10] These textiles were all made on a rectangular tabletop loom, and the resulting design resembles the spokes of a wheel.[11]

Metalworking is another craft known from the Kooskia camp, but it was decidedly not a permitted activity. When guard Alfred Keehr was on duty

Fig. 54. Oil painting of the Kooskia Internment Camp by the Japanese timekeeper, known only as "Take" [pronounced "Taki"]. Courtesy Janie Fluharty and the LDKRS.

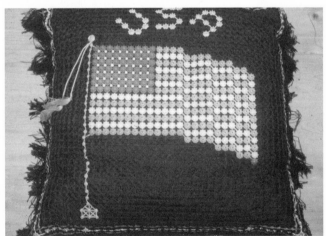

Fig. 55. Pillow cover made by a Kooskia internee, probably the dentist, Dr. Hiromi Tojo. Photograph by Mike Misner. Courtesy AACC.

100

one night he discovered one of the Japanese mechanics shaping a car part into a machete, with holes bored through it to attach a wooden handle. The next day Keehr reported the incident to Merrill Scott, the officer in charge, who had the offender removed, probably to Fort Missoula.[12]

Other internees practiced plastic carving. A relative of USBPR employee Ralph Willhite owns two finger rings made by internees at the Kooskia camp.[13] They are laminated, multicolored plastic, probably Bakelite.[14] Kits for making Bakelite jewelry were "especially popular in the 1940s."[15]

The detainees at the Kooskia camp also did stonecrafting, meaning that they collected colored stones to make, or decorate, various craft projects (Fig. 56). The day after his arrival at the Kooskia camp, internee Tommy Yoshito Kadotani observed, "Some fellows is already enjoying in stone hunting."[16] This had been a popular activity at Fort Missoula,[17] and probably at other camps as well. Some of the items made by the Kooskia internees included a bird and a floor lamp base.[18]

Four examples of wood-working are known so far from the Kooskia Internment Camp. One was an inkwell, carved for the son of USBPR employee Lawrence Hall.[19] Another is a full-size cabinet. It has three shelves enclosed by two glass doors and was made by an unknown Japanese internee for USBPR employee Ralph Willhite and his wife, Violet.[20] Another man made two miniature chests of drawers for DeAnn Jacks, the young daughter of employees Amelia and Ed Jacks (Fig. 57).[21] One chest has a painted design of cherry tree branches and blossoms. The other has Japanese writing on some of the drawers.[22] Transliter-

Fig. 56. Vase made of colored stones at the Fort Missoula detention camp by a friend of Kooskia internee Kyutaro Nakamura. Owned by Nakamura's sister, Chiyo Endo. Photograph by Rich Iwasaki, Portland.

ated, it reads, *Ichi nichi no gakumon sensai no takara. Fugetsu,* meaning, "One day's learning is a treasure that lasts a thousand years," [signed, or by] "Fugetsu."[23] There is another motto in English on the bottom drawer, reading, "Knowledge is power," above "G. H. H." If those are the initials of

Fig. 57. Miniature chests of drawers made by George Hitoshi Hanamoto. Top left and left, chest with writing; top right, chest with painted design. Each chest is about 11 in. high by 10 in. wide by 5 in. deep. Images courtesy Joan Pills.

the chest's craftsman, that person was surely George Hitoshi Hanamoto, a laborer and journalist from Honolulu.[24]

Two former Kooskia camp employees seemed surprised that woodworking was possible, since the internees "didn't have any tools."[25] However, the men may have created the necessary implements. In the War Relocation Authority (WRA) camps, for example, detainees made scissors, pliers, and tin snips from scrap metal; turned old files into chisels; and fabricated knives from found metal and scrap wood.[26]

The Canteen

During their leisure time, the internees could visit the camp's canteen (Fig. 58), a facility provided under the terms of the Geneva Convention. According to Articles 11 and 12 of that document, and included in the INS's "Instructions concerning the treatment of enemy aliens," the internees were entitled to establish a canteen, with the items sold subject to approval by the officer in charge. Detainees were allowed to run the canteen, if competent to do so; in that case, the INS required that an INS employee audit the canteen accounts.[27] Profits from the canteen were "divided among internees and all is used for the welfare of the internees."[28]

The canteen was across Canyon Creek from the main camp area. There was a footbridge to it, as well as a bridge for service vehicles.[29] Measuring twenty by thirty-two feet, it originally was a storage room and workshop.[30] The canteen sold cigarettes, gum, candy, and "novelties and trinkets."[31] It also stocked some slacks, sport jackets, shirts, and even slippers.[32] Depart-

Fig. 58. Kooskia camp canteen interior. Visible merchandise includes snacks, neckties and other clothing, boxed cards, a ukulele, and toiletries. Courtesy Scrapbook, PG 103-16-2.

ing internees apparently gave their unwanted belongings to the canteen for resale; in October 1944 Hozen Seki bought a shirt there for $1, commenting, "Second hand but splendid wool."[33]

The terms of the Geneva Convention required the canteen to contain certain items, specifically "soap, dentifrices, shaving materials, writing materials, sewing materials, and tobacco." These supplies, even tobacco, would be furnished to "detainees not financially able to supply their own needs"; i.e., the camp workers, because they earned less money than the road workers.[34] They received a canteen credit of $3 per month for extra food, tobacco, soap, and toothpaste, as well as for "matches, soda pop, beer, and general miscellaneous items … ."[35]

Tobacco requirements speciified that "detainees must be permitted to smoke under proper regulations. The tobacco furnished shall be good grade pipe or cigarette tobacco, and the equivalent of ten cigarettes a day shall be issued" (Fig. 59).[36] Tobacco for the canteen was part of the supply procurement process. In early June 1943 the Kooskia camp requested that Fort Missoula include this item in their own bids, in order to get a better price.[37]

Beer was readily available at the canteen (Fig. 60).[38] In February 1944 Fort Missoula sent Kooskia ninety-nine cases of beer at $2.50 per case.[39] Another time, employees Amelia and Ed Jacks drove to Missoula in a Kooskia camp truck "and brought back a load of beer for the camp."[40] From the few beer bottle labels that are visible in Kooskia Internment Camp photographs (Fig. 61), the beer served at the canteen was most likely Highlander Beer from the Missoula Brewing Company in Missoula, Montana (Fig. 62).[41]

Dance, Drama, and Music

People of Japanese ancestry confined in internment and incarceration

camps continued to participate in many of their traditional cultural practices.[42] Although only one mention of performance activities was located in archival documents, Hozen Seki's diary reports many instances when the internees participated in dance, drama, and music, and several photographs depict musical groups and amateur theatricals at the Kooskia camp (Fig. 63).

Fig. 59. Truckload of men heading off to work; several are smoking cigarettes. Courtesy Scrapbook, PG 103-38-3.

Fig. 60. Canteen interior. Four unidentified men stand in front of counter, three with beers and two holding cigars. Two unidentified canteen attendants sit behind counter. Sign reads, [koo]skia camp [c]anteen. Courtesy Scrapbook, PG 103-19-2.

Fig. 61. Bottle of Highlander beer stands on shelf in front of canteen window. Courtesy Scrapbook, PG 103-19-1.

Fig. 62. Bottle of Highlander beer. Photograph courtesy Steve Armstrong.

In mid-September 1944 Seki commented that the celebration for the opening of the new recreation hall would be held on the final Saturday of the month, and added, "The committee asked to me for dancing," and he practiced that afternoon.[43] From then until the end of the month he was busy with preparations. One night, following dinner, he "practiced the dance 'Okasa [*sic*, for Osaka] *odori*'" (Fig. 64).[44] He also composed a play for the dedication celebration,[45] and he and the other actors practiced it several times, once "all night."[46] On September 30, Seki wrote, "All quit their work at 3 o'clock, prepared the stage and decorationed [*sic*] the new hall. It was a big succes[s]ful celebration."[47]

Several of the internees appreciated the musical opportunities that were available at the Kooskia camp.[48] Besides the recreation room piano, some men had their own instruments. Minoru Jo Wazumi, a clerk from Stamford, Connecticut, practiced in the music room

Fig. 63. Performance of internee Hozen Seki's play to celebrate opening of new recreation building. Courtesy Scrapbook, PG 103-24-2. Characters above the stage transliterate as "Ku-oo-su-ki Shingekidan," or "Kooskia New Theatrical Company." Characters to the left read "oden," meaning a Japanese street food that people can buy and eat immediately. Characters on the sign at right transliterate as "tabi," meaning "travel." Translations courtesy Ikuyo Suzuki.

Fig. 64. Dance performance to celebrate opening of new recreation building. Courtesy Scrapbook, PG 103-24-1.

every evening after work, and commented, "I am still playing 'Meditation of Thais.' That is my only happiness."[49]

In early October 1943 the Kooskia camp obtained some surplus musical instruments from Fort Missoula. They included two flutes, an oboe, a piccolo, a French horn, and four saxophones - baritone, alto, and two tenors. The Kooskia camp reimbursed Fort Missoula for $154.40, the cost of repairing the instruments.[50] Internee spokesman James I. Yano practiced on one of the tenor saxophones,[51] and Yuji Kawamoto "practiced his flute ... so hard and [so] concentrated that he memorized the entire score of 'The Flight of [the] Bumble Bee.'"[52] By July 1944 the musicians had formed an orchestra and entertained their fellow internees with concerts.[53]

There was also a violin at the Kooskia camp. Although it was not his, Hozen Seki practiced on one several times, chiding himself for forgetting how to play it.[54] The only Japanese musical instrument known to be there was the three-stringed *samisen* that dental technician Keiji Kijima received in May 1944.[55]

Food Gathering and Cooking

Very soon after their arrival the internees began to explore the surrounding forest. There they found, and gathered, various wild foods. In late May 1943 internee Tommy Yoshito Kadotani wrote a friend, "Some fellows is already enjoying brake-hunting [gathering edible ferns]."[56] Former internee spokesman James I. Yano later recalled that they participated in "wild mushroom hunting."[57]

The terms of the Geneva Convention permitted the internees to cook familiar delicacies. That document states, "Prisoners shall also be afforded the means of preparing for themselves such additional articles of food as they may possess."[58] For confirmation, the inspection report prepared by the Spanish vice-consul following his March 1945 visit to the Kooskia camp provides a "Yes" answer to the question, "Can detainees prepare additional national food?"[59] Although detainees in the WRA camps sometimes made clandestine sake using leftover or burnt rice from the mess halls, there is no evidence that the Kooskia internees practiced this skill.[60]

Games and Surreptitious Gambling

The recreation room was mostly intended for athletics, but had space at both ends for other activities. The men played cards there or just relaxed.[61] They also played dominoes. In one photograph, four men are seated at a table, with three bottles of beer visible (Fig. 65). Two of the men are playing dominoes.[62] The photograph also depicts several bowls, two with chopsticks lying across them, and a glass jar containing more chopsticks.

Fig. 65. Two unidentified internees with beers in front of them play dominoes while two others observe, and a fifth man drinks a beer. Bowls and chopsticks are also present on the table. Courtesy Scrapbook, PG 103-18-3.

Checkers and chess were available,[63] and the men also played Japanese board games. A photograph taken inside one of the barracks shows two men playing the Japanese strategy game of *go*; three other men are observing (Fig. 66). Like their countrymen interned on road gangs in Canada, the Kooskia internees may also have played *shogi*, Japanese chess.[64]

As mentioned earlier, the internees were only allowed to have $10 in cash in their possession at any one time, and some of them gambled with it.[65] One night the gambling led to a fight. That was very unusual, because ordinarily "you would never hear them arguing amongst themselves."[66]

Gardening and Landscaping

The internees' main vegetable garden was near the employee housing at Apgar, one-half mile up the road. One man cultivated the garden as his full-time job, and also tended it during his free time.[67] Many of the vegetables served with meals were grown there (Fig. 67).[68]

Because a number of the Kooskia detainees had been gardeners prior to internment, it is not surprising that they tried to beautify their surroundings even more. One notable feature was a garden near the entrance to the camp, on a man-made island in the middle of Canyon Creek, first built by the federal prisoners. Measuring some eight feet by ten feet, the garden was used for vegetables at first, and later only for flowers.[69]

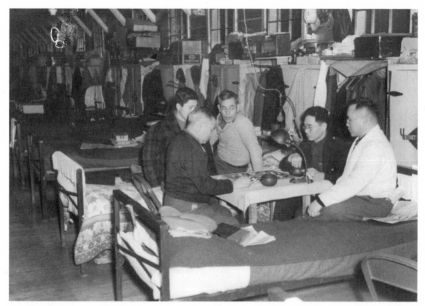

Fig. 66. Internees playing and observing the Japanese strategy game of go *inside their barracks after removal of top bunks. Players are, left, Katsuji Onishi and right, Kizaemon Ikken Momii. Observers, from left to right, are unknown; Kiichi Sanematsu; and the camp dentist, Dr. Hiromi Tojo. Courtesy Scrapbook, PG 103-05-3.*

The internees' gardening efforts also made a very favorable impression on one official visitor, who commented,

The Japanese, with their special aptitude for such work, have extensively landscaped and beautified both banks of the creek and even the small island directly opposite of the administration buildings.

Fig. 67. Acorn squash raised in the internees' garden at Apgar. Courtesy Scrapbook, PG 103-17-3.

Whether covered with its blanket of snow as the writer found it last December or displaying the velvet green of mid-summer July which the visitors have just enjoyed, this camp, in an invigorating climate, is always attractive.[70]

Movies and Radio

Following their successful petition for improvements in recreation facilities, internees could view movies twice a week, on Wednesday and Saturday.[71] A third evening was "employee night," when camp employees, USBPR personnel, and family members attended, as well as other local residents.[72] Because he had had experience running a movie projector at the New York Buddhist Church, internee Hozen Seki was responsible for operating the equipment.[73]

A bulletin board in English and Japanese kept everyone informed of the scheduled movies. There was always a feature film, and one or more "shorts" (Fig. 68). Seki's diary entries mention some of the movies that he showed, together with his critiques of them. In mid-April 1944 he wrote, "Movie night. Title 'Too Many Girls.' Musical comedy. Not so good."[74] Occasionally the films were even in Spanish, for the benefit of the Spanish-speaking internees.[75]

Fig. 68. *Unidentified internee seated in front of blackboard advertising films in English and Japanese. The feature film is* [Road to] Zanzibar *and the shorts are* Rumba Land *and* New York World's Fair. Road to Zanzibar *(1941) starred Bing Crosby, Bob Hope, and Dorothy Lamour. Courtesy Scrapbook, PG 103-14-5.*

The internees could listen to the radio in their leisure time, and Seki sometimes made a note of what they had heard. In the afternoon of April 12, 1945, he learned that President Roosevelt had died. The following Saturday the road workers got the afternoon off in memory of him.[76]

Pets and Other Animals

The internees had a few pets, raised some pigs, and interacted with other animals. Former internee spokesman James I. Yano recalled, "since we didn't have any fences around the camp, some wild animals and birds came in and stayed with us."[77] Their main pet was a fawn named Mary. Its mother reportedly "abandoned" it near camp and the guards allowed the internees to capture it.[78]

During the summer of 1944 the camp had some puppies, and that winter a cat stayed around the garage.[79] About the puppies Hozen Seki wrote, "The babys of dog became big. ... Mr. Higo likes them so much that he buys dog's [food]."[80] Another internee kept four ground squirrels in a cage, but they were definitely not happy. One of them tried to escape, and scratched its nose. Seki observed, "It looks miserable."[81] Taming small animals, such as chipmunks, was also common in Canada's road work detention camps.[82]

Some of the Kooskia internees raised pigs for food; a sketch map of the camp shows an area between the road and the river labeled "where hogs were raised" (Fig. 28, page 47).[83] Cecil Boller and fellow guard Ed Denton helped the internees by obtaining the young pigs and taking the adults to the slaughterhouse. The internees, and Boller, greatly enjoyed the pork, but the pig farming unfortunately came to an abrupt halt. "Somebody" found out that the government had not inspected the pigs before they were killed, so put a stop to the pig raising; Boller thought that the butcher in town might have complained,[84] thus stifling any competition.

The camp also had horses. Three were kept in a barn near the employees' housing at Apgar,[85] and a photograph shows two employees on horseback (Fig. 19, page 30). In September 1944 Hozen Seki helped shoe two of the horses.[86] To feed them, the camp obtained oats from Fort Missoula and hay from local suppliers.[87]

Reading, Studying, and Writing

The INS's "Instructions concerning the treatment of alien enemy detainees" allowed the internees to possess books, magazines, and other reading materials. Camps were supposed to supply these, wherever possible. Internees could also receive books and other reading matter, "subject to censorship."[88] The Kooskia camp's library began with several hundred English-language fiction titles purchased from the prison camp.[89] Augmenting these were additional works of fiction, "true story" titles, and "some science."[90] Another two hundred books in Japanese, "all censored," belonged to the internees.[91] In mid-1944 the library was placed in the newly completed recreation building (Fig. 69).[92]

On the whole, the Kooskia internees were "very educated,"[93] and some subscribed to newspapers and magazines. T. Mitsu Shiotani, a "domestic" from New York, received the *New York Times*,[94] and Hozen Seki subscribed to *Reader's Digest*. An article on Abraham Lincoln in the February 1945 issue moved Seki to tears.[95] Other internees attended classes, particularly English, during their leisure time.[96] By mid-July 1944 internee Katsuji Onishi, an importer-exporter from New York, had organized additional learning opportunities in business English, Japanese, Buddhism, Biblical studies, and Spanish (Fig. 70).[97]

Several journalists were interned at the Kooskia camp, so it is not surprising that they put out a newspaper;[98] guard Cecil Boller remembered that it was in Japanese.[99] It was probably mimeographed, since a mimeograph machine would have been available in the office. Unfortunately, no issues of the Kooskia camp newspaper have been located.

To compensate for being separated from their relatives, the men at the Kooskia camp kept in close touch with other family members, many of whom were themselves confined in the WRA incarceration camps. Besides

Fig. 69. Kooskia camp library. Note Japanese magazines on table and burning cigarette in ashtray. Courtesy Scrapbook, PG 103-21-1.

Fig. 70. Ten internees attending a class. Left to right, Ittetsu Watanabe, possibly Frank Hiyo Yamamoto, Katsuji Onishi, unknown, Tetsuzo Iwazumi, unknown, possibly Kichinojo Shirai, possibly Mikisaburo Izui, Bunji Iwaya, possibly Yasajiro Shimizu. Courtesy Scrapbook, PG 103-22-3.

writing and receiving personal letters, the Kooskia internees also conducted correspondence relating to business matters.

Hozen Seki learned to type at the Kooskia camp. In the evenings, he wrote letters for other internees and to his own family.[100] One letter to his eight-year-old son Hoken, dated February 8, 1943 [*sic*, for 1944], reads,

Hoken,

I am sure you are a nice boy. Few days ago we had a lot of snow. It was a very beautiful rural scene. Shall I tell you about the view?

Shut your eyes, dear, and try to picture it in your busy little mind. There are many pine trees, which have pretty pine needles and white snow around our houses. A number of birds gathered for their feeding at the front of my dwelling place. I gave them the rest of my bread. Suddenly I wished you were here with me.

Love, Daddy.[101]

Because some Kooskia internees had sons who were contemplating becoming soldiers, the war was of great concern to their fathers. In June 1943 Kizaemon Ikken Momii wrote to his son, Rikito (Rick) Momii, at the WRA's Topaz incarceration camp in Utah:

When are you slated to be inducted? Hope sincerely that your New World will welcome you with open arms. When time comes, rid yourself of the worries for those you'll leave behind and act to the credit of the Japanese stock. If on the field of battle, behave as a brave American soldier. Forget blood-ties. Fight loyally for the United States. My parting wishes. [Signed], Your Dad, Kizaemon Momii.[102]

A week later, Momii sent Rick a reminder:

I want you to remember what I wrote you last. Once you put on the uniform of the U.S. Army, your body your mind have nothing more to do with Japan. You belong completely to America. Don't do anything that's ridiculous or cowardish. Bloody war awaits you. Go with strong resolve that you are to give all, to fight well, for the defen[s]e of your country. Up to now, indecision might have made me utter weakly sentiment. No more of that. I send you off as true soldier's father should, telling you to go bravely and to fight wholeheartedly.[103]

A subsequent letter from Momii to his son was especially poignant, in that it recalled the death of Matsuko Momii, Rick's mother, at the Topaz incarceration camp the previous January (Fig 5, page 11): "As to mother's urn, I first thought you might keep it with you but perhaps that is not practical. I want you to ask Mr. Yoshida to keep it for us until I shall join the boys [Rick's younger brothers] there [at the Topaz camp]."[104]

Besides personal correspondence, the internees conducted business through the U.S. mail. One way to demonstrate their patriotism was by purchasing defense stamps and bonds.[105] These represented the nation's indebtedness to individuals who had lent money to the U.S. government to build up the armed forces in order to resist Axis aggression. In 1942 defense bonds were renamed U.S. War Savings Bonds and the U.S. Treasury Department issued a directive permitting internees to purchase them.[106] While at the Kooskia camp, detainee James Denkichi Urabe sent two war bonds to his wife, Hattie. Each cost $18.75; at maturity in ten years their full value would be $25 apiece.[107]

In other business correspondence, just prior to being paroled, Urabe wrote to Colonel Ralph Hutchins, commanding officer at Fort Meade, Maryland, where Urabe was previously interned. Urabe forcefully expressed his loyalty to the U.S.:

... My supreme desire is to serve the United States Army as a cook soon as my case is clear: so I am ready to serve under your commanding at any place and my health is a perfect condition[.] Let me have an opportunity to prove my sincerity and loyalty to the United States of America and fight for SAVE American principles and I am ready to sacrifice for the protection of American flag. Respectfully yours, [signed] J. Urabe.[108]

A few internees practiced creative writing. Although little is known about this activity, there are a few hints in Hozen Seki's diary that some of the internees wrote essays and poetry. Seki, for example, composed sermons in English,[109] and was once asked to "decide [the] prize for literature works of internees."[110] While at the Kooskia camp, fellow internee Frank Eizo Yanagi, an engraver and artist from Chicago, gave Seki a poem that he wrote in English, using "very nice penmanship."[111]

Religious Observances

Many Buddhist ministers and priests were arrested following the bombing of Pearl Harbor, and there were several at the Kooskia camp, including Hozen Seki, from New York, and Yoshio Hino and Sokan Ueoka, from Hawai'i. Despite a provision in the Geneva Convention providing for the "observance of the Sabbath day," the camp had no official resident spiritual advisor, although a priest or minister occasionally visited.[112] When that happened, "a goodly number" attended. One internee commented that they found it comforting, stating, "We did not think so much about religion when there was no trouble in our lives," remarking, "It is different now."[113]

Following completion of the new recreation room, religious services took place there.[114] The internees were mostly Buddhist, while others were Protestant, Catholic, and Shinto; several were "no religion."[115] Hozen Seki's participation in religious observances at the Kooskia camp included planning a service for Buddha's birthday in early April 1944 and conducting Buddhist services in "Basic English" on Sunday evenings from then on.[116]

Visits from Friends and Relatives

The INS's interpretation of Geneva Convention regulations required camps to establish regular visiting hours for internees' relatives, friends, lawyers, and others, up to two hours per week. An INS employee supervised the visit, except in the case of "a representative of a Protecting Power or the Department of State," who was exempt from surveillance.[117] In November 1943 the Spanish Embassy requested that visiting hours be lengthened to two hours each morning and afternoon, especially if visitors had made "long and costly trips."[118]

We know that some of the Kooskia internees did have visitors. In early August 1943 Tad Sato spent a day at the Kooskia camp with his father, Kosaku Sato, a second-hand dealer from Seattle.[119] Tad saw his father at work on the road gang, visited his living accommodations, and had dinner in the mess hall. He recalled that "the food was great."[120]

Kooskia internee Kinzo Asaba, a candy store owner from Seattle,[121] received a visit from his son Wataru (Watson), age twenty-four, and daughter Yoshi, age seventeen, who were incarcerated at Minidoka (Fig. 71). On the trip, "everyone stared at them, and they were so uncomfortable and afraid that they hardly ate on the way to and from the camp."[122] When they reached the end of the bus route, a car took them to the Kooskia camp. Yoshi Asaba, now Yoshi Mamiya, does not have many memories of the visit, because it was such a stressful time for her. She described it as "the low point of my life" and "a

Fig. 71. Wataru "Watson" Asaba and his sister, Yoshi Asaba, in front of Block 36, Barrack 7, "Apartment" A, Minidoka incarceration camp, ca. 1943 or 1944. Courtesy Yoshi Asaba Mamiya.

very stressful and sad experience" for a teenager, especially when they had to leave their father at the Kooskia Internment Camp and return to Minidoka.[123]

The internee dentist's wife visited him from another camp,[124] and other wives would "come up once in a while and see their husbands." They took a train to the town of Kooskia and then someone from the camp picked them up in a station wagon.[125]

Altogether then, the Kooskia internees found diversion in many creative, entertaining, and uplifting ways. They appreciated opportunities to use their leisure time productively or amusingly; any activity was welcome if it could make their enforced confinement pass more quickly.

They also enjoyed participating in sports and games, whether actively or as spectators.

Sports Activities

According to Articles 13, 17, and 56 of the Geneva Convention, as interpreted by the INS in their instructions for the treatment of alien enemies, detainees were entitled to "Exercise and Fresh Air." Even internees who were being disciplined "must be allowed to exercise or to stay in the open air at least two hours each day. In all other cases, weather permitting, exercise in the open air must be permitted for longer periods and at least twice daily."[126]

Besides exercise, detainees could "engage in sports." The INS interpreted Geneva Convention requirements to mean that they must furnish "suitable recreational and exercise equipment, both outdoor and indoor";[127] Japanese internees at Fort Missoula even golfed.[128] At the Kooskia Internment Camp, the initial sports facilities were "inherited" from the prison camp in that the INS purchased most of the prison camp's recreational supplies. These included apparatus for baseball, basketball, football, handball, horseshoes, paddle tennis, softball, table tennis, and volleyball.[129] The camp already had a baseball/softball diamond and a tennis or handball court, and the men could also go fishing and swimming in the river.[130]

Even before beginning their road work, the internees began participating in the available sports opportunities. Writing to a friend, Tommy Yoshito Kadotani mentioned several possibilities and commented, "I believe there isn't a single person who is not satisfied."[131]

Boating and Fishing

As soon as they arrived at the Kooskia camp, some of the internees eagerly anticipated the potential for fishing opportunities. In late May 1943 Yoshie Charles Yoshikawa, a cook from Vermilion, Ohio,[132] excitedly wrote a friend at the Santa Fe Internment Camp:

> River runs down near our camp and stream run by barrack. We almost could do our trout fishing from bed, but the river are high right now. But in the very near future we could do fishing. According to officer's explanation there are plenty trout here. Oh, Boy! It won't be long before we have live trout for our parties.
>
> Our camp are surrounding by mountains and trees, river. I am already feel just like having summer vacation. Fishing Trips. Last night I dreamed myself already caught thousands trouts.[133]

In early June 1943 Dave Aldridge, assistant officer in charge at the Kooskia camp, sought permission for the men to fish in the Lochsa River because that activity would "contribute in no small measure to the morale of the internees." Bert Fraser, officer in charge at Fort Missoula, agreed, saying, "it is worth trying in view of the fact that the Japanese are so fond of fishing." He suggested that Aldridge get permission from the Forest Service first and then approach the Idaho Fish and Game Commission.[134]

By July 1944 forty-eight internees had each purchased a fishing license costing $2 per year.[135] They bought the licenses at the canteen, which also sold fishing tackle.[136] One Sunday, at 4:00 a.m., some twenty internees left by truck to go fishing, and returned by lunchtime.[137]

One internee "found a river boat," which revived his "old memories about summer vacation for fishing trips at northern part of Idaho."[138] Other internees built boats and rafts to help them pursue fishing opportunities. One photograph shows seven such vessels, one named "Lima," after the home of some of the Peruvian Japanese internees (Fig. 72). Another depicts a board raft with a box for a seat (Fig 31, page 53).

The internees cooked the fish that they caught. In fact, their trout fishing was so successful that they asked the camp kitchen to reduce the dinners of purchased fish from three to two per week.[139] Sashimi may have been one of the foods they prepared, although neither government documents nor

Fig. 72. Internees built boats and rafts having wooden boxes for seats. Unidentified internee sits on the boat Lima *and fishes in the Lochsa River. Courtesy Scrapbook, PG 103-03-3.*

Hozen Seki's diary mention it. In comparison, however, a Japanese Canadian internee working on the Yellowhead-Blue River Highway project in British Columbia under similar circumstances reported, "In the clear stream which flows in front of our camp, ... you will find trout in great numbers which make excellent sashimi."[140]

Sports and Competitions

The doctor and dentist who inspected the camp in mid-June 1943 found the recreational facilities "almost totally lacking." They reported that these "consist of one rock-strewn, weedy baseball diamond."[141] However, from an internee account, we know that softball, handball, and table tennis were available when the men first arrived.[142] It was not until a year later that the internees erected a building that served as an indoor recreation room. The report of a visit to the Kooskia Internment Camp by an International Red Cross representative stated that the men "most often play Japanese games," but did not specify what those games were.[143]

Government documents, oral interviews, and Hozen Seki's diary mention many of the opportunities for sports and games that were available to the internees. Baseball and softball equipment sold to the INS in early June 1943 and intended for the Kooskia camp included thirty-two bats, a line marker, two fielders' gloves for baseball, one hard baseball, and twenty softballs.[144] Other equipment may already have been on site, such as protective gear for the catcher and additional gloves. A photograph captioned "Sunday

Softball" shows a group of thirty-seven internees posing for the camera. Twenty-one are wearing headgear, including sixteen with visors or baseball caps. Several men have bottles of beer, and one is smoking a cigarette. Some of their equipment is visible, including five bats and one ball. Eight men hold or wear baseball gloves, whereas the catcher wears a chest and groin protector and his mitt rests on the ground in front of him (Fig. 73).

Two of the guards recalled that the internees boxed and wrestled.[145] Cecil Boller mentioned one internee in particular, a jolly "moose of a man" who was good at wrestling. Everybody, even the other Japanese, called him "Big George" because he was so big, burly, and husky; "he'd wrestle two or three of them at a time, just giggle and laugh the whole time."[146] Although nine

Fig. 73. Group of internees with softball gear; several beers are visible. Peruvian internee Arturo (Arthur) Shinei Yakabi is second from right in the front row, with white cap; George Tamaki, or "Big George" is probably the large man kneeling, second from left; Kiichi Sanematsu is second from the top, in the center, behind the man in the black sweater; others are unidentified. Courtesy Scrapbook, PG 103-21-3.

of the Kooskia internees were named George, either as a first name or a nickname, "Big George" was probably George Tamaki, from Juneau, Alaska, who weighed 180 pounds and was five feet, nine inches tall.[147]

Other sports, such as Japanese martial arts, may not have been "allowed" at the Kooskia camp. Another possibility, of course, is that they were practiced but not recognized for what they were. When the guards observed "wrestling" they may actually have been watching jujitsu, a Japanese martial art emphasizing ground wrestling whereas judo emphasizes throws.[148]

Several internees who were proficient in Japanese martial arts were surely interned for that reason. Goro Mochizuki is one example. Born in Japan in 1902, he had arrived in Seattle, Washington, by 1924. Between 1928 and 1930 he entered various judo tournaments and won trophies at several of them.[149] When he was arrested in Portland, Oregon, on April 9, 1942, his subsequent "Basic Personnel Record" lists his occupation as "Jiu Jitsu Instructor,"[150] while a document prepared two years later identifies him as a "Jujitsu & fencing [i.e., kendo] instructor."[151] This occupation would have been enough to cause him to come under suspicion and to be interned.

The Japanese martial art, kendo, "originated in the Japanese feudal ages as training for the samurai class and is based on the techniques of the two-handed sword of the samurai."[152] Before World War II, it was a recreational activity popular with both first-generation Japanese immigrants, the Issei, and their second-generation offspring, the Nisei.[153] According to martial arts historian Joseph Svinth, all kendo clubs in North America closed immediately following Japan's attack on Pearl Harbor because government agents in both the U.S. and Canada began arresting club leaders "on suspicion of being agents of a foreign government."[154] In Svinth's opinion, kendo was "the activity most likely to get a fellow into trouble."[155] This was partially true for California newspaperman Kizaemon Ikken Momii (Fig. 74), author of the book *Hokubei Kendo Taiken* (North American Kendo Clubs),[156] and especially accurate for Umajiro Imanishi, an "Express man" from Seattle, Washington, and for Joe Kozo Uenishi, a bookkeeper and department store helper, also from Seattle.[157]

Fig. 74. Kizaemon Ikken Momii at the time of his arrest. The number he is holding, "123," is not known. It is not part of his Internee Serial Number or of his Department of Justice number; E271, Momiu [sic, for Momii], Kizaemon; Photographs of Enemy Aliens (negatives) [Box 4]; RG85, NARA I.

Hokubei ("North American") Butoku Kai ("Military Virtue Society") was an offshoot of the parent organization, Dai Nippon ("Japan") Butoku Kai.[158] Umajiro

Imanishi's Federal Bureau of Investigation (FBI) file contains information provided by Confidential Informant SE-201; that person advised the FBI that Imanishi was "an expert and instructor in the Dai Nippon Butoku-Kai (fencing club), and that [he] has extreme pro-Japanese ideas."[159] The informant's latter statement was absolutely contradicted by Imanishi's own behavior, namely, that he had never returned to Japan following his arrival in the U.S., and by statements, from several American citizen family members, attesting to his loyalty.

Using the Freedom of Information Act, researcher Guy Power obtained some FBI files related to that agency's investigations into kendo in the Pacific Northwest. Power compiled them into a paper, "FBI Reports on Kendo in Seattle and Portland before WWII," which contains "characterizations of several Japanese individuals who were formerly active in the Dai Nippon Butoku Kai or the Hokubei Butoku Kai."[160] According to the FBI documents, Umajiro Imanishi acted as secretary for the Dai Nippon Butoku Kai. Following his arrest on February 21, 1942, the FBI interviewed him about his kendo activities. Imanishi told the investigators that the group met twice a week for kendo practice, "and he said that although in Japan the members of the Dai Nippon Butoku Kai bow in reverence to the Japanese Emperor before commencing to fence, the members in Seattle bow only to each other." He "claimed that their motto or code was 'to make strong the mind, heart and character.'" Another member, when interviewed,

> advised that the actual members of the organization were the children who participated in the Kendo practice. The parents of the children attending the meetings paid $1 per month if they had one child participating, $1.50 if two children, and $2.25 per month if three children.

A few of the first generation Japanese (the Issei) also participated in the kendo; Imanishi was one of them.[161]

Following Imanishi's arrest, he eventually arrived at the Kooskia Internment Camp in September 1943. He was not there long. In mid-November he had a hearing before the Alien Enemy Special Hearing Board. Following the hearing, the Board reported that they were "... absolutely convinced that the subject is a good man, willing to work in any capacity to help the United States win the war against Japan, has no desire to return to Japan, and wishes the United States to win the war." In early January 1944 Imanishi was paroled to join his family at the Minidoka incarceration camp in Idaho.[162]

Joe Kozo Uenishi was one of the Dai Nippon Butoku Kai's two co-treasurers, along with Kintaro Nakashima, a Seattle restaurant owner who was also a Kooskia internee. Like Imanishi, Uenishi participated in kendo and was also interviewed by the FBI in late April 1942.[163] The FBI report on him stated, with reference to the kendo ritual:

> ... in Japan the Kendo participants follow a ritual of bowing to the shrine of some Japanese god. He [Uenishi] stated the local Japanese organization follows this form of ceremony by bowing to the south side of the gymnasium in which they are engaged in Kendo, because that is the place where the shrine of this god would be located if they had such a shrine. After bowing to the south side of the gymnasium they then bow to one another and commence to fence.[164]

Uenishi indicated that in Japan the Dai Nippon Butoku Kai "emphasizes loyalty to the Japanese Emperor and obedience to parents." The Seattle organization, however, "emphasizes only obedience to parents and such military virtues as courage, honor, loyalty, etc. He said the Kendo Club in Seattle has not attempted to instill in its young members the idea of loyalty to the Japanese emperor."[165]

Given the interest and expertise in kendo that some of the Kooskia internees possessed, it would not be surprising to learn that they practiced that sport at the Kooskia camp. If they did, however, it would have been surreptitiously, and without the proper equipment. Given the anti-Japanese bias that considered kendo to be a manifestation of a Japanese political organization rather than as a legitimate sport, any practitioners at the Kooskia camp must have been extremely discreet.

Foot racing was another activity practiced at the Kooskia camp. One Fourth of July, probably in 1944, the internees celebrated with a picnic at a site up the river from their camp. Guard Al Keehr recalled that they purchased about $200 worth of prizes to award at the event.[166] A photograph probably taken that day shows seven men lined up at the start of a foot race, with two other men standing as observers or acting as officials (Fig. 75).

Hiking was another activity the internees enjoyed, but it was confined to a three-mile area around the camp.[167] In late February 1945 Hozen Seki reported in his diary, "After a beef-steak dinner, Mr. Yanagi [Frank Eizo Yanagi] & I took a walk [for] an hour because it was so nice warm day as a real spring. How comfortable it was!"[168] In early March Seki wrote, "this afternoon Ishizaki [Ichimatsu Ishizaki, a waiter from New York], Koda [Motokichi Koda, a domestic worker from Pennsylvania] & I took a walk to the mountain path. It was very comfortable. It too[k] us two hours."[169]

Table tennis was already available at the Kooskia camp when the first internees arrived.[170] Shortly thereafter, the Kooskia camp supplemented their table tennis equipment with six paddles, three nets, and fourteen dozen Ping-Pong balls.[171] In July 1944 a visiting representative from the International Red Cross (IRC) confirmed that the men played Ping-Pong,[172] and a

Fig. 75. Fourth of July foot race. Courtesy Scrapbook, PG 103-25-2.

photograph shows two of them participating in that activity (Fig. 76).

The internees could also play tennis and paddle tennis. In May 1943 the INS bought one tennis net, one paddle tennis net, and nine tennis balls for the Kooskia camp.[173] Perhaps that facility had tennis rackets already, left over from the prison camp. We do know that the internees did play tennis, because the same

Fig. 76. Two unidentified internees playing Ping-Pong in recreation building. Note stack of wrestling mats, back left. Courtesy Scrapbook, PG 103-22-2.

IRC representative reported that it was one of the games they preferred.[174] Today, at the camp site, there is a concrete slab on a slope off the present Forest Service No. 107 Trailhead. Ayden Thomas, a former mining claim owner at the site, stated that "it was used as a tennis court or handball court by the prison [and] … it had a wooden bounce board on one side."[175]

Other sports for which there was equipment at the Kooskia camp included basketball, football, handball, horseshoes, and volleyball, but little is known about internee participation in these activities. Internee Tommy Yoshito Kadotani reported that handball was one of several activities available when the internees first arrived in May 1943.[178] The following month, an order for sports equipment included six handballs, four pairs of horseshoes, two volleyball bladders, one volleyball, and two volleyball nets.[179]

In early June 1943 the Kooskia camp administration ordered a basketball net and two basketballs, as well as two footballs.[176] The IRC representative also observed that there was an athletic field where the internees could play football. His report noted, however, that they preferred less strenuous sports, since "they are not so very young."[177]

Although the available documents do not mention soccer or any equipment for it, some of the younger men may have played that game. Arthur Shinei Yakabi, a Kooskia internee kidnapped from Peru, played soccer at Fort Missoula before he came to the Kooskia camp.[180]

The Kooskia internees thus filled their leisure hours with many pastimes that benefited their bodies, minds, and morale. Just as Hozen Seki's diary and later reminiscences from former employees all illuminate the internees' recreational opportunities, their insights also enhance our understanding of internee-employee perceptions of the camp experience.

Chapter Seven
Candid and Outspoken:
Internee and Employee Perspectives on the Kooskia Internment Camp

In every place where there are prisoners of war, they shall be allowed to appoint agents entrusted with representing them directly with ... authorities ... .

Geneva Convention, Article 43.

The Japanese aliens' response to their unjust incarceration must often have found expression in the phrase, *shikata-ga-nai*, meaning, "it cannot be helped," and in the word *gaman*, "persevere." Resigning themselves to conditions that they could not control, some sought to improve their circumstances, and gain a measure of power over their own lives, by volunteering for assignment to the Kooskia Internment Camp. Although there is no Japanese language equivalent for the American idiom, "when life hands you lemons ... ," the men who volunteered for the Kooskia camp did indeed "make lemonade."[1]

The internees' generally positive attitudes are reflected in diary entries by Reverend Hozen Seki, a Buddhist minister and founder of the New York Buddhist Church. After being at the Kooskia camp for six months or so, Seki obtained a blank, five-year diary, possibly as a present from his wife or a friend. Each page in the diary is headed by a month and date and is ruled into five sections of four lines each, all beginning with "19," thus leaving it to the writer to designate the year. Since Seki's native language was Japanese, it is a remarkable achievement that his diary entries are always in English, except for occasional words in Japanese. For Seki, the diary was another way to improve his command of the English language, together with the reading and studying accomplishments that he often described.

Seki's first diary entry is on January 1, 1944,[2] after which he set the diary aside for the next three months. Beginning on April 1 he wrote in it daily for several years. The entries from then until late May 1945 illuminate Seki's time at the Kooskia camp. Many of his comments on daily life there have already been incorporated as appropriate into previous chapters, especially those on living and working conditions and on leisure activities. His diary entries also reveal other aspects of camp life, particularly internee organization and self-government, internee-employee relations, and holiday celebrations. Seki's observations touch additional subjects of concern to him, such as his own philosophy about his experience and his home and family life.

Although the internees' perspectives are of primary importance, Kooskia camp employees also provided valuable observations on the overall experience. Interviews with former guards Alfred (Al) Keehr and Cecil Boller offer additional dimensions to daily life at the Kooskia camp.

Internee Organization and Self-Government

Articles 42 and 43 of the Geneva Convention, as interpreted by the Immigration and Naturalization Service (INS), specified that the detainees "shall have their own camp organization." They could also "manage the internal affairs of the camp relating to work, recreation, education, and general welfare ... ." To do so, they elected representatives and formed committees, whose work was "properly supervised" by an INS employee.[3]

Internees could also appoint a spokesman to represent them with the administration and with any visitors from the "Protecting Powers," neutral countries overseeing alien welfare. The INS required that the officer in charge of each camp "make himself available to the detainee representative not less often than once each day." If the spokesman had any complaints, these were to receive immediate attention, and the spokesman was also entitled to write the Central Office in Philadelphia if he wished.[4] At the Kooskia camp the spokesman had "an office ... which is attractively arranged and furnished" (Fig. 77).[5]

All these arrangements, from the elected governing committee to the spokesman's access to the officer in charge, to the provision for writing to the top INS administration, helped sustain the internees' morale and encouraged them to believe that, although incarcerated, they still had some control over their lives and circumstances. Even the office provided for the spokesman was an unspoken INS acknowledgment that the spokesman needed "face," or prestige, to function effectively with, and on behalf of, his fellow internees.

Fig. 77. Bunji Iwaya, an elected Kooskia Internment Camp spokesman, in the spokesman's office in early to mid-1944. Iwaya, who spoke Japanese, English, and some Spanish, did not win subsequent quarterly elections. Courtesy Scrapbook, PG 103-28-4.

In May 1943 the Kooskia internees elected James I. Yano as their first spokesman because of his education and his command of the English language.[6] Following Yano's parole to the War Relocation Authority's Topaz, Utah, incarceration camp in early 1944,[7] Hozen Seki became the next internee spokesman, probably because Seki was "such a prominent person."[8] The spokesman's responsibilities included representing the internees in dealings with the administration, mediating disputes between internees, and presiding over internee meetings. In early April 1944 the men had a meeting to decide the "inside" workers' salary. Because the kitchen and other "inside" workers received a lower salary than the road workers did, the latter contributed part of their pay to the camp workers, thus making the two groups' wages more equitable. Seki also shared issues of health and safety with the other internees, such as when the new German internee physician, Dr. Hans Werner Kempski, showed him a tick.[9]

The Kooskia camp also had an assistant internee spokesman, another elected officer who served as the spokesman's secretary. Four times a year the internees voted for those two positions as well as for the other members of the governing committee, those in charge of work, education, and the canteen. Together, these men oversaw the detainee population's general welfare.[10]

While there is no list of internee officers over the life of the Kooskia Internment Camp, Seki's diary mentions some of the winners of the quarterly elections and other names appear in official reports. In July 1944 Sakaye Ed Yoshimura, a photographer from California, was spokesman and supervisor of education; Yoneji Imamura, a lumber mill worker from Washington, was in charge of work; and Gitaro Kozima, an importer/exporter from California, oversaw the canteen.[11] The Kooskia internees also elected barracks representatives. Only a few of them are known, mostly through Seki's diary; at the end of June 1944 "Mr. Onishi [Katsuji Onishi, an importer/exporter from New York] was elected as captain of this room."[12]

Elections usually took place on Sunday, the men's only day off, and Seki sometimes recorded the results. In late September 1944 he wrote, "Election day for spokesman. Kozima 40. Onishi 30. Seki 18. Watanabe 10. It was interesting."[13] As the December 1944 elections approached, the internee governing committee met, hoping to solve an important problem: the canteen had run out of cigarettes. They decided to collect $5 from each smoker to buy tobacco from the Army.[14] At mid-month, the committee met again, to discuss "the problem of New Year's dinner, and Tabacco [*sic*]."[15] Following the vote Seki commented, "After dinner we have a meeting that elected next spokesman & vice spokesman. Kojima & I elected."[16] In February another Sunday mass meeting caused Seki to note, "I was the chairman. There were many problems, but everything was O. K."[17]

In early March 1945 the officers were Gitaro Kozima, spokesman and canteen; Naoichi Maeda, work; and Katsuji Onishi, education.[18] At the next quarterly election, on March 25, the men elected Seki "the chairman of the board as before."[19] Some board meetings discussed plans for the imminent closure of the camp, whereas others promoted tidiness in the dormitories. Following one of the latter meetings, Seki wrote, "As [a] result, to-day I have cleaned my bed. I shall keep like this, it looks so comfortable."[20]

Internee and Employee Relationships

In April 1944 Seki noted that guard Henry Boyer had come back from Montana, observing. "He is fat, and very kind man."[21] Seki later recorded the arrival of a new staff member that month, writing, "Mr. Kashino ... arrived here as a[n] officer of censor for letters."[22]

Paul Shoichi Kashino was born in Denver, Colorado, in 1912 and was educated in Japan from 1917 until about 1930 (Fig. 78).[23] Following Pearl Harbor, the Federal Bureau of Investigation (FBI) and the INS, knowing of his bilingual education, requested his services as interpreter and censor at Fort Missoula; the alternative was being drafted to serve in the South Pacific. Kashino complied, and arrived at Fort Missoula in January 1942.[24]

While there Kashino unknowingly endured an unwarranted attack on his character. In early May 1942 W. F. Kelly, then chief supervisor of the

Fig. 78. Paul Kashino, the Kooskia camp's censor, interpreter, and translator. Courtesy Virginia Kashino Tomita.

Border Patrol, based at the Justice Department's INS office in Philadelphia, wrote the acting supervisor at Fort Missoula with implications that maligned Kashino's integrity. Kelly expressed surprise that the central office had received from Fort Missoula "very few ... letters, or excerpts," that revealed "subversiveness on the part of the writers." In contrast, the Santa Fe, New Mexico, internment camp, "where, it is believed, the Japanese in detention are of approximately the same classes as you have in detention at Fort Missoula," sent such reports "almost daily." Kelly continued, "This naturally raises a question concerning the care and efficiency with which censorship is being handled at Fort Missoula, and it is desired that you investigate and submit a report." With reference to Kashino, Kelly wrote, "... if you do not have complete confidence in his ability and integrity it is suggested that you have one of the Korean interpreters go over the mail he has passed, without his knowing that that is being done, in order that you may be satisfied he is doing his work properly."[25]

Fort Missoula's acting supervisor, P. R. McLaughlin, replied to Kelly stating that he had investigated the handling of Japanese mail and that he felt "such mail is being properly examined." He noted that Kashino only worked with mail in Japanese, whereas a "white" employee censored letters in English. McLaughlin promised to conduct an investigation.[26] On May 22 he wrote Kelly stating, "... after an intensive and careful check of Japanese mail censored by Interpreter Paul Kashino, it would appear that he is doing a thorough and conscientious job." McLaughlin continued, "During the check which was without his knowledge, of course, he called [an INS officer's] attention ... to a questionable letter, and this letter was included with the batch of mail referred to Korean Interpreter Kim for checking. It was the only communication which Kim was able to find that was in any way questionable." McLaughlin concluded, "to be candid and frank, I am satisfied that our mail is being properly and thoroughly handled."[27]

Before Fort Missoula closed in July 1944 Paul Kashino transferred to the Kooskia Internment Camp as interpreter, translator, and censor. In early October Kashino married Hattie Maniwa in Denver, and their first home together was at the Kooskia camp, in the employees' housing at Apgar (Fig. 79).[28] Hozen Seki observed their arrival and wrote about it in his diary: "Mr. Kashino arrive[d] with his new wife who is lovely. He look[s] so happy."[29]

Fig. 79. Hattie Kashino in front of the Kashinos' cottage at Apgar. Courtesy Virginia Kashino Tomita.

Seki had a cordial relationship with Kashino and occasionally mentioned him elsewhere in his diary.[30]

Seki's Caucasian supervisor for his work in the garage was a "Mr. Pauline." Little else is known about this man, and at times their relationship was less than amicable. Pauline's surname first appears in Seki's diary in July 1944, when Seki commented, "Mr. Pauline must go to Missoula. We checked all bad tires."[31] Besides needing good tires for the difficult journey, he may have been taking the bad tires to Missoula to exchange for better ones, or to get them fixed. Following Pauline's return at the end of July, he and Seki "went to Mrs. Waki for repairing her car."[32] "Mrs. Waki" was Miss Amy Wachter, an office worker at the Kooskia camp.

In August Seki wrote, "This afternoon I get mad when washing the car because of Pauline's interfere[nce] during the work." Seki regretted what must have been an outburst, writing, "I must more improve my mind." A few days later his problems were solved temporarily when Pauline had to go to Spokane where his wife was in the hospital. On Friday Seki wrote, "There is not any interfer[ence] during my work. It was pleased to me."[33]

Pauline returned later that month.[34] The following Saturday, Seki reported on an accident Pauline caused: "While working with Pauline, he turned the wheel, then my breast was clashed [crushed] against the fender and wheel. It was a heart-rending sight."[35] On Sunday, the internees' day off, Seki "… slept all day because of the hit of breast, but not so bad. To-morrow, it will be cured."[36] In fact, the injury took several weeks to heal.[37]

During the third week in September Seki wrote, "This morning Pauline went to Missoula, then we were rather leasure [*sic*]." By November the two men had achieved a better relationship. Early in the month Seki commented, "At the evening Mr. Pauline who came back from hunting called me to his room. He is so kind though his talking [makes me] laugh sometime[s]." They must have worked together harmoniously for the next several months because Seki does not mention any more problems. Finally, in March 1945 he wrote, "This morning, Pauline suddenly quited [quit] and returned home to Missoula."[38]

Despite his early disagreements with Pauline and once with an internee whom he scolded for breaking the movie projector in a fit of temper, Seki was seen as a peacemaker who could help resolve disputes. In the fall of 1944 he wrote, "Last night there was a little quar[r]el which I settled this afternoon." Later that month he "scol[d]ed Mr. Hoshiko who broked [*sic*] the movie set [projector] in his temper."[39]

Even when he was not the spokesman, Seki sometimes interceded with the administration on behalf of specific internees, not always successfully. In early October 1944 ten men were scheduled for transfer to the Santa Fe Internment Camp. Seitaro Higo, a laborer from California, did not want to leave the Kooskia camp. Seki wrote, … I consult[ed] with Mr. Scott on this matter. He [Higo] will go there." Following a subsequent mass meeting Seki observed, "Any how, I hope a good harmony in this camp."[40]

At the beginning of 1945, potential problems surfaced with a change in the road supervisors. U.S. Bureau of Public Roads (USBPR) employee Bailey Rice, previously the "powder monkey" in charge of blasting operations, became a foreman for the road work. According to Seki, the men were "talking about Mr. Rice … . They say he doesn't like Japanese."[41] Subsequently, Seki did not mention any problems with him, so perhaps none materialized.

After Merrill Scott became superintendent of the Kooskia camp, in response to the internees' petition for better living and working conditions, several official visitors commented on his fine character. In late July 1944 Captain Antonio Martin of the Spanish Embassy and Charles C. Eberhardt of the State Department inspected the Kooskia camp. Eberhardt's subsequent report spoke of the internees' high respect and esteem for Scott.[42] In Martin's report to the Spanish Ambassador, he wrote that the internees "request me to thank the officer in charge[,] Merrill H. Scott[,] for the new canteen, the recreation hall, office [for] spokesman, and his understanding cooperation in solving the daily problems of the camp."[43]

Scott enjoyed fraternizing with the internees and was not afraid to get his hands dirty working with them, nor did he worry about any loss of dignity.

In November 1944 Hozen Seki noted in his diary, "Repaired the battery with Mr. Scott."[44]

Although the internees regarded the superintendent quite highly, some of the employees disliked Scott intensely. Former Kooskia camp guard Al Keehr recalled that Scott tried to get him to drink on night duty. Scott "had a room there himself and he'd be drinking ... and you could smell [it], ... and he'd offer, want me to drink with him! Well, you know that that was no good. ... He'd offer me a drink and I told him, 'No, Scott, ... you know I ain't supposed to be drinking when I'm on [duty].' But that's the way he was."[45] Guard Cecil Boller got along with Scott better than Keehr did. He recalled that one of his duties was to do a bed check at night, and that Scott put a stop to it when the internees complained that the guard's flashlight woke them up.[46]

Holidays and Other Celebrations

The Kooskia internees eagerly anticipated holidays and special events for the welcome diversion and morale boost these brought to their daily routine. In 1943 and 1944 they celebrated the Fourth of July, Thanksgiving, and Christmas. They greeted the New Year in 1944 and 1945, and held an anniversary picnic in May 1944 after they had been at the Kooskia camp for a year. They also enjoyed other social gatherings from time to time.

The men participated enthusiastically in these typical American holidays and events, ones that were celebrated at the behest of the INS administration. Some internees, particularly those married to Japanese American women, probably were accustomed to these celebrations. For others, the experience must have been new to them. One exception was New Year's Day, which is "the most important national holiday in Japan"[47] as well as at the Kooskia camp.

Fourth of July

In 1944 the Fourth was on a Tuesday. Seki observed, "Afternoon everybody rested as it is the independent day."[48] Although Seki did not mention a special event, perhaps because he did not attend it, Keehr described that year's Fourth of July outing.[49] The guards took over one hundred internees up the river to a campground several miles away where "they had a big feed."[50] Later that day Keehr had an unpleasant run-in with Superintendent Scott, one that worked to the internees' advantage. Even though the guards "were supposed to have the day off," Scott said they could not because he needed them to supervise the detainees' picnic. Scott told the internees that they could fish one-half mile above and below the picnic grounds. If they got beyond that, the guards had the authority to pick them up and take them back to the picnic area. Keehr observed that "a lot of white people didn't really go for that with them fishing all along the river." As Keehr sat and talked to several other guards he noticed that one Japanese fisherman had wandered outside the permitted boundary. Keehr brought the man back, even though the internee said there were no fish where he was supposed to be. When Scott arrived at the picnic, "so drunk he couldn't hardly stand up," the internees complained that the guards would not allow them to fish. Scott said to the four guards, "I understand there was a little misunderstanding between you and these boys." Keehr replied, "No, there's no misunderstanding. I done just what you told me to." Scott then told the guards that after dinner they had to "take a truck up river 4-5 miles and the other one go down the river 4 miles and unload all them that wants to fish ... and then follow them back up to the camp." In Keehr's opinion, "he just made a joker out of us guys."[51]

Thanksgiving

Although most of the holidays celebrated at the Kooskia camp are well-documented in government records, Thanksgiving is not. The only mention of it, and just for 1944, occurs in Hozen Seki's diary. On November 23, 1944, he wrote, "Thanksgiving's dinner was a splend[id] turkey dinner."[52]

Christmas

In mid-December 1943 Fort Missoula sent the Kooskia Internment Camp a shipment of holiday foods, including dressed turkey, mixed candy, and mixed nuts.[53] During the Christmas season the Kooskia internees received other special privileges. The canteen stocked gift items for them to buy and mail to relatives and friends. In early December 1944 two internees employed in the canteen went shopping in Lewiston with chief clerk Albert Stark.[54]

The men also sent Christmas cards. In the fall of 1944 the INS central office offered to furnish cards to the Kooskia camp and Scott ordered 650 of them. They were postcards, and some were in Spanish for the convenience of the Japanese Latin Americans (Fig. 80).[55] The men could send up to twelve Christmas postcards in addition to their regular mail quota for December.[56] In mid-December Seki "wrote several greetings card to my friends."[57]

Besides having a holiday dinner, the internees also decorated the mess hall and had Christmas trees both indoors and outdoors, including one near the canteen (Fig. 81). On December 25 Seki commented, "It was wonderful dinner. Mr. Scott donated wine and Kashino [contributed] beer. Everybody enjoyed."[58]

Former employee Amelia Jacks had splendid memories of life at the Kooskia Internment Camp, especially at Christmas. There, "Christmas was a real holiday, filled with celebration and good cheer." The Japanese internees

Deseo a Ud. y Familia
FELICES PASCUAS
y un
Próspero Año Nuevo.
Kooskia, 25 de Dic. de 1944

Fig. 80. Christmas postcard in Spanish, December, 1944: "Wishing you and your family a Merry Christmas and a Prosperous New Year." Perhaps because "Felices Pascuas" can also mean Easter or Passover, today "Feliz Navidad" [sometimes "Felices Navidades"] is more common; AN85-58A734, FN56125/27j, Box 2409, RG85, NARA I. Image courtesy Robert Ellis.

helped immeasurably, by doing the cooking and cleaning up afterwards. She recalled, "The guards' families had our Christmas dinner in the community hall, all of us, about 30 adults and 10 kids … . It was simply gorgeous with all the snow, and the Christmases were just wonderful there. … We'd have real feasts; just send in an order and you'd get what you wanted, rationed or not rationed, … You know, I thoroughly enjoyed living there; it just didn't feel like we were at war at all."[59]

The employees' idyllic experience contrasted sharply with that of the internees. Although they made the best of this holiday time far from their homes and families, and, if Buddhist, they would not have celebrated Christmas at all, they would much rather have been reunited with their loved ones. For them, that would have been the real celebration.

New Year's

Of all the holidays observed at the Kooskia camp, New Year's was the most important. The men decorated the mess hall for it and had a special meal (Fig. 82). They sent New Year's greetings to their friends and relatives on postcards provided by the camp administration (Fig. 83).[60] The internees also observed the custom of *mochitsuki*, meaning the ceremonial pounding of steamed *mochigome* (sweet or glutinous rice) to make *mochi* (sweet rice cakes). *Mochi* are "essential to the Oshōgatsu or New Year's celebration."[61] In October 1943 Fort Missoula ordered a shipment of *mochigome* but had not received it by December 21.[62] The rice finally arrived just in time and they

Fig. 81. Three unknown internees decorate the camp's outdoor Christmas tree. Courtesy Scrapbook, PG 103-18-2.

sent the Kooskia camp a one-hundred-pound sack.[63] The Kooskia internees then gathered to prepare it as they would have done previously in Japan or in Japanese American communities and households.

Although there is no information on the actual *mochi*-making in 1943, the 1944 event is depicted in photographs and mentioned in Hozen Seki's diary. On December 20 Seki wrote that the internees began preparations: "one man made a *usu* [a mortar made from a cross-section of log] for *mochitsuki*."

Fig. 82. Kitchen workers set out a special holiday meal. Courtesy Scrapbook, PG 103-10-2.

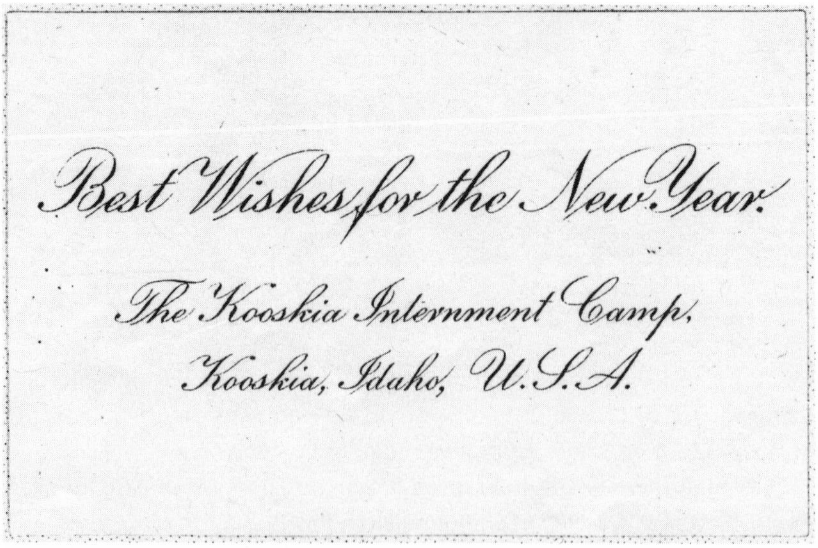

Best Wishes for the New Year.

The Kooskia Internment Camp,

Kooskia, Idaho, U.S.A.

Fig. 83. Kooskia Internment Camp New Year's postcard; AN85-58A734, FN56125/27j, Box 2409, RG85, NARA II. Image courtesy Robert Ellis.

On December 30 he commented, "At 1 p.m. they make *mochi*."[64] According to one account, "[m]ochitsuki is an all day event which requires many hands, long hours, and physical labor, but it is also a time of fellowship and social- izing."[65] The day before *mochi*-making, participants wash the special rice and place it in large containers to soak overnight. The next morning they steam it over boiling water in *seiro* (wooden steaming frames), stacked several atop one another (Fig. 84). After the rice is cooked, it is put into the *usu*.[66]

A photograph from the Kooskia Internment Camp shows some of the internees posing with their wooden *usu* (Fig. 85). It is decorated with a *shimenawa*, "a sacred rope of rice straw hung from shrines and other places important in Shinto religion. This rope is believed to have the power to ward off evil spirits. Hanging from this is cut and folded paper called *gohei*. These are hung on *shimenawa* ... to invoke the presence of the *kami* [the gods]."[67]

The hot cooked rice in the *usu* is pounded with a *kine* or wooden mallet (Fig. 86). With enthusiasm and force, the *mochi* is pounded until the mass of rice is smooth and shiny, with no discernible indi- vidual grains of rice. An essential participant in the pounding is the person assisting who quickly darts his or her hand into the *usu* and turns the rice before the next rhythmic pound (Fig. 87).

Fig. 84. Preparations for making mochi *(sweet rice cakes). Right, soaking* mochigome *(sweet or glutinous rice) in large kettles. Left, steaming soaked* mochigome *in wooden steamers,* seiro. *Courtesy Scrapbook, PG 103-12-1.*

Fig. 85. Mochi-making crew poses with their decorated usu (wooden mortar) *before beginning to pound the steamed* mochigome. *Courtesy Scrapbook, PG 103-12-3.*

Fig. 86. Two men pound mochigome *in* usu. *Courtesy Scrapbook, PG 103-11-2.*

Fig. 87. One man pounds mochigome *in* usu *while another man reaches in to turn it. Courtesy Scrapbook, PG 103-12-2.*

"The smooth, consistent mass of *mochi* is turned onto a cloth or paper covered table, already spread with a thin layer of *mochiko* (sweet rice flour). This makes the sticky mass easier to handle. An adept person pinches off small portions of the steaming hot *mochi* for others, who quickly form them into flattened bun shapes with their hands"[68] (Fig. 88).

The rounded bun shape represents the traditional Japanese mirror, *kagami*, which itself is the emblem of the Shinto goddess Amaterasu o mikami, the Sun Goddess.[69] After the formed *mochi* has cooled it is ready to eat.[70] Its elasticity symbolizes strength, and its color, white, represents purity.[71]

Celebrants prepare special *kagami mochi* by obtaining small, raised trays, *sanbo*, and placing a sheet of white paper, representing purity, on each. Participants then flatten the individual *mochi* and stack them at

Fig. 88. Men form mochigome *into bun-shaped* mochi. *Courtesy Scrapbook, PG 103-10-1.*

least two high on the trays. Then they place a tangerine or other small, bitter orange fruit, on top of the stacked *mochi*. The fruit, *daidai* ("generation to generation"), represents longevity.[72]

On New Year's Eve 1944 Seki wrote, "At night, Mr. Ishizaki [Ichimatsu Ishizaki, a waiter from New York] had invited me to the Canteen. At midnight Sochu hit the gong 108 [to wipe out the 108 sins of the past year]. It was very special day ... ."[73]

Surprisingly, there were several quarrels among the internees on New Year's Day. The following morning, the committee settled them peacefully. That accomplished, the New Year celebrations continued for several days. On January 6, 1945, Seki commented, "To-night we had a new year party again."[74]

In contrast, Japanese internees in British Columbia had a very lonely and meager New Year:

> We did not have a drop of *omiki* [a sake toast to the gods], no decorative *omochi* [i.e., *mochi*], ... no color - only the *kado matsu* [*kado*, "gate," or doorway framed with *matsu*, "pine trees" or pine boughs (Fig. 89)], a camp full of men and the wilderness around, empty of human life. At no time have we felt so much the loneliness of our life separated from the ordinary world.[75]

Anniversary Picnic

Another important event was the anniversary picnic. It took place in late May 1944, one year after the camp opened for Japanese detainees. On Sunday, May 7, Seki wrote in his diary, "In the morning we 20 people went to W.P.A. Camp for looking to the picnic of the end of this month."[76]

Sunday, May 28, was "that day which internees arrived here one years [*sic*] ago from Santa Fe. We have

Fig. 89. Doorway (kado) *decorated with pine branches* (matsu). *Courtesy Scrapbook, PG 103-47-4.*

Picnic. They enjoyed."[77] The Japanese arranged the event as a way to show appreciation for the Caucasian construction personnel who supervised their work. The internees planned the activities and prepared Japanese food. It included plants, such as fiddlehead ferns, harvested from the local woods. The guests enjoyed themselves very much, and power shovel operator Milt Barton described the meal as "quite a banquet!"[78]

Several group photographs were taken that day (Fig. 90, Fig. 91). Lists accompanying them contain the names of 101 Japanese internees, the German internee doctor, and some of the camp employees.[79] The three images were taken beside a creek strewn with distinctive large boulders (Fig. 92). Although the location should be identifiable today, the exact spot has proven elusive, so perhaps it was destroyed by subsequent road construction. In early June the photographs became available for purchase and Seki bought a copy of each.[80]

Fig. 90. Group photo taken at anniversary picnic, May 28, 1944. Left to right, Seizo Takahashi, Keiji Kijima, Otosaburo Sumi, German internee doctor Hans Werner Kempski, superintendent Merrill Scott, Yusaku Kaniyashiki, Yoshitaro Nikki, head mechanic Ralph Willhite, Torajiro Imahashi, George Hideji Tamaki, Jinichiro Ooka, Takashi Kono, Ichimatsu Ishizaki, Shohei Tsutsumi (seated), Naoichi Maeda (seated), Shinkyu Taira, Yoji Taira, Daisuke Oyama, Itaru Akiyama, Yasuichi Ushiroji, Saburo Uehara, Saiki Goya, Ryoichi Nagai, Yoneji Imamura (front, standing), Eikichi Sakoda, Unosuke Shibata, Shigeru Mori. Courtesy Scrapbook, PG 103-25-1.

Fig. 91. Group photo taken at anniversary picnic, May 28, 1944. Courtesy Scrapbook, PG 103-23.

Other Social Activities

When detainees received paroles and left the Kooskia camp for good, Seki noted that their fellow internees had parties for the lucky ones. One Sunday in early July 1944, "we have a fare-well party which was so successful. About 80 persons gathered." The event celebrated the departure of Shiro Abe, Yoshio Hino, Takashi Joe Kono, and George Tamaki, who left at 11 a.m. the next morning.[81] On October 14 "we had a little farewell party in my room" for eleven internees who were transferring to Santa Fe.[82]

Other gatherings were more intimate. Earlier, on July 7, Seki wrote, "Mr. Higo bought three beers for Kijima. Him and I drink it."[83] Towards the end of that month a gear broke on the movie projector. Since the Saturday night film could not be shown until a new part arrived, Seki and several others "gathered … at the porch of Canteen to drink and talk … ."[84]

In early November 1944, Seki wrote, "Mr. Ishizaki invited me [to] his birthday celebration at night. He & I, 4 beers, that's all."[85] The following March, Dr. Kempski asked Seki to his birthday party. The two men conversed "cheerfully about all subject[s]," and Seki called it a "comfortable night." A few evenings later, after one of the movie showings, Ishizaki invited Seki to the Canteen. Several others gathered there and they "were so happy that

[we] forgot the time. 12:15." The night watchman had to tell them to go to bed.[86]

These social gatherings were not just with other internees. Another evening, again after a movie, Seki drank beer at the canteen with Scott, Amy Wachter, and a fellow internee.[87]

Hozen Seki's Philosophy

Despite his undeserved imprisonment, Seki's diary entries reveal that he seems to have adjusted quite well to his life as an internee. On April 1, 1944, he began writing his daily observations of internment camp life. That date's note reads, "since January 11, this year I stayed in side at Camp Kooskia,

Fig. 92. Group photo taken at anniversary picnic, May 28, 1944. The fifteen Japanese men pictured are (roughly left to right): Sokichi Hashimoto, Nahokichi George Kobayashi, Tomosaburo Kato, Goro Mochizuki, Ichita Yoshida, Haruyuki Nagamine, Tatsuo ("Jumbo") Nishimura, Yoneji Imamura, Motokichi Koda (barely visible behind the tree, top center), Hisashi Imamura, Riichi Kinugawa, Seisaburo Yogi, Eiichi Morita, Masashi Yamamoto [Chiyogi Okamoto], and Keiji Kijima. The four Caucasian men pictured are: top center, left, power shovel operator Milt Barton, and top right, head mechanic Ralph Willhite, both U.S. Bureau of Public Roads employees; squatting, lower right, is superintendent Merrill Scott; immediately above Scott is German internee doctor Hans Werner Kempski. Courtesy Mickey Barton.

but To-day, have wor[k]ed at outside. It was very pleasure to me. Labour is sacred." Perhaps Seki lost his position as internee spokesman, as happened several times, and returned to working outdoors. In the ensuing days he writes that he is becoming more used to the outdoor work, and describes feeling "nearly comfortable" and "comfortable" after work.[88]

In mid-April his duties changed. The work "foreman, Mr. Imamura [Yoneji Imamura, a lumber mill laborer from Washington] told me to work as mechanic." After Seki had washed a couple of cars and repaired some tire chains, he wrote, "It is my own profit. Lear[n]ing is useful." He continued to acquire skills on the job, and to appreciate the experience. On learning to fix a car's water pump, he commented, "Everything will build up my knowle[d]ge."[89]

On April 22, 1944, Seki felt a real touch of spring, writing, "there are many little wild flowers which peeped out for lovely sunshine." He added, "& beer made me O.K." By May 3, the mountains and hills became clad in a soft, green garment of grass, strawberries blossomed, and Canyon Creek's turbulence increased daily.[90]

Despite these enjoyments, Seki never forgot that he was interned. In the fall of 1944, he helped shoe two of the camp's horses. He wrote, "When I took one horse to his cage, he cried at look another horse, even animal[s] wish to [be] free." The following month, when some internees gained their paroles and left the camp, Seki "felt so melanc[h]oly that I couldn't say good-bye."[91]

A rumored camp closure caused Seki to remark, "Sometimes, dream become at present," meaning, dreams can become reality. Seki became the assistant spokesman in December 1944, and continued working in the garage. He enjoyed this experience, commenting, "To-day, I feel that I am so happy because I can study and work under this my position. I should study with all my might and main."[92] When no vehicles needed repair, he still used his time profitably, for study.

In mid-January 1945 Seki had a rehearing to see if he should be paroled.[93] Sadly, the INS did not release him.

Hozen Seki's Home and Family Life

In his diary, Seki often mentions his wife, Satomi, and his two sons, Hoken and Hoshin, who lived in New York City. In mid-April 1944 he received a poem in a letter from Satomi: "Life is a constant parting, One more the stream has crossed, But think as ye stand weeping, Of that which ne'er is lost."[94] Seki also noted that his older son, Hoken, "got lots of A['s] in his report card."[95]

At the end of April Seki "bought pencils and handkerchiefs for Hoken & others at the Canteen." Internee Kasanu Kodaka, a domestic worker from

New York, received a parole and took the gifts with him. In early May Seki sent his wife $10 as a Mother's Day present. When Satomi wrote that Hoken was promoted to the fourth grade, Seki was so proud that he bragged to his roommates, joking, "father promotes his son."[96]

On July 17, 1944, Seki wrote, "it is my father's memorial day." He received two letters from friends, one of whom wrote an essay that Seki found "very interesting. I appreciated him so much."[97] In October Seki "Wrote to Hoken because he sent me a nice letter yesterday." Shortly thereafter, Satomi sent him a photograph of herself and the boys (Fig. 93). When he received it Seki commented, "How wonderful my boys are!" In early November Satomi

Fig. 93. Hozen Seki's wife, Satomi, and their two sons, Hoshin, center, and Hoken, right. Photograph sent to Seki in October 1944 and mentioned in his diary on October 28: "How wonderful my boys are!" Embossed "Soichi Sunami New York." Courtesy Hoshin Seki.

sent him "a parcel of foods." Later that month, Hoken wrote his father praising young Hoshin's verbal skills, saying, "He understands everything," and reporting that Hoshin wished his father "were there to play with him."[98]

In March 1945 Seki received some very exciting news from his wife; she was coming to visit him at the Kooskia camp for a week during early April. Because Satomi was bringing their two sons, Seki received permission from the Kooskia camp's new superintendent, William R. Beecher, to house them in a vacant employee cottage at Apgar.[99] On April 1 Seki visited it with a fellow internee and pronounced it "perfectly all [right]."[100] The following morning he drove to Kooskia to get Pres-to-logs. There he learned that his family would arrive on April 4.[101]

The family visit was a great success. Seki wrote, "Hoken & Hoshin [were] enjoyed so much they say we are in honey moon. It is not, I believe, mistake." His diary for the following week is full of his family's activities. On April 5, "My family is living comfortably and happy with me in the cottage. Hoshin [about four years old] talk everything, Hoken [about ten years old] is busy to play around."[102] The next day Seki "took Hoken, Hoshin to the bath in camp. They enjoy so much. Internees gave them candy and etc."[103] On Saturday, Seki's friend Ishizaki brought over some food. "Hoken & Hoshin became friend[s] with Mr. Stark's & Jacks' children [Larry Stark and DeAnn Jacks]. Satomi & I wrote … letters to the kind people of N.Y."[104]

Sunday it rained, so several of Seki's friends brought food to the family;[105] in later years, Satomi Seki recalled that all their meals were brought to them.[106] On Monday, "Hoken went to mountain with George Tahara [Shunichi Tahara, a cook; also from New York City]. Everybody in camp were so kind to boys. They gave them [a] lot of gifts."[107] One internee gave Hoshin a model boat that he had made.[108]

On the evening of April 10, "… whole family saw the picture [movie]. Afterwards, Ed Jacks gave them a ride back to the Apgar cottage. Although it rained the next day, "Hoken & Hoshin are enjoying the country-life. [It is] so good for them. After noon our whole family went to Camp."[109] Finally, on April 12, "At 10:30 a.m. my family went back to N.Y."[110] They reached home safely and "in good spirits" on April 18.[111]

During her visit, Satomi Seki obtained an appointment with Superintendent Beecher to discuss her husband's hoped-for parole.[112] Although Seki was not released from the Kooskia Internment Camp, other internees did receive hearings that resulted in a happier outcome.

Chapter Eight
Surviving External Scrutiny:
Inspections, Rehearings, and Releases

Representatives of the protecting Power ... shall be permitted to
go to any place, without exception, where prisoners of war are
interned. They ... may interview them ... .

Geneva Convention, Article 86.

While at the Kooskia camp, the internees explored the available avenues that might allow them to be released for employment elsewhere and/ or to rejoin family members. One way was to request a hearing or rehearing before an Alien Enemy Control Unit (AECU) Hearing Board. These boards, which met both at Fort Missoula and at the Kooskia camp, examined, or reexamined, internees' case files to determine if continued internment was "justified" by the "evidence." Although most detainees continued to be incarcerated, a few men were released, paroled, or transferred. Repatriation to Japan was another way to achieve freedom, and some of the Kooskia internees took advantage of that option; others were forced to do so.

The possibility of liberty, or even a parole to a War Relocation Authority (WRA) incarceration camp, gave the Kooskia camp internees hope for the future - any one of them could be the next person to rejoin family members. Although the men remaining behind were happy for their friends who left, and were encouraged that they might be successful themselves, it was very disheartening for those whose appeals were repeatedly denied.

During World War II the United States severed diplomatic relations with enemy nations. Subsequently, the government of Spain, a self-professed neutral country, agreed to act for Japan in a diplomatic capacity in the U.S., with the objective, in this context, of ensuring that citizens of Japan who resided here were treated fairly. As a result, a Spanish official visited the Kooskia Internment Camp several times to check on the welfare of the Japanese aliens there. Other official visitors, for the same purpose, included representatives from the International Red Cross (IRC) and from the War Prisoners Aid of the Young Men's Christian Associations (YMCA).

Inspections and Official Visits

In response to Geneva Convention provisions governing the care of internees, the Immigration and Naturalization Service (INS) issued "Instructions concerning the treatment of alien enemy detainees."[1] One paragraph stipulated, "Reports as to our treatment of alien enemy detainees are made from time to time to the belligerent nations by diplomatic representatives of the protecting Powers (the Swiss for Germany and Italy, the Spanish for Japan)." Other organizations, such as the IRC, were allowed to visit internees. When that happened, "full access must be accorded and opportunity afforded to talk to internees and to receive any complaints they may care to make."[2]

Spanish Government Visits

Antonio R. Martin, the Spanish vice-consul, made several visits to the Kooskia camp to check on the Japanese internees' welfare. Charles C. Eberhardt of the U.S. State Department usually accompanied him, and both men prepared reports afterwards.[3] Their first visit was on December 19, 1943.[4] In preparing for it, Bert Fraser, officer in charge at Fort Missoula, wrote a humorous letter to Whitney Young of the Department of State stressing the difficulties in journeying to this remote outpost (Fig. 94):

> I have just returned from a trip to Kooskia [via] Alaska and Siberia and it took such a long time I am now in my second childhood (or "The One Government Man who Grew Old in the Service").
>
> There is a pre-historic train which leaves Spokane at 9 p.m. and arrives in Lewiston, Idaho[,] at the pleasant hour of 2 a.m. (Only members of the State Department up to no good, and respectable ornithologists who get up before the chickens are about at this hour.)
>
> From Lewiston there is a streamlined piece of junk locally known as the "Galloping Goose" which takes one to the town of Kooskia. From this metropolis of some 25 inhabitants one proceeds by auto car for 31 miles to the camp, providing 4 tires can be found or stolen which can stand the trip.[5]

Fraser's letter continued in a more serious vein, presenting what was a logistical ordeal and providing several suggestions for overcoming it. Transportation possibilities depended on whether the representatives wished to visit the Kooskia camp first or Fort Missoula first, and if they wanted to

travel by train or automobile. Whatever method was chosen, travel to the Kooskia camp required a lengthy journey from Montana.[6]

Martin and Eberhardt visited Fort Missoula first, and Fraser was very concerned about some of the complaints from internees confined there. On December 20 he responded with a "Confidential Memorandum" to Fort Missoula's six department heads, instructing them to

do everything possible to keep down and prevent complaints made by the Japanese. The Japanese government has issued an ultimatum to the effect that they will not repatriate any more of our people [Americans interned in Japan] unless the reports from the Spanish Government on the treatment of Japanese in this country show improvement. It is very evident that the Japanese are not at all interested in whether or not any more Japanese are repatriated from America. This attitude thus places us on the defensive.

Naturally we have not mistreated these people [Fraser seems to be unaware of genuine mistreatment at Fort Lincoln and even Fort Missoula],[7] and we are not expected to give in to their every whim, but I do believe that every employee should keep in mind that the fate of thousands of Americans yet in Japan may very definitely depend upon our actions right at Fort Missoula. One wrong act may undo all that we have done and prove disastrous … .

The Japanese complaints at Missoula have never been numerous, but it was very evident that they had increased decidedly at the last and very recent visit of the Spanish Representative. In fact, the representative commented on this fact himself. I believe we are taking too much for granted and paying too little attention to this internee group.[8]

Fraser asked the department heads to <u>not</u> post the memorandum, but to bring it to the attention of all employees, including "patrol inspectors, guards, clerks," stressing that "every employee having anything to do with Japanese [should] do the very best they can to establish cooperative and pleasant relations with [them]." Although employees were welcome to discuss the memo among themselves, they should not allow aliens to overhear such discussion because that "would be defeating our purpose."[9]

Fraser's concern with continued repatriation stemmed, on the one hand, from the need to exchange as many internees as possible for Americans held in Japan. If Japan refused to continue the exchanges, American prisoners would suffer. On the other hand, feeding, clothing, and housing the Japanese internees was an expensive drain on wartime coffers.

In view of the internees' unhappiness at Fort Missoula, and because the Kooskia camp's Deane A. Remer, officer in charge, had just been replaced by Merrill Scott, it is unfortunate that no report from Martin and Eberhardt's first inspection of the Kooskia camp was located. However, there is a full account of their second visit, which occurred on July 31, 1944. On that date, the camp held 124 Japanese internees, and Sakaye Ed Yoshimura, a photographer from California, was the internee spokesman. Each inspector prepared a report, both of which were overwhelmingly favorable. Martin stated that the "Prisoners' opinion of food" was "Very Satisfactory," and there were no requests or complaints.[10] In a personal letter to Willard F. Kelly, assistant commissioner for alien control, based in Philadelphia, Martin commented,

On arrival at Kooskia we found a camp especially well and efficiently administered with no important problems presented and the most contented group that could be imagined in circumstances such as surrounded them. For the first time in my experiences in visiting such camps and centers I was requested by the Spokesman to advise our Ambassador of the thanks and appreciation of the entire group of detainees for the efforts on their behalf by the Officer in Charge . [Merrill Scott]."[11]

Martin said that he and Eberhardt left the Kooskia camp "in a very satisfied frame of mind over conditions in general" there. He admitted that "the wonderful scenery at and near the camp, in contrast to the arid deserts which we had visited may have contributed toward this state of mind," but concluded, "we are convinced that Kooskia is today one of the prize places in this crazy and war-torn world (Fig. 95)."[12]

Eberhardt's report stated, "the only semblance of a guard is the American truck man who drives them to and from their work along the highway who, however, treats them and is treated by them more as a chum than as a guard or keeper."[13] He added,

> [The camp] is also unusually well administered in all details by the Officer in Charge, Mr. Scott. He seems to know every internee by name; has direct and personal contacts with all of them; they hold him in highest respect and esteem, in appreciation of which they directed through their spokesman a letter to Captain Martin from which the following lines are quoted: 'It is my obligation, as the spokesman on behalf of the Japanese internees in the camp, to inform you of the generosity and considerate efforts of Mr. M. H. Scott, the Officer in Charge of the camp, in training us and I especially wish to emphasize of his eagerness to see that we are as happy and pleasant as possible in this circumstances.'
>
> 'I further wish to assure you that we all feel fortunate to be in custody of a real American as decent and benevolent as Mr. Scott

Fig. 95. Kooskia Internment Camp, about 1944. Foreground, administrative buildings. Background, right, barracks; center, canteen and recreation building. Note garden island in Canyon Creek, left foreground. Courtesy Scrapbook, PG 103-02-2.

and request that this fact be transmitted to the Japanese authorities in charge of the American nationals interned in various places in Japan."[14]

Martin and Eberhardt visited the Kooskia Internment Camp one more time, on March 4, 1945. At that time, Gitaro Kozima, an importer/exporter from California, was the internee spokesman, and only 103 Japanese internees still remained there. Martin indicated that he received "no complaints whatsoever" from the internees, and that the "health conditions" were "excellent."[15]

International Red Cross Visit

As a neutral organization, the IRC, headquartered in Geneva, Switzerland, provided assistance during World War II to anyone who might need its services. One important function was that of conveying brief messages to and from family members in warring countries. They also helped with the acquisition of Japanese foods, such as rice, tea, and *shoyu* (soy sauce).[16]

On July 11 and 12, 1944, Paul Schnyder of the IRC's U.S. delegation paid an official visit to the Kooskia camp, to investigate the treatment of its 128 Japanese internees. In his diary on July 11, Hozen Seki commented only, "International R. C. man visited."[17] Afterwards, Schnyder wrote Scott, "I was very impressed by the beauty of your surroundings and the way your camp is run."[18] A report of his visit did not become available until the following spring. It began, "This camp has been in existence for a long time, but it had not yet been visited because it is difficult of access," and concludes, "Mr. Scott, who is the Chief of the camp, does everything to satisfy the Japanese internees. The latter could not be better treated. Their camp is very fine."[19]

War Prisoners Aid of the Young Men's Christian Associations Visit

The War Prisoners Aid group of the YMCA also assisted internees in various ways. In mid-April 1944, for example, they sent the Kooskia camp a box of unspecified "athletic equipment."[20] Luis Hortel of that organization visited the Kooskia camp in early 1945.[21] The only mention of it is in Hozen Seki's diary, when he states, "Mr. Stark [chief clerk Albert Stark] introduced me [to] a gentleman who visited from Y.M.C.A. I talked with him late this night. He promised to call my family in N.Y. [New York]." Seki spoke with the YMCA representative again the following day.[22]

Rehearings, Releases, and Repatriation

Despite glowing recommendations from official inspectors, the Kooskia internees were, of course, still prisoners. IRC representative Schnyder commented, tellingly, "The internees enjoy all privileges that could possibly be accorded, except freedom."[23] Notwithstanding their idyllic surroundings, the men naturally enough sought their liberty, whether to leave for other occupations outside the camp or to rejoin family members. A successful rehearing sometimes enabled them to achieve these objectives. Other internees accepted repatriation to Japan.

Rehearings and Releases

Following their arrest and transfer to an internment camp, the Kooskia internees had had a hearing before an AECU Hearing Board. However, because wartime hysteria and prejudice prevented those interrogations from being fair and impartial, the men continued to be incarcerated, often for reasons that today seem rather absurd. In early June 1943 the Kooskia internees received an opportunity to request a rehearing at Fort Missoula, and fifty-seven men applied.[24] Disappointingly, men from Alaska, Hawai'i, and Panama later learned that they would not receive a rehearing after all because the AECU had no jurisdiction over their cases.[25]

U.S. Attorney Attilio di Girolamo began hearings at Fort Missoula for Kooskia internees on or about September 23, 1943.[26] Perhaps because there were so many requests from the Kooskia camp detainees, di Girolamo decided to postpone some of their hearings until a later date when he could conduct them at the Kooskia facility.[27] The hearings there began on Monday, November 8. A group from Los Angeles consisting of "Mr. and Mrs. Loyd Wright[;] Mr. and Mrs. [d]i Girolamo, their five year old son, Vincent[;] and Miss Adele Vanden Heuvel" traveled to the Kooskia camp in Wright's car. Other members of the hearing board, making their own travel arrangements, were Gardner Turrill of Los Angeles and Garret McEnerney II of San Francisco.[28] Fraser also planned to attend, saying, "Remer [D. A. Remer, the Kooskia camp's officer in charge] can accommodate all of party and will have files and typewriter."[29] The hearing board was still convened at the Kooskia camp on November 11, when Fraser reported that "they desire to see me if I can possibly get over there."[30]

Kooskia internee James I. Yano received a hearing at the Kooskia Internment Camp and also acted as an interpreter in other hearings. He recalled that di Girolamo "spoke English with a strong foreign accent."[31] Because there was not yet an official interpreter at the Kooskia camp, Remer recommended Yano to the Board in that capacity "as a person to be trusted and of good character." The Board agreed; members found Yano to be "fair and honest."[32]

Yano's own hearing took place on November 14. The "Summary of Facts and Opinion" for his case stated, "The camp record at Kooskia shows that the subject is a good worker, driving a heavy truck, and very cooperative." During his hearing, Yano "stated with considerable emotion and sincerity to the Board that he would give his life for the United States and regrets that he cannot be a citizen, but in spite of such an impossibility he is still loyal to the United States and hopes that some day the laws will change as to make him a full American citizen."[33]

The Board recommended that Yano be released, stating, "the subject has absorbed too much of the American way of living to wish anything else but an American victory in this war, and ... if he were released he would not constitute a menace to the internal security."[34] In April 1944 Yano joined his brother and family at the WRA's Topaz incarceration camp in Utah.[35] Although now with relatives, he had merely exchanged one prison for another.

Detainees desiring a rehearing had to write a letter applying for one. Although some letters were elaborate, others were quite brief, such as that from Kooskia internee Kosaku Sato, a second-hand dealer from Seattle (Fig. 96). In August 1943 he wrote to the officer in charge at Fort Missoula, "Dear Sir: If it is possible, I wish to be granted an opportunity of having a rehearing. Truly yours, Kosaku Sato."[36]

Sato's original hearing after his arrest was at Fort Missoula on April 29, 1942.[37] At that time, the Board denied release because Sato had served in the Japanese army for two years between late 1899 and late 1901 and "admitted membership in Hinomaru Kai" (a Japanese veterans' organization). Since his mother and sister were in Japan, and his son was in the United States, "he did not want either country to win the war."[38] Following Sato's first hearing, "the board recommended internment [despite stating] "that there was hardly a case" for it.[39]

On November 13, 1943, Sato appeared before the Alien Enemy Special Hearing Board at the Kooskia Internment Camp. A "Report and Recommendation to the Attorney General" included a "Summary of Facts and

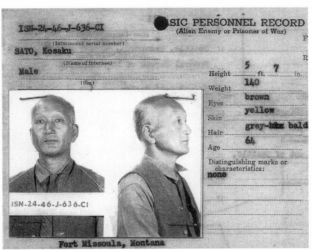

Fig. 96. Kosaku Sato, from his "Basic Personnel Record (Alien Enemy or Prisoner of War)" card, undated [1942], 1; E466F, Sato, Kosaku; OPMG, RG389, NARA II.

Opinion," stating that "at Kooskia his work is fair due to his age [65] and he is considered very cooperative." Sato "never wants to go back to Japan and wishes to remain in this country and help this country win the war against Japan. The subject appears to be younger than his age and impressed the board as being sincere and prompt in his answers." The Board recommended unanimously that Sato be released.[40]

Although the U.S. Attorney's office felt Sato should "be paroled to a relocation center,"[41] Kooskia superintendent Remer reported that he requested to "go any where that he can find employment. However, he would rather stay at the Internment Camp than go to a Relocation Center pending arrangements for employment."[42] In mid-March 1944 Sato was released to Spokane, Washington.[43] From there he went out to work with a railroad gang, but the work was "too tough" for someone of his advanced age, so he went back to Spokane, lived in a "cheap hotel," and cut up vegetables for the Davenport Hotel's kitchen.[44]

Internee Seiichi Yoshinaka, a farmer from Washington, had a rehearing at the Kooskia camp on November 16, 1943.[45] He was originally interned mainly because, on a visit to Japan in the winter of 1940, he took with him a large quantity of drill bits worth over $2,500 that he had bought at the request of two friends there.[46]

Yoshinaka's wife, eldest son, and youngest son sent letters of support for his release. Akiko Yoshinaka wrote that her husband "did not join any clubs or associations of [a] secretive nature." She continued,

My husband having concentrated all his time and efforts toward successful farming of his land and rearing of our children to be good citizens of the United States, I know he has had no opportunity to do anything that would have benefited Japan or to be detrimental to the welfare of the United States.[47]

Yoshinaka's eldest son, Kazuo, wrote,

Since food plays a vital part in this world conflict and its outcome, I am putting in many acres of produce such as potatoes, onions, carrots, turnips, and other vegetables. Last year I had a very difficult time getting sufficient farm labor. If this situation continues this year, I shall be compelled to farm on a smaller scale. With my father here, I should be able to maintain the larger scale of farming.[48]

Kazuo Yoshinaka also wanted his father released because "he knows so much more about farming than I do. He has been farming for nearly thirty years. ... His presence would enable me to avoid a great deal of the trouble I experienced last year for I do not have his years of experience and knowledge." The writer also revealed that he would soon get married and move to a different household, and that his father was needed "so that he could take care of my stepmother and my four brothers and two sisters."[49]

Even Yoshinaka's youngest son, Jimmy, age eight, wrote a letter of support for his father (Fig. 97). At the time, he had not seen his father for two years. The family was then in Moses Lake, Washington, because the government had exercised its "powers of eminent domain" in 1943 to seize their farm at Ringold, together with many other homes and farms, for the Hanford Nuclear Reservation.[50]

The Special Hearing Board agreed "that the type of the tools and the amount involving altogether $2,500 can hardly be considered to be made on behalf of the Japanese government or in a quantity to arouse suspicion."[51] Their "Report and Recommendation" continued,

> Subject has a wife and eight children (Fig. 98) in the State of Washington, five of whom are boys and one of them was rejected for military service on account of his eyes. [He stated] that he is willing

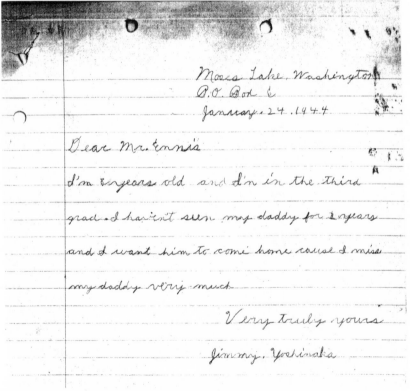

Fig. 97. Copy of letter to Edward J. Ennis, director of the Department of Justice's Alien Enemy Control Unit, from Jimmy Yoshinaka, age eight, requesting his father's release from custody. CLCF, Seiichi Yoshinaka, 146-13-2-81-14; RG60, NARA II.

Fig. 98. Seiichi Yoshinaka and his family, about 1938. Front row, left to right, Mariko, Seiichi, Jimmy, Kenji, wife Akiko, Kiyoshi; back row, left to right, Masato, Yuki, Kazuo, Takeko, and cousin, Harold Yoshinaka. Courtesy Yoshinaka family.

for any of his children to serve in the United States Army because it is his desire to remain in this country and help this country win the war against Japan. … The subject appears to be a very rugged farmer, frank and sincere, and one whose children are his chief interest, and in the Board's opinion incapable of committing any act detrimental to the internal security of the United States, and therefore recommends that he be released so that he can join his family and be of some value to the manpower program."[52]

The Yoshinaka family's persistence achieved the hoped-for result when the U.S. Department of Justice paroled Seiichi Yoshinaka. On February 8, 1944, he left Kooskia for Spokane.[53] Two days later he reunited with his family in Moses Lake.[54]

Releases, Including Paroles and Transfers

While the term "parole" could mean release, usually to a Caucasian sponsor, it could also mean "transfer" in the sense of moving to another internment camp or to a WRA incarceration camp. As demonstrated, some paroles occurred because a detainee's case was reviewed in a subsequent hearing. Once the initial war hysteria had subsided, the Hearing Board members could see that age, length of time in the U.S., family ties, and demonstrated loyalty trumped supposed suspicious circumstances. Other internees won partial freedom in other ways.

In early March 1944, the Kooskia camp received notification that fourteen of their internees had obtained paroles under unspecified conditions. These probably resulted from the rehearings held at Fort Missoula and at the Kooskia camp in September and November, respectively.[55] Two and a half months later, the names of two of these former Kooskia internees appeared on a list of "Japanese Aliens on Parole within Immigration District No. 10," meaning Idaho and eastern Washington. Henry Kiichi Akagi, a cannery worker from Alaska, was at Anderson Ranch Dam, and Shohei Arase, a delivery truck driver from Seattle, was in the Emmett, Idaho, vicinity.[56]

Akagi was first released to the Minidoka incarceration camp in southern Idaho in early December 1943. In February 1944 he was further paroled in care of Mr. V. A. Roberts, to work on helping build Anderson Ranch Dam.[57] Its construction provided employment for an unknown number of other Japanese aliens and Japanese American citizens paroled from their confinement at Minidoka, the WRA incarceration camp at nearby Hunt.[58]

Arase was also paroled to Minidoka, arriving there in mid-January 1944. Several weeks later he was granted a month's leave to visit his daughter in Denver "and to investigate relocation possibilities there." In mid-April 1944 he was "paroled under the sponsorship of Mr. Dewey Bowman of Emmett, Idaho," where he lived and worked on Bowman's farm.[59] Arase's daughter, Betty Okamura, remembered that one of her father's jobs was picking apples. That would have been in the fall; other Arase family members, in the Minidoka incarceration camp, were paroled for apple picking during September and October 1942.[60]

In December 1943 Fort Missoula's Bert Fraser supported one detainee's desire for relocation to the family camp at Crystal City, Texas. Despite having the reputation of being one of several "dangerous troublemakers" at the WRA's Manzanar incarceration camp in California, Genji George Yamaguchi, a landscaper and insurance salesman from Los Angeles, later a Kooskia internee, was a "model internee" at Fort Missoula. Fraser felt that "immediate action should be taken to permit Genji Yamaguchi to be joined with his family, as he has patiently waited for months, and his wife has three small babies, which naturally worries him considerably."[61] Yamaguchi did achieve parole to Crystal City, and in January 1945 his wife had another child, deplorably called an infant "alien enemy" despite being an American citizen by birth.[62]

Kidnapped Peruvian internees Koshio Shimabukuro, later Koshio Henry Shima, and his father, Taro Shimabukuro, also transferred to the same place after having been at the Kooskia camp for only three weeks. They learned that Teruko Shimabukuro, Koshio's sister and Taro's daughter, had arrived in the United States from Peru, so they joined her at the Crystal City camp.[63] Shima commented that they did not know she was coming to the U.S. also, or they would not have gone to the Kooskia camp for such a short time.[64]

In mid-July 1944 Hozen Seki noted in his diary, "3 persons who came [from] S. A. [South America] have transferred to the family camp [Crystal City], Texas. Mr. Watanabe who slept upper bed of mine, too went, his baby dead on the way."[65] This was Harukichi Watanabe, a businessman who was also kidnapped from Peru. Later, his destitute family followed him to the United States, suffered the baby's sad death, and were reunited with him at the Crystal City camp.[66] Kooskia camp guards Bud Nicholson and Ed Jacks accompanied Watanabe and the Shimabukuros to Texas.[67]

Surprisingly, at least one paroled internee returned for a visit. In early January 1945 Tadao Kawahara, originally a farm laborer from Montana, came back to recruit workers for jobs with the railroad.[68] Kawahara could speak both Japanese and English and had been a foreman on the road project, skills that ensured his release to a railroad maintenance gang.[69] Following Kawahara's visit, Kazuo Takesaki, a laundry worker from Oakland, California, mentioned it in a letter to Sakaye Ed Yoshimura, who by then had transferred back to the Santa Fe, New Mexico, detention station: "'Chino' Kawahara came here a week ago. There were railroad jobs available then. Many people were hired. If too many people want jobs, availability is questionable. Hiring started yesterday. Anyway the number of people [at the Kooskia camp] will decline from now."[70]

Repatriation

Repatriation to Japan was another avenue the internees could use to enjoy greater freedom. The U.S. government encouraged, even coerced, this action, because for every Japanese citizen who repatriated, the Japanese government would return an American citizen held in Japan. The internees who accepted repatriation traveled to New York where they boarded the Swedish vessel *Gripsholm*.[71] This ship took people of Japanese descent to neutral locations where they were exchanged for Americans held by Japan. Entire families often made the journey; some Peruvian Japanese family groups consisted of as many as nine members, including American-born infants.

Sometimes the Japanese government requested the return of named individuals; those designated could accept or refuse. In other instances detainees sought repatriation by completing a form given to them by the internment camp administration. These decisions were agonizing. On the one hand, the men desired to regain their freedom and rejoin relatives, especially elderly parents, in Japan. On the other hand, leaving would mean renouncing contact with family members in the U.S.

While at the Kooskia camp, at least two internees received official notification that the Japanese government desired their return. On June 21, 1943, the INS's Philadelphia office wrote Fort Missoula:

The following aliens, presently interned at Kooskia, Idaho, are to be informed that the Japanese Government has requested their repatriation:

KADOTANI, Tommy Yoshito

SEIKE, Masayuki (Fig. 99)

Please ascertain from them whether they desire to be repatriated, forwarding to this office, in quadruplicate, petitions for repatriation, or signed statements refusing repatriation, whichever the case may be. If repatriation is desired, it is possible that it may be effected in the next sailing ... .

Please inform this office by telegraph ... which aliens desire repatriation and which refuse.[72]

On June 29, 1943, Fraser wired Philadelphia, "MASAYUKI SEIKE REQUESTS REPATRIATION AND TOMMY YOSHITO KADOTANI REFUSES."[73] In early July, Kadotani wrote to Miss M. Kadotani, probably his sister, at the WRA's Poston incarceration camp in Utah, "Although I received the order of my repatriation from the Japanese Government on last 28th, I have refused it after careful consideration about you all."[74] Kadotani subsequently received a parole to the Poston camp.[75]

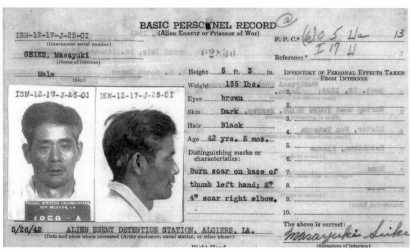

Fig. 99. *Masayuki Seike, from his "Basic Personnel Record (Alien Enemy or Prisoner of War)" card, May 26, 1942, 1; E466F, Seike, Masayuki; OPMG, RG389, NARA II.*

Besides Seike, five other Kooskia internees also wished to be repatriated at the same time. Understandably, they wanted to learn the names of other repatriates, so the internee spokesman, James I. Yano, requested a list of them. On July 26, Remer wrote Fort Missoula, stating, "several of the detainees have received letters from other camps informing them that such a list has been announced. If a list is available, please send us one."[76] Fort Missoula's acting officer in charge, Francis M. Burns, replied, "please be informed that this Service does not make a practice of informing the interned Japanese of the names of any of the repatriates, other than those in the camp where such internees are held. Therefore, such a list will not be furnished the Japanese spokesman at Kooskia."[77]

In late July 1943, Louis Yorikatsu Kakiyama, a barber kidnapped from Panama (Fig. 100), signed a statement refusing repatriation:

I, KAKIYAMA, Louis Yorikatsu, hereby, decline repatriation to Japan. Reasons are as follows:

1. I have never applied for repatriation.

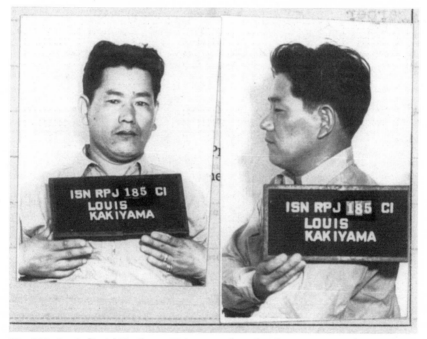

Fig. 100. Louis [Luis] Yorikatsu Kakiyama, from his "Basic Personnel Record (Alien Enemy or Prisoner of War)" card, undated [1942], 1; E466F, Kakiyama, Louis; OPMG, RG389, NARA II. On the sign he is holding, "ISN" means Internee Serial Number, "RPJ" stands for Republic of Panama Japanese, and "CI" is Civilian Internee.

2. I have my family which consists of my wife and four children in Panama.

3. My only request is to be joined with my family in Panama.[78]

In mid-August, Kakiyama again signed a similar statement refusing repatriation, as did Tokuhei Akena.[79] Despite their refusals to be repatriated, both men were sent back to Japan without explanation. On August 26 they did some pre-trip shopping at the Missoula Mercantile Company. Receipts in their names show that Akena purchased eight handkerchiefs, a jacket, a shirt, two pairs of "sox," two sweaters, a belt, and three ties, for $31.20. Kakiyama bought five shirts, one pair "sox," and two belts for $14.00.[80] On August 29 both men left Fort Missoula to be repatriated.[81]

For her second such voyage, the *Gripsholm* departed from New York on September 2, 1943. The sailing list contained the names of 1,340 Japanese passengers, of whom six had been at the Kooskia Internment Camp. Besides Tokuhei Akena and Louis Yorikatsu Kakiyama, both kidnapped from Panama, they were Kuromitsu Banba, from Hawai'i; Jinji Emori, from Alaska; Shiro Matsukawa, from the U.S. (the shrimp boat *Fuji* out of Louisiana); and Masayuki Seike, also from the U.S. (the shrimp boat *Young Bride* out of Louisiana).[82] Despite Kakiyama's plea to rejoin his family, no wives or children accompanied these men.

Marmagao in Portuguese India (Goa) was the *Gripsholm*'s destination, which she reached on October 16. There the repatriates were exchanged for prisoners who had arrived from Japan aboard the *Teia Maru*. The *Gripsholm* then returned to the U.S., arriving in New York on December 1.[83] Nothing is known about the fate of any former Kooskia detainees once they reached Japan.

A few Kooskia internees achieved repatriation, parole, or even outright release. For most, however, those goals remained elusive. Their best alternative was to continue working at the Kooskia Internment Camp, fighting anti-Japanese sentiment through hard work, positive attitudes, and occasional friendships with receptive Caucasian acquaintances.

Chapter Nine
Friends or Enemies?:
Internees Interact with the "Home Front"

Prisoners of war ... must at all times be humanely treated and protected, particularly against acts of violence, insults[,] and public curiosity.

Geneva Convention, Article 2.

How did neighboring residents perceive the Japanese at the Kooskia camp? Did they view the camp's inmates through an anti-Japanese lens, realize the incarceration's unfairness, or simply see the camp as a means to an end, i.e., completing the road?

Following Japan's bombing of Pearl Harbor, anti-Japanese prejudice was extremely virulent throughout the United States. Idaho's elected officials, in common with those in many other states, generated political capital through inflammatory rhetoric. Unfortunately, their public statements failed to distinguish between Japan-the-enemy and law-abiding Japanese Americans.

Anti-Japanese Sentiment

In early March 1942, in an outrageously racist diatribe, an Idaho newspaper demanded that the Pacific Coast's Japanese residents, "little brown hissing Orientals," should be conscripted for military road construction from Montana through Canada and into Alaska. The editorial completely ignored the fact that most of the Japanese on the West Coast were loyal U.S.-born Japanese Americans.[1] Later that month, in a letter to the editor of the *Kamiah Progress* and perhaps to other newspapers as well, Idaho governor Chase A. Clark wrote, "The state of California is crawling with Japanese. They contribute nothing to the standard of life - but undermine it. In a hundred years they will overrun us to the Rocky Mountains, unless checked. I want them put in concentration camps and kept under guard so that they can be taken back under guard."[2]

While Clark realized that there were "honest, patriotic Japanese," he suggested that those born in the U.S.

are more dangerous that those born in Japan because the latter, to some extent, may appreciate their escape from despotism, but those born here are taught that Japan is heaven and their Emperor is the Almighty.

Clark did "not want to work any hardship on any Japanese who are loyal American citizens," but he was against allowing people of Japanese ancestry "to establish [themselves] permanently" in Idaho.[3]

Despite his desire to keep Japanese people from settling there, Clark welcomed them for temporary laboring pursuits. His letter appeared in the same newspaper as an article about him headlined, "Would Work Jap Aliens on Lewis and Clark Highway."[4]

Clearly, local newspapers helped fan the flames of racial animosity. Articles and editorials commonly used the racist epithet, "Jap," to refer to any Japanese, and, in common with politicians, most newspaper editors equally failed to distinguish the enemy in Japan from United States citizens or permanent resident aliens of Japanese ancestry.

Regional papers printed vitriolic anti-Japanese remarks made by prominent elected officials, particularly Governor Clark, who continued his anti-Japanese rant. In May 1942 the *Idaho County Free Press* reported on Clark's address to the Grangeville, Idaho, Lions Club: "'Send them all back to Japan, then sink the island,' he recommended. 'They live like rats, breed like rats, and act like rats. We don't want them in Idaho.' Club members approved the governor's remarks with a hearty round of applause."[5]

Other anti-Japanese propaganda appeared in advertisements. A drawing of a mosquito with a caricatured Japanese head exhorted readers to "Slap That Jap!" by buying U.S. war bonds and stamps (Fig. 101).[6] The artist, "Dr. S.," is none other than Theodor Seuss Geisel. As "Dr. Seuss," Geisel authored *The Cat in the Hat* and many other beloved children's books, but he is far less famous for his many anti-Asian cartoons.[7]

Such quotes and stereotypes, appearing in trusted local newspapers, could only reinforce prevailing attitudes. These resulted in a few malicious incidents involving the Japanese interned at Kooskia. In one instance, Robert Ashburn recalled that a railroad train carrying Japanese to the Kooskia Internment Camp "spent the night on a siding at Kooskia and when they woke up, swastikas had been painted on the outside of the train."[8]

Regional Attitudes towards the Japanese

Despite their confinement in the Kooskia Internment Camp, the Japanese internees had occasional opportunities to interact with members of the Caucasian population. Some contacts occurred during their internment, such as with Immigration and Naturalization Service (INS) personnel and with U.S. Bureau of Public Roads (USBPR) employees. Finally, additional interactions occurred with residents of nearby communities.

When the Kooskia camp opened, many of the Caucasians who lived in the region undoubtedly mirrored the wartime attitudes that prevailed in the rest of the United States. Because most did not personally know any Japanese people, it was easy for local residents to be of the same mentality as those government officials who had ordered the incarceration of the West Coast's Japanese residents. For example, a columnist for a newspaper in a nearby community reported, "Well folks, the Japs are here! No, they have not invaded us, but the first contingent of Japanese internees arrived at Kooskia by train Thursday afternoon around five o'clock ... ." The reporter wondered what local residents were thinking, "especially those who have relatives in war battling the Japs abroad, and now, we have these to contend with in our beautiful forests of Idaho."[9]

Others were more sympathetic to the imprisoned Japanese Americans and resident aliens. Arthur Deschamps, Jr., of Missoula, Montana, worked for the American Crystal Sugar Company from the late 1930s. During World War II he had a job recruiting sugar beet laborers out of the various camps, and referred to the "War Relocation" program as "one of the most bizarre and demoralizing experiences of my life." In September 1942 he and another man went to Stockton, California, to recruit people from the Stockton

Fig. 101. "Slap That Jap!" cartoon, by "Dr. S," i.e., Dr. Seuss (Theodor Seuss Geisel), Idaho County Free Press, August 6, 1942, 5. Racist language and caricatures frequently appeared in newspapers during wartime. These encouraged readers to unfairly equate Japanese Americans with the enemy. Courtesy Idaho County Free Press, Grangeville, ID. Used with permission.

"Assembly Center" at the San Joaquin County Fairgrounds. In later years, Deschamps recalled,

> ... the sight that I saw there ... [will] really stay in my mind for the rest of my life. Here was this spectacle of American citizens behind barbed wire being guarded by men in uniforms[,] and a little group of Boy Scouts, who were waiting within the compound with their scout banner and their little uniforms and the American flag. The contradictions of that spectacle [were] so [horrible] and bizarre that I just never forgot it. To think that in this great country of ours, that such a thing could happen, but it did happen.[10]

Even in early May 1945, when the Japanese left the Kooskia camp, a newspaper headline still referred to them inappropriately: "Japs to Leave Camp Tomorrow."[11] However, the intervening two years had provided some local residents, particularly those who worked at the camp or who interacted with the internees in other ways, with an opportunity to get to know Japanese people a bit better, and on a personal, one-to-one basis. This helped to change attitudes. USBPR employee Milton Barton has already been recognized as someone who commented favorably on the attitude, work ethic, learning abilities, and productivity of the Japanese internees.[12] Some Caucasians, who were children at the time, remember how the internees shared cookies and candy bars with them.[13] Today, others describe the entire internment and incarceration camp experience as "a shameful thing."[14]

Caucasian Friends and Former Employers

Letters in some internees' files indicate that they kept in touch with Caucasian friends and previous employers. One such case involved internee Jinjiro Inuzuka, a gardener from southern California, who tried to learn what had become of his furniture and truck after he was arrested. Mrs. N. O. Talbot, one of his former employers, attempted to find out on his behalf. A letter from the Spanish Consulate in San Francisco followed Inuzuka to the Kooskia camp from the Santa Fe Detention Station. It contained a copy of a letter from Talbot, for whom Inuzuka had worked for eleven years. She went to considerable trouble to help him, inquiring about his belongings with some of Inuzuka's other employers and with the local INS office.[15] Talbot closed her letter by saying, "We all thought it very unkind the way the Immigration people acted."[16]

The file of Minoru Jo Wazumi, a clerk from Connecticut, contains an extensive correspondence between him and several Caucasian women friends. Some letters appear in their entirety, while a few consist of just censored lines or paragraphs, copied or cut out from the original letters. Ruth Miller was a friend sympathetic to the plight of the Japanese. In one letter she mused, "I wonder if our paths will ever cross again. Will you be deported at the end of the [w]ar? It is maddening to me to lose such fine friends as you and Gene [another Japanese alien] before I have an opportunity really to know you."[17]

Wazumi also exchanged letters with Elizabeth Nesbitt, "Beth." She wrote, romantically,

Perhaps it is because you are going away and I shall never see you again, that I continuously feel sunk - or sinking - as though giant waves, one after another, were rolling over me, and in spite of myself, I keep saying why, why, why? In the minutes before sleep comes[,] hundreds of pleasant memories come before my eyes. I can see you swinging around in the Penna. Station [Pennsylvania train station in New York City] looking this way and that, then catching a glimpse, coming smilingly and happily toward me. ... Perhaps instead of lamenting a future without those wonderful days, I should cherish them and be thankful for having had them. But they hurt--don[']t they?[18]

Perhaps depressed at his imprisonment, Wazumi applied for repatriation to Japan. As the weeks passed, Nesbitt seemed to become resigned to his leaving, writing, "Minoru, I want you to know that ... you will always be among my most precious memories. ... From a clear sky you came into [my] life at exactly the right moment, and since then I have learned, through you, many things. I couldn't estimate how awful existence would have been without your cheerful companionship." She continued,

Even though the breadth of this Continent is between us and we never meet until we pass over, I shall always be able to think of you with a smile, and to laugh in pleasant memories for many of our happy hours together. Needless to say, you have my best wishes for health, happiness, and all good things of life. Somewhere along the way some fine young girl will come forth to make life interesting and worthwhile for you.[19]

In August 1942, just before she expected Wazumi to leave on the prisoner exchange ship, Nesbitt sent him a "final" letter. The censor retyped it, adding the underlined comments: "<u>Original typed in green</u>" with "<u>In this corner, the lipstick imprint of small, upraised lips</u>." "Beth" also enclosed, "... <u>wrapped in a slip of paper upon which is written 'care please', a lock of blond hair</u>."[20]

Whether or not because of Nesbitt's interest in him, Wazumi subsequently withdrew his request for repatriation. He also requested a rehearing of his case.[21] While he waited, he seized the opportunity to transfer to the Kooskia Internment Camp via Fort Missoula.

Other internee/Caucasian contacts were between detainees and their lawyers, or with governmental agencies. Takeshi Okazaki was an importer

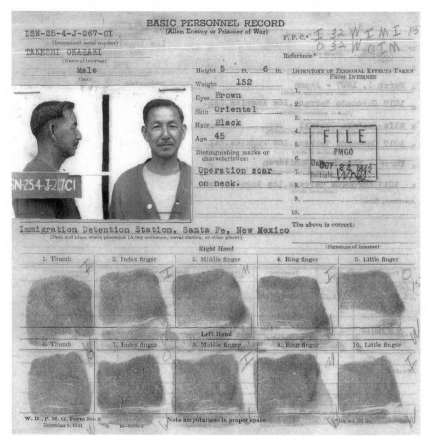

Fig. 102. *"Basic Personnel Record (Alien Enemy or Prisoner of War)" card for Takeshi Okazaki, undated [1942], 1; E466F, Okazaki, Takeshi; OPMG, RG389, NARA II.*

from Los Angeles (Fig. 102). His file contains a letter to the Provost Marshal General in Washington, DC, from Clarence L. Belt, a Los Angeles attorney. It is dated September 24, 1942, when Okazaki was at the Santa Fe Internment Camp in New Mexico. From the letter's content, it is not clear whether Belt is writing as a friend of the Okazaki family or in his professional, legal capacity. Apparently Okazaki had heard a rumor that the Santa Fe camp was to be turned into a family camp. If so, he wished to be reunited with his family there. Okazaki's son and daughter were in the WRA's Manzanar, California, incarceration camp, while his wife, "a white woman, a native of Austria," lived in Los Angeles. Belt reported, "It is their hope that they can all be together, either in this camp at Santa Fe, New Mexico, or some other camp."[22]

On a later petition refusing repatriation, Okazaki listed his family as wife Barbara, age 44, a housewife; daughter Florence, age 20, and son Takeshi, age 18, were both students.[23] The government's cruel and unjust internment and incarceration camp policies had first separated this father from his family and then removed the children from their mother.

Working with INS and USBPR Employees

Guard Cecil Boller developed an excellent rapport with the Japanese internees. After Al Keehr quit, Boller drove the truck to Kooskia every day to get groceries and to pick up the mail. He also did personal shopping for the men, usually "some stationery or some toiletry at the drugstore." He "really wasn't supposed to do it, but did [it] anyway."[24] Boller benefited from that arrangement, saying that the Japanese kitchen staff "took a little better care of me than they did the rest of them [guards]. I could have a T-bone or whatever I wanted. ... [T]hey took care of me. I kind of liked that." Thus pampered by the grateful Japanese internee cooks, Boller gained twenty or thirty pounds in two years.[25]

Boller was also more adventurous than most regarding opportunities for eating Japanese food. "Big boxes of halibut" arrived at the Kooskia train station "once a week or so. They ate lots of fish." Boller recalled that the Japanese prepared the fish in a way that was new to him. At first he could "hardly eat [it], they baked it in squares ... they'd just bake it plumb black and then they'd put that soy sauce over it. I couldn't hardly hack it." However, Boller grew to like fish prepared that way. Eventually, when he was the night watchman, he would go in the kitchen, "get me three or four of them squares and put them in my pocket and eat them cold! I could eat anything they cooked."[26]

Another experience with Japanese food, just as memorable but not so successful, occurred when Boller escorted the Kooskia camp's Japanese dentist to Texas.[27] Boller remembered many details about that trip, mainly because it was just the two of them; when a few men transferred out at a time, several guards went with them, so could socialize among themselves. Boller described his journey as "the worst trip I ever had in my life! ... they sent me with him alone and we didn't have too much in common."[28] The two men went by train, but because they had so little conversation, Boller remembered the journey as the "slowest train I think that ever existed." On arrival in Texas, the internee showed his appreciation by treating Boller to a meal. The dentist, whose native Japanese lacked the "L" sound, always called him "Mr. Ceeso," for Cecil, and never attempted the more difficult "Boller:"

'Mr. Ceeso, I buy you best meal money can buy!' I says, 'I'm all for it!' We got down there and of course we shopped around and found

a Japanese restaurant which was alright, I liked their food there. So
he done the ordering. I says, 'I'll try the same thing you do.' 'Okay,
Mr. Ceeso.' So here it comes, a big platter -- reminded me of strips
of bacon. Raw fish, cut in strips. He'd stick his fork in one of them,
roll it up, stick it in a little black soy sauce in the middle, and put her
in, and boy ... . He'd go chew on that old thing and I ... well heck,
I'll try it. And I put one in. I chewed on it, it got so big I couldn't get
... . I couldn't go that raw fish to save my soul! 'Mr. Ceeso, you don't
appear to like the raw fish.' I says, 'I can't take her!' Well he ordered
something else, it must have been a good meal there. I ate that, didn't
worry about that. But he'd spear one of them and roll it up on his fork
and dip it, dunk it, in that little bowl of black sauce. And he ate both
of [them]. He ate the one that we got for me and him too. He was
hungry for that.[29]

Guard Al Keehr didn't think it was fair that families were separated.
Referring to four internees from Alaska, he commented,

The way they went up there, a bunch of Federal men, of course,
had to go and pick them up, and their wives was down in Oregon
in that camp down there, an intensive camp ["Camp Harmony," the
temporary detention "Assembly Center" at Puyallup, Washington],
and they didn't know for three months where their husbands were.
I don't think that was fair. ...They should have let them write or ...
something.[30]

Kooskia employee Amelia Jacks recalled that "the relations between
guards and captives [were] pleasant." She added, "It was very cordial, they
treated us well and we treated them well - but we did keep our distance since
we weren't allowed in the camp area."[31]

Cecil Boller related a story about an interaction between one of the
Japanese internees and J. W. Gillmore, the USBPR's head project engineer
and overall manager:

Yeah, he [Gillmore] was a hard-charging old guy and thought the
world would quit turning if it wasn't for him gouging everybody in
the hi[nd] end to keep him a goin.' ... There was one old Japanese, ...
little old guy, and they'd been packing powder [explosives] up high
on the hill, getting ready to shoot off and widen a chunk of road.
And the old [Japanese man] come down off the hill and he sat down
on a rock, and Gillmore says ... he called him a name, too, but I
can't remember what it was. [The Japanese man] says, 'Mr. Gillmore,
when you see me sittin' down that's a sign I've been working and I'm
tired!' Old Gillmore, he shook his head and walked off and everybody
laughed. It tickled me.[32]

Jan Boyer, daughter of guard Henry Boyer, was about five years old when her family lived in the employee cottages at Apgar. One winter the snow was so deep that the internees had to dig them out from the house to the road. She commented, "The guards that worked there always had good things to say about the internees." The detainees reciprocated those sentiments; on her father's birthday one year, an internee "made him a green birthday cake."[33]

Mickey Barton, son of USBPR power shovel operator Milt Barton, commented, "There was a mutual respect and understanding between the internees and those they worked with."[34] The elder Barton once compared the Japanese workers with their predecessors, the convicts. He described the Japanese as "by far the best," and "cooperative."[35] The younger Barton observed that the "relationship between the construction group and the Japanese" was excellent, adding,

My father was impressed with the attitude and work ethic of the Japanese. Though lacking in highway construction skills, they were fast learners, demonstrating very little animosity as a result of being inter[n]ed. He thought the productivity of the Japanese was greater than that of the prison convicts that preceded them.[36]

Newspaper Publicity about the Camp

Once the internees had begun working, newspapers in the region began to take notice of them. In early July 1943 the regional forester, Evan W. Kelley, wrote B. J. Finch, the USBPR's district engineer: "As surmised, some agitation is being started against assignment of labor to that project [Lewis-Clark Highway] at this time." Kelley enclosed an editorial from the Spokane, Washington, *Spokesman-Review*. It read, in part:

MISAPPLIED USE OF WAR PRISON LABOR

The government has put 250 interned Japanese to work building a highway between Missoula and Lewiston over the Lolo pass route. A good many people question the judgment of the authorities in undertaking this road project at this time and employing labor on it that could be used to so much greater advantage in agricultural work where there is a critical shortage of help.

If no agricultural community is willing to employ Japanese labor, these internees could be put to work cutting wood for fuel, which the OPA [Office of Price Administration] has ordered rationed in this timbered region because of an allegedly prospective shortage next fall.

It does seem that war prisoner labor could be used to better advantage during this war-time man power shortage than on construction that is not presently essential, and which probably will be needed to provide work for jobless Americans later on.[37]

As with the rationed wood fuel discussed above, wartime rationing meant that the "home front" endured shortages of many accustomed items, both necessities and luxuries. Some local residents became very resentful that Japanese internees were able to get things that they could not obtain, particularly beer. Most people were not aware that the Geneva Convention, governing the treatment of both prisoners of war and internees, entitled them to anything a U.S. soldier could obtain at his base camp. Bert Fraser, the officer in charge at Fort Missoula, reported to W. F. Kelly, the INS's assistant commissioner for alien control at Philadelphia, that an unnamed Kooskia Internment Camp employee

... had the malicious habit of going to [the town of] Kooskia [and] spreading stories on how the Japanese were mollycoddled, until finally the Spokane papers blasted the camp because of a letter received from a Kooskia woman on how truckload after truckload of beer was hauled into the camp and yet the white people in the general region could not purchase a bottle of beer.[38]

The woman's letter as printed in the *Spokesman-Review* brought up many concerns of the "home front" regarding supposed privileges enjoyed by the Japanese, such as beer, candy, and more and better food (Fig. 103).[39] Following the letter's appearance in the newspaper, Fraser explained to his superior what the INS had done in the matter of "damage control." Acting in the absence of officer in charge D. A. Remer, camp administrator Walter C. Wood contacted the letter writer, Mrs. Harvey Gumm of Kooskia. He explained matters to her and arranged for her to see the camp, after which "she wrote

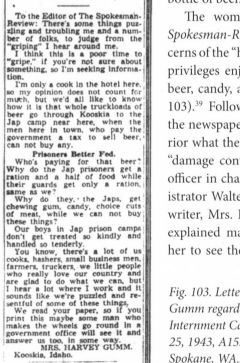

JAPS GET BEER; REST GET LEFT

Kooskia Cook Asks Pointed Questions About Rations at Internment Camp.

To the Editor of The Spokesman-Review: There's some things puzzling and troubling me and a number of folks, to judge from the "griping" I hear around me.

I think this is a poor time to "gripe," if you're not sure about something, so I'm seeking information.

I'm only a cook in the hotel here, so my opinion does not count for much, but we'd all like to know how it is that whole truckloads of beer go through Kooskia to the Jap camp near here, when the men here in town, who pay the government a tax to sell beer, can not buy any.

Prisoners Better Fed.

Who's paying for that beer? Why do the Jap prisoners get a ration and a half of food while their guards get only a ration, same as we?

Why do they, the Japs, get chewing gum, candy, choice cuts of meat, while we can not buy these things?

Our boys in Jap prison camps don't get treated so kindly and handled so tenderly.

You know, there's a lot of us cooks, hashers, small business men, farmers, truckers, we little people who really love our country and are glad to do what we can, but I hear a lot where I work and it sounds like we're puzzled and resentful of some of these things.

We read your paper, so if you print this maybe some man who makes the wheels go round in a government office will see it and answer us too, in some way.

MRS. HARVEY GUMM.
Kooskia, Idaho.

Fig. 103. Letter to editor from Mrs. Harvey Gumm regarding beer at the Kooskia Internment Camp, Spokesman-Review, *July 25, 1943, A15. Courtesy* Spokesman-Review, *Spokane, WA. Used with permission.*

another letter to the newspaper retracting the statements and stating that she had been misinformed."[40]

Cecil Boller remembered the incident. He commented, "Yeah, they stirred up a little stink over that once or twice, but heck, … us guards if we wanted a beer we could go up there, at [the] commissary up there and buy it and drink it just the same as they did."[41]

Following the editorial and letters in the *Spokesman-Review*, the *Lewiston Morning Tribune* contacted the Kooskia camp administration requesting the privilege of doing a feature story on the camp. In early August 1943 reporter Tish Erb wrote Fraser for his approval: "I am certain we can get a story that will have a human interest angle and create a better feeling" about Japanese being placed on the Lewis-Clark Highway project. She thought readers would like to know where the Japanese came from and what were their pre-war occupations, since "we understand that a number of them are college graduates and that some were engaged in rather large business enterprises. We should like to know by talking with their leader, or leaders, what they think of the project on which they are working."[42]

Erb also wanted to learn about the internees' menu, recreation, and religion. Besides those topics, she was interested in the skill with which they handled machinery and in "how much [more] work they are able to accomplish than their predecessors at the camp, the federal prisoners who were handicapped by short hours and a rather inconstant population."[43]

Fraser replied a week later, agreeing to the project, "especially the human interest angle." Certain restrictions would apply to the story, namely that no Japanese internees' names could be mentioned and no pictures would be permitted. Fraser also wanted to examine the article before publication "to make sure there is nothing objectionable about it" so that neither he nor the reporter would "get into any difficulty over such a story."[44]

In early September Erb submitted her completed article to Fraser for his approval.[45] In mid-September Fraser returned it to her, having "made a few corrections which are trivial."[46]

The published version appeared in late September 1943.[47] The INS administration must have been delighted with its lengthy and accurate description of internee life and conditions. Erb dispelled some rumors that were "repeated by the uninformed, fostered by antipathy for the race and denoting a misunderstanding of the international regulations observed by the United States in the treatment of internees." She then continued:

> The Kooskia internment camp … is the first experiment in this country in the utilization of Japanese alien labor on government construction. The satisfactory progress made in the short time the camp has been in existence gives evidence of the benefit to be de-

rived from an expansion of the program to other internee groups or prisoners of war.[48]

In playing up the "human interest" angle for her readers, Erb reminded them of the "industrious habits of the Japanese, all of whom lived in this country prior to the war and made their living by the sweat of their brow or the exercise of their intellect." In previous camps, the internees "spent their time within fenced enclosures under heavy guard in idleness." However, once they came under the provisions of the Geneva Convention, they received the same treatment as "prisoners of war pertaining to work, rations and wages:"

> Aliens cannot be compelled to work. There are those who will disagree with this tenet of the Geneva conference ... and in their animosity will advocate slavery for enemy aliens or prisoners ... .
> When it is pointed out that Japan does not extend humane treatment to American aliens or prisoners, it must be remembered that Japan did not ratify the Geneva [C]onvention and that Japanese living standards, both civilian and military, are inferior to those of Christian nations like America.[49]

Erb summarized details of the internees as a group, writing,

> Some ... have been in the United States for more than 40 years, some are graduates of American universities, and some do not speak English. Their average age is 37 and their average residence here is 25 years. Their families are strung from Maine to Mexico. ... Some of them are fathers of American-born sons serving in the United States army ... .[50]

Most aspects of the internees' lives were highly regulated. Erb observed that "the daily routine begins with the crisp clang of a sounding gong cutting the clear, clean air. At the sound the aliens arise promptly, make their toilet and tidy their quarters." Detailed bedmaking instructions ensured that all bunks had a uniform appearance. Erb also commented on the internees' morning schedule:

> At the breakfast signal, the men march to the mess hall, a long building furnished with tables and benches manufactured by Prison Industries, Inc., and installed when prisoners occupied the camp. The Japanese line up at the steam table with their plate and cup and are served. The kitchen is a model of cleanliness, the same as other parts of the camp.[51]

The workers quit for "dinner," the noon meal, at 11:30 and returned to camp for it. Afterwards, at 12:25, "the work signal again [was] sounded" and they went back out on the road. The internees worked until 4:30, "having completed the number of hours of work permissible under the international rules," i.e., eight hours. They then returned to camp, and went to their barracks to shower or wash up for supper, which was served at 5:00.[52]

Contacts with Area Residents

Sometimes internees accompanied Boller when he went to town for the mail and any needed groceries. Most often, internees got a trip to Kooskia to load up a shipment of Pres-to-logs.[53] Occasionally a guard would take some detainees to Lewiston for shopping, with luggage and fishing gear being their main purchases.[54] Although area residents surely noticed the Japanese in their midst, there are no known instances of overt hostility towards them.

In most cases, local Caucasians reported favorably on the Japanese internees whom they encountered. Some Caucasians even expressed unhappiness with what they perceived as the unfair treatment of Japanese American citizens and Japanese aliens during wartime.

When the first internees arrived in Lewiston by train they ate a meal prepared by the widow who ran the nearby White Front Cafe.[55] Helen Kalinoski, later Helen Thiessen, recalled that the food she served the earliest group of detainees included ham.[56] This caused quite a controversy. Because of rationing, ham had not been available to Lewiston residents. However, when Thiessen went to the butcher to get some meat for the internees' meal, the butcher fortuitously had ham, so she bought it. She was the first person to obtain any in quite some time, and local Caucasian residents were aggravated that the internees got it before they did. She got "quite a panning" for that; people were still talking about it a long time afterwards, even after the war.[57] Her son, Irving Kalinoski, had similar memories, recalling that he and his mother "pret' near got crucified because we fed them ham."[58]

A contentious point with local residents was the question of whether the road running beside the camp should be closed to the public. USBPR engineer Finch made the suggestion, believing it to be "in the interest of the internees." Acting regional forester C. S. Webb put forward the proposal to Fraser, but stated, "We placed a gate on the road last year on account of the prison camp. Mr. Crocker [the forest supervisor, based in Grangeville, Idaho] tells me the plan was none too successful and resulted in many difficulties and lost time in the conduct of official business and was the cause of some resentment and criticism by the public."[59]

Fraser replied, stating that he believed it was "much wiser to permit the highway to remain open." There was very little traffic on it, and "any travelers who show evidence of curiosity or intent to molest the Japanese can be dealt with by the guards." He continued, "I know there was considerable criticism by the public last year and I believe it wise to prevent this if possible. This blocking is also a nuisance to the Forest Service and to our Service and I therefore recommend that no gates be placed along the highway."[60]

Interactions between Japanese internees and individual Caucasians sometimes occurred in settings outside the Kooskia Internment Camp. One series in particular took place at St. Joseph's Hospital in Lewiston when Kooskia internee Sakaye Ed Yoshimura, a photographer from California, was admitted in late July or early August 1944 for an unknown medical condition requiring surgery. Mae Betty Piersol, now Rainville, had just entered nurse's training there in June, age 18 (Fig. 104). That summer she worked on floor 5 North, the surgery floor, where she met Yoshimura. Rainville recalled,

> I remember the other nurses could not get him to say much. I took it as a challenge to get him to talk and he must have sensed I was sincere in my conversations. I told him of the two Japanese families who lived beside us in Nampa, Idaho. My sister and I would walk to and from grade school together [with the Japanese children]. I'm not sure of the spelling now but one family was Koyama and the other [Miyaki]. I asked him if any of the men in Camp had that name. He said no, not to his knowledge. He began to talk softly, I told him of the beautiful vegetable gardens the two families raised and of us exchanging gifts at Christmas time. I found he spoke very good English and was so appreciative of everything you did for him. When asked what he wanted for bed time snack he said "Ice Cream." He said they didn't get ice cream in camp. I tried to give him Ice Cream every time I cared for him and reported that to the charge nurse so she would order more. Ed started to be more open and communicative with the rest of the staff.
>
> ...
>
> Ed was very somber on the day of his discharge. He would not say goodbye to any one. He sent me a letter from camp thanking me for my kindness and care. He asked me to write to him and I did answer his one letter August 22, 1944. I never heard from him again.[61]

Piersol's letter and envelope (Fig. 105), now in a private collection, bear the stamp, "Detained Alien Enemy Mail Examined." In her letter, Piersol referred to Yoshimura's leaving the hospital: "Do you know I kind of miss you. Just a little of course, ha ha. That 215 [his room number] sure seems empty," and, "When you left, the way you acted, I didn't think you would write." She also referred to Yoshimura's love of ice cream: "Say, I sure could go for some ice cream right now. Why don't you drop over in about five mins. and bring some with you. OK? OK!!!"[62]

In later life, elderly Lewiston residents expressed sympathetic feelings for the Japanese whom they knew, and empathized with the plight of others. Dick Riggs related a comment made by his then-ninety-two-year-old mother, Laura Riggs, regarding the well-respected Kaisaki family, truck

gardeners of Japanese ancestry who were prewar residents of Lewiston. She suggested that "if it [incarceration] was ever tried on the Kaisaki family there would have been a pretty good uprising here."[63]

Fig. 104. Mae Betty Piersol, RN. She graduated from St. Joseph's Hospital School of Nursing, Lewiston, Idaho, in 1947. As a student nurse, she cared for Kooskia internee Sakaye Ed Yoshimura during his stay in the hospital. Engstrom photo. Courtesy Mae Betty Rainville.

Fig. 105. Envelope, Mae Betty Piersol to Ed Yoshimura, Camp Kooskia, postmarked August 23, 1944. Note censor's stamp, "Detained Alien Enemy Mail Examined." Courtesy Carl Sasaki.

After viewing slide presentations about the Kooskia Internment Camp, and seeing photographs of internees drinking beer and otherwise enjoying themselves, some people have commented that the internees seem to have had a pretty easy life there. What those people are forgetting is that these men were imprisoned simply because they were Japanese aliens who were perceived as potential saboteurs, even through some had sons fighting in the U.S. Army. Most of them were aliens only because racist U.S. laws would not allow them to become citizens. They had never committed any crimes and were not accused of any. As a result of this unjust detention, they lost their businesses and homes, and were separated from their families.

Helen Thiessen, who, as Helen Kalinoski, served many of the Japanese internees in and from her White Front Cafe in Lewiston, recalled, at ninety-four, that they were "polite" and "nice, gentle people" who "didn't seem to be angry" and who "had a wonderful attitude." She thought that what had happened to them "was a sad thing for the Japanese that were good working people." Thiessen concluded, "I hope that never happens again."[64]

Chapter Ten
Back to Barbed Wire and Beyond:
Closure, and Aftermath, of the Kooskia Internment Camp

In case of transfer, prisoners of war shall be officially notified of
their new destination in advance; they shall be allowed
to take with them their personal effects ... .
Geneva Convention, Article 26.

After Fort Missoula closed in early July 1944 it was inevitable that the Immigration and Naturalization Service (INS) would also consider shutting the Kooskia camp. In fact, such rumors had begun to circulate among the Kooskia internees by late June, nearly a year before the Kooskia camp finally ceased operating.[1] In mid-February 1945 Superintendent Merrill Scott attended an internee committee meeting to inform the group that the camp would indeed close in the near future and that they would all be transferred to New Mexico.[2]

Although reasons for the camp's closure were not communicated to either the internees or the media, contemporary INS publications provide two explanations. Despite the laborers' progress being "satisfactory" on this first, and only, U.S. "experiment" employing Japanese alien internee workers on a construction project for the government, both "the diminishing population ... due to the number of paroles that have been granted" and "deterioration of equipment and the impossibility of securing replacements" for it forced the camp's closure.[3]

Local Residents Challenge the Camp's Closing

On April 20, 1945, work stopped so the men could prepare for their move on April 25 to the INS camp at Santa Fe.[4] Hozen Seki and his colleagues talked about getting up a petition to delay the departure, but instead they concentrated on packing.[5] On April 22 Seki wrote, "By the young men's help, I have packed whole my stock. Total pound was 697 lb. & 18 boxes. Everyone was examined."[6] The next day the internees learned that their departure would be delayed for over a week because local citizens were greatly surprised, and displeased, to learn that the camp would close, thus halting the road-building activity.[7] They persuaded Idaho's U.S. Congressman Compton I. White to hold a hearing into the matter.[8]

On April 26 a large official contingent, including Idaho's governor, Charles C. Gossett, visited the camp.[9] The following day, White convened a formal hearing in Lewiston to protest shutting down the project.[10] Seki commented, "Jacks, Kozima, and I went to Lewiston for the Congressman White's hearing about the road work."[11] After the inquiry, White "questioned the Japanese spokesman [Seki] from the camp" in a closed session.[12] Seki bragged in his diary, "I was a fine act."[13] White and Gossett concluded that the Japanese could leave, but that their camp should be retained for possible future use with a highway project.[14]

Internees Removed to Santa Fe INS Camp

The evening following the Lewiston hearing the internees learned that they would leave for Santa Fe on the morning of May 2.[15] On May 1 Seki wrote his wife about his impending departure. He also conducted the last mass meeting of his tenure as spokesman, noting, "Everyone busy."[16] At 11:00 a.m. on May 2 the men left the camp for the town of Kooskia. Arriving that night by train in Spokane, Washington, they were excited to see neon signs again.[17]

Transfer of Camp Supplies

In early March 1945 William R. Beecher had replaced Merrill Scott as Kooskia camp superintendent with the specific assignment of closing the camp.[18] After the internees left, some of the administrative personnel remained to take care of logistical details involving the closure.[19] This included the transfer of all remaining food supplies to Fort Lincoln, the INS internment camp at Bismarck, North Dakota. The receiving supply officer castigated the shipment as "Misrepresented Surplus Property." He observed that some of the items were "vermin infested" and that "much of the canned goods … were bulging and leaking and it was apparent from the exterior that the merchandise was inedible; yet it was sent here."[20] I. P. McCoy, Fort Lincoln's officer in charge, fired off a scathing memo to the INS's W. F. Kelly in Philadelphia, complaining, "I can see some purpose in trying to wish off useless or valueless articles on another agency but there is no excuse for us doing it among ourselves."[21] Clearly, nothing had changed in the two years since the Kooskia camp itself refused to accept the Army's offer of thirteen hundred pairs of deteriorated shoes left over from World War I.[22]

The Aftermath of Closure

Following termination of the Kooskia camp in early May 1945, its employees found other jobs within the INS, with other government agencies such as the Bureau of Prisons, or in the private sector. Over the next few years, the buildings were gradually removed, gold mining resumed at the site, and the Lewis-Clark Highway was finally completed.

On August 19, 1962, numerous dignitaries met at Packers Meadow near Lolo Pass on the Idaho-Montana border.[23] They dedicated the highway before a Sunday crowd of some five thousand people and "an eight-teepee encampment of Nez Perce Indians."[24] Tennessee Senator Albert Gore, chairman of the Senate Subcommittee on Roads and Highways, was the featured speaker in honor of his support for substantial appropriations to complete the road (Fig. 106). He told his audience that he was "'for the wilderness' for its scenic attractions. 'Some of the people in the East have never seen a virgin forest,' he declared. 'In Tennessee we say that a tourist is worth more than a bale of cotton and [is] a lot easier to pick.'"[25]

Fig. 106. Senator Albert Gore of Tennessee, father of former U.S. vice president Al Gore, orating at the dedication of the Lewis-Clark Highway (U.S. Highway 12), August 19, 1962. Courtesy Idaho Transportation Department, Boise.

Forgetting the Kooskia Internment Camp

All the excitement about final completion of the Lewis-Clark Highway eclipsed the previous history of its earliest builders: the federal prisoners and the Japanese internees. Older residents of the vicinity, who knew about the prison and internment camps from their inception and perhaps had even worked there, did not often share their knowledge or experiences with their descendants, perhaps thinking it unimportant or too short-lived to be memorable. For different reasons, mostly involving a desire to forget what had happened to them, the former internees also did not talk about the camp to their relatives. The Kooskia Internment Camp thus became largely unknown to succeeding generations, the descendants of the former internees and employees.

Although secondary sources sometimes discussed the major World War II INS internment camps, such as Fort Missoula, Montana, that housed Japanese and other "enemy" aliens, the Kooskia camp was seldom mentioned, whether on maps or in lists of other INS alien detention camps.[26] It risked being completely forgotten.

Documenting the Kooskia Internment Camp

Soon there was little to be seen at the former Kooskia Internment Camp. Although Canyon Creek, clear and ice-cold, still gushes into the Lochsa River, the bridges to the canteen are gone, as are all the structures.[27] The land is presently owned by the Clearwater National Forest (CNF), a unit of the U.S. Forest Service (USFS), and is recorded as an archaeological site. Except for the tennis or handball court's concrete slab surface, and level areas that held the former buildings and the baseball diamond, almost nothing remains to remind us of the Kooskia Internment Camp's contribution to American, and Japanese American, history.

During the 1970s the USFS directed the CNF and other forests to research archaeological sites on their lands. This resulted in archaeological surveys of the Kooskia camp and some interviews with now-deceased informants.[28] In later years, the site records received occasional additions, and in 1982 the CNF made an effort to document the internment camp phase in greater detail with more interviews, documents, and photographs.[29] However, the interviews were only with Caucasian employees, not with Japanese internees. Employee perceptions, while certainly very important, do not necessarily reflect what the detainees themselves thought of the experience. In that context, it is helpful to remember that the internees, although volunteers, were unjustly incarcerated.

Past and Potential Archaeological Work at the Site

The camp site itself is especially significant, and not just because it housed the Kooskia Internment Camp. Previous occupiers were the Canyon Creek Prison Camp and the Civilian Conservation Corps (CCC) Camp F-38; the site was also used as a Nez Perce campground and is associated with the rescue of the ill-fated Carlin hunting party in 1893.[30]

Since mining or other development activities do not currently threaten the site, salvage archaeology is not necessary, so any excavations done there are likely to be productive. In 1978 Forest Service archaeologists collected ceramic artifacts from the surface, including, but not specifically mentioned in the report, the base of a Japanese rice bowl marked "MADE IN JAPAN" (Fig. 107a).[31] In the early 1990s, while visiting the site, the son of a former internment camp guard found the base of a Japanese teacup with an identical mark (Fig. 107b).[32]

Fig. 107a, b. Artifacts collected from the Kooskia Internment Camp site. a., base of a Japanese rice bowl marked "MADE IN" above "JAPAN," collected by Forest Service employees in 1979; b, base of a Japanese teacup with an identical mark, collected in the 1990s by the son of a former guard. a, courtesy Laboratory of Anthropology and Asian American Comparative Collection, University of Idaho, Moscow; b, courtesy Micheal Moshier.

In December 2006, to preserve and interpret U.S. sites where Japanese Americans were detained during World War II, the U.S. Congress established the Japanese American Confinement Sites grant program (Public Law 109-441).[33] An appropriation of $1 million for fiscal year 2009 allowed the National Park Service to solicit grant proposals to benefit qualifying entities. One of those was the Kooskia Internment Camp, and the University of Idaho received nearly $16,500 to undertake archaeological testing there in 2010.[34]

Historical Research on the Site

The Forest Service investigations coincided with a national movement that obtained redress and an apology for Japanese Americans, both citizens and permanent resident aliens of Japanese ancestry, who were victimized by racism and war hysteria and put into internment and incarceration camps. Beginning in 1997 one federal and two state grants supported the present author's research on the camp.[35] This took place in archival repositories, such as the National Archives in Washington, DC, and through oral or written interviews with former Kooskia detainees and employees as well as with relatives of deceased internees and employees. For the first time, research focused on the internees' perspectives of their experiences.

Progress continues to be made in recognizing the national significance of the Kooskia Internment Camp. In February 2005 the National Park Service issued a draft National Historic Landmark Theme Study entitled *Japanese Americans in World War II.*[36] It recommended that the Kooskia Internment Camp "should be studied for possible listing in the National Register."[37] Two newspaper articles in early 2007 reported the need for a nomination to the National Register of Historic Places and for an interpretive sign.[38] Shortly thereafter, a CNF employee indicated that an interpretive sign "has been on our long term ... plan for some time."[39]

Internee Accomplishments

Information on the actual road distance built and/or improved by the Kooskia internees remains elusive since it is often combined with statistics from the federal prisoners' achievements or those of later workers who came after the Kooskia internees. For example, one document indicates that a 6.25 mile segment of the road, from Old Man Creek to Fish Creek, was begun in 1942 and completed by 1952.[40]

Some of the internees' other accomplishments, while less measurable, are more significant. In particular, the Kooskia Internment Camp was a successful experiment in utilizing Japanese alien internees as volunteers for building a portion of the Lewis-Clark Highway between Idaho and Montana. Besides helping a much-needed road progress towards completion, the project enabled the undeservedly incarcerated internees to once again become productive members of society. Although the work was tiring, difficult, and sometimes even dangerous, the men appreciated the opportunity to receive fair wages in exchange for performing useful work.

Unlike friends and relatives in the War Relocation Authority (WRA) incarceration camps, detainees in the custody of the INS enjoyed better treatment under the Geneva Convention. Since the road building project could not function without the internees, their knowledge of, and petition for, their rights and privileges accorded them by the Geneva Convention was crucial in compelling the INS to agree to their demands, thus contributing to the establishment of a symbiotic relationship between the detainees and the Kooskia camp administration.

It is evident that, once their early grievances were resolved, the internees became exemplary workers, earning praise and respect from most of their Caucasian work supervisors and from INS administrative personnel. After Captain Antonio Martin of the Spanish Embassy and Charles C. Eberhardt of the State Department visited the Kooskia camp in late July 1944, Eberhardt's report contained an emphatic tribute, not only to the excellent, and humane, conditions that prevailed there, but also to the internees' determination to demonstrate their cooperation despite being deprived of their civil rights. Eberhart wrote that Martin had stated, "For the first time in my experience in visiting such camps and centers, I was requested by the [internee] spokesman to advise our Embassy of the thanks and appreciation of the entire group of detainees for the efforts on their behalf by the Officer in Charge."[41]

Doing the road work allowed the men to regain much of the self-respect that many of them must have lost through the humiliation of having been so unjustly interned. At 92, former internee spokesman James I. Yano commented, "We worked hard because we enjoyed the job we were doing, and I'm very happy to say I was one of them."[42]

Legacies of the Kooskia Internees

The story of the Kooskia Internment Camp would be incomplete without investigating what happened to the internees in the intervening sixty-five years since the camp closed. In recent years information has emerged about the postwar experiences of some of the Japanese aliens held at the Kooskia camp, in particular the Japanese Peruvian detainees.

The incarceration experience had adverse consequences for most, if not all, of the Japanese internees and their families. Nevertheless, several men overcame those difficulties to be recognized for their national importance, while others' contributions remain to be learned. Since many were reticent about the experience, even with family members, few details are known about most internees' later lives. In some cases, their relatives still may not even know that they were interned at the Kooskia camp. Hozen Seki and Toraichi Kono are two former Kooskia internees whose lasting legacies are known. In addition, Koshio Henry Shima, formerly Koshio Shimabukuro, will be remembered for his struggles to obtain justice for the kidnapped Japanese Latin Americans.

Hozen Seki (Fig. 108)

Prior to his internment, Reverend Hozen Seki had founded the New York Buddhist Church. Following his release, he co-founded the American Buddhist Academy (ABA) in New York City, an institute that "offered Americans

Fig. 108. Hozen Seki, founder of the New York Buddhist Church and the American Buddhist Academy, both in New York City. This photograph, taken around 1962 during his visit to the Santa Barbara, California, Buddhist Temple, shows him in his Buddhist robe. Courtesy Hoshin Seki.

the opportunity to study and learn Buddhism."[43] Seki also returned to Japan to request donations for the American Buddhist Academy Library. Many Japanese temples, individuals, and private libraries contributed to the cause. In 1950 the National Diet Library of Japan shipped nearly ten thousand volumes of Buddhist texts, manuscripts, and sutras to New York.[44]

Hozen Seki and his wife, Satomi, retired to Hawai'i where he died in 1991. In 2000 the ABA was reincorporated as the American Buddhist Study Center (ABSC); it recognizes, honors, and continues Seki's seminal work through monthly book discussion groups, lecture series, and Japanese cultural events that relate to Buddhism.[45] In 2001 the ABSC published *A Spark of Dharma: The Life of Reverend Hozen Seki.*[46]

Toraichi Kono (Fig. 109)

Even before World War II ended with victory over Japan on August 14, 1945, President Harry S Truman issued Proclamation 2655, allowing the U.S. to continue to deport "alien enemies" believed "to be prejudicial to the future security or welfare of the Americas."[47] This edict affected some of the Japanese who had been detained at the Kooskia camp, among them Toraichi Kono.

Kooskia internee Toraichi Kono's enduring significance is assured; a forthcoming documentary film about his life is in preparation.[48] Best known first as chauffeur and then personal secretary to the famous movie comedian, Charlie Chaplin, from 1916 to 1934,[49] Kono was suspected of involvement in espionage activities in early 1941. He reportedly arranged a meeting between Al Blake, a U.S. Navy seaman and former Chaplin employee, and Itaru Tachibana, an officer in the Imperial Japanese Navy.[50] On June 7, 1941,

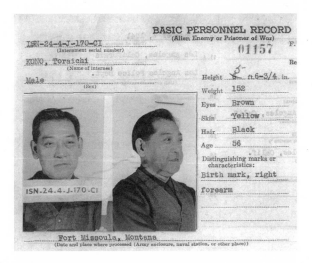

Fig. 109. Toraichi Kono, from his "Basic Personnel Record (Alien Enemy or Prisoner of War)" card, undated [1942], 1; E466F, Kono, Toraichi; OPMG, RG389, NARA II.

exactly six months before Japan attacked Pearl Harbor, the FBI arrested Tachibana and picked up Kono the following day. When Tachibana admitted he was a spy, Kono was implicated, but the U.S. Attorney in Los Angeles dismissed the complaint against him later that month.[51] Following Pearl Harbor, Kono was rearrested. He arrived at the Kooskia camp in September 1943 and remained there until early April 1944.[52]

At war's end Kono was interned at Santa Fe, New Mexico. When he tried to win his postwar release, the old allegations resurfaced.[53] In mid-December 1945 Kono appeared before a Repatriation Hearing Board. This group decided he should be deported to Japan, based on the accusation that he "was involved in espionage activities in 1941" because he facilitated the Blake/Tachibana meeting.[54] Kono protested that he was innocent of any espionage and had merely been trying to help a friend who knew that Tachibana wanted to visit a film studio, and who had approached Kono because he "was once Chaplin's secretary and knew all the big film people."[55]

Kono's grown children, Spencer Kono and Yuriko Nadaoka, visited Washington, DC, and wrote innumerable letters, even one to President Truman, seeking to cancel their father's deportation.[56] In October 1946 Kono transferred to Seabrook Farms in New Jersey under "relaxed internment."[57] The following March, although he was not from Peru, Kono was included in a class action lawsuit, discussed later, brought by attorney Wayne Collins, an attorney for the American Civil Liberties Union (ACLU) in San Francisco, on behalf of some Japanese Latin Americans who wished to remain in the U.S.[58]

Collins was ultimately successful in enabling Toraichi Kono to avoid deportation; in late September 1947, Kono was paroled under Collins' sponsorship.[59] In August 1948 Kono finally received a document vacating the

1946 order directing that he be deported to Japan, but ironically, that paper still referred to him as an "alien enemy."[60] Toraichi Kono died in March 1971.[61] Thirty-five years later, in March 2006, the Chaplin Society of Japan hosted a Chaplin-Kono Conference in Kyoto. Its objective was "to reassess the relationship of Charlie Chaplin" with Kono.[62]

War's end thus did not mean mass release of internees. In particular, the INS internment camps at Santa Fe, New Mexico, and Crystal City, Texas, continued to hold Japanese alien internees from the Kooskia camp and elsewhere into mid-1946 and late 1947 respectively.[63] Many at the latter camp were Japanese Peruvians.

Japanese Peruvians after the Kooskia Internment Camp

Continuing its prewar prejudice against people of Japanese ancestry, the Peruvian government declined to permit the return of many of the expelled Japanese Peruvians.[64] Instead, Peru proclaimed that in order to be eligible for return to that country, a person had to have been born in Peru, be a naturalized citizen of Peru, or be married to a Peruvian;[65] even so, those conditions did not guarantee return.

For Japanese Peruvians deemed ineligible for return, the result was a government-imposed dilemma. They had no passports; U.S authorities had compelled them to surrender those documents but had never returned them.[66] Once the war ended, at least thirteen hundred Japanese Peruvian "illegal aliens" remained in the United States. Lacking their passports, they were stateless, but neither the U.S. nor Peru wanted them. Therefore, and to get on with their lives, nine hundred of them endured deportation to Japan. Taro Shimabukuro, a former Kooskia internee, was one of them.

Koshio Henry Shima [Koshio Shimabukuro]

Taro's son, Koshio, later Koshio Henry Shima, was one of the other four hundred people, primarily Peruvian citizens or permanent resident aliens, who still hoped to return to Peru eventually. Therefore, they needed to stay in the U.S., but also had to fight deportation to Japan.[67] At war's end they had nowhere to go, so remained at the Crystal City, Texas, internment camp into 1947.[68]

Official negotiations with Peru continued, but Peru resisted taking the Japanese back. W. F. Kelly, the INS's assistant commissioner for alien control, favored paroling the Japanese Peruvians if Peru would not readmit them, particularly since "Collins" might be able to halt deportation proceedings in court.[69] From the mid-1940s well into the 1960s, Wayne M. Collins (Fig. 110), fought vigorously for the rights of many thousands of Japanese aliens and American citizens of Japanese ancestry.[70] He and his associates kept hundreds of Japanese aliens from being forcibly removed under Truman's

Fig. 110. American Civil Liberties Union attorney Wayne M. Collins. From the mid-1940s well into the 1960s he fought for the rights of thousands of Japanese aliens and American citizens of Japanese ancestry, including some Kooskia internees. Courtesy San Francisco Chronicle.

Fig. 111. Koshio Shimabukuro in New Jersey, 1947. Courtesy Koshio Henry Shima.

various proclamations mandating deportation of "alien enemies."

Due to Collins' tireless support and persistence,[71] some two hundred Japanese Latin Americans were released from internment and paroled to Seabrook Farms in New Jersey; there they worked either on the company's truck farm or in the frozen foods plant.[72] Koshio Shima was one of them (Fig. 111).[73] Others were released from Crystal City to American citizen sponsors in California and elsewhere[74]; Shima eventually became a gardener in southern California.[75] The Peruvian government never compensated Taro Shimabukuro for his property, so Shima lost his potential inheritance.[76] Subsequently, as will be discussed, he would play an important role in attempts to achieve justice for interned Japanese Latin Americans.

In 1954, the U.S. Congress allowed the Japanese Latin Americans one year to apply for residency, made retroactive to their arrival during the war. About one hundred people thus attained permanent residency and citizenship. Others never learned of the legislation or missed the application deadline. For them, a later remedy was to leave the U.S. and then return legally. In this way, most of the remaining Japanese Latin Americans did achieve permanent residency. Unfortunately, their official date of entry was not made retroactive to their actual wartime arrival,[77] which decades later was used to justify denying them redress.

Naturalization, Redress, Apology, and Reparations

Beginning in the 1950s, the nation began to take bipartisan steps towards righting previous wrongs committed against Japanese Americans. In 1952 the U.S. Congress passed the McCarran-Walter Act. One of its provisions "nullified the racial restrictions of the 1790 naturalization law," making Japanese aliens eligible to apply for naturalization.[78] On February 19, 1976, the thirty-fourth anniversary of Roosevelt's Executive Order 9066, President Gerald Ford rescinded EO9066; that order had led to the mass exclusion and incarceration of some one hundred twenty thousand Americans of Japanese descent.[79]

Subsequently, in 1980, Congress created the Commission on Wartime Relocation and Internment of Civilians (CWRIC) partly to investigate the official government claim that the internment of Japanese Americans was "justified by military necessity." The Commission took testimony from many former internees, both citizens and permanent resident aliens, including former Kooskia internee Tatsuji Mitsu Shiotani from Riverdale, NY, then age 84. He stated, "I do not feel bitter because of this experience. I still have much love and respect for America, and prefer to live here over any other place in the world."[80] In 1983 CWRIC concluded that the internment "was not justified by military necessity." Instead, it was caused by "race prejudice, war hysteria, and a failure of political leadership."[81] In recent years "wartime hysteria" has received primary blame as the dominant instigator.

Legal scholar Natsu Taylor Saito offers a differing viewpoint. She asserts that the chief motivating factor, rather than "wartime hysteria," was actually racial animosity fueled by economic jealousy. Even today, many people still believe that the wartime incarceration of Japanese Americans was "an unfortunate but understandable response to a perceived national security crisis," thereby mitigating racism's role in the tragedy. If "wartime hysteria" truly applied to people of Japanese descent, it should also have applied equally to individuals of German or Italian ancestry, but it did not. Unlike the Japanese, neither Germans nor Italians were incarcerated *en masse*.[82] Saito argues that internment and incarceration of Japanese Americans "was not an aberration" but was "quite consistent with the historical treatment of Asian Americans and other racially subordinated groups."[83]

On August 10, 1988, President Ronald Reagan signed the Civil Liberties Act of 1988.[84] It awarded an apology and a redress payment of $20,000 to surviving Japanese American detainees, both citizens and aliens, and established a public education fund. However, most of the kidnapped Japanese Latin Americans were excluded, because they were not legal "permanent [U.S.] residents or citizens at the time of their internment."[85] The only ones who qualified were those who had taken advantage of the 1954 law granting retroactive residency to those who applied for it in time.

In 1991 six Japanese Peruvian families in Northern California founded the Japanese Peruvian Oral History Project (JPOHP) both to collect oral histories from the survivors and to assist in their struggle for redress.[86] With the formation of the Campaign For Justice: Redress Now for Japanese Latin Americans! (CFJ) in 1996, a lawsuit, *Carmen Mochizuki et al. v. The United States*, was filed on behalf of the Japanese Latin American internees, with five named plaintiffs, including Koshio Henry Shima (former Kooskia internee Koshio Shimabukuro), seeking redress by inclusion under the Civil Liberties Act of 1988.[87] The timing was urgent, because the Civil Liberties Act of 1988 would expire on August 10, 1998.[88]

In June 1998 the U.S. Court of Federal Claims gave preliminary approval of a settlement agreement in the *Mochizuki* case, which would affect former internees whether living in the U.S., Japan, or Peru. However, their redress payment would be only $5,000, not the $20,000 granted to Japanese Americans. What is worse, payment of the smaller amount was not even guaranteed, because insufficient funds remained in the 1988 Civil Liberties Act redress account.[89]

Nevertheless, the majority of the Japanese Latin American internees accepted the "take it or leave it" settlement offer; many felt it was important to have admission of governmental wrongdoing on record along with an apology which could be presented to the elderly internees before they died. Seventeen of the internees rejected the settlement agreement.[90] They included Shima, one of the plaintiffs in the *Mochizuki* lawsuit.[91] In late August 1998 he filed suit against the U.S. government in federal court in Los Angeles for equal treatment with Japanese American internees, including the token monetary payment of $20,000.[92] He also submitted two additional claims, to the Justice Department and to the State Department, for full compensation in excess of $10 million dollars.[93] Shima sought recompense for his unlawful abduction, "for his imprisonment, loss of Peruvian citizenship and violation of his equal protection rights," and for the continued refusal of the U.S. to apologize or grant redress for over 50 years. As his attorney explained, "Mr. Shima is not even interested in one penny. What he would like is what happened to have never have happened to him."[94] But since that was impossible, resolution of this lawsuit in Shima's favor would serve as a deterrent to future government misconduct and to strengthen the rule of law, both constitutional and international, in the U.S.

Those who accepted the $5,000 settlement had to meet an eligibility deadline of August 10, 1998, to qualify for payment; some seven hundred former internees complied.[95] When the Office of Redress Administration began sending checks, to the oldest survivors first,[96] the funds were soon exhausted, leaving many deserving recipients unpaid. On May 21, 1999, President Clinton signed a $15 billion supplemental emergency appropriations bill that reallocated $4.3 million to replenish the Civil Liberties Public Education Fund in order to pay $5,000 apiece to some five hundred Japanese Latin Americans, as well as $20,000 each to a group of Japanese American internees.[97]

Even so, not all who deserved redress received it. Many potentially eligible claimants could not be located in time to file a claim by the deadline. Those who refused the unfair $5,000 settlement, such as Shima, could not obtain justice in U.S. courts. In 2000, his case was dismissed and in 2001 the Ninth Circuit Court of Appeals denied him a hearing.[98] Shima died, uncompensated, in early 2005.[99]

In her book, *From Chinese Exclusion to Guantánamo Bay*, Natsu Taylor Saito argues that the U.S.'s treatment of the Japanese Latin Americans was a particularly egregious violation of international law. In kidnapping, deporting, interning, holding hostage, and forcibly repatriating Japanese Peruvians, the U.S. committed a number of war crimes that have gone unpunished.[100]

In addition, the U.S.'s refusal to compensate the victims violates "a fundamental principle of customary law," that of "the right to redress an international wrong." As Saito observes, the U.S. has insisted on compensation for other World War II war crimes, including that for Holocaust survivors victimized by Swiss banks that laundered looted gold for the Nazis and for people who performed slave labor for Volkswagen. Activists for Korean and other "comfort women" used as sex slaves by the Japanese military also demand "an apology and reparations from Japan."[101]

The examples in the previous two paragraphs demonstrate a paradox, in that the U.S. espouses "selective compliance" with international law while still insisting on participation "in the development and promotion of the global rule of law." In other words, this "American exceptionalism" means that "other countries should comply with international law, but the United States need not do so."[102]

Persisting Consequences for the Internees and Their Families

Dispersed in different states and even other countries, the Kooskia camp's Japanese internees rarely, if ever, shared their incarceration experiences with family members. Teresa Watanabe's grandfather, her *jichan*, was Kooskia internee Yoshitaka Watanabe, a former fruit and vegetable merchant at Seattle's Pike Place Market. In an article about him, she wrote, "We never knew what his experience was like. We never asked him about it, and he never volunteered any information. He died with his secrets."[103] Contributing to his silence may have been certain traditional "Japanese cultural values," among them *shikata-ga-nai* (it cannot be helped) and *hazukashi* (shame), as well as "*giri* (obligation, duty), *gimu* (duty, responsibility), *enryo* (reserve, restraint), *gaman* (patience, perseverance)[,] and *unmei* (fate)."[104]

Scholar Amy Iwasaki Mass argues that the incarceration camp and internment camp experiences had a "profound impact" on Japanese Americans' self image, resulting in "psychological defense mechanisms that were used to maintain a sense of integrity and worth."[105] To acknowledge that the government they trusted had betrayed that trust "was so difficult that [their] natural feelings of rage, fear, and helplessness were turned inward and buried." These became manifested in "deep depression, a sense of shame, [and] a sense of 'there must be something wrong with me.'" Mass further observes that "the psychological responses of depression and shame are similar to those used by children who have abusive parents."[106]

Once the federal government assumed responsibility for wartime injustices to Japanese Americans by providing an apology and redress payments, Mass concludes that Japanese Americans no longer needed to employ the defenses of denial and rationalization. Instead, they "can feel an inner sense of honor and integrity that is validated and confirmed by the larger society"; this "sense of self-worth is vital to mental health."[107]

For many of the Kooskia internees, arrest by the Federal Bureau of Investigation (FBI) came at their homes. Not surprisingly, impressionable young children often witnessed this terrifying event. The fathers were removed to a jail, were kept incommunicado from their families, and were subject to "hearings" that were little more than "kangaroo courts" with predetermined outcomes; it is no wonder that the internees felt shamed and did not want to discuss their experiences. Especially galling was to have a later hearing and learn, from FBI reports presenting "evidence," that one's internment was based on subjective judgments, faulty logic, or erroneous intelligence from unnamed "confidential informants."[108] The stigma of arrest and incarceration remained.

Incalculable harm befell families whose head of household was imprisoned in an internment camp. Not only were family members deprived of his financial support, they also lacked his moral authority and discipline. Younger children, especially boys, often would "run wild," especially once they were confined in the WRA incarceration camps.[109] Documents available today from the National Archives, such as "Basic Personnel Record (Alien Enemy or Prisoner of War)" cards, bear the fingerprints of the individual as well as two head-and-shoulders photographs, the classic front and side view "mug shots" taken of lawbreakers. When Teresa Watanabe first saw that document as created for her grandfather, she thought he was a criminal (Fig. 112).[110]

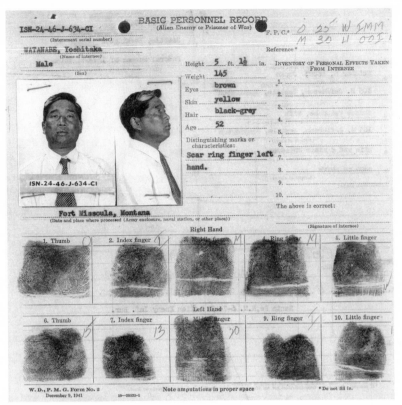

Fig. 112. Yoshitaka Watanabe's "Basic Personnel Record (Alien Enemy or Prisoner of War)" card, undated [1942], 1; E466F, Watanabe, Yoshitaka; OPMG, RG389, NARA II.

The Kooskia Internees' Geneva Convention Legacy and Post-9/11 Comparisons

The Geneva Convention of 1929 governed the treatment of the Japanese detainees at the Kooskia Internment Camp. There are actually four Geneva Conventions, international treaties drafted and revised at different times in Geneva, Switzerland, and subsequently ratified by some 191 nations, including the U.S. These treaties protect the wounded and sick on land (Geneva I, 1864/1949); at sea, including people shipwrecked (Geneva II, 1906); prisoners of war (Geneva III, 1929/1949, extended to internees in World War II); and civilians (Geneva IV, 1949).[111]

Ironically, because of the 1929 Geneva Convention agreement, Japanese noncitizen internees at the INS internment camps received better treatment than did their Japanese American citizen relatives in the WRA incarceration camps. For example, Article 11 specified that internees were entitled to receive a food ration "equal in quantity and quality to that of troops at base camps."[112] In contrast, because the 1929 Geneva Convention did not apply to the WRA's prisoners, they experienced decidedly substandard food and living conditions compared with those provided for the internees.

A lasting legacy of the Kooskia Internment Camp lies in the internees' knowledge and use of the 1929 Geneva Convention. This document empowered the Kooskia internees in ways not seen since. Their realization of their rights under it led them to petition the INS administration for, and ultimately to achieve, better living and working conditions, including replacement of the camp superintendent. Only one other group of internees, at Lordsburg, New Mexico, used this information to such great advantage.[113] The power it gave the Kooskia internees to have some control over their lives is so impressive that it is no wonder that the U.S. government fought hard to have its provisions denied to current prisoners at our Guantánamo Bay detention facility in Cuba.[114]

Humane Warfare

On Christmas Day 1776 George Washington's troops won the Battle of Trenton and captured hundreds of Hessian soldiers. He ordered his lieutenants to "treat them with humanity." For over two hundred years, the U.S. followed that principle, so much so that Scott Horton, president of the International League for Human Rights, could state, "The very idea of humane warfare in modern times started here in the United States."[115]

Civil liberties lawyer Joseph Margulies agreed, writing, "Throughout the twentieth century, the United States military continued to define itself by the humanitarian conviction that war—despite its inevitable horrors—should not be a senseless descent into anarchy." During World War II, with respect to the 1929 Geneva Convention, the U.S. "announced that it would comply [with it] and frequently invoked that compliance to distinguish the nobility of our actions from the enemy's unprincipled rapacity."[116] Ironically, because the 1929 Geneva Convention required similar housing for prisoners of war (POWs) and U.S. soldiers, some POW camp authorities in the U.S. even went so far as to move U.S. soldiers from barracks into tents when delays in construction of proper POW facilities necessitated tents for newly arrived POWs. The U.S.'s treatment of internees and POWs was independent of enemy countries' management of similarly detained U.S. citizens in Japan, Germany, and Italy, despite numerous documented atrocities committed against U.S. prisoners, particularly by Japan.[117]

In 1949 nations again assembled in Geneva to update the Geneva Convention. Because Korea and the U.S. had not ratified the agreement, North Korea did not respect it during the Korean War. Following that conflict, and despite inhumane treatment of captive U.S. soldiers by their Korean guards, the U.S. did ratify the 1949 Geneva Convention in 1955. Reasons given for ratification included maintaining the U.S.'s "moral leadership in the international community," as well as helping "to ensure that U.S. troops would not be mistreated in future conflicts."[118] Sadly, the Vietnam War also saw massive abuse of American prisoners, even though the U.S. officially applied the 1949 Geneva Convention to captured North Vietnamese.[119] Later, in Grenada, Haiti, Panama, and in the first Gulf War, we continued to abide by its principles.[120]

Post-9/11 Modifications

Following the horrific events of September 11, 2001, everything changed. On that day, nineteen militant, Islamic, suicide hijackers commandeered four commercial jetliners and flew them into the twin towers of New York's World Trade Center and into the Pentagon, the Arlington, Virginia, headquarters of the U.S. Department of Defense. The fourth airplane, possibly intended for the U.S. Capitol, crashed into a field in Pennsylvania. Besides the nineteen hijackers, another 2,973 people died and twenty-four are still missing but presumed to be dead.[121] Direct costs related to the destruction and subsequent cleanup amounted to at least 27.2 billion dollars.[122]

Immediately after the attacks, the U.S. government detained over twelve hundred people.[123] Many were arrested secretly, were not charged with any crime, and some were badly beaten. In other cases, local vigilantes assaulted or even killed men of, or thought to be of, Middle Eastern descent. Of more than five thousand arrests within two years, of which "hundreds were tried in closed hearings," not one person was convicted of terrorism.[124] By mid-2006, other hundreds of detainees at the U.S.'s detention facility at Guantánamo Bay, Cuba, were still not charged with any crimes.[125]

The 9/11 tragedies also stimulated a tremendous U.S. effort to combat terrorism, as well as new rules for "enemy combatants." One commentator observed that the administration of President George W. Bush "sought to redefine what counts as 'torture' and find exceptions to the Geneva Conventions rules against abusive treatment."[126] Examples include a January 2002 Justice Department memo "arguing that Geneva Convention provisions for POWs did not apply in the war on terrorism,"[127] and another from then-U.S. Attorney General Alberto Gonzales to President Bush calling portions of the Geneva Convention "obsolete" and "quaint."[128] In mid-2006, in a five to three vote, the U.S. Supreme Court blocked the administration's proposal to try detainees at the U.S.'s Guantánamo Bay, Cuba, detention camp before military tribunals. The Defense Department then issued a memo that "instructs recipients to ensure that all Defense Department policies, practices[,] and directives comply with Article 3 of the Geneva Conventions governing the humane treatment of prisoners."[129]

In his *Enemy Aliens: Double Standards and Constitutional Freedoms in the War on Terrorism*, David Cole describes how the "concept of emergency detention of suspicious people made a comeback" in 1986 when "an anti-terrorism task force comprised of high-level Justice Department officials considered an INS 'Contingency Plan'" which included "the use of immigration law to intern 'alien terrorists' and 'alien activists' in a federal detention center in Oakdale, Louisiana." Once the "Contingency Plan" became public knowledge, "the government quickly backed away from it, insisting that such a program was just a "thought experiment.""[130]

Concluding Observations

The success of the Kooskia Internment Camp is a tribute to both the indomitable spirit of the Japanese detainees and to the humane treatment they received from the Kooskia camp employees and administrators, particularly Merrill Scott. His sincere concern for the internees and their welfare communicated itself to them; they in turn rewarded his interest with a genuinely cooperative attitude and a desire to distinguish themselves through their hard work and their dedication to the task at hand.

Future work related to this notable site must include nominating it to the National Register of Historic Places, erecting an interpretive sign at or near the site, and continuing presentations of illustrated talks to the general public. In addition, archaeological investigations will take place at the site in 2010. All these projects will further ensure that the Kooskia Internment Camp and its history are not forgotten. Unfortunately, there are still people who do not appreciate the sacrifices made by the unjustly imprisoned Japanese alien internees in the INS camps and those of their unconstitutionally incarcerated Japanese American families in the WRA incarceration camps. For example, one person, who still does not "get it," wrote that life in such camps "was not much different than conditions for a lot of Americans in [19]41 nor the American farms most of them came from …. Today's generation of TV producers portray them as victims, a view I don't share."[131]

That critic forgets that he had a choice in how and where he lived and worked. During World War II, Japanese American citizens and permanent resident aliens of Japanese ancestry largely did not. They all made incalculable sacrifices, both emotionally and financially, when they were forcibly removed from their once-secure surroundings of neighborhoods, homes, and businesses. They lost their jobs, their family life, their pets, and their possessions, and were "relocated" at the whims and vagaries of a prejudiced, hysterical government. The U.S. Constitution and their elected political leaders had all failed them, dismally and abysmally. Ultimately, passage of the Civil Liberties Act of 1988, and its included apology, $20,000 redress payment, and education fund, announced to the U.S. and to the world that the U.S. government had made a severe blunder and was making partial restitution to the victims of that mistake.[132]

In later life attorney Wayne Collins observed, "No other nationality would have taken with such forbearance treatment so dastardly. Under our American democracy, even alien enemies, to my concept of constitutional interpretation, should have been entitled to basic constitutional immunities." Collins further denounced the U.S. government actions, and concluded,

> The damage done to these innocent people without cause was utterly evil. It was a war crime from which our nation proceeded to divert attention by harassing and mercilessly executing individuals like [Japan's World War II] General Yamashita for allegedly condoning crimes of subordinate officers of which he probably knew nothing. What is then to be said of our own Generals and civilian officials who not only condoned governmental crimes against our native-born citizens but systematically aided and abetted them?[133]

Even after his former clients had forgiven the U.S. government, he could not, saying, "I still feel bitter about the evacuation. It was the foulest god-dam [*sic*] crime the United States has ever committed against a wonderful people."[134] Collins, who died in 1974, had cause to view his government with suspicion. In 1973, nearly thirty years before the disastrous events and consequences of September 11, 2001, Collins prophesied, "Given another manufactured hysteria over 'national security' or some such expediency to justify ends, citizens can again be carted off at the point of bayonets. That is America's evacuation legacy."[135]

His prophecy, that "another manufactured hysteria over 'national security'" would result, again, in people being "carted off at the point of bayonets," came true more than thirty years after his death following the tragic events of September 11, 2001, often called the "Pearl Harbor of the twenty-first century."[136] Once again, the U.S. government sought to target people of certain ethnicities, including citizens, resident noncitizens, and foreign nationals, by deeming them "Other," i.e., potentially "sympathetic to the enemy." As the "Other" they were thus deserving of unequal treatment, including kidnapping, incarceration, and indefinite detention, under the guise of "emergency measures necessary to safeguard the lives, property, and fundamental freedoms of Americans from attack by those who 'hate us.'"[137]

As Saito asks us, "Who or what is being protected? Clearly some citizens are being sacrificed, presumably for the protection of the remainder. What distinguishes those worthy of protection from those who are not?"[138]

From 1937 to 1945, Germany imprisoned Lutheran pastor Martin Niemöller (1892-1984) in Sachsenhausen and Dachau concentration camps for opposing the Nazis' state control of the churches.[139] His poem reminds us to be vigilant in protecting our civil rights:

First they came for the Communists, and I didn't speak up, because I wasn't a Communist.

Then they came for the Social Democrats, and I didn't speak up, because I wasn't a Social Democrat.

Then they came for the Trade Unionists, and I didn't speak up, because I wasn't a Trade Unionist.

Then they came for the Jews, and I didn't speak up, because I wasn't a Jew.

Then they came for me, and by that time there was no one left to speak up for me.[140]

Today, the U.S. continues to violate international law by ignoring post-World War II agreements, such as the United Nations' Universal Declaration of Human Rights and the Convention Relating to the Status of Refugees, as well as the U.S. Congress-approved International Covenant on Civil and Political Rights and the International Convention on the Elimination of All Forms of Racial Discrimination.[141] Here, let us allow Natsu Taylor Saito to speak out on the implications of the Japanese American and Japanese Latin American internment and incarceration experience as they apply to future events. She cautions us, "If we have learned anything from [those] 'mistakes' … , it is that we should not take claims of military necessity at face value but must look at the larger social, political, and economic dynamics at work." Indefinite detention of Japanese American citizens, permanent resident noncitizens, and people kidnapped from other countries "is most accurately attributed not to military necessity or even 'wartime hysteria' but to decades of anti-Asian sentiment and to the economic and political interests of those in power."[142]

Sixty years after Pearl Harbor, in the immediate aftermath of the September 11, 2001, calamity, the Japanese American community took an unpopular stand by bravely stepping forward to condemn the government's linking of Muslim American citizens and noncitizens to the 9/11 tragedy. Once again, "race prejudice, war hysteria, and a failure of political leadership" had contributed to knee-jerk reactions towards people from a particular ethnic or religious group. Because of Japanese Americans' own experiences with internment and incarceration, and their empowering movement for government accountability which resulted in historic apology and redress, they were able to sway public opinion away from the wholesale imprisonment of an entire group of people who, once again, had done nothing wrong.

Appendix:
List of All Men at the Kooskia Internment Camp

Last Name	First Name	Other/Middle/ Alias	Kooskia Number[1]	Date of Birth	Residence	Occupation
Abe	Shiro		195	Mar. 11, 1901	Brooklyn, NY	Chauffeur/household
Akagi	Henry	Kiichi	[151]	Oct. 5, 1881	Killisnoo, AK	Cannery
Akena	Tokuhei		[120]	Apr. 15, 1900	David, Chiriqui, Panama	Barber
Aketa	Masaji		[250]	Apr. 20, 1916	Lima, Peru	Barber
Akimoto	Roy	Naoyoshi	1	June 1, 1900	Seward, AK	Laundry/farming
Akiyama	Itaru		105	Nov. 4, 1913	West Long Branch, NJ	Cook/pantryman
Aragaki	Shibasuke		212	Feb. 28, 1901	Sullana, Peru	Barber
Arase	Shohei		[153]	Apr. 21, 1893	Seattle, WA	Delivery truck driver
Arashiro	Munehisa		150	Apr. 16, 1912	Kakaha, Kauai, HI	Electrician
Asaba	Kinzo		228	Nov. 17, 1888	Seattle, WA	Store owner
Baba	Hiroshi		[134]	July 8, 1903	New York, NY	Gardener
Banba	Kuromitsu		2	Dec. 11, 1901	Honolulu, HI	Waiter
Borovicka[2]	Ludwig	René Pons	[137]	July 26, 1893	Chicago, IL	Doctor [Italian]
Deki	Miyanoshin		106	Oct. 17, 1901	Brooklyn, NY	Restaurant business
Emori	Jinji		3	May 17, 1916	Dutch Harbor, AK, "Wilhelmina"	Radio operator
Endo	Unosuke		[251]	May 15, 1892	Terminal Island, CA	Fisherman

201

Surname	Given	Alt.	No.	Date	Place	Occupation
Eto	Shosuke		[215]	Mar. 20, 1891	Catacaos, Peru	Mechanic
Fujii	Ginichi		4	Apr. 4, 1886	Fairbanks, AK	Minister/cooking
Fujimura	Kihachiro		107	Aug. 3, 1893	New York, NY	Domestic worker
Fukasawa	Kazuo		[252]	Aug. 15, 1908	Lima, Peru	Merchant
Furuki	Shizuo		5	June 8, 1903	Altadena, CA	House servant/gardener
Goya	Saiki		214	June 1, 1910	Casapalca, Peru	Baker
Hamada	Jisaku		6	Sept. 3, 1890	Los Angeles, CA	Cook
Hanamoto	George	Hitoshi; Hiroshi	7	Oct. 14, 1903	Honolulu, HI	Laborer/journalist
Haneda	Jiro		[108]	Dec. 7, 1908	New York, NY	Domestic servant
Hara	Takuzo		8	Apr. 24, 1899	Terminal Island, CA	Fisherman
Haraguchi	Tome		9	Jan. 2, 1881	Port Townsend, WA	Railroad worker
Hasegawa	Minoru	See **Kaniyashiki**				
Hashimoto	Kaichi		[155]	Mar. 1, 1885	Seattle, WA	Laborer
Hashimoto[2]	Sokichi	Harry	229	Jan. 27, 1900	Los Angeles, CA	Vegetable packer/landscaper
Hayashi	Haruo		[216]	Feb. 26, 1900	Piura, Peru	Barber
Higa	Matsu		196	July 25, 1887	Montclair, NJ	Butler
Higashi	Kiyusaburo		10	Feb. 6, 1888	Portland, OR	Hotel owner
Higo	Seitaro		152	Feb. 12, 1892	Terminal Island, CA	Laborer
Hino	Yoshio		197	Nov. 16, 1889	Oahu, HI	Buddhist priest
Hirabayashi	Hamao		[144]	May 1, 1888	Seattle, WA	Grocer/butcher
Hiratsuka	Joe		[156]	Mar. 22, 1875	Ekuk Spit, AK	Fish cannery worker
Honma	Katsumi		11	Apr. 12, 1903	El Paso, TX	Taxidermist

Surname	Given name		No.	Date	Place	Occupation
Hori	Kishiro		12	Jan. 8, 1885	McGill, NV	Laborer
Hoshiko	Hitoshi		13	Mar. 27, 1885	McGill, NV	Laborer
Iizuka	Shotaro		154	Apr. 10, 1894	Visalia, CA	Farmer
Ikegami	Joe	Unosuke	14	Dec. 9, 1892	Ketchikan, AK	Laundry worker/tailor
Imahashi	Mitsui	Mitsuye	N/A	N/A	N/A	N/A
Imahashi[2]	Torajiro		15	Sept. 26, 1905	Ensenada, Mexico	Fisherman
Imakiire	Zenji		16	Jan. 15, 1889	[Wailuku, HI?] Harvey, LA (shrimp boat *King Tut*)	Fisherman
Imamoto	Jusaku		17	Jan. 1, 1878	Seattle, WA	Bartender
Imamura	Hisashi		18	Mar. 20, 1896	Santa Monica, CA	Gardener
Imamura	Yoneji		19	Jan. 26, 1907	Eatonville, WA	Lumber mill laborer
Imanishi	Umajiro		[178]	Oct. 23, 1891	Seattle, WA	Express man
Inamine	Seiho		[138]	Jan. 7, 1915	Lima, Peru	Merchant
Inouye	Rokuro		20	May 20, 1890	Juneau, AK	Laundryman
Inuzuka	Jinjiro		21	Jan. 10, 1896	San Diego, CA	Farmer/gardener
Ishihara[3]	Takuzo		N/A	N/A	N/A	N/A
Ishikawa	Yasaku		22	Sept. 14, 1902	Terminal Island, CA	Fisherman
Ishima	Kazuyoshi		[139]	Jan. 15, 1899	Hawthorne, CA	Farmer
Ishizaki	Ichimatsu		109	Nov. 6, 1904	New York, NY	Waiter
Iwashima	Sokichi		230	Oct. 21, 1889	Terminal Island, CA	Fisherman
Iwaya	Bunji		23	Feb. 8, 1883	Cloudcroft, NM	Truck farmer
Iwaya	Suemitsu		[110]	Oct. 25, 1898	Stamford, CT	Cook
Iwazumi	Tetsuzo		143	May 1, 1888	Philadelphia, PA	Wholesaler
Izui	Mikisaburo		[157]	Jan. 28, 1882	Seattle, WA	Pharmacist

Surname	Given name		Number	Date	Location	Occupation
Kadotani	Tommy	Yoshito	24	July 10, 1903	Santa Cruz, CA	Gardener
Kagawa	Shotaro		25	July 1, 1885	Los Angeles, CA	Nursery worker
Kage	Mantaro		[218]	Apr. 2, 1888	Chulucanas, Piura, Peru	Cafe owner
Kaijima	Tony	Toyomatsu	26	c. 1881	Ketchikan, AK	Laundry
Kakiyama	Louis, Luis	Yorikatsu	[121]	Nov. 26, 1900	David, Panama	Barber
Kamesaka	Sancho		27	Jan. 20, 1881	Denver, CO	Farm worker
Kanashiro	Kiyomasa		[253]	Nov. 17, 1913	Callao, Peru	Restaurant owner
Kanashiro	Ricardo		[254]	Oct. 20, 1920	Lima, Peru	Clerk
Kaniyashiki[2]	Yusaku	M. Hasegawa	211	June 6, 1897	Terminal Island, CA	Fisherman
Kato	Tomosaburo		28	Dec. 9, 1890	Los Angeles, CA	Gardener
Kawahara	Tadao	"Chino"	29	Apr. 1, 1898	Whitefish, MT	Farm laborer
Kawamoto	Yuji		[111]	Oct. 18, 1912	New York, NY	Architect
Kawanaka	Keiichi		[198]	Sept. 19, 1896	New York, NY	Waiter
Kawauchi	Rinosuke		30	June 1, 1902	Ensenada, Mexico	Fisherman
Kayano	Harvey	Mitaro	31	Mar. 15, 1882	Chicago, IL	Cook
Kempski	Hans	Werner	227	Mar. 1, 1910	Bolivia, Argentina	Doctor [German]
Kihara	Ichimatsu		[185]	Dec. 7, 1893	Seattle, WA	Wholesaler
Kihara	Kisaku		217	Mar. 2, 1891	Paita, Peru	Merchant
Kiijiki	Goro		32	Apr. 1, 1876	Ketchikan, AK	Laundry laborer
Kijima	Keiji		135	July 21, 1898	New York, NY	Dental mechanic
Kinugawa	Riichi		200	June 22, 1898	New York, NY	Chauffeur/gardener/cook

Kisanuki	Tatsu	See **Nishimura**				
Kishida	Jisaburo		[255]	Jan. 3, 1894	Seattle, WA	Warehouseman
Kito	Tom	Tamokazu	[158]	Jan. 11, 1899	Petersburg, AK	Shrimp cannery worker
Kiuchi[2]	Genji		33	c. 1898	New Orleans, LA	Fisherman
Koba	Katushi		122	July 4, 1885	Seattle, WA	Restaurant owner
Koba	Tsuneyoshi		[148]	June 12, 1900	Baltimore, MD	Medical student
Kobayashi	Nahokichi	George	34	Sept. 19, 1892	El Centro, CA	Card dealer in club/laborer
Kobayashi[3]	Shigeru		N/A	N/A	N/A	N/A
Kobayashi	Toshiyo	T. Komatsu	35	Feb. 19, 1893	Seattle, WA	N/A
Koda	Motokichi		199	Mar. 15, 1887	Philadelphia, PA	Domestic
Kodaka	Kasanu		[232]	Mar. 23, 1894	New York, NY	Domestic
Koga	Hichiro	Nakano	[112]	Mar. 10, 1895	New York, NY	Domestic/odd jobs
Komatsu	Shigeru	See T. **Kobayashi**	[145]	Sept. 1, 1888	Sacramento, CA	Farm worker
Komatsu	Toshio					
Komoto	Ikutaro		36	Nov. 7, 1882	El Paso, TX	Farmer
Kono	Takashi	Joe	37	July 4, 1910	Juneau, AK	Waiter
Kono	Toraichi		[160]	Mar. 3, 1885	Los Angeles, CA	Not given
Kozima	Gitaro		38	Jan. 25, 1886	Hollywood, CA	Exporter-importer
Kunihiro[2]	Jitsuichi	José	[231]	Dec. 23, 1889	Sullana, Piura, Peru	Watch repairman
Kurata	Itsuo		[203]	Feb. 12, 1889	Terminal Island, CA	Fisherman
Kurisu	Jinhichi		39	Sept. 12, 1886	Port Townsend, WA	Railway worker
Kurisu	Koichi		159	Feb. 28, 1902	Honolulu, HI	Store manager

Kurita	Tsunejiro	George	40	Jan. 21, 1893	Seattle, WA	Laborer/confectioner
Kuroda	Katsuto		[161]	Apr. 3, 1894	Monterey, CA	Laundry worker
Kuroiwa	Tsunezo		[256]	Sept. 7, 1901	Chosica, Peru	Barber
Kuroki	Uichiro		219	July 29, 1900	Frias Piura, Peru	Storekeeper
Kusuyama	Shinichi	Harry	[162]	Oct.16, 1892	Santa Barbara, CA	Butler
Kuwamoto	Torihey		41	Apr. 24, 1884	Juneau, AK	Lumber mill worker
Maeda	Naoichi		42	Feb. 5, 1887	Terminal Island, CA	Fisherman
Makino[2]	Kuhei		[235]	Apr. 3, 1889	Long Island, NY	Cook
Masuoka	Baiichi		[163]	May 3, 1884	Portland, OR	Hotel manager
Matsubayashi	Kojiro		[164]	Oct. 10, 1878	Juneau, AK	Cannery worker
Matsuda	Ryuzo		202	Aug. 26, 1904	New York, NY	Assistant bookkeeper
Matsuishi	Yorimichi		[113]	Apr. 24, 1903	Ridgefield, CT	Treaty merchant
Matsukawa	Shiro		43	c. 1895	Sandy Point, LA (shrimp boat *Fuji*)	Fisherman
Matsushita	Shichigoro		44	July 3, 1898	Terminal Island, CA	Fisherman
Matubara	Seiiti		45	Sept. 27, 1919	Ensenada, Mexico	Laborer
Mayeda	Henry	Ichi	[166]	July 13, 1885	Hoonah, AK	Cook
Minato	Inao		46	Aug. 3, 1888	Walnut Grove, CA	Farm laborer
Mishima[3]	Toyoji		N/A	N/A	N/A	N/A
Miura	Genpei		233	Mar. 25, 1894	Kapoho, Puna, Hawai'i, HI	Cane planter/Japanese school teacher
Miya	Takeshi		[123]	July 17, 1876	Seattle, WA	Money collector
Miyagishima[2]	Umeo		234	Dec. 14, 1897	McGill, NV	Railroad laborer
Miyagishima[2]	Yonezo		[242]	Feb. 2, 1905	McGill, NV	Railroad worker

Miyamoto	Satoru		[220]	July 10, 1896	Piura, Peru	Barber
Miyasato	George	Kameichi	[168]	July 5, 1897	Wrangell, AK	Cook
Miyashita	Toshiyuki		47	Feb. 6, 1912	Tacoma, WA	Cook
Mochizuki	Goro		48	Apr. 7, 1902	Portland, OR	Jiu-jitsu instructor/greengrocer
Momii	Kizaemon	Ikken	[124]	Nov. 29, 1894	San Francisco, CA	Newspaper publisher
Mori[2]	Shigeru		[206]	Oct. 20, 1905	Bronx, NY	Housework/cook
Morita	Eiichi		49	Mar. 23, 1896	Guadaloupe, CA	Farm laborer
Morita	Moku		50	Feb. 12, 1895	Auburn, CA	Farmer
Moto	George	Tsurumatsu	[170]	Jan. 1, 1871	Deering, AK	Prospector
Motoyama	Masao		51	Aug. 5, 1896	Guadaloupe, CA	Seed company laborer
Murai	Suyematsu		52	Oct. 2, 1898	San Francisco, CA	Domestic
Murakami	Seishichi		165	Jan. 18, 1889	Terminal Island, CA	Fisherman
Murakoshi[2]	Kazuo		[171]	Oct. 10, 1886	Oakland, CA	Housecleaning/laborer
Murata	Frank	Torataro	167	Nov. 5, 1879	Anchorage, AK	Cook
Nagai	Ryoichi		53	Sept. 30, 1906	Ensenada, Mexico	Fisherman/laborer
Nagamine	Haruyuki		54	Oct. 15, 1880	Los Angeles, CA	Wholesale produce business
Nagasaki	Hajime	Jimmy	[147]	Jan. 4, 1888	Seattle, WA	Stationary engineer
Nagashima	Yohachi		55	Aug. 12, 1899	Bingham Canyon, UT	Railroad trackman
Nagayori[3]	Kaku		N/A	N/A	N/A	N/A
Nakaike	Frank	Eiikichi	56	Feb. 2, 1877	Fairbanks, AK	Cook
Nakamura	Kokichi		125	Feb. 10, 1887	Maui, HI	Mail carrier
Nakamura	Kyutaro		[126]	Oct. 30, 1904	Milwaukee, OR	Farmhand

Nakamura	Teiji		[127]	Sept. 19, 1886	Miami, FL	Gardener/clerk
Nakashima	Kintaro		[179]	Aug. 1, 1881	Seattle, WA	Restaurant owner
Nambu	Genya		57	Aug. 30, 1891	Sacramento, CA	Newspaperman
Namikawa	Shirokichi		236	May 28, 1899	Terminal Island, CA	Fisherman
Niino	Shikamatsu		[249]	July 5, 1878	Layton, UT	Railroad trackman
Nikki	Yoshitaro		58	Feb. 15, 1902	Ensenada, Mexico	Fisherman
Nishibata	Kinbei		59	Dec. 25, 1903	Terminal Island, CA	Fisherman
Nishimura	Tatsuo	"Jumbo"	60	Dec. 24, 1910	Los Angeles, CA	Gardener
Nishiyama	George	Shigematsu	61	Dec. 8, 1878	Seward, AK	Janitor
Nomura	Giichi		169	May 11, 1895	Honolulu, HI	Stonemason
Nose	Masao		62	Jan. 12, 1905	Gaston, OR	Farmhand
Numamoto	Ototaro		63	Nov. 15, 1892	Chula Vista, CA	Farm laborer
Obata	Kigoro		[172]	Mar. 11, 1890	Seattle, WA	Cashier
Ohta[2]	Minoru		204	June 18, 1886	Los Angeles, CA	Cook
Oishi	Ichimatsu		64	Feb. 1, 1884	Terminal Island, CA	Craftsmanship
Okada	Sakuichi		237	Mar. 21, 1886	Salt Lake City, UT	Pantry cook
Okamoto[2]	Chiyogi	M. Yamamoto	246	Oct. 12, 1909	Terminal Island, CA	Fisherman
Okazaki	Takeshi		[190]	Mar. 1, 1897	Los Angeles, CA	Importer
Okuda	Isamu	T.	65	Feb. 4, 1899	Seattle or Tacoma, WA	Railroad laborer
Omura	Roy	Minoru	66	Dec. 25, 1892	Sitka, AK	Laundry
Onaga	Rincho		[191]	Sept. 5, 1895	Kauai, HI	Barber
Onishi	Katsuji		205	Apr. 30, 1896	Pelham Manor, NY	Importer/exporter
Ooka	Jinichiro		67	Sept. 4, 1914	Ensenada, Mexico	Fisherman

Oura	Mutsuichiro		[173]	Jan. 15, 1897	Terminal Island, CA	Fisherman
Oyama	Daisuke		221	Oct. 22, 1886	Trujillo, Peru	Farmer/storekeeper
Ozaki²	Hachiro		238	Feb. 23, 1903	San Pedro, CA	Fisherman
Pons	René	See **Borovicka**				
Saito	Harry	Kogi; Yukiharu	68	Apr. 15, 1895	Nome, AK	Restaurant operator
Saito	Ippachi		[176]	Feb. 5, 1899	Idaho Falls, ID	Photographer
Saito	Shigetoshi		[192]	Nov. 15, 1885	Seattle, WA	Printer
Sakai	Masaji	James	69	June 19, 1878	Magna, UT	Janitor
Sakamoto	Cuzo		70	May 13, 1883	Petersburg, AK	Cook
Sakoda	Eikichi	Luis	222	Sept. 5, 1890	Piura, Peru	Barber
Sakuma	Toimon		[140]	Feb. 12, 1887	Ogden, UT	Trackman
Sakurada	Sansaku		71	Feb. 26, 1907	Terminal Island, CA	Fisherman
Sanematsu	Kiichi		72	May 27, 1894	Riverside, CA	Gardener
Sano	Shichiro		[213]	Dec. 16, 1896	New York, NY	Cook
Sarae	Hirai		73	June 10, 1898	Terminal Island, CA	Fisherman
Sato	Chuji	John C.	174	Jan. 25, 1889	Shaker Heights, OH	Cook/butler
Sato	Kosaku		[128]	May 28, 1878	Seattle, WA	Second-hand dealer
Sato	Ryuji		207	Oct. 16, 1881	New York, NY	Domestic
Sato	Sataro		175	Feb. 17, 1900	Gresham, OR	Farm laborer
Seike	Masayuki		74	Sept. 26, 1899	Harvey, LA (shrimp boat *Young Bride*)	Fisherman
Seki	Hozen		136	Dec. 15, 1903	New York, NY	"Missionary"/Buddhist minister
Seko	Idayu		75	Nov. 11, 1899	Terminal Island, CA	Fisherman

Surname	Given name	Alt. name	No.	Date	Place	Occupation
Shibata	Unosuke		76	Mar. 12, 1880	Wrangell, AK	Shrimp picker
Shigekuni	Aisuke		[141]	July 23, 1888	Oahu, HI	Contractor
Shimabukuro	Koshio	Henry Shima	[257]	Sept. 17, 1923	Lima, Peru	Businessman
Shimabukuro	Taro		[258]	Jan. 25, 1897	Lima, Peru	Merchant
Shimizu	Yasajiro		[181]	March 4, 1882	Seattle, WA	Railroad laborer
Shiotani	Tatsuji	Mitsu	[114]	Mar. 31, 1897	Westchester, NY	Domestic
Shirai	Kichinojo	Harry	77	c. 1885	Ketchikan, AK	Cook
Suga	Yasuo		78	Aug. 20, 1908	Ensenada, Mexico	Fisherman
Sugiyama	Katsujiro		79	Apr. 15, 1888	McGill, NV	Laborer
Sumi	Otosaburo		80	Apr. 12, 1908	Terminal Island, CA	Fisherman, carpenter
Sumida	Toshio		177	Sept. 23, 1909	Los Angeles, CA	Student
Suzuki	Bunichi		81	May 6, 1899	Los Angeles, CA	Cook
Tahara	Shunichi	George	208	Nov. 1, 1899	New York, NY	Cook
Taira	Yojo	Yotsuni; Yoji; Yojyo	241	Mar. 6, 1886	Maui, HI	Laundry operator
Taira[2]	Shinkyu	Carlos	223	Feb. 24, 1901	Chiclayo, Peru	Farmer
Takahashi	Seizo		82	Sept. 29, 1889	Minneapolis, MN	Jiu-jitsu teacher
Takahashi	Tei		115	July 31, 1888	Trucksville, PA	Caretaker
Takamori	Masataro		83	June 5, 1882	Guadaloupe, CA	Laborer
Takamura	Victor	Kaichiro	224	Nov. 18, 1888	Piura, Peru	Taxi owner
Takehara[2]	Renichi		239	Apr. 2, 1908	New York, NY	Cook/waiter
Takemoto	Yasuo		84	Nov. 18, 1899	Los Angeles, CA	Gardener
Takenaka	Gaichi, Goichi	George	85	May 1, 1878	Valdez, AK	Cook
Takesaki	Kazuo		86	Nov. 20, 1901	Oakland, CA	Laundry worker

Takeuchi	Shimpachi		[142]	Sept. 3, 1886	Newtonville, MA	Domestic worker
Takeuchi	Taro		240	Feb. 22, 1881	New York, NY	Manager of restaurant
Tako	Kokichi		[259]	Nov. 2, 1911	Callao, Peru	Merchant
Tamaki	George	Hideji	87	Feb. 14, 1908	Juneau, AK	Sawmill worker
Tamura	Shinkichi		88	Apr. 17, 1917	Los Angeles, CA	Student
Tanagi	Koi		[193]	Aug. 10, 1881	Seattle, WA	Grocery store owner
Tanaka	Ryohei		[129]	June 15, 1886	Los Angeles, CA	Hotel proprietor
Tanaka	Satsuki		89	June 29, 1903	Fresno, CA	Cook
Tanaka	Toyokuma		90	Apr. 3, 1883	Portland, OR	Hotel Keeper
Tanaka	Yuzo	Harry	[116]	Mar. 12, 1883	New York, NY	Domestic worker
Teraoka	Hisahiko		91	Feb. 8, 1921	Ensenada, Mexico	Fisherman
Teraoka	Takehiko		92	Mar. 23, 1895	Ensenada, Mexico	Fisherman
Terasaki	Mannosuke		93	Dec. 30, 1904	Ensenada, Mexico	Fisherman
Toguri	Makoto		94	Aug. 20, 1889	Gardena, CA	Laborer
Tojo	Hiromi		[243]	Apr. 2, 1890	Washington, DC	Dental porcelain worker
Tokuda	Seichi		[130]	Aug. 15, 1897	Terminal Island, CA	Fisherman
Tokumi	Ushichiro		[149]	July 13, 1891	New York, NY	Inventor/writer
Tokushi	Gagi		95	c. 1883	Kilgore, TX	Cook
Tomikawa	Seikichi		[260]	Nov. 27, 1908	Peru	Schoolteacher
Toyofuku	Tanzo		[183]	Apr. 14, 1898	Los Angeles, CA	Horticultural contractor
Tsujiuchi	Shunichi		[245]	Mar. 23, 1899	Garden Grove, CA	Fisherman
Tsutsumi	Shohei		180	Apr. 10, 1886	Delano, CA	Farmhand
Uchiyama	Asaichi		225	Jan. 1, 1893	Chiclayo, Peru	Merchant

Surname	Given name		No.	Date	Location	Occupation
Uehara	Saburo		244	Aug. 8, 1907	Honolulu, HI	Laborer
Uema	Somatsu		226	Jan. 12, 1897	Piura, Peru	Baker
Uenishi	Joe	Kozo	[184]	June 23, 1900	Seattle, WA	Bookkeeper/dept. store helper
Ueoka	Sokan	Raymond	[131]	Sept. 6, 1905	Maui, HI	Minister
Umeda	Motoharu		132	Sept. 13, 1909	Seattle, WA	Cook
Urabe	James	Denkichi	[117]	Aug. 11, 1896	Bloomsburg, PA	Chef
Ushiroji	Yasuichi		96	May 14, 1909	Ensenada, Mexico	Fisherman/laborer
Uyechi	Harry	Kenji	[182]	Mar. 3, 1908	Honolulu, HI	Laborer
Wakabayashi	Saichiro		209	July 1, 1892	Bethlehem, PA	Domestic
Wakamatsu[2]	Yoshiji		[248]	May 17, 1880	Seattle, WA	Manager, chop suey house
Waki	Shigeyoshi		97	Oct. 17, 1901	Seattle, WA	Cook
Watanabe[2]	Harukichi		[261]	Feb. 23, 1901	Peru	Merchant
Watanabe	Ittetsu		247	Mar. 28, 1893	Maui, HI	Salesman
Watanabe	Yoshitaka		[186]	Oct. 8, 1889	Seattle, WA	Vegetable dealer
Wazumi	Minoru		[118]	Mar. 29, 1906	Stamford, CT	Clerk
Yakabi	Arturo, Arthur	Shinei	146	Jan. 4, 1922	Callao, Peru	Bakery employee
Yamade	Kay	Keitaro	[188]	Dec. 22, 1882	Ketchikan, AK	Planing mill worker
Yamaguchi	Asataro		[194]	Dec. 19, 1892	Cincinnati, OH	Perfume manufacturing
Yamaguchi[2]	Genji	George	[187]	Sept. 7, 1902	Los Angeles, CA	Landscaper/insurance sales
Yamaguchi	Shiro		98	Jan. 11, 1901	San Antonio, TX	Cafe operator
Yamamoto	Frank	Hiyo	99	Sept. 1885	Juneau, AK	Cook
Yamamoto[3]	George		N/A	N/A	N/A	N/A

Yamamoto	Masashi	See Okamoto				
Yamamoto	Tadayoshi		[201]	Oct. 15, 1899	Delano, CA	Ranch foreman
Yanagi	Frank	Eizo	210	Nov. 20, 1892	Chicago, IL	Engrosser (copyist)/artist
Yano	Isao	James; James I., Jimmy	100	Oct. 1, 1905	Houston, TX	Japanese Foreign Trade Bureau
Yogi	Seisaburo		101	Apr. 21, 1908	Honolulu, HI	Waiter/businessman
Yokota	Seiichi		102	Nov. 22, 1900	Havre, MT	Boiler washer
Yoshida	Ichita		133	Jan. 18, 1903	Tacoma, WA	Laborer
Yoshikawa	Yoshie	Yoshio; Charles	103	Aug. 8, 1899	Vermilion, OH	Cook
Yoshimura	Sakaye	Ed; Eddie	104	Apr. 18, 1904	San Diego, CA	Photographer
Yoshinaka	Seiichi		[189]	Apr. 2, 1890	Ringold, WA	Farmer
Yuri	Katsumoto		119	July 1, 1901	Stamford, CT	Butler

Except where noted, information is from internees' "Basic Personnel Record (Alien Enemy or Prisoner of War)" card, Entry 466G (Germans) or Entry 466F (Japanese), Records Relating to (German) (Japanese) Civilian Internees during World War II, 1941-1946; Records of the Office of the Provost Marshal General, RG389, NARA II. Because the names are transliterated from Japanese, there may be alternative spellings for some of them.

N/A means not available and c. is circa.

[1] The first group, Nos. 1 through 104, arrived on May 27, 1943. The second group, Nos. 105 through 119, arrived on May 28, 1943. The third group, Nos. 120 through 133, arrived on June 7, 1943. More men came between then and September as individuals or small groups, Nos. 134 through 148. The fourth group arrived September 20, 1943, Nos. 149 through 184. Other individuals, Nos. 184 through 194, followed from then until the end of January 1944. Men in the fifth group, which arrived February 1, 1944, had Nos. 195 through 211. Group 6 came on February 7, 1944, and received Nos. 212 through 227. The seventh group, Nos. 228 through 248, arrived on March 17, 1944. The eighth group, Nos. 249 through 261, came on June 7, 1944. Numbers lacking brackets are known. Numbers within brackets are approximate and were inferred from lists or other data.

[2] No "Basic Personnel Record" was located for this individual; the information is from other documents in the National Archives.

[3] No "Basic Personnel Record" or any other documents were located for this individual; the information is courtesy Yosh Shimoi.

List of Abbreviations

1000/8 = Sanitation Recommendations.

1000/F = 1000/F, Hospital [Box 1].

1000/K = 1000/Kooskia.

1000/K(1) = 1000/Kooskia (1) [Box 4, first white folder].

1000/K(2) = 1000/Kooskia (2) [Box 4, second white folder].

1000/K(4) = 1000/Kooskia [Box 4].

1000/K(5) = 1000/Kooskia [Box 5].

1000/K(6) = 1000/Kooskia [Box 6, Envelope #3].

1000/S(1) = 1000/Stations [Box 6, Envelope #1, 1000/Kooskia].

1000/S(2) = 1000/Stations [Box 6, Envelope #2, 1000/Kooskia (1)].

1000/S(3) = 1000/Stations [Box 6, Envelope #3, 1000/Kooskia].

1001/A = Personnel-General Correspondence, 1943-1944 [Box 10].

1014/E = Cooperation with Other Federal Agencies.

1016/A = Investigations, General Correspondence.

1021/Z = Memoranda, Labor Division.

1022/Q = Visiting of Detainees, [Box 24].

1022/X = Geneva Convention [Box 24].

1025/A = Censorship, General Correspondence.

1025/F = Censorship, Telegrams.

1035/G = Mess Analysis, Alien Mess (10 Day Reports)

1036/A = Detainees, General Correspondence.

AACC = Asian American Comparative Collection, University of Idaho, Moscow.

ACAC = Assistant Commissioner for Alien Control.

AcACAC = Acting Assistant Commissioner for Alien Control.

ACLU = American Civil Liberties Union.

AdG = Attilio di Girolamo, USDJ, AECU, Los Angeles, CA, and Washington, DC.

AECU = Alien Enemy Control Unit.

AEHB = Alien Enemy Hearing Board.

AEIB = Alien Enemy Information Bureau.

AHS = A. H. Stark, Chief Supply Officer, KIC.

AN = Accession Number.

APA = Asian Pacific American.

ARM = Captain Antonio R. Martin, Spanish Vice Consul.

ARP = Ardith R. Pugh, Staff Assistant, CWRIC, Washington, DC.

Asst. = Assistant.

Attn. = Attention.

BHF = Bert H. Fraser, OICFM.

BJF = B. J. Finch, District Engineer, USBPR, Ogden, UT.

Box 2059 = Civilian [Alien] Internee Case Files, 1941-1945.

Box 2402 = Interpreter, Japanese, Employment of.

Box 2405 = Supplies for Internment Camps.

Box 2406 = Correspondence to and from Alien Enemy Detainees.

Box 2409 = Correspondence Re: Censorship of Mail and International Phone Calls.

Box 2412 = Alien Enemy Funds, Regulations Pertaining to.

Box 2436 = INS Records/Inspection Reports Re: Visits to Detention Facilities.

Box 2438 = Involuntary Repatriation of Alien Enemies from Latin America.

Box 2451 = Contracts, Expenses, Utilities, etc., KIC.

BP = Bureau of Prisons.

BPR = "Basic Personnel Record (Alien Enemy or Prisoner of War)."

c. = circa.

cc. = carbon copy.

CCC = Civilian Conservation Corps.

CCE = Charles C. Eberhardt, Special War Problems Division, Department of State, Washington, DC.

CCIC = Crystal City Internment Camp, Crystal City, TX.

CEW = C. E. Waller, Chief Budget and Fiscal Control Section (place not given).

CFH = C. F. Hiser, Senior Clerk, BP, USDJ, Federal Prison Camp, Kooskia, ID.

CH = Conrad Hoffmann Jr., War Prisoners Aid of the YMCA, New York, NY.

CHPW = Camp Harmony "Assembly Center," Puyallup, WA.

CINS = Commissioner, INS, Philadelphia, PA.

CLB = Clarence L. Belt, Attorney at Law, Los Angeles, CA.

CLCF = Closed Legal Case File.

CNFSO = Clearwater National Forest Supervisor's Office, Orofino, ID.

C/o, c/o = In care of.

CO = Central Office, INS, Philadelphia, PA.

CoS/AE = Change of Status, Alien Enemy.

CoS/DAE = Change of Status, Detained Alien Enemy.

CoS/DEA = Change of Status, Detained Enemy Alien.

CSW = C. S. Webb, Acting Regional Forester [Missoula, MT].

CWRIC = Commission on Wartime Relocation and Internment of Civilians.

DA = Dave Aldridge, KIC (title not given).

DA-AcOICKIC = Dave Aldridge, Acting OIC of Alien Detentions, KIC.

DA-AsOICKIC = Dave Aldridge, Assistant OIC of Alien Detentions, KIC.

DA-OICKIC = Dave Aldridge, OIC of Alien Detentions, KIC.

DAR = D. A. Remer, OIC, KIC.

DJ = Department of Justice.

DJG = D. J. Griffin, FBI, San Francisco, CA.

DJH = D. J. Hale, Chief Supply Officer, FLIC.

DSL = Daniel S. Lane, District Parole Officer, USDJ, INS (place not given).

E271 = Entry 271, Records of Enemy Alien Internment Facilities, World War II, Miscellaneous Records 1942-1945.

E291 = Entry 291, Records of Enemy Alien Internment Facilities, World War II, Fort Missoula, MT, General Files, 1942-1945.

E303 = Entry 303, Detainees, General Treatment, General Files, 1942-1945, Kenedy, TX.

E306 = Entry 306, Detainees, memos to, #1, Index to General Files, 1942-1945, Old Raton Ranch Camp, Fort Stanton, NM.

E465 = "Sailing List - Japanese Embarked for Second Voyage of *Gripsholm* - New York - September 2, 1943."

E466F = Entry 466F, Records Relating to Japanese Civilian Internees during World War II, 1942-1946.

EDD = E. D. Dickinson, Chairman, Alien Enemy Repatriation Hearing Board, Santa Fe, NM.

EGH = Earl G. Harrison, Commissioner, USDJ, INS, Philadelphia, PA.

EJC = Edwin J. Clapp, Jr., FLIC.

EJE = Edward J. Ennis, Director, AECU, USDJ, Washington, DC.

EJM = Emilio J. Morelli, Acting OIC, KIC.

EJO = Edward J. O'Connor, member; Alien Enemy Repatriation Hearing Board, Santa Fe, NM.

EMS = Edgar M. Scott, Jr. MD, Assistant Surgeon (Retired), USPHS, Medical OICFM.

EVA = Earl V. Adams, MD, Acting Assistant Surgeon, USPHS, OICFM.

EWK = Evan W. Kelley, Regional Forester, USDA, Northern Region, Missoula, MT.

FB = Francis Biddle, Attorney General, Washington, DC.

FBI = Federal Bureau of Investigation.

FdA = F. de Amat, Consul of Spain, San Francisco, CA.

FFT = Frank F. Thweatt, Jr., Senior Surgeon, Assistant Chief, Hospital Division, Federal Security Agency, USPHS, Washington, DC.

Fiset = Louis Fiset kindly provided Wegars with photocopies of many KIC documents that he obtained when working on his book, *Imprisoned Apart: The World War II Correspondence of an Issei Couple* (Seattle: University of Washington, 1997). Subsequently, Wegars relocated many of these in the National Archives; those she did not find are credited to Fiset.

FLD = Frank L. Davis, Senior Officer Special, KIC.

FLD-KIC = Frank L. Davis, Acting Internal Security Officer, KIC.

FLIC = Fort Lincoln Internment Camp, Bismarck, ND.

Fluharty = Photocopy kindly provided by Janie Fluharty.

FMB = Francis M. Burns, FMIC (title not given).

FMB-AcOICFM = Francis M. Burns, Acting OIC, FMIC.

FMB-AsOICFM = Francis M. Burns, Assistant OIC, FMIC.

FMIC = Fort Missoula Internment Camp, Missoula, MT.

FN = File Number.

FVB = Frank V. Brown, Assistant Surgeon (Retired), USPHS, Medical OICFM.

FVF = Frederick V. Follmer, United States Attorney, Lewisburg, PA.

GHA = George H. Asdell, FBI (place not given).

GT = Gardiner Turrill, member, USDJ, Alien Enemy Special Hearing Board, and Junior Vice President, California Bank, Los Angeles, CA.

HCD = Hamilton C. Dowell, FBI, Seattle, WA.

HKB = H. K. Bishop, Chief, Division of Construction, Federal Works Agency, Public Roads Administration, Washington, DC.

HMK = Harry M. Kimball, FBI, USDJ, Washington, DC.

HVS = Henry V. Stallings, Acting OICFM.

IBA = "Invitation, Bid, and Acceptance (Short Form Contract)."

IC = Internment Camp.

IN = Invitation Number.

INS = Immigration and Naturalization Service.

IPM = I. P. McCoy, OIC, FLIC.

IW = Ivan Williams, OIC, INS, SFIC.

JA = John Atkinson, FBI, New York, NY.

JACL = Japanese American Citizens League.

JAK = J. A. Koppang, Financial Officer, FMIC.

JANM = Japanese American National Museum.

JCD = J. Charles Dennis, United States Attorney, USDJ, Western District of Washington, Seattle, WA.

JDC = James D. Crawford, Relocation Program Officer (place not given).

JGH = John G. Hunter, Relocation Adviser, Colorado River War Relocation Project, Poston, AZ.

JHT = James H. Terry, member, Alien Enemy Repatriation Hearing Board, Santa Fe, NM.

JLA = Japanese Latin Americans.

JLO = J. L. O'Rourke, District Director or OIC, CCIC.

JLS = John L. Slattery, Chairman, AEHB, Northern District of California.

JP(1) = John Penery, Relocation Division, Washington, DC.

JP(2) = Joseph Prendergast, Assistant Chief, Civil Defense Section, Special Defense Unit (place not given).

JPL = Julian P. Langston, Chief Internal Security Officer (place not given).

JPO = James P. O'Connor, FBI (place not given).

JPOHP = Japanese Peruvian Oral History Project.

JS = Joseph Savoretti, Deputy Commissioner/Assistant Commissioner for Adjudication, USDJ, INS, Washington, DC.

JWG = J. W. Gillmore, Resident Project Engineer, USBPR.

JWP = J. W. Pehle, Assistant to the Secretary, Treasury Department, Washington, DC.

KIC = Kooskia Internment Camp, USDJ, INS, Kooskia, ID.

KR = Karl Roenke, Forest Archaeologist, CNFSO.

LAF = Lloyd A. Fortune, Chief Supply Officer, FMIC.

LBS = Lemuel B. Schofield, Special Assistant to the Attorney General, USDJ, INS, Philadelphia, PA.

LDKRS = Lochsa District, Kooskia Ranger Station, Kooskia, ID.

LHJ = Loyd H. Jensen, OIC or Acting OIC, INS, SFIC.

LRB = Ludwig R. Borovicka, MD (Italian internee physician), USPHS, KIC.

LW = Loyd Wright, Chairman, Alien Enemy Special Hearing Board (place not given).

MAEIB = Memorandum for: Alien Enemy Information Bureau.

MG = Manuscript Group.

MHS = Merrill H. Scott, OIC, KIC.

MHS-OICTC = Merrill H. Scott, OIC, TC.

MSL = M. S. Lombard, MD., Medical Director, USPHS, Spokane, WA.

n. = Note.

N/A = Not applicable/Not available.

NARA I = National Archives and Records Administration, Washington, DC.

NARA II = National Archives at College Park, College Park, MD.

NCRR = National Coalition for Redress/Reparations [now Nikkei for Civil Rights & Redress].

N. d., n.d. = No date.

NDC = N. D. Collaer, Chief, Deportation and Detention Section, INS, Philadelphia, PA.

NDC-AcACAC = N. D. Collaer, Acting Assistant Commissioner for Alien Control, INS, Philadelphia, PA.

NNB = N. N. Blackwell, Chief, Detention, Deportation and Parole Section, USDJ, INS.

OIC = Officer in Charge.

OICFM = OIC, FMIC.

OICKIC = OIC, KIC.

OICSF = OIC, SFIC.

OPMG = Office of the Provost Marshal General, War Department, Washington, DC.

PMG = Provost Marshal General, Washington, DC.

PMO = Perry M. Oliver, Director of Administrative Services, USDJ, INS, Philadelphia, PA.

PRM = P. R. McLaughlin, Acting Supervisor of Alien Detentions, USDJ, INS, FMIC.

PS = Paul Schnyder, Assistant to the Delegate, International Committee of the Red Cross, Geneva, Switzerland, Delegation to the United States of America, Washington, DC.

PSK = Paul S. Kashino, official censor, translator, and interpreter, FMIC; interpreted, censored, copied, excerpted, and/or translated the original communication.

RG60 = Record Group 60, General Records of the USDJ, NARA II.

RG65 = Record Group 65, Records of the FBI, NARA II.

RG85 = Record Group 85, Records Related to the Detention and Internment of Enemy Aliens during World War II, Records of the INS, NARA I.

RG389 = Record Group 389, Records of the OPMG, NARA II.

RGP = Ray Garrett Phillips, FBI, New York, NY.

RH = Ralph Hutchins, Colonel, Quartermaster Corps, and Commanding Officer, Fort George G. Meade, MD.

RHA = R. H. Armstrong, Canyon Creek Prison Camp, Kooskia, ID.

RLF = R. L. Flanders, FBI (place not given).

RRM = R. R. Mitchell, Senior Highway Engineer, USBPR, Ogden, UT.

SAAG = Special Assistant to the Attorney General, INS, Philadelphia, PA.

Sato = Photocopy kindly provided by Tad Sato.

Scrapbook = Kooskia Internment Camp Scrapbook, Historical Photograph Collection, University of Idaho Library.

SFIC = Santa Fe Internment Camp, Santa Fe, NM.

SFN33 = U.S. Standard Form No. 33 (Revised), "Invitation, Bid, and Acceptance (Short Form Contract)."

SFN36 = Standard Form No. 36, "Standard Government Form of Continuation Schedule for Standard Form 31 or 33 (Supplies)."

SFN1036 = Standard Form No. 1036-Revised, "Statement and Certificate of Award."

SFPC = Superintendent, Federal Prison Camp [Canyon Creek Prison Camp], Kooskia, ID.

SFT = Sterling F. Tremayne, FBI, Seattle, WA.

TC = Tuna Canyon Detention Station, Tujunga, CA.

TCC = Tom C. Clark, U.S. Attorney General, USDJ, Washington, DC.

TE = Tish Erb, Assistant City Editor, *Lewiston Morning Tribune*, Lewiston, ID.

TMC = Thomas M. Cooley, II, Director, Alien Enemy Control Unit.

TRM = T. R. Martinez, Chief, Investigation and Deportation Section, USDJ, INS, Philadelphia, PA.

UC = Ugo Carusi, Commissioner of Immigration, Philadelphia, PA.

USBPR = U.S. Bureau of Public Roads.

USDA = U.S. Department of Agriculture.

USDJ = U.S. Department of Justice.

USPHS = U.S. Public Health Service.

WCCA = Wartime Civil Control Administration, San Francisco, CA.

WCW = Walter C. Wood, KIC (title not given).

WCW-AcOICKIC = Walter C. Wood, Acting OIC, KIC.

WCW-AcAsOICKIC = Walter C. Wood, Acting Assistant OIC, KIC.

WCW-AsOICKIC = Walter C. Wood, Assistant OIC, KIC.

WFK = W. F. Kelly, Assistant Commissioner for Alien Control, USDJ, INS, Philadelphia, PA.

WFK-BP = W. F. Kelly, Chief Supervisor, U.S. Border Patrol, INS, Philadelphia, PA.

WFM = W. F. Miller, Acting Assistant Commissioner for Alien Control, or Chief of Border Patrol Section, Philadelphia, PA.

WHW = W. H. Wagner, Assistant to Director of INS, FMIC.

WJK = William J. Keenan, Medical Technical Assistant, USPHS, KIC.

WMC = Wayne M. Collins, Attorney at Law, San Francisco, CA.

WRA = War Relocation Authority.

WRB-AcOICKIC = W. R. Beecher, Acting OIC. KIC.

WTH = W. T. Hammack, Assistant Director, BP (place not given).

WY = Whitney Young, Department of State, Washington, DC.

YMCA = Young Men's Christian Association.

Endnotes

For abbreviations, see pages 215 to 222.

Foreword

1. In contrast to the U.S., where people born in Japan were forbidden from becoming naturalized citizens until the law changed in 1952, Japanese immigrants in Canada could apply for Canadian (British) citizenship after three years' residency.

Preface

1. Author's recollection of the question posed to an invited speaker at Washington State University, probably late 1996 or early 1997. Had I realized that comment would provide the impetus for a decade of research, I would have documented it more carefully at the time.

2. Author's recollection of the speaker's response. Following publicity about the camp in local newspapers, the original questioner telephoned and thanked me for validating her memory. The original speaker is now aware of the Kooskia camp.

3. The former Immigration and Naturalization Service (INS) is now part of the Department of Homeland Security.

4. Kooskia is a contraction of a Nez Perce word related to the local rivers, see Cort Conley, *Idaho for the Curious* (Cambridge, ID: Backeddy Books, 1982), 127, and Lalia Boone, *Idaho Place Names: A Geographical Dictionary* (Moscow, ID: University of Idaho, 1988), 212, for contradictory meanings. The town of Kooskia, today a community of some seven hundred persons at the confluence of the Middle Fork and the South Fork of the Clearwater River, is about thirty miles west of the former Kooskia Internment Camp. Although the camp was actually several miles east of the hamlet of Lowell, it was named after the larger community, probably because Kooskia, on the railroad, was the closest real town.

5. Yoshito Kadotani, KIC, to Sanzo Aso, SFIC, May 28, 1943; E291,1000/K(2), RG85, NARA I, PSK.

6. [Kooskia internees] to BHF, July 7, 1943, [3]; E291, RG85, NARA I, Fiset, PSK.

7. Information on the CCC in northern Idaho is available in various issues of the *Kamiah (ID) Progress* and the *Kooskia (ID) Mountaineer* between early May and mid-October 1933, and in the *Tree Troopers' Tattler* (Lewiston, ID, District Headquarters, Civilian Conservation Corps), July and August 1933, photocopy at Idaho State Historical Society Library and Archives, Boise. CCC Camp F-38, at the confluence of Canyon Creek with the Lochsa River, housed nearly two hundred recruits from New York State. Life at the Canyon Creek Prison Camp is detailed in various issues

of the *Lochsa (ID) Pioneer*, an inmate publication produced at the camp between November 1939 and August 1941. Ludwig (Lud) Freier's article "Bitter-Loot [*sic*; probably a pun] Trail," in *Lochsa (ID) Pioneer* 1:8 (June 1940), 30, was reprinted as "Bitter-Root Trail" by the Nez Perce County Historical Society, Lewiston, ID, in *The Golden Age* 26:1 (Spring/Summer 2006), 15-18.

8. The exact number is not certain because available lists are incomplete. Several men suspected of being confined at the Kooskia Internment Camp could not be located in records at the National Archives in Washington, DC, or College Park, MD.

9. For a list of the INS and U.S. Army camps, see Asian American Comparative Collection, The Kooskia Internment Camp Project, "Justice Department and U.S. Army Internment Camps and Detention Stations in the U.S. during World War II," available at http://www.uiweb.uidaho.edu/LS/AACC/JusticeCampsWWII.htm (accessed November 17, 2009).

10. The Nez Perce Trail is also called the Nee-Mee-Poo or Nimipuu ["The People"] Trail.

11. Johnny Johnson, "'The Time Had Come to Celebrate End of the 'Missing Link,'" *The Golden Age* 16:1 (Spring/Summer 1996), 11.

12. Ralph S. Space, *The Clearwater Story: A History of the Clearwater National Forest* ([Missoula, MT]: USDA Forest Service, Northern Region, 1979), 72.

13. *Lewiston (ID) Morning Tribune*, 'Prison Labor Helped Open Canyon Route,' in "Lewis & Clark Highway Edition," August 19, 1962, sec. 2, p. 22.

14. *Kamiah (ID) Progress*, "Interest Shown in Lewis-Clark Route," 33:28 (May 26, 1938), 1.

15. Freier, "Bitter-Loot Trail" and his "Bitter-Root Trail."

16. Harry K. Honda, "A Personal Search of the Public Archives Uncovers Lives of WWII Japanese Canadians," draft typescript, April 22, 2000, prepared for the U.S. Nisei visiting Canada, copy in AACC, and Yon Shimizu, *The Exiles: An Archival History of the World War II Japanese Road Camps in British Columbia and Ontario* (Wallaceburg, ON: Shimizu Consulting and Publishing, 1993).

17. There is an extensive literature on this topic, e.g., Barry Broadfoot, *Years of Sorrow, Years of Shame: The Story of Japanese Canadians in World War II* (Toronto, ON: Doubleday Canada, 1977), and Bill Waiser, *Park Prisoners: The Untold Story of Western Canada's National Parks, 1915-1946* (Saskatoon, SK: Fifth House, 1995). As one writer noted, Canada's removal of Japanese Canadians from the West Coast began in January 1942 "and may have had a decisive influence on the [U.S.] War Department's decision to proceed similarly ... but, in many ways, discriminatory measures imposed on the Canadian Japanese were more arbitrary and severe," Michi Weglyn, *Years of Infamy: The Untold Story of America's Concentration Camps* (New York: William Morrow, 1976), 56. Canada's harsher actions included confiscation and sale of people's property and belongings, since the Canadian Japanese actually had to help pay for their confinement. Although the war ended in 1945, they were forbidden to return to British Columbia until March 1949, ibid., 57.

18. Thanks to Micheal Moshier for calling his father's album to my attention. The album, called a "scrapbook" because it includes two drawings in addition to the photographs, is now housed in the University of Idaho Library Special Collections, with the call number PG 103. The photographer, who is unknown, could have been an employee or even an internee; two internees were former photographers. To view all the items in the scrapbook, visit "Kooskia Internment Camp Scrapbook," University of Idaho

Library Digital Collections, available at http://contentdm.lib.uidaho.edu/cdm4/browse.php?CISOROOT=/spec_kic (accessed February 16, 2010).

19. See Asian American Comparative Collection, The Kooskia Internment Camp Project, "Obtaining Department of Justice (DOJ) Closed Legal Case Files (CLCF) from the National Archives and Records Administration (NARA)," available at http://www.uiweb.uidaho.edu/LS/AACC/CLCF.htm (accessed November 17, 2009).

20. E.g., Lillian Baker, *American and Japanese Relocation in World War II: Fact, Fiction, & Fallacy* (Medford, OR: Webb Research Group, 1990); Michelle Malkin, *In Defense of Internment: The Case for 'Racial Profiling' in World War II and the War on Terror* (Washington, DC: Regnery, 2004).

21. See James Hirabayashi, "'Concentration Camp' or 'Relocation Center:' What's in a Name?," *Japanese American National Museum Quarterly* 9:3 (Autumn 1994), 5-10, and Roger Daniels, "Words Do Matter: A Note on Inappropriate Terminology and the Incarceration of the Japanese Americans," in *Nikkei in the Pacific Northwest: Japanese Americans and Japanese Canadians in the Twentieth Century,* ed. Louis Fiset and Gail M. Nomura (Seattle: Center for the Study of the Pacific Northwest in association with University of Washington Press, 2005), 190-214.

22. Greg Robinson, *By Order of the President: FDR and the Internment of Japanese Americans* (Cambridge, MA: Harvard University, 2001), 56-57, 61.

23. Ibid., 61.

24. Ibid., 131.

25. Ibid., 2, citing Press and Radio Conference #982, November 21, 1944, FDR Library. Robinson provides several more instances where the term was used by Roosevelt and other government officials, 65-69, 75, 88-89, 133, 191, 203. Idaho politicians also used similar rhetoric. In March 1942, Idaho Governor Chase A. Clark stated, "I have urged that Japanese who may be sent here be placed under guard and confined in concentration camps for the safety of our people, of our state, and the Japanese themselves," Chase A. Clark, letter to editor, "Clark Defends Stand on Aliens," *Kamiah (ID) Progress* 37:17 (March 19, 1942), 1. Incarceration was ordered despite the official government belief, prior to Pearl Harbor, that the Issei (first generation Japanese immigrants) were "weakened in their loyalty to Japan by the fact that they have chosen to make this their home and have brought up their children here," and found the Nisei (U.S.-born second-generation of Japanese descent) "pathetically eager" to show their loyalty to the U.S., Robinson, *By Order of the President*, 67.

26. As legal scholar Natsu Taylor Saito points out, however, "death camps and concentration camps ... [are] distinct phenomena" because they "not only had fundamentally different missions (liquidation versus confinement or forced labor) but were situated in different locations and operated under separate administrative structures," Natsu Taylor Saito, *From Chinese Exclusion to Guantánamo Bay: Plenary Power and the Prerogative State* (Boulder: University Press of Colorado, 2007), 59. All the death camps were in occupied Poland, whereas the nearly two hundred concentration camps were mostly within Nazi Germany, ibid. Although the notorious Dachau was a concentration camp rather than a death camp, the death rate there was still 36 percent, ibid., 270-271n58.

27. Some have argued, convincingly, that the term "concentration camp" is now so associated with Nazi Germany's World War II concentration camps that it can no longer be used in any other way, e. g., Daniels, "Words Do Matter," 204-205, citing historian Alice Yang Murray. For additional discussion of this topic, see Karen L. Ishizuka, *Lost*

and Found: Reclaiming the Japanese American Incarceration (Urbana: University of Illinois, 2006), 11-13.

28. Christopher Smith, "Park Service Asks to Cut 'Internment' from WWII Prison Camp Name," *Moscow-Pullman (ID-WA) Daily News* 91:148 (June 24-25, 2007), 7A.

29. Densho: The Japanese American Legacy Project, available at http://www.densho. org/; see particularly "A Note on Terminology," available at http://www.densho. org/default.asp?path=/assets/sharedpages/glossary.asp?section=home (accessed November 4, 2009), and *Densho: The Japanese American Legacy Project, 2006 Annual Report* (Seattle: Densho), [3].

30. Smith, "Park Service." The name changed to Minidoka National Historic Site in May 2008 per Sec. 313c of the Consolidated Natural Resources Act of 2008.

31. Ibid.

32. Only one other group of internees, at Lordsburg, New Mexico, used the Geneva Convention to such great advantage; they held a successful strike to protest a violation of it, Yasutaro Soga, *Life Behind Barbed Wire: The World War II Internment Memoirs of a Hawai'i Issei* (Honolulu: University of Hawai'i, 2008), 76. The Lordsburg camp superintendent was ultimately replaced, Tetsuden Kashima, "Introduction," in Soga, *Life Behind Barbed Wire*, 8.

33. Gerald R. Ford, *Presidential Proclamation 4417* rescinding EO9066, available at http://www.ford.utexas.edu/LIBRARY/SPEECHES/760111p.htm (accessed November 17, 2009).

34. Asian American Comparative Collection, available at http://www.uiweb.uidaho. edu/LS/AACC/ (accessed November 17, 2009).

35. E.g., Priscilla Wegars, ed., *Hidden Heritage: Historical Archaeology of the Overseas Chinese* (Amityville, NY: Baywood. 1993).

36. E.g., Priscilla Wegars, *Polly Bemis: A Chinese American Pioneer* (Cambridge, ID: Backeddy, 2003).

37. In Japanese, the phrase is *nidoto nai yoni*, Ken Mochizuki, "Bainbridge Island Memorial: Let It Not Happen Again," *International Examiner (Seattle, WA)* 33:7 (April 5-18, 2006), 4.

38. Moustafa Bayoumi, "Choose the Wrong Faith, and Go Directly to Jail," *Lewiston (ID) Tribune*, July 2, 2006, 4F.

39. Ibid.

40. In September 2007 the Islamic Cultural Center of Fresno (ICCF) presented the Japanese American Citizens League (JACL) with a "Spirit of Abraham Award" "for its defense of Muslim Americans' civil rights in the aftermath of the Sept. 11th terrorist attacks," *Pacific Citizen (Los Angeles, CA)*, "APAs in the News," "JACL to be Honored with Spirit Award," 146:5 (September 7-20, 2007), 5. Subsequently, in the spring of 2008, the ICCF presented its "Voices of Courage Award" to Floyd Mori, national executive director and former president of the JACL, for "speaking out against racial profiling of Muslim and Arab Americans following 9/11," Islamic Cultural Center of Fresno, Media Coverage about ICCF, "JACL Director Honored by Islamic Cultural Center," from Hokubei.com, May 8, 2008, available at http://www.icfresno. org/multimedia/04e.htm (accessed December 22, 2009).

41. Amnesty International USA, "Threat and Humiliation: Racial Profiling, National Security, and Human Rights in the United States," available at http://www. amnestyusa.org/us-human-rights/other/rp-report----threat-and-humiliation/page. do?id=1106664 (accessed November 17, 2009).

42. Tom Henderson, "Evil Spirits of 1941 Still Hovering over America," *Lewiston (ID) Tribune*, July 10, 2006, 8A.

Chapter One: Anti-Japanese Attitudes: Foreshadowing Japanese American Internment and Incarceration

1. The chief need for a road in this remote location was to shorten the distance between Fort Missoula, Montana, and Portland, Oregon/Vancouver, Washington, and facilitate transportation to the Puget Sound area; see D. Worth Clark, John Thomas, Compton I. White, Henry C. Dworshak, Walter M. Pierce, and Homer D. Angell to Honorable Harry H. Woodring, Secretary of War, February 5, 1940, with attached Memorandum for U.S. War Department Concerning Lewis and Clark Highway, by M. A. Means, President, Lewiston Chamber of Commerce, Lewiston, Idaho; 1000/K(4), E291, RG85, NARA I. Clark (D) and Thomas (R) were Idaho's U.S. Senators, while White (D) and Dworshak (R) were Idaho's two delegates to the U.S. House of Representatives. Angell and Pierce represented Oregon in the U.S. House of Representatives, Terry Abraham, comp., *A Union List of the Papers of Members of Congress from the Pacific Northwest* (Pullman, WA: Washington State University Library, 1976), 9, 46. See also Woodring's reply, Harry H. Woodring, Secretary of War, War Department, Washington to Honorable Compton I. White, House of Representatives, February 17, 1940; 1000/K(4), E291, RG85, NARA I; *Kamiah (ID) Progress*, "L-C Highway Gets Important Boost," 35:14 (February 22, 1940), 1.

2. Naturalization was legally closed to immigrants of Asian descent through the provisions of the Naturalization Act of 1790, amended in 1870 and upheld by a 1922 U.S. Supreme Court decision, John Joel Culley, "Enemy Alien Control in the United States during World War II: A Survey," in *Alien Justice: Wartime Internment in Australia and North America*, ed. Kay Saunders and Roger Daniels (St. Lucia, Queensland, Australia: University of Queensland, 2000), 138. Naturalization only applied to "free white" persons who had lived in the U.S. for at least two years, Library of Congress, "A Century of Lawmaking for a New Nation: U.S. Congressional Documents and Debates, 1774 - 1875," Statutes at Large, 41st Congress, 2nd Session, 103-104, 'An Act to establish an [*sic*] uniform Rule of Naturalization,' available at http://memory.loc.gov/cgi-bin/ampage?collId=llsl&fileName=001/llsl001.db&recNum=226 (accessed November 5, 2009). In 1868 U.S.-born African-Americans gained citizenship under Section 1 of the 14th Amendment to the Constitution, "All persons born or naturalized in the United States, ... are citizens of the United States ... ," Wikipedia: The Free Encyclopedia, "Fourteenth Amendment to the United States Constitution," available at http://en.wikipedia.org/wiki/Fourteenth_Amendment_to_the_United_ States_Constitution (accessed November 5, 2009). African-Americans born in Africa were added to the naturalization laws in 1870; see Library of Congress, "Century of Lawmaking," 254-256, 'An Act to amend the Naturalization Laws and to punish Crimes against the same, and for other Purposes,' available at http://memory.loc. gov/cgi-bin/ampage?collId=llsl&fileName=016/llsl016.db&recNum=289 (accessed November 5, 2009). Section 7 states, "*And be it further enacted,* That the naturalization laws are hereby extended to aliens of African nativity and to persons of African descent." There was no need to mention "whites" in this document because they were covered by the Naturalization Act of 1790. Similarly, the law does not mention Asians; they continued to be excluded because they were neither "white" nor "African."

In 1943 the repeal of the 1882 Chinese Exclusion Act allowed U.S. residents born in China to become naturalized. For Japanese-born aliens, naturalization did not become possible until passage of the 1952 McCarran-Walter Immigration Act.

3. For a lengthy discussion of this topic, with reference to anti-Japanese alien land laws, see Chapters 4 and 5 in Roger Daniels, *Asian America: Chinese and Japanese in the United States since 1850* (Seattle: University of Washington, 1988), 100-155.

4. Culley, "Enemy Alien Control," 144.

5. Franklin D. Roosevelt, *Executive Order 9066*, available at http://www.foitimes.com/internment/EO9066.html (accessed November 5, 2009).

6. Michi Weglyn, *Years of Infamy: The Untold Story of America's Concentration Camps* (New York: William Morrow, 1976), 71-72.

7. Franklin D. Roosevelt, *Executive Order 9102*, available at http://www.nps.gov/manz/eo9102.htm (accessed November 5, 2009).

8. Military Areas No. 1 and No. 2, established on March 2, 1942, included, in No. 1, the western halves of Washington, Oregon, and California, together with the southern half of Arizona, whereas No. 2 comprised the eastern halves of the first three states, Robert C. Sims, "The 'Free Zone' Nikkei: Japanese Americans in Idaho and Eastern Oregon in World War II," in *Nikkei in the Pacific Northwest*, ed. Fiset and Nomura, 251n3. Only Californians were subsequently removed from their state's Military Area No. 2, CWRIC, *Personal Justice Denied: Report of the Commission on Wartime Relocation and Internment of Civilians*, foreword by Tetsuden Kashima (Washington, DC: Civil Liberties Public Education Fund and Seattle, University of Washington, 1997), 107, 111-112. Military Areas Nos. 3 through 6, from which Japanese Americans were not removed, were Idaho, Montana, Nevada, and Utah, respectively, U. S. Army, *Public Proclamation No. 2* (San Francisco: Headquarters Western Defense Command and Fourth Army, 1942), 2. The Japanese American citizens living in other states were also not threatened with incarceration.

9. Sims, "'Free Zone' Nikkei," 236, 242, 244. The more than nine hundred "restricted areas" in eight western states were places near "strategic" installations such as airports, bridges, canals, dams, radio stations, sawmills, tunnels, and other facilities vulnerable to imagined "sabotage"; people of Japanese descent were not allowed to live in the vicinity. Even in states where Japanese Americans were not sent to incarceration camps, some were forced to move because their homes and businesses were in areas labeled "restricted."

10. The usual number given for the World War II WRA incarceration of Japanese Americans and Japanese resident aliens is 120,313 people, CWRIC, *Personal Justice Denied*, 150. However, except for 1,735 individuals who transferred into WRA camps from INS camps, that total does not account for the 17,477 people of Japanese descent who were held by the INS for the Justice Department, Tetsuden Kashima, *Judgment without Trial: Japanese American Imprisonment during World War II* (Seattle: University of Washington, 2003), 124-125. Some of the latter number, especially renunciants from the continental U.S., may also be counted in the WRA total of 120,313. Actual numbers may never be conclusively known.

11. CWRIC, *Personal Justice Denied*, 112.

12. Kanshi Stanley Yamashita, "The Saga of the Japanese Americans: 1870-1942," *American Baptist Quarterly* 13:1 (March 1994), 4.

13. CWRIC, *Personal Justice Denied*, 150. Thirteen were in California, and with one each in Arizona, Oregon, and Washington, 137. This source provides names of

the "assembly centers," their maximum populations, and the dates they were oc-cupied, 138. Former inmates testified to the deplorable living conditions in these facilities, 138-139. "Military control of the Western Defense Command [WDC] Area (Arizona, California, Idaho, Montana, Nevada, Oregon, Utah, and Washington) was established in March 1942 by Executive Order 9066. The WDC at first tried to implement a voluntary evacuation of Japanese-Americans. However, only about 5,000 of the approximately 120,000 Japanese-Americans living in the affected area agreed to evacuate. The WDC then created the Wartime Civil Control Administra-tion [WCCA] to enforce a mandatory evacuation through the issuance of a series of exclusion orders. The WDC was in charge of the initial evacuation of Japanese-Americans to temporary Assembly Centers, the operation of the centers, and the transfer of Japanese-Americans to permanent Relocation Centers operated by the War Relocation Authority. When internees reached the Relocation Centers, military jurisdiction ceased," National Archives and Records Administration (NARA), Japa-nese Americans during WWII: Relocation & Internment, "Check Military Records Related to the Relocation and Internment of Japanese-Americans during World War II," available at http://www.archives.gov/research/japanese-americans/military.html (accessed February 2, 2010).

14. James Masao Mitsui, *Crossing the Phantom River* (Port Townsend, WA: Graywolf, 1978), 31. Used with permission.

15. No administrative relationship existed between the INS's Kooskia Internment Camp, in north central Idaho, and the WRA's Minidoka incarceration camp, some four hundred miles away, near Twin Falls.

16. For some German Americans who did, see Arthur D. Jacobs, *The Prison Called Hohenasperg* (N.p.: Universal Publishers, 1999).

17. Roger Daniels, "The Conference Keynote Address: Relocation, Redress, and the Re-port, A Historical Appraisal," in *Japanese Americans: From Relocation to Redress*, ed. Roger Daniels, Sandra C. Taylor, and Harry H. L. Kitano (Salt Lake City: University of Utah, 1986), 6. See also discussion in Roger Daniels, "The Internment of Japanese Nationals in the United States during World War II," in *Halcyon* 17 (1995), 66.

18. U.S. Code, Section 21, Title 50, "An Act Respecting Alien Enemies," section 1, ap-proved July 6, 1798, United States Statutes at Large, available from The Avalon Project at http://avalon.law.yale.edu/18th_century/alien.asp (accessed November 5, 2009).

19. Paul Frederick Clark, "Those Other Camps: An Oral History Analysis of Japanese Alien Enemy Internment during World War II" (master's thesis, California State University, Fullerton, 1980), 6.

20. Kashima, *Judgment without Trial*, 29-32.

21. John J. Culley, "The Santa Fe Internment Camp and the Justice Department Program for Enemy Aliens," in *Japanese Americans*, ed. Daniels, Taylor, and Kitano, 57; Greg Robinson, *By Order of the President: FDR and the Internment of Japanese Americans* (Cambridge, MA: Harvard University, 2001), 64. The term "ABC lists" appears in two letters, dated December 2009, to the author from an FBI employee, so is the designation used here.

22. CWRIC, *Personal Justice Denied*, 54. Other sources give "top billing" to "fishermen, produce distributors, Shinto and Buddhist priests, farmers, influential business-men, and members of the Japanese Consulate," whereas suspects in Groups B and C included Japanese-language teachers, Kibeis, martial arts instructors, community servants, travel agents, social directors, and newspaper editors ... ," Bob Kumamoto, "The Search for Spies: American Counterintelligence and the Japanese American

Community 1931-1942," *Amerasia Journal* 6:2 (1979), 58; Robinson, *By Order of the President*, 64-65. As Kashima, *Judgment without Trial*, 29, explains, people on the "A" list were considered the most dangerous to national security, those on the "B" list were "less dangerous," and individuals on the "C" list were "least dangerous." Although Kumamoto is often cited for Buddhist clergy being on the "A" list, he may have inferred a person's placement on that list based on the order in which he or she was arrested, rather than from an actual list of names kept by the FBI. Otherwise, if Buddhist clergy were all on the "A" list, why was Reverend Hozen Seki not arrested until September 24, 1942? Confusingly, Peter Irons, *Justice at War* (Berkeley: University of California, 1993), 21-22 and 383n39, appears to cite <u>both</u> Kumamoto <u>and</u> CWRIC in the context of Buddhist clergy being on the "A" list.

23. Culley, "Santa Fe Internment Camp," 57.

24. Robinson, *By Order of the President*, 65.

25. In November 2009, I wrote a Freedom of Information/Privacy Act (FOIPA) request to the FBI to obtain the specific occupations on the individual lists. The information received was not conclusive; an appeal for more is pending.

26. Culley, "Santa Fe Internment Camp," 57; the Justice Department kept this information on punch cards.

27. E. P. Hutchinson and Ernest Rubin, "Estimating the Resident Alien Population of the United States," *Journal of the American Statistical Association* 42:239 (September 1947), 385. One source states, "Of the total number of registered aliens, 1,100,000 were classified as 'enemy aliens' [to mean that they were aliens of an enemy nation] at the outbreak of war on December 7, 1941," Arthur D. Jacobs, "Chronology - Suspicion, Arrest, and Internment: The War Years, Alien Registration Background," April 1, 1942, *The Freedom of Information Times*, available at http://www.foitimes. com/internment/chrono.htm (accessed November 4, 2009).

28. LBS by JS, November 27, 1941; AN85-58A734, FN56125/15, Box 2402 [possibly misfiled here], RG85, NARA I. The capital letters emphasized the personal and confidential nature of the communication.

29. CWRIC, *Personal Justice Denied*, 54; Culley, "Santa Fe Internment Camp," 58. The wording read, "alien enemies deemed dangerous to the public health or safety of the United States by the Attorney General or Secretary of War"; their property could also be confiscated, CWRIC, *Personal Justice Denied*, 54. Proclamations 2526 and 2527 referred to German and Italian aliens respectively, ibid., 370n25. Franklin D. Roosevelt's *Presidential Proclamation No. 2525, Alien Enemies - Japanese*, is available at http://www.foitimes.com/internment/Proc2525.html (accessed November 5, 2009).

30. Don Whitehead, *The FBI Story: A Report to the People* (New York: Random House, 1956), 183; no citation is provided.

31. A similar directive was issued the following day, December 8, ordering FBI agents to apprehend German and Italian aliens without regard to their list status, Arthur D. Jacobs, "Chronology," December 8, 1941.

32. Robinson, *By Order of the President*, 57.

33. Stephen S. Fugita and Marilyn Fernandez, "Religion and Japanese Americans' View of Their World War II Incarceration," *Journal of Asian American Studies* 5:2 (June 2002), 116. Two excellent studies of the internment of Buddhist clergy are Duncan Ryūken Williams, "Camp Dharma: Japanese-American Buddhist Identity and the Internment Experience of World War II," in *Westward Dharma: Buddhism beyond*

Asia, ed. Charles S. Prebish and Martin Baumann, 191-200 (Berkeley: University of California, 2002), and Williams' "Complex Loyalties: Issei Buddhist Ministers during the Wartime Incarceration," *Pacific World: Journal of the Institute of Buddhist Studies*, Third Series (5, 2003). I am grateful to Roger Daniels for suggesting Williams' articles.

34. Culley, "Santa Fe Internment Camp," 58; thanks to Stan Flewelling for helping me clarify this discussion.

35. Ibid.

36. CWRIC, *Personal Justice Denied*, 55.

37. Jerre Mangione, *An Ethnic at Large: A Memoir of America in the Thirties and Forties* (New York: G. P. Putnam's Sons, 1978), 320.

38. Kashima, *Judgment without Trial*, 124-125. Similar statistics are in a memo dated August 9, 1948, from W. F. Kelly, Assistant Commissioner, Immigration and Naturalization Service, to Mr. A. Vulliet, World Alliance of Young Men's Christian Associations, available at http://home.comcast.net/~eo9066/1948/IA102.html (accessed November 4, 2009). The numbers given there "of persons received by the Immigration and Naturalization Service under the alien enemy program, including those received from outside continental United States and those who were voluntarily interned in order to join the internee-head of the family," are Germany, 10,905; Japan, 16,849; Italy, 3,278; Hungary, 52; Romania, 25; Bulgaria, 5; other, 161.

39. Mangione, *Ethnic at Large*, 321. By due process, Mangione was referring to the Fifth Amendment to the Bill of Rights, part of the U.S. Constitution, which states that "No person shall ... be deprived of life, liberty, or property, without due process of law ... ." As one writer has observed, "this Amendment has been interpreted to mean that all individuals who are ... deprived of their civil liberties should have the opportunity to be heard prior to incarceration," Diane Matsuda, Director, California Civil Liberties Public Education Program, Sacramento, CA, letter to Tim Fought, ed., *Herald and News (Klamath Falls, OR)*, May 15, 2003, 2, AACC.

40. Bill Hosokawa, *Nisei: The Quiet Americans*, rev. ed. (Boulder: University Press of Colorado, 1992), 216.

41. Ibid.

42. Betty Arase Okamura, letter to author, May 29, 1998.

43. HCD, [report on] Shohei Arase, March 23, 1942; CLCF, Shohei Arase, 146-13-2-82-485; Stack 230/25/34/3, Box 701, RG60, NARA II; Okamura, letter.

44. HCD, [report on] Shohei Arase, March 23, 1942, 1-3.

45. Okamura, letter.

46. LBS, MAEIB, OPMG, "In Re: CoS/DEA," Arase, Shohei, March 21, 1942; CLCF, Shohei Arase.

47. Okamura, letter, citing information from her older sister, Hana Yamaguchi.

48. HCD, [report on] Shohei Arase, March 23, 1942, 3-4.

49. Ibid., 3, and Kumamoto, "The Search for Spies," 57-58.

50. USDJ, AEHB No. One, Western District of Washington, "In re The Detention of Shohei Arase," April 20, 1942; CLCF, Shohei Arase. Those who accused Arase of disloyalty, SE-249 on March 30, 1942, and SE-250 on April 9, 1942, "advised they had known subject personally for a substantial length of time, and that there was no question in their minds that he was definitely pro-Japanese in his sympathies," SFT, [Report], May 11, 1942; CLCF, Shohei Arase.

51. Yosh Shimoi, telephone conversation with author, November 13, 2003.

52. Brian Niiya, ed., "Inu," *Japanese American History: An A-to-Z Reference from 1868 to the Present* (New York: Facts on File, 1993), 177.

53. Kashima, *Judgment without Trial*, 23.

54. Ibid., 227n42.

55. Rikito (Rick) Momii, letter to author, answers to questions dated March 30, 1998. Ikken Momii had also authored a book on kendo (Japanese fencing) clubs; see chapter 6.

56. DJG, "Apprehension Report" for Kizaemon Ikken Momii, March 2, 1942, 2; CLCF, Kizaemon Ikken Momii, 146-13-2-11-32; Stack 230/25/2/5, Box 171; RG 60; NARA II.

57. LBS by JS, Memorandum for JP(2), "In re: CoS/DEA Kazaemon [*sic*] Nomii [*sic*]," December 30, 1941; CLCF, Kizaemon Ikken Momii.

58. Form 52, Medical Department, U.S.A. (Revised March 15, 1938), Register No. 34003, October 13, 1942; Entry 466F, Kizaemon Ikken Momii, RG389, NARA II.

59. Yasu Momii, e-mail to author, September 10, 2000. Mrs. Momii "had emergency surgery in camp. The surgery seemed to have been successful, but she died of complications." Ten days later, her death was reported in the Topaz camp newspaper simply as DEATH: MOMII--Mrs. Matsu Momii, [Block]5-[Barracks]8-[Room]E, age 44, 8:10 AM, Jan. 6, *Topaz (UT) Times/Weekly Saturday Times* 2:13 (January 16, 1943), 4.

60. EGH, MAEIB, OPMG, "In Re: CoS/DEA," August 3, 1942; CLCF, Kizaemon Ikken Momii.

61. "Memorandum for the Chief of the Review Section," February 24, 1943, 1; E291, 1016A, [misfiled at 1014/E], RG85, NARA I. Jeffrey F. Burton and others, *Confinement and Ethnicity: an Overview of World War II Japanese American Relocation Sites*, Publications in Anthropology, no. 74 (Tucson, AZ: Western Archeological and Conservation Center, National Park Service, U.S. Department of the Interior, 1999), 172-173, has more information on this incident.

62. "Memorandum," February 24, 1943, 2.

63. Burton and others, *Confinement and Ethnicity*, 172.

64. "Memorandum," February 24, 1943, 2-5, 14, and "Hearing of Sokichi Harry Hashimoto, Japanese Alien, Fort Missoula, Montana," December 10, 1943; both E291, 1016A, RG85, NARA I, and CLCF, Sokichi Harry Hashimoto, 146-13-2-12-4232; Stack 230/25/10/4, Box 200, RG60, NARA II.

65. EGH, MAEIB, OPMG, "In Re: CoS/DEA," March 24, 1943; CLCF, Sokichi Harry Hashimoto.

66. BHF to EJE, Attn. EJC, December 11, 1943; E291, 1016A, RG85, NARA I.

67. EGH, MAEIB, OPMG, "In Re: CoS/DEA," August 26, 1943; CLCF, Genji George Yamaguchi, 146-13-2-12-4230; Stack 230/25/10/4, Box 200, RG60, NARA II and EGH, MAEIB, OPMG, "In Re: CoS/DEA," April 10, 1944; CLCF, Sokichi Harry Hashimoto.

68. Kocho Fukuma, *A Spark of Dharma: The Life of Reverend Hozen Seki*, ed. Hoshin Seki (New York: American Buddhist Study Center, 2001), iv, 5, 36, 41, 74.

69. JA, "Hozen Seki," September 25, 1942, 1-2; CLCF, Hozen Seki, 146-13-2-51-2146; Stack 230/25/24/3, Box 490, RG60, NARA II.

70. Ibid., 10, 12.

71. Hozen Seki, [Diary], 1944-1948, front flyleaf. I am grateful to Hoshin Seki for providing a photocopy of his father's diary.

72. JA, "Hozen Seki," September 25, 1942, 12.

73. RGP, "Report," Hozen Seki, October 7, 1942; CLCF, Hozen Seki.

74. BPR, Seki, Hozen, December 7, 1942, 2; E466F, Seki, Hozen, RG389, NARA II, and Fukuma, *Spark of Dharma*, 47.

75. Fukuma, *Spark of Dharma*, 78.

76. Seki, [Diary], front flyleaf.

77. Kashima, *Judgment without Trial*, 125.

78. Marilyn George, "Tom Kito Looks Back: A Cannery Worker and Then Some," *Alaska Fisherman's Journal* (November 1996), sec. 2, p. 31; BPR, Kito, Tamakuju, January 14, 1942; E466F, Kito, Tom, RG389, NARA II.

79. George, "Tom Kito Looks Back," 31.

80. Marilyn George and Pamela Cravez. "Forced from Their Homes … Petersburg's Kitos Remember Prison Camps," *Senior Voice* (February 1990), 9; BPR, Kito, Tamakuju, January 14, 1942; E466F, Kito, Tom.

81. Marilyn George, "Petersburg's Oldest Citizen Looks Back on a Happy Life," *Alaskan Southeaster* (1996?), 11, and her "Tom Kito Looks Back," 32.

82. For general information on Hawaiian internees and their experiences, see Patsy Sumie Saiki, *Ganbare! An Example of Japanese Spirit* (Honolulu, HI: Kisaku, 1982). All of the Kooskia internees from Hawai'i, except Zenji Imakiire, are listed in her Appendix 3, 221-228. For an individual Hawaiian internee's experiences, see Yasutaro Soga, *Life Behind Barbed Wire: The World War II Internment Memoirs of a Hawai'i Issei* (Honolulu: University of Hawai'i, 2008).

83. Ibid., 30-31. There were also eleven Japanese females, mainly newspaperwomen or priestesses.

84. Ibid., 46-47, 73.

85. Ibid., 73-74.

86. Ibid., 80, 84.

87. Ibid., 87; e.g., Individual Pay Data Record, Civilian Enemy Alien or Prisoner of War, June 5, 1943; E466F, Uehara, Saburo, RG389, NARA II.

88. Saiki, *Ganbare!*, 100.

89. Ibid., 117-118, 179.

90. Roger Daniels gives a figure of 2,264 Latin American Japanese, "Internment of Japanese Nationals," 69. According to C. Harvey Gardiner, *The Japanese and Peru 1873-1973* (Albuquerque: University of New Mexico, 1975), 87, the countries participating in this outrage were Bolivia, Colombia, Costa Rica, the Dominican Republic, Ecuador, El Salvador, Guatemala, Haiti, Honduras, Nicaragua, Panama, and Peru. Thomas Connell, *America's Japanese Hostages: The World War II Plan for a Japanese Free Latin America* (Westport, CT: Praeger, 2002), 117, adds Mexico and Cuba to Gardiner's list. In an apparent contradiction, Gardiner states that "Honduras could find no Japanese in her roundup of Axis nationals," 88. The most complete work on this atrocity is Gardiner's later *Pawns in a Triangle of Hate* (Seattle: University of Washington, 1981). Other useful sources are Thomas Connell, III, "The Internment of Latin American Japanese in the United States during World War Two: The Peruvian Japanese Experience" (PhD diss., Florida State University, Tallahassee, 1995) and his *America's Japanese Hostages*. Additional information is in CWRIC,

"Latin Americans," in *Personal Justice Denied*, 305-314, and in Edward N. Barnhart, "Japanese Internees from Peru," *Pacific Historical Review* 31:2 (May 1962). A personal view of the experience is Seiichi Higashide, *Adios to Tears: The Memoirs of a Japanese-Peruvian Internee in U.S. Concentration Camps* (Honolulu, E&E Kudo, 1993; reprinted Seattle: University of Washington, 2000).

91. Kumamoto, "The Search for Spies," 48, Daniels, "Internment of Japanese Nationals," 69, and Greg Robinson, *A Tragedy of Democracy: Japanese Confinement in North America* (New York: Columbia University, 2009), 148, all mention fears for the safety of the Panama Canal as a factor in the expulsions. According to CWRIC, *Personal Justice Denied*, 307, "the model of the Latin American deportation and internment program was developed in Panama" prior to the U.S.'s entrance into World War II. Panama built an internment camp for enemy aliens, and the internees were later transferred to the U.S. "to be traded for Western Hemisphere nationals held in Japan," ibid.

92. Gardiner, *Japanese and Peru*, 87.

93. For a scholarly account of German Latin American internees, see Max Paul Friedman, *Nazis and Good Neighbors: The United States Campaign against the Germans of Latin America in World War II* (New York: Cambridge University Press, 2003). For a personal narrative about a German family deported from Costa Rica, see Heidi Gurcke Donald, *We Were Not the Enemy: Remembering the United States' Latin-American Civilian Internment Program of World War II* (New York, iUniversie, 2006). I am grateful to Karl Gurcke for calling my attention to both.

94. Gardner, *Pawns*, 69-70; Clifford Uyeda, "Japanese Peruvians and the U.S. Internment Camps," *Nikkei Heritage* 5:3 (Summer 1993), 4.

95. Connell, *America's Japanese Hostages*, 73.

96. Ibid., 100, 167.

97. E.g., Leah Brumer, "Stealing Home," *The East Bay Monthly* 29:2 (November 1998), 29.

98. Gardiner, *Japanese and Peru*, 87-88.

99. Gardiner, *Pawns*, 73; Arthur Shinei Yakabi, "My New Beautiful Country," manuscript (Papers of Arthur S. Yakabi, Research Library -- Historical Museum at Ft. Missoula, MT, 1978), 1-3.

100. For information on Panama's and Mexico's treatment of their Japanese residents, see Robinson, *Tragedy of Democracy*, 145-149.

101. Carol Bulger Van Valkenburg, *An Alien Place: The Fort Missoula, Montana, Detention Camp 1941-1944* (Missoula, MT: Pictorial Histories, 1995), 2.

102. John Christgau, *"Enemies": World War II Alien Internment* (Ames: Iowa State University, 1985), 20.

103. E.g., Asian American Comparative Collection, The Kooskia Internment Camp Project, "Justice Department and U.S. Army Internment Camps and Detention Stations in the U.S. during World War II," available at http://www.uiweb.uidaho.edu/LS/AACC/JusticeCampsWWII.htm (accessed November 5, 2009).

104. Clark, "Those Other Camps," 8.

105. Van Valkenburg, *Alien Place*, 2.

106. Clark, "Those Other Camps," 7.

107. Ibid. Because of these transfers of jurisdiction, information in the National Archives on former detained aliens can be found both in Justice Department/INS records and also in War Department/Provost Marshal General records. Record Group 60,

General Records of the Department of Justice, includes CLCFs for alien internees. They are housed in the National Archives at College Park, College Park, MD. Also at College Park is Record Group 389, Office of the Provost Marshal General; it includes Records Relating to Japanese Civilian Internees during World War II, 1942-1946.

108. Kashima, *Judgment without Trial*, 63; Clark, "Those Other Camps," 7.

109. Mangione, *Ethnic at Large*, 322; Charles I. Bevans, comp., "Prisoners of War," in *Treaties and Other International Agreements of the United States of America 1776-1949*, vol. 2, Multilateral, 1918-1930 (U.S. Government Printing Office, Washington, DC, 1969), "Geneva Convention," Article 2, 938. It was signed at Geneva, Switzerland, hence its shortened title, "Geneva Convention." Its exact title is "Convention of July 27, 1929, Relative to the Treatment of Prisoners of War," Bevans, *Treaties*, 932. For the text of the Geneva Convention, see http://www.icrc.org/IHL. nsf/52d68d14de6160e0c12563da005fdb1b/eb1571b00daec90ec125641e00402aa6?O penDocument (accessed July 30, 2009). The agreement to extend the Geneva Convention to internees was brokered by the Red Cross, which had the right to inspect the internment camps, Culley, "Enemy Alien Control," 140-141.

110. Mangione, *Ethnic at Large*, 323, and a clarification from Roger Daniels, e-mail to author, June 18, 2009.

111. Clark, "Those Other Camps," 8, Van Valkenburg, *Alien Place*, 3.

112. Van Valkenburg, *Alien Place*, 10.

113. Clark, "Those Other Camps," 8.

114. Culley, "Santa Fe Internment Camp," 58-59. It did not close permanently until May 1946.

115. Kashima, *Judgment without Trial*, 117.

116. Roger Daniels, "The Conference Keynote Address," 6.

117. Bevans, *Treaties*, 938, 940-941, 945-946.

118. Culley, "Santa Fe Internment Camp," 59; Tetsuden Kashima, "American Mistreatment of Internees during World War II: Enemy Alien Japanese," in *Japanese Americans: From Relocation to Redress*, ed. Roger Daniels, Sandra C. Taylor, and Harry H. L. Kitano (Salt Lake City: University of Utah, 1986), 54.

119. Kashima, "American Mistreatment of Internees," 54-56 and 56n21. Testimony in 1948 at the Japanese war crimes trials established that although Japan agreed to abide by the Geneva Convention, they did not intend to do so, using it, instead, "as a means to secure good treatment for Japanese who might become prisoners of war or be interned by the Allied Powers," Howard S. Levie, ed., "United States and Others v. Sadao Araki and Others (International Military Tribunal for the Far East [IMTFE], 4-12 November 1948)," in "Documents on Prisoners of War," Naval War College, Newport, RI, *International Law Studies* 60 (Newport, RI: Naval War College, 1979), 458-459; 465. Levie compares death rates of American and British POWs captured by the Italian and German forces (9,348 deaths or 4 percent of 235,473 POWs) vs. those in Japanese hands (35,756 deaths or 27 percent of 132,134 POWs), 440, and documents Japanese massacres of civilian internees; no Americans are mentioned among the latter, 444. For a Japanese American soldier's experiences in Japanese prison camps, see Frank Fujita, *Foo, A Japanese-American Prisoner of the Rising Sun: The Secret Prison Diary of Frank "Foo" Fujita* (Denton, TX: University of North Texas, 1993).

120. Hyung-ju Ahn, "Koreans as Interpreters at Japanese Enemy Alien Detention Centers during World War II," in *Guilt by Association: Essays on Japanese Settlement, Intern-*

ment, and Relocation in the Rocky Mountain West, ed. Mike Mackey (Powell, WY: Western History Publications, 2001), 108.

121. Ibid., 108-109. The four men were on temporary assignment from Fort Missoula to deal with "tougher cases" of supposedly "uncooperative internees," 107-108.

122. Ibid., 110-111. As a result of the investigation, the INS dismissed a third official, from Fort Missoula. For a more extensive account of the occurrence, see ibid., 107-111. Sumi's available files contain few mentions of the abuse, mostly allusions to it in the context of needing dental treatment as a result. Karl I. Zimmerman, Chief Supervisor of Immigration, interviewed Sumi about the incident at Fort Lincoln, Bismarck, North Dakota, on June 9, 1942. Sumi's complete testimony is provided as Appendix A in Hyung-ju Ahn, *Between Two Adversaries: Korean Interpreters at Japanese Alien Enemy Detention Centers during World War II* (Fullerton, CA: California State University, 2002), 85-99.

123. Teruko Teddy [Ogami], Section C, Block 2, Apt. 26, CHPW, to Teiichi Ogami, FMIC, May 12, 1942, 1; E291, 1025A, RG85, NARA I. For more on the Puyallup temporary detention center, see Louis Fiset, *Camp Harmony: Seattle's Japanese Americans and the Puyallup Assembly Center* (Champaign, IL: University of Illinois, 2009). One scholar has observed, "Because the ACs [assembly centers, operated by the Wartime Civil Control Administration, WCCA, under the Fourth Army's Western Defense Command] were under the aegis of the Army, and hastily built, living conditions were severe and grim, and rules and regulations for the incarcerated [were] strict. The ACs indeed bore great similarities through makeup and administration to POW [prisoner of war] camps," Peter T. Suzuki, *Linguistic Change in a Unique Cohort: Isseis, Kibeis, and Niseis in the WWII Internment Camps* (Omaha: School of Public Administration, University of Nebraska, 2005), 12.

124. Hisahiko Teraoka, KIC, to Tsueemon Tsuji, SFIC, June 2, 1943; E291, 1000/K(2), RG85, NARA I, PSK.

Chapter Two: Anticipating Internee Arrival: Establishing the Kooskia Internment Camp

1. "Curious Crowd Watches Arrival of 104 Japs under Armed Guard," *Lewiston (ID) Morning Tribune*, May 28, 1943, 14; the onlookers also included "one Chinese." Although the article stated that the men were "both citizen internees and aliens," none were U.S. citizens.

2. WFK's rarely-used given name was Willard.

3. WFK to OICFM, radiogram, February 22, 1943; E291, 1000/K(4), RG85, NARA I.

4. BHF to WFK, March 1, 1943, 1-2; E291, 1000/K, RG85, NARA I. Fraser referred to it as the "Kooskia Federal Prison Camp."

5. Ibid., 2.

6. Potlatch Corporation, Pres-to-log Division, Records, 1933 to 1989, University of Idaho Library Special Collections, Moscow, ID, Manuscript Group 388, with additional information in MG 135, MG 139, and MG 192. Pres-to-logs required one-quarter the space of the original wood. Besides feeding the boilers, Pres-to-logs fired up the kitchen ranges.

7. BHF to WFK, March 1, 1943, 2. Two sixteen-hundred-gallon tanks held the gasoline for the vehicles and oil for the diesel engines.

8. Ibid., 2-3.

9. Ibid., 3.

10. Ibid., 4.

11. All were eventually recaptured.

12. Ibid., 3-4.

13. WFK to OICFM, March 23, 1943; E291, FN56149/443, RG85, NARA I, Fiset.

14. BJF to BHF, April 2, 1943; E291, RG85, NARA I, Fiset.

15. Ibid. The INS actually paid the men's wages and then received reimbursement from the USBPR, which was in turn reimbursed by the Forest Service.

16. WFK to OICFM, March 23, 1943, 1.

17. BHF to WFK, April 5, 1943, 1-2; E291, 1000/K, RG85, NARA I.

18. Ibid., 2-3.

19. Ibid., 1-2.

20. John J. Culley, "The Santa Fe Internment Camp and the Justice Department Program for Enemy Aliens," in *Japanese Americans: From Relocation to Redress*, ed. Roger Daniels, Sandra C. Taylor, and Harry H. L. Kitano (Salt Lake City: University of Utah, 1986), 59.

21. LBS, "Instruction No. 58, Instructions Concerning the Treatment of Alien Enemy Detainees," April 28, 1942, 1-2; E291, 1022/X, RG85, NARA I; also available at http://home.comcast.net/~eo9066/1942/42-04/IA119.html (accessed November 9, 2009).

22. Ibid., 2.

23. DA-AcOICKIC to OICFM, May 31, 1943; E291, 1000/K(4), RG85, NARA I.

24. Ibid.

25. BHF to DA-OICKIC, June 4, 1943; E291, 1000/K, RG85, NARA I. Aldridge left in early July, DA to NDC, July 2, 1943; together with "Memorandum for Mr. Remer," no date [probably July 2, 1943]; both E291, 1000/K(1), RG85, NARA I.

26. BHF to CINS, June 14, 1943; E291, 1000/K(4), RG85, NARA I.

27. DA-AsOICKIC to OICFM, June 9, 1943, 1; E291, 1000/K(4), RG85, NARA I. They were George E. Barron, Henry F. Boyer, Thomas R. Fifield, Clyde A. Hexum, Jack E. Metcalf, Elgin D. Moshier, George F. Parkins, Albert H. Stark (clerk), and Stanley A. Thomas. Frank L. Davis and Deane A. Remer were not on the list but continued to work at the camp.

28. DA to OICFM, May 29, 1943; together with "BP, List of Employees at Camp 5-29-43," May 29, 1943; E291, 1000/K(4), RG85; NARA I; WFK to OICFM, telegram, July 8, 1943; E291, 1001/A, RG85, NARA I; DAR to WFK, June 24, 1943; E291, 1000/K(1), RG85; NARA I.

29. WFK to OICFM, telegram, July 8, 1943; E291, 1001/A, RG85, NARA I.

30. DAR to OICFM, no date, before July 17, 1943; E291, 1000/K(4), RG85, NARA I.

31. Alfred Keehr and Dorothy Keehr, interview by Ramona Alam Parry, July 12, 1979, transcript, 1, CNFSO, 1. Keehr, Cecil Boller, Bert Blewett, George McClanahan, and Ed Denton were five of the seven. Other Kooskia camp employees were Bill Pataja and Bud Nicholson, guards Bill Kruger and Walter Pataja, and secretaries Marguerite Pataja and Amy Wachter, Amelia Jacks and Edwin Jacks, interview by Dennis Griffith, March 25, 1982, transcript, [2, 13], LDKRS. Hozen Seki's diary often mentioned a Mr. Pauline as his supervisor in the camp garage, e. g. Hozen Seki, [Diary], 1944-1948, July 20, 1944. Jim Yenney was another guard, Cecil Boller, interview by author, June 7, 2000, transcript, 4, 6, AACC.

32. Beginning July 1, the date the INS officially took control of the camp, the INS apparently provided meals to their employees at no cost, BHF to CINS, Attn. WFK, June 7, 1943; E291, 1000/K(4); RG85; NARA I.

33. DAR to WFK, June 24, 1943; E291, 1000/K(1); RG85, NARA I.

34. DA-AsOICKIC to BHF, June 3, 1943; E291, 1000/K(4), RG85, NARA I.

35. DA-AcOICKIC to OICFM, June 11, 1943; E291, 1000/K(4), RG85, NARA I.

36. Keehr and Keehr, interview, 5.

37. Cecil Boller, telephone conversations with author, August 20 and September 15, 1997.

38. DAR to PSK, October 30, 1943; E291, 1000/K(4), RG85, NARA I. The letter bears the initials "aj" after "DAR," indicating that Amelia Jacks typed the letter for D. A. Remer.

39. Ken Jacks, e-mail message to author, October 16, 1997; Dennis Griffith, "Reply to: 2360 Special Interest Area. Subject: History of Japanese Internment Period: Canyon Creek Prison Camp Site," photocopy of handwritten document, [2, 4], LDKRS [1982], "[Duties of] Financial Officer," n.d.; copy in AACC.

40. Amelia Jacks, telephone conversation with author, August 20, 1997.

41. Griffith, "Reply to: 2360 Special Interest Area," [3-4].

42. Keehr and Keehr, interview, 17. Groceries came from Gilroy's in Kooskia, Jacks and Jacks, interview, [1, 9].

43. Jacks and Jacks, interview, [12].

44. Ibid., [1, 9]; Jacks, e-mail.

45. Griffith, "Reply to: 2360 Special Interest Area," [4]. This was originally Alfred Keehr's responsibility. Jacks seems to have replaced Keehr in this capacity after Keehr quit.

46. WFK to OICFM, April 27, 1943; E291, FN56149/443, RG85, NARA I, Fiset.

47. Ibid., 1-2. The rate of pay that was offered fluctuated from $45 per month, and an assumption that necessary extra clothing would be provided, to $55 per month, with $10 per month deducted for the clothing.

48. WFK to OICSF, April 27, 1943, 2-3; E291, FN56149/443, RG85, NARA I, Fiset.

49. LHJ to WFK, May 4, 1943; E291, FN1300, RG85, NARA I, Fiset. The agreement may only have applied among the original 104 men from Santa Fe, and not to others who came later from other camps.

50. Ibid.

51. WFK to OICFM, April 27, 1943; E291, FN56149/443, RG85, NARA I, Fiset.

52. WTH to RHA, May 24, 1943, 1; E291, 1000/K(4), RG85, NARA I.

53. Ibid., 1-2.

54. Kooskia Internment Camp is the name most commonly used on official documents obtained at NARA I. It was sometimes called the Canyon Creek Internment Camp or the Canyon Creek Prison Site, e.g., "Work Roster-Daily Time Report, Canyon Creek Internment Camp, May," Orofino, ID, CNFSO, 1944, and H[oward] Watts and Fred Kuester, "Cultural Site Record [for] 10-IH-870," Orofino, ID: CNFSO, 1979.

55. "Jap Contingent Goes to Lochsa Road Job," *Clearwater Tribune (Orofino, ID)* 31:12 (May 27, 1943), 1.

56. Ibid.; "Curious Crowd," 14.

57. E.g., "Jap Camp Gets 14 More Men," *Lewiston (ID) Morning Tribune*, June 8, 1943, 10.

58. WFK to SFPC; District Director of INS, El Paso, Texas; and OICSF and OICFM, May 20, 1943; together with "The following itinerary [of trains, stops, dates, and times]," May 19, 1943; E291, 1000/K(4), RG85, NARA I.

59. Eddie Webster, "Peep at a Camera-Shy Jap" [photograph], *Lewiston (ID) Morning Tribune*, May 29, 1943, 10.

60. "Curious Crowd," 14.

61. Irving Kalinoski, telephone conversation with author, August 20, 1997; "Curious Crowd," 14.

62. Helen Thiessen, telephone conversation with author, August 21, 1997.

63. Ibid.

64. Not all the men stayed the entire two years. Some were released to other jobs, or to join family in the WRA camps, such as Minidoka, in southern Idaho, and Topaz in Utah, or in the INS family camp at Crystal City, Texas. Other groups, and individuals, occasionally arrived to replace men who had departed.

65. Sakaye Ed Yoshimura, KIC, to Mr. & Mrs. D. S. Yoshimura, Poston WRA, Poston, AZ, June 1, 1943; E291, 1000/K(2), RG85, NARA I.

66. "Roster of Japanese Civilian Internee Volunteers, transferred from Third Service Command, Fort Meade IC, Fort George G. Meade, MD, to Immigration & Naturalization Service," c/o SFPC [June 1, 1943]; E291, 1000/K(4), RG85, NARA I.

67. "16 Japs, Under Guard of Army, to Prison Camp," *Lewiston (ID) Morning Tribune*, May 29, 1943, 10. The actual number was fifteen. Helen Thiessen also fed Italian internees who came through Lewiston on their way to other camps.

68. Kalinoski, telephone conversation.

69. DA-AcOICKIC [on Federal Prison Camp stationery] to OICFM, June 8, 1943; E291, 1000/K(4), RG85, NARA I, and "Japanese Enemy Aliens Transferred to Kooskia, Idaho from Fort George G. Meade, MD ... Santa Fe, New Mexico ... Camp Livingston, Louisiana"; no date, possibly about June 8, 1943; E291, 1000/K(4), RG85, NARA I.

70. "Lochsa Prison Camp Holds 134 Japanese," *Clearwater Tribune (Orofino, ID)* 31:14 (June 10, 1943), 8. The total was actually 135, unless one internee had already left.

71. Tish Erb, "Jap Internees Work Hard, Well Treated, at Kooskia Road Camp," *Lewiston (ID) Morning Tribune*, September 26, 1943, sec. 2, p. 1.

72. Ibid.

73. Ibid.

74. James I. Yano, letter to author, answers to questions dated January 18, 1997, 1.

75. Yasuo Suga, KIC, to Mrs. Misae Maeshiba, Poston, AZ, June 21, 1943; E291, 1000/K(2), RG85, NARA I, PSK.

76. Yoshi Asaba Mamiya, telephone conversation with author, December 13, 1997; Betty Arase Okamura, letter to author, May 29, 1998.

77. LW and GT, "In the Matter of the Detention of Kosaku Sato," November 13, 1943, Sato.

78. James I. Yano, letter to author, answers to questions dated January 18, 1998, 1.

79. Koshio Henry Shima, telephone conversation with author, April 13, 1998.

Chapter Three: No Barbed Wire: Living Conditions at the Kooskia Internment Camp

1. Sakiko Nakashima, CHPW, to Kintaro Nakashima, FMIC, May 11, 1942, 1; E291, 1025/A, RG85, NARA I.

2. LBS, "Instruction No. 58, Instructions Concerning the Treatment of Alien Enemy Detainees," April 28, 1942, 6-7; E291, 1022/X, RG85, NARA I; also available at http://home.comcast.net/~eo9066/1942/42-04/IA119.html (accessed November 9, 2009).

3. Louis Fiset, "Censored!: U.S. Censors and Internment Camp Mail in World War II," in *Guilt by Association: Essays on Japanese Settlement, Internment, and Relocation in the Rocky Mountain West*, ed. Mike Mackey (Powell, WY: Western History Publications, 2001), 69-100, and Louis Fiset, "Return to Sender: U.S. Censorship of Enemy Alien Mail in World War II," *Prologue* 33:1 (Spring 2001), 21-35.

4. The numbers of outgoing letters allowed changed from time to time, Fiset, "Return to Sender," 26, and "Censored!," 77.

5. ARM to unknown, "Visit to Japanese Internees, Detainees or Evacuees," July 31, 1944, 11; AN85-58A734, FN56125/157, Box 2436, RG85, NARA I.

6. LBS to all district directors, "Examination of the postal, telegraphic, and cabled communications of detained alien enemies," April 15, 1942; E291, 1025A, RG85, NARA I. In his diary, Hozen Seki told of the internees receiving the letters. He wrote, "At night we had a lots for stationarys [lots of letters] which came from R. C. [Red Cross]. I had not it. [I did not get one.]," Hozen Seki, [Diary], 1944-1948, February 23, 1945.

7. LBS to all district directors, "Examination," 3.

8. The Korean censors could speak, read, and write Japanese because they were forced to learn it during Japan's occupation of their country. See Hyung-ju Ahn, "Koreans as Interpreters at Japanese Enemy Alien Detention Centers during World War II," in *Guilt by Association*, ed. Mackey, 101-116, and Ahn's *Between Two Adversaries: Korean Interpreters at Japanese Alien Enemy Detention Centers During World War II* (Fullerton, CA: California State University, 2002).

9. BHF to DAR, June 2, 1943; E291, 1000/K, RG85, NARA I.

10. Ibid.

11. E.g., BHF to OICKIC, June 16, 1943, and BHF to DA-OICKIC, June 10, 1943; both E291, 1000/K(2), RG85, NARA I.

12. Y. Yoshikawa, KIC, to H. Takiguchi, SFIC, May 28, 1943; E291, 1000/K(2), RG85, NARA I.

13. Inao Minato, KIC, to Katsutaro Sera, Lordsburg, NM, May 28, 1943; E291, 1000/K(2), RG85, NARA I, PSK.

14. In February 1942, before the Kooskia camp even opened, an article in the Japanese-language *North American Times*, published in Seattle, had a headline reading, "One Letter for Every Ten Days to Detainee is Proper," PSK to NDC, about February 16, 1942; E291, 1025F, RG85, NARA I. This was an attempt to voluntarily restrict the incoming correspondence to a more manageable amount.

15. BHF to CO, July 3, 1943; E291, 1000/K, RG85, NARA I.

16. DA-AsOICKIC to OICFM, May 31, 1943; E291, RG85, NARA I, Fiset. The incoming and outgoing correspondence was logged onto index cards, one for each internee, Fiset, "Return to Sender," 22.

17. Louis Fiset, e-mail to author, April 2, 1998; he has examples of the letters with the appropriate postmarks. Missoula was 177 miles away, over the mountains. For infor-

mation on the transportation networks, see BHF to WFK, March 1, 1943, 2, 4; E291, 1000K, RG85, NARA I. In late April 1944, prior to Fort Missoula's closure on July 1, censor Paul Kashino transferred to the Kooskia Internment Camp, Virginia Kashino Tomita, letter to author, March 25, 1998, and Seki [Diary], April 26, 1944.

18. As listed on some of the letters, they were "Officer in Charge, Central Office, Alien Enemy Control Unit, General, File Office, and Barrack #32"; the latter three locations are not known.

19. Rev. Hozen Seki, KIC, to Rev. Y. Tamai, Denver, CO, postcard, June 29, 1943; E291, 1000/K(1), RG85, NARA I.

20. Minoru Wazumi, KIC, to Miss Elisabeth Nesbitt, Philadelphia, PA, May 28, 1943; E291, 1000/K(2), RG85, NARA I, PSK.

21. Hisahiko Teraoka, KIC, to Tsueemon Tsuji, SFIC, June 2, 1943; E291, 1000/K(2), RG85, NARA I, PSK.

22. Yoshito Kadotani, KIC, to Sanzo Aso, SFIC, May 28, 1943; E291, 1000/K(2), RG85, NARA I, PSK. Aso did not transfer to the Kooskia camp.

23. Sakaye Yoshimura, KIC, to Mr. & Mrs. D. S. Yoshimura, Poston WRA, Poston, AZ, June 1, 1943; E291, 1000/K(2), RG85, NARA I, PSK.

24. Sakaye Yoshimura, KIC, to Saima Yokota, SFIC, June 11, 1943; E291, 1000/K(2), RG85, NARA I, PSK.

25. LBS, "Instruction No. 58," 2-3.

26. Teraoka to Tsuji.

27. Kadotani to Aso.

28. Kuromitsu Banba, KIC, to Sutematsu Endo, SFIC, May 28, 1943; E291, 1000/K(2), RG85, NARA I, PSK.

29. Dennis Griffith, "Internee Housing Area," sketch map based on drawing by Amelia and Ed Jacks, LDKRS [1982].

30. Dennis Griffith, "History Lower Canyon Creek Mines/Prison Camp - Oral Interview with Ayden Thomas," Lochsa Ranger District, 2360 - Special Interest Areas, LDKRS, April 26, 1982, 4.

31. PMO by WHW, radiogram, July 1, 1943, together with SFN33, IN44-6K, BHF to OICKIC, June 16, 1943; AN85-58A734, FN56125/288, Box 2451, RG85, NARA I.

32. WHW to MHS, Attn.: AHS, July 19, 1944; together with SFN33, IN28345-3, MHS, May 10, 1944; both AN85-58A734, FN56125/288, Box 2451, RG85, NARA I.

33. BHF to WFK, March 1, 1943, 2; E291, 1000/K, RG85, NARA I.

34. Cecil Boller, interview by author, June 7, 2000, transcript, 3, AACC.

35. Seki, [Diary], August 29, 1944.

36. Ibid., September 25, 1944.

37. Ibid., November 21, 1944.

38. Takeo Ujo Nakano, *Within the Barbed Wire Fence*, with Leatrice Nakano (Toronto: University of Toronto, 1980), 16.

39. Charles I. Bevans, comp., "Prisoners of War," in *Treaties and Other International Agreements of the United States of America 1776-1949*, vol. 2, Multilateral, 1918-1930 (Washington, DC, U.S. Government Printing Office, 1969), 940-941.

40. LBS, "Instruction No. 58," 3.

41. BHF to OICKIC, Attn.: DA, June 2, 1943; E291, 1000/K(4), RG85, NARA I.

42. WFM to OICKIC, July 12, 1943; E291, 1000/K(1), RG85, NARA I.

43. BHF to CINS, telegram, May 19, 1943; E291, 1000/K(4), RG85, NARA I. For a table showing how rationing applied to certain foods, visit Asian American Comparative Collection, The Kooskia Internment Camp Project, "Tables Related to Food and Clothing," available at http://www.uiweb.uidaho.edu/LS/AACC/FoodClothing.htm, number 1 (accessed November 10, 2009).

44. LBS, "Instruction No. 58," 3-4.

45. EGH "Instruction No. 123," February 24, 1943; E303, RG85, NARA I. For a table showing the types and amounts of foods that internees could expect to receive, visit Asian American Comparative Collection, The Kooskia Internment Camp Project, "Tables Related to Food and Clothing," available at http://www.uiweb.uidaho.edu/LS/AACC/FoodClothing.htm, number 2 (accessed November 10, 2009).

46. LAF to unknown, "Memorandum Covering the Food Allowance Expressed as Pounds Per Man Per Day for the Use of Alien Detainees Held under Jurisdiction of the United States Immigration and Naturalization Service at Kooskia, Idaho," May 19, 1943, 1; E291, 1000/K(4), RG85, NARA I.

47. Ruth and Estella [Hoshimiya] to My Dear Father, May 21, 1942, 1-2; AN85-58A734, FN56125/27x1, Box 2406, RG85, NARA I.

48. Teraoka to Tsuji.

49. Kuromitsu Banba, KIC, to Sutematsu Endo, SFIC, May 28, 1943; E291, 1000/K(2), RG85, NARA I, PSK.

50. DA-AcOICKIC to OICFM, June 9, 1943, 2-3; E291, 1000/K(4), RG85, NARA I.

51. Brown was retired from the U.S. Public Health Service and Reineke was a retired dentist.

52. FVB to BHF, June 19, 1943; E291, 1000/8, RG85, NARA I.

53. For a table comparing food poundage and cost for two successive recording periods, visit Asian American Comparative Collection, The Kooskia Internment Camp Project, "Tables Related to Food and Clothing," available at http://www.uiweb.uidaho.edu/LS/AACC/FoodClothing.htm, number 3 (accessed November 10, 2009).

54. *Lewiston (ID) Morning Tribune*, "Work to Be Continued on L-C Highway," April 28, 1945, 10.

55. H[oward] Watts and Fred Kuester, "Cultural Site Record [for] 10-IH-870," Orofino, ID: CNFSO, 1979, [4].

56. Fort Missoula, "Japanese Mess Menu List," January 20-29, 1942; E291, 1035/G, RG85, NARA I.

57. Ibid. Where "butter" is mentioned, oleomargarine was more commonly served. Because of shortages and rationing, butter was difficult to obtain. The available documents for the Kooskia camp only show one order for butter, but there are many requests for oleomargarine from Fort Missoula.

58. Ibid.

59. Fort Missoula, "Japanese Mess Menu List."

60. Tish Erb, "Jap Internees Work Hard, Well Treated, at Kooskia Road Camp," *Lewiston (ID) Morning Tribune*, September 26, 1943, sec. 2, p. 1.

61. Ibid.

62. During World War II the United States severed diplomatic relations with enemy nations. Subsequently, the government of Spain, a self-professed neutral country, agreed to act for Japan in a diplomatic capacity in the U.S., with the objective of ensuring that citizens of Japan who resided here were treated fairly. As a result, a

Spanish official visited the Kooskia Internment Camp several times to check on the welfare of the Japanese aliens there.

63. MHS to WFK, August 15, 1944, 1; AN85-58A734, FN56125/157, Box 2436, RG85, NARA I.

64. Ibid.

65. Tatsuji Shiotani [T. Mitsu Shiotani], "Testimony of Mr. Tajitsu [*sic*] Shiotani for the Commission on Wartime Relocation and Internment of Civilians, November 23, 1981, New York City," photocopy of typescript, 2, AACC.

66. FMB-AcOICFM to OICKIC, Attn.: DA, June 26, 1943; E291, 1000/K(1), RG85, NARA I. For a table showing the weight and amounts of some of these products, visit Asian American Comparative Collection, The Kooskia Internment Camp Project, "Tables Related to Food and Clothing," available at http://www.uiweb.uidaho.edu/ LS/AACC/FoodClothing.htm, number 4 (accessed November 10, 2009).

67. FMB-AsOICFM, "Supplemental Inventory of Stores Sold to Immigration & Naturalization Service," June 4, 1943; E291, 1000/S(3), RG85, NARA I.

68. FMB-AcOICFM to OICKIC, June 26, 1943.

69. BHF to OICKIC, July 22, 1943, and BHF to OICKIC, July 26, 1943; both E291, 1000/S(3), RG85, NARA I. The cheese represented 1,470 ration points.

70. BHF to OICKIC, November 15, 1943; E291, 1000/S(1), RG85, NARA I.

71. HVS to OICKIC, March 4, 1944; E291, 1000/S(3), RG85, NARA I.

72. BHF to DA-OICKIC, June 16, 1943; E291, 1000/K(4), RG85, NARA I.

73. DA-AsOICKIC [on Federal Prison Camp stationery] to OICFM, June 2, 1943; E291, 1000/K(4), RG85, NARA I.

74. DAR, SFN1036, June 15, 1943; together with DAR, SFN33, June 15, 1943; both AN85-58A734, FN56125/288, Box 2451, RG85, NARA I.

75. Ibid., together with DAR, SFN33, June 13, 1943; all AN85-58A734, FN56125/288, Box 2451, RG85, NARA I.

76. DAR, SFN1036, July 25, 1943; together with DAR, SFN33, July 21, 1943; both AN85-58A734, FN56125/288, Box 2451, RG85, NARA I.

77. DAR, SFN33, August 1, 1943; AN85-58A734, FN56125/288, Box 2451, NARA I.

78. Information from DAR, IBA, June 25, 1943; together with SFN36, both AN85-58A734, FN56125/288, Box 2451, RG85, NARA I, and SFN33 between BHF for KIC and Pacific Fruit & Produce Co., Lewiston, ID, June 10, 1943; E291, 1000/S(3), RG85, NARA I. For a table showing the amounts and prices for the fresh produce, visit Asian American Comparative Collection, The Kooskia Internment Camp Project, "Tables Related to Food and Clothing," available at http://www.uiweb.uidaho.edu/LS/AACC/Food Clothing.htm, number 5 (accessed November 10, 2009).

79. DAR, SFN33, IN44-28, September 6, 1943; AN85-58A734, FN56125/288, Box 2451, RG85, NARA I.

80. Ibid.

81. DAR, "Purchase Order," to Carstens Packing Company, Spokane, WA, May 21, 1943; E291, 1000/S(3), RG85, NARA I.

82. DAR, SFN1036, July 1, 1943; together with DAR, SFN33, July 1, 1943; and together with SFN36; all AN85-58A734, FN56125/288, Box 2451, RG85, NARA I. For a table showing the amount provided and cost per pound of some of these meats over a four-week period in mid-1943, visit Asian American Comparative Collection, The

Kooskia Internment Camp Project, "Tables Related to Food and Clothing," available at http://www.uiweb.uidaho.edu/LS/AACC/FoodClothing.htm, number 6 (accessed November 10, 2009).

83. BHF, SFN33, "Invitation," June 11, 1943; AN85-58A734, FN56125/288, Box 2451, RG85, NARA I.

84. Carol Bulger Van Valkenburg, *An Alien Place: The Fort Missoula, Montana, Detention Camp 1941-1944* (Missoula, MT: Pictorial Histories, 1995), 85.

85. BHF to MHS, April n.d., 1944; E291, 1000/S(3), RG85, NARA I.

86. BHF to MHS, May 2, 1944; E291, 1000/S(3), RG85, NARA I.

87. BHF to OICKIC, April 19, 1944; E291, 1000/S(3), RG85, NARA I.

88. BHF to MHS, May 20, 1944; E291, 1000/S(3), RG85, NARA I.

89. DAR, SFN1036, Mason Ehrman Company, Lewiston, ID, June 19, 1943; AN85-58A734, FN56125/288, Box 2451, RG85, NARA I.

90. DAR, SFN1036, Pacific Fruit and Produce Company, Lewiston, ID, June 19, 1943; AN85-58A734, FN56125/288, Box 2451, RG85, NARA I.

91. HVS to CO, telegram, March 8, 1944; E291, 1000/S(3), RG85, NARA I.

92. Alfred Keehr and Dorothy Keehr, interview by Ramona Alam Parry, July 12, 1979, transcript, 9, CNFSO.

93. DA-AsOICKIC to OICFM, June 2, 1943; E291, 1000/K(1), RG85, NARA I.

94. BHF to OICKIC, Attn.: DA, June 2, 1943; E291, 1000/K(4), RG85, NARA I. For a table showing amounts and prices of Asian foods from Fort Missoula sent to the Kooskia Internment Camp, visit Asian American Comparative Collection, The Kooskia Internment Camp Project, "Tables Related to Food and Clothing," available at http://www.uiweb.uidaho.edu/LS/AACC/FoodClothing.htm, number 7 (accessed November 10, 2009).

95. DAR to BHF, July 2, 1943; E291, 1000/S(3), RG85, NARA I.

96. BHF to OICKIC, July 5, 1943; E291, 1000/S(3), RG85, NARA I.

97. DA-AsOICKIC to OICFM, June 2, 1943.

98. BHF to OICKIC, July 22, 1943; and BHF to OICKIC, July 26, 1943; both E291, 1000/S(3), RG85, NARA I.

99. HVS to CO, telegram, March 8, 1944.

100. FMB-AsOICFM, "Supplemental Inventory," June 4, 1943.

101. DAR by AHS to OICFM, September 24, 1943; E291, 1000/S(3), RG85, NARA I.

102. BHF to OICKIC, telegram, October 1, 1943; E291, 1000/S(3), RG85, NARA I.

103. HVS to CO, telegram, March 8, 1944.

104. BHF to MHS, April 1944.

105. Ibid.

106. BHF to OICKIC, April 19, 1944.

107. Amelia Jacks and Edwin Jacks, interview by Dennis Griffith, March 25, 1982, transcript, [3-4], LDKRS. They indicated the incinerator on their sketch map.

108. LBS, "Instruction No. 58," 3.

109. ARM to unknown, March 1, 1945, 3; AN85-58A734, FN56125/157, Box 2436, RG85, NARA I.

110. Arthur Deschamps, Jr., interview by Susan Buchel, November 20, 1979, transcript, tape 67-2:1, Historical Museum at Fort Missoula, Missoula, MT.

111. For Canada see, for example, Yon Shimizu, *The Exiles: An Archival History of the World War II Japanese Road Camps in British Columbia and Ontario* (Wallaceburg, ON: Shimizu Consulting and Publishing, 1993), 176, describing a Japanese traditional bath in a work camp. Bill Waiser, *Park Prisoners: The Untold Story of Western Canada's National Parks, 1915-1946* (Saskatoon, SK: Fifth House, 1995), 191, states that the Japanese internees at the Geikie camp "insisted on the construction of traditional bathhouses with large soaking tubs."

112. Nakano, *Within the Barbed Wire Fence*, 34.

113. Seki, [Diary], April 6, 1944.

Chapter Four: "A Real He-Man's Job": Work Assignments and Working Conditions

1. Minoru Wazumi, KIC, to Miss Elisabeth Nesbitt, Philadelphia, PA, May 28, 1943; E291, 1000/K(2), RG85, NARA I, PSK.

2. Tish Erb, "Jap Internees Work Hard, Well Treated, at Kooskia Road Camp," *Lewiston (ID) Morning Tribune*, September 26, 1943, sec. 2, pp. 1, 5.

3. Cecil Boller, telephone conversation with author, August 20, 1997.

4. Yoshimura, Sakaye, KIC, to Mr. & Mrs. D. S. Yoshimura, Poston WRA, Poston, AZ, June 1, 1943; E291, 1000/K(2), RG85, NARA I, PSK.

5. DA-AsOICKIC to JWG, "General Order #2, Instructions for crew leaders on road construction," June 5, 1943; E291, 1000/K(4), RG85, NARA I.

6. Sakaye Yoshimura, KIC, to Saima Yokota, SFIC, June 11, 1943; E291, 1000/K(2), RG85, NARA I, PSK.

7. Erb, "Internees Work Hard." Although Erb visited the camp much earlier, her later illness delayed publication of the story for several months.

8. Ibid., 1.

9. T. Mitsu Shiotani, KIC, to Mrs. J. Frank Conwell, Lincolndale, NY, June 19, 1943; E291, 1000/K(2), RG85, NARA I, PSK.

10. Milton (Mickey) Barton, letter to author, March 30, 1998, 2-3.

11. Erb, "Internees Work Hard," 1; Milton (Mickey) Barton, e-mail to author, September 23, 2004, 3.

12. Barton, e-mail, 2-3.

13. Amelia Jacks and Edwin Jacks, interview by Dennis Griffith, March 25, 1982, transcript, [10], LDKRS.

14. BJF to JWG, July 23, 1943; E291, 1000/K(4), RG85, NARA I.

15. Barton, letter, 3.

16. James I. Yano, letter to author, October 4, 1997, 2.

17. BJF to BHF, June 12, 1943; E291, 1000/K(1), RG85, NARA I.

18. BHF to Attn. of WFK, June 14, 1943; E291, 1000/K(4), RG85, NARA I.

19. Jo Minoru Wazumi, KIC, to Miss Ruth Miller, New York, NY, June 16, 1943; E291, 1000/K(2), RG85, NARA I, PSK.

20. BHF to Attn. of WFK, June 14, 1943.

21. BJF to JWG, July 23, 1943.

22. Alfred Keehr and Dorothy Keehr, interview by Ramona Alam Parry, July 12, 1979, transcript, 10, CNFSO.

23. C. Harvey Gardiner, *Pawns in a Triangle of Hate* (Seattle: University of Washington, 1981), 97-98.

24. Ibid. Besides Wazumi and Yakabi, another jackhammer operator was Otosaburo Sumi, the young man who was severely beaten at Fort Lincoln, FLD-KIC, to EJE, Re: Otasuburo [*sic*, for Otosaburo] Sumi, July 12, 1944, 3; CLCF, Otosaburo Sumi, 146-13-2-12-2282; Stack 230/25/9/1, Box 35; RG60, NARA II.

25. Jacks and Jacks, interview, [10].

26. Shiotani to Conwell.

27. DA-AsOICKIC to OICFM, May 31, 1943; E291, RG85, NARA I, Fiset.

28. DA-AsOICKIC to JWG, "General Order #2," June 5, 1943.

29. Ibid.

30. BHF, Attn.: WFK, April 20, 1943; together with BHF to DAR, BP, April 20, 1943; together with DAR, BP, to BHF, April 18, 1943; together with "Restriction on Enemy Aliens and Persons of Japanese Ancestry with Respect to Explosives or Explosive Ingredients" [from Federal Register], undated; all E291, 1000/K(4), RG85, NARA I. Gillmore's initials appear in DA-AsOICKIC to OICFM, June 3, 1943; E291, 1000/K(4), RG85, NARA I; his surname is often misspelled "Gilmore" in official documents.

31. WFK to OICFM, June 18, 1943; E291, 1000/K(4), RG85, NARA I.

32. DAR to FMB-AcOICFM, June 28, 1943; E291, 1000/K(4), RG85, NARA I.

33. Barton, letter, 2-3.

34. Jacks and Jacks, interview, [10].

35. FVB to BHF, June 19, 1943, 3-4; E291, 1000/8, RG85, NARA I, Fiset.

36. Ibid.

37. Ibid., 4.

38. FVB to WJK, June 25, 1943; E291, 1000/F, RG85, NARA I. Curiously, although Hozen Seki arrived at the Kooskia Camp on June 15, 1943, Hozen Seki, [Diary], 1944-1948, front flyleaf, his name is not on the list of men whom the doctor examined on June 21; perhaps the Fort Missoula doctor had already examined him.

39. Shiotani to Conwell.

40. Barton, letter, 3. There were no deaths at the Kooskia camp.

41. Keehr and Keehr, interview, 10.

42. DAR by WCW to OICFM, July 21, 1943; E291, 1000/K(1), RG85, NARA I.

43. [Unknown], "Strictly Confidential Memorandum" to BHF, no date, received at Fort Missoula July 5, 194[3]; E291, 1000/K(4), RG85, NARA I.

44. James D. Urabe, Alien Detention Camp, Fort George G. Meade, MD, to FVF, September 4, 1942, 2; E466F, Urabe, James D., RG389, NARA II.

45. "Alien Enemy Property Receipt," July 22, 1942, E466F, Urabe, James D.

46. BPR, undated [1942], 2; E466F, Urabe, James D. Having an African-American wife may have made Urabe look more suspicious to the FBI; that group feared, erroneously, that Japanese spies would collude, for subversive purposes, with blacks disaffected, and thus disloyal, because of racial segregation, Bob Kumamoto, "The Search for Spies: American Counterintelligence and the Japanese American Community 1931-1942," *Amerasia Journal* 6:2 (1979), 51, 54.

47. Hattie E. Urabe, Bloomsburg, PA, to James Urabe [Fort George G. Meade, MD], typed copy of handwritten letter, July 22, 1942; E466F, Urabe, James D.

48. James D. Urabe, Area "D," Fort George G. Meade, MD, to RH, July 24, 1942, 2; E466F, Urabe, James D.

49. Cecil Boller, interview by author, June 7, 2000, transcript, 3, AACC.

50. DAR, "Organization of Fire Brigade," July 16, 1943; E291, 1000/K(4), RG85, NARA I.

51. ARM to unknown, "Visit to Japanese Internees, Detainees or Evacuees," March 1, 1945 [*sic*, for March 4], 2; AN5-58A734, FN56125/157, Box 2436; RG85, NARA I.

52. DAR, "Organization of Fire Brigade."

53. Jacks and Jacks, interview, [10].

54. Seki, [Diary], April 18-20, 24-25, 1944.

55. Ibid., May 26, 1944.

56. Ibid., March 6, 1945.

57. In a "stake" truck, upright wooden slats form the sides of the truck bed.

58. "Motor Vehicle Expense Report for the Month of May 25 to 31 Inclusive," undated [probably May 31, 1943]; E291, 1000/K(4), RG85, NARA I.

59. BHF to Supply Officer, U.S. Army, Fort William Henry Harrison, Helena, MT, June 29, 1943; E291, 1000/K(4), RG85, NARA I.

60. ARM to unknown, March 1, 1945 [*sic*, for March 4], 4.

61. Keehr and Keehr, interview, 4.

62. LBS, "Instruction No. 58, Instructions Concerning the Treatment of Alien Enemy Detainees," April 28, 1942, 4; E291, 1022/X, RG85, NARA I; also available at http://home.comcast.net/~eo9066/1942/42-04/IA119.html (accessed November 9, 2009). A "Turkish" towel is a type of towel, usually cotton, having a thick pile or a rough surface, such as modern bath towels.

63. BHF to OICKIC, January 26, 1944; E291, 1000/K(6), RG85, NARA I.

64. Jacks and Jacks, interview, [10]; ARM to unknown, "Visit to Japanese Internees, Detainees or Evacuees," July 31, 1944, 1, 5; AN5-58A734, FN56125/157, Box 2436, RG85, NARA I.

65. FVB to BHF, June 19, 1943, 3-4; E291, 1000/K(5), RG85, NARA I.

66. ARM to unknown, July 31, 1944, 5.

67. Seki, [Diary], April 10, 1944.

68. FMB-AsOICFM, "Supplemental Inventory of Stores Sold to Immigration & Naturalization Service," June 4, 1943; E291, 1000/S(1), RG85, NARA I.

69. WFM to OICKIC, July 22, 1943; AN85-58A734, FN56125/23d, Box 2405, RG85, NARA I.

70. LHJ to CO, Attn: WFK, cc. to OICKIC, July 26, 1943; AN85-58A734, FN56125/23d, Box 2405, RG85, NARA I. The shoes were "hob-nail field issue" and their sizes were 9½ to 12.

71. DAR to WFM, August 7, 1943; AN85-58A734, FN56125/23d, Box 2405, RG85, NARA I.

72. BHF to KIC, October 15, 1943; E291, 1000/S(3), RG85, NARA I.

73. Keehr and Keehr, interview, 13.

74. FMB-AsOICFM, "Supplemental Inventory."

75. CFH to FMB-AsOICFM, May 25, 1943; E291, 1000/K(4), RG85, NARA I.

76. FMB-AsOICFM to DA-OICKIC, June 7, 1943, 2; E291, 1000/K(4), RG85, NARA I.

77. BHF to OICKIC, November 16, 1943; E291, 1000/S(3), RG85, NARA I. For a table showing for the sizes, quantities, and costs of these items, visit Asian American Comparative Collection, The Kooskia Internment Camp Project, "Tables Related to Food

and Clothing," available at http://www.uiweb.uidaho.edu/LS/AACC/FoodClothing. htm, number 8 (accessed November 10, 2009).

78. BHF to OICKIC, November 25, 1943; E291, 1000/S(3), RG85, NARA I.

79. Ibid.

80. BHF to OICKIC, December 13, 1943; E291, 1000/S(3), RG85, NARA I.

81. BHF to OICKIC, January 26, 1944; E291, 1000/K(6), RG85, NARA I.

82. BHF to WHW, March 15, 1944; E291, 1000/K(4), RG85, NARA I. For a table showing details of these shipments, visit Asian American Comparative Collection, The Kooskia Internment Camp Project, "Tables Related to Food and Clothing," available at http://www.uiweb.uidaho.edu/LS/AACC/FoodClothing.htm, number 9 (accessed November 10, 2009).

83. BHF to CINS, Attn.: WFK, June 14, 1943; E291, 1000/K(4), RG85, NARA I.

84. DAR to OICSF, August 21, 1943; E291, 1000/K(4), RG85, NARA I; LHJ to OICFM, radiogram, September 17, 1943; E291, 1000/K(1), RG85, NARA I; "More Japs at Kooskia Camp," *Lewiston (ID) Morning Tribune*, September 22, 1943, 12.

85. Barton, letter, 1-2, 5-6; Sharon Hall, e-mail message to author, November 27, 2006.

86. Barton, letter, 2; Hall, e-mail; and Donald Weseman, letter to author, undated but about October 23, 2006. "Cat skinner," for bulldozer operator, derives from the manufacturer's name, Caterpillar, and from nineteenth century mule or bull teams whose drivers were called "mule skinners" or "bull skinners."

87. "Conference at Kooskia Camp," May 21, 1943, together with "Memorandum of Agreement" between the BP and the INS [May 21, 1943]; E291, 1000/K(4), RG85, NARA I.

88. DA-AsOICKIC, May 31, 1943; E291, 1000/K(4), RG85, NARA I.

89. Barton, letter, 3.

90. "[Duties of] Financial Officer" n.d.:[3]; copy in AACC.

91. Amelia Jacks, e-mail to author via Ken Jacks, November 25, 1997.

92. Lists of men detained at Kooskia provide their occupations. These can be spelled out or written in a 3-digit code. Where a man has both types of notations, on different documents, they correlate closely. To decipher the codes, see U.S. Department of Labor, *Dictionary of Occupational Titles Part II, Group Arrangement of Occupational Titles and Codes*, prepared by the Job Analysis and Information Section, Division of Standards and Research (Washington, DC: U.S. Government Printing Service, 1939), ix-xviii.

93. BJF and BHF, "Agreement," undated, approximately May 25, 1943; E291, 1000/K(5), RG85, NARA I.

94. BJF to BHF, August 14, 1943; together with sample time sheet listing nine names and their jobs, undated [August 14, 1943?]; E291, 1000/K(4), RG85, NARA I.

95. James I. Yano, letter to author, answers to questions dated December 11, 1997, 3.

96. WFK to OICFM, June 1, 1943, 1, and PMO to OICFM, April 28, 1943; FN56149/443 and FN56149/482; E291, RG85, NARA I, Fiset.

97. Keehr and Keehr, interview, 10-11.

98. Malvern Hall Tillitt, "Army-Navy Pay Tops Most Civilians': Unmarried Private's Income Equivalent to $3,600 Salary," *Barron's National Business and Financial Weekly*, April 24, 1944, 1-2, available at http://www.usmm.org/barrons.html (accessed November 10, 2009). There is a long history of tying internee pay to what a soldier received.

99. *New York Times*, "Help Wanted - Male," July 21, 1944, 30.

100. Tillitt, "Army-Navy Pay," 1.

101. WFK to OICFM, telegram, July 8, 1943; E291, 1001/A, RG85, NARA I.

102. DA-AsOICKIC to OICFM, May 31, 1943.

103. Keehr and Keehr, interview, 9.

104. BHF to DAR, July 17, 1943; E291, 1000/K(1), RG85, NARA I.

105. DAR by WCW to OICFM, July 21, 1943.

106. DA-OICKIC to OICFM, June 17, 1943; E291, 1000/K(1), RG85, NARA I.

107. WFK to OICFM, June 26, 1943; E291, 1000/K(4), RG85, NARA I.

108. HKB to WFK, July 7, 1943; E291, 1000/K(1), RG85, NARA I.

109. BHF and BJF, Modification of Agreement, July 15, 1943; E291, 1000/K(1), RG85, NARA I.

110. BJF and DAR [signed by WCW, AsOICKIC], "Agreement," August 2, 1943; E291, 1000/K(4), RG85, NARA I.

111. BJF to BHF, August 5, 1943; E291, 1000/K(4), RG85, NARA I.

112. RRM to BJF, July 6, 1943, 5; E291, RG85, NARA I, Fiset.

113. BJF to BHF, August 14, 1943; together with sample time sheet, [August 14, 1943?].

114. Ibid.

115. Torajiro Imahashi, KIC, to Tosuke Sukegawa, SFIC, July 7, 1943; E291, 1000/K(2), RG85, NARA I, PSK.

Chapter Five: A Powerful Petition: Internees Protest Deteriorating Conditions at the Kooskia Camp

1. BHF to DAR, June 1, 1943; E291, 1000/K(4), RG85, NARA I.

2. DA-AsOICKIC to OICFM, May 31, 1943; E291, 1000/K(4), RG85, NARA I; BHF to DA-OICKIC, June 4, 1943; E291, 1000/K, RG85, NARA I.

3. DA-AcOICKIC to OICFM, June 9, 1943, 1; E291, 1000/K(4), RG85, NARA I.

4. Ibid.

5. WFK to OICFM, June 14, 1943; E291, 1000/K(1), RG85, NARA I.

6. DA-AcOICKIC to OICFM, June 9, 1943, 3.

7. Ibid., 3-4.

8. DA to BHF, telegram, June 16, 1943; E291, 1000/K(1), RG85, NARA I.

9. JAK to OICFM, June 29, 1943, 1-2; E291, RG85, NARA I, Fiset.

10. LBS, "Instruction No. 58, Instructions Concerning the Treatment of Alien Enemy Detainees," April 28, 1942, 7; E291, 1022/X, RG85, NARA I; also available at http://home.comcast.net/~eo9066/1942/42-04/IA119.html (accessed November 9, 2009).

11. Unknown, USDJ, INS, Missoula, MT, to unknown, June 23, 1943, through July 5, 1943, 1; E291, 1000/K(4), RG85, NARA I.

12. Ibid.

13. Ibid., 2.

14. Ibid.

15. DA-AsOICKIC to OICFM, June 5, 1943; E291, 1000/K(4), RG85, NARA I.

16. BHF to DA-OICKIC, June 8, 1943; E291, 1000/K(4), RG85, NARA I.

17. Unknown to unknown, June 23, 1943, through July 5, 1943, 2.

18. "Affidavit and Certificate" of WCW-AcAsOICKIC, July 2, 1943; E291, 1000/K(4), RG85, NARA I.

19. Unknown to unknown, June 23, 1943, through July 5, 1943, 2.

20. Ibid., 2-3.

21. Ibid., 2.

22. N. D. [also referred to as Nick or Donald] Collaer was the former superintendent at Fort Missoula.

23. DA to NDC, July 2, 1943; E291, 1000/K(1), RG85, NARA I.

24. DA-AsOICKIC, Confidential to OICFM, June 3, 1943; E291, 1000/K(4), RG85, NARA I.

25. Ibid.

26. Ibid.

27. RRM to BJF, July 6, 1943, 1-3; E291, RG85, NARA I, Fiset. However, Chapter 4 presents evidence showing that Japanese internees did in fact work with explosives in defiance of regulations.

28. Ibid., 1-4.

29. Ibid., 6.

30. Ibid.

31. Ibid.

32. FVB to BHF, June 19, 1943, 3-4; E291, 1000/8, RG85, NARA I.

33. LBS, "Instruction No. 58," 9-10.

34. Yoshito T. Kadotani, KIC, to Miss M. Kadotani, Poston, AZ, July 1, 1943; E291, 1000/K(5), RG85, NARA I.

35. DA to NDC, July 2, 1943; E291, 1000/K(1), RG85, NARA I.

36. [Kooskia internees] to BHF, July 7, 1943, 1; E291, RG85, NARA I, Fiset, PSK.

37. The internees' names do not appear on the English translation.

38. The camp did have a movie projector that had formerly belonged to the prison camp, but perhaps it was broken. In addition, movies had not yet been provided as originally promised.

39. The available documents contain no other mention of this incident. Evidently, only the guards supervising the road crews carried guns. Henry Boyer's daughter recalled, "One day he had to shoot a bear ... with his hand-gun," Jan Boyer, e-mail to author, September 9, 2005.

40. [Kooskia internees] to BHF, July 7, 1943.

41. Yasutaro Soga, *Life Behind Barbed Wire: The World War II Internment Memoirs of a Hawai'i Issei* (Honolulu: University of Hawai'i, 2008), 76. Tetsuden Kashima, "Introduction," in Soga, *Life Behind Barbed Wire*, 8, adds, "their protest eventually led to the transfer of this particular camp commander out of the Lordsburg center," which also happened at the Kooskia camp.

42. IPM to OICFM, radiogram, July 8, 1943; E291, 1000/K(4), RG85, NARA I. I. P. McCoy was the officer in charge at the Fort Lincoln Internment Camp.

43. LRB to MSL, July 22, 1943; and FFT to FVB, July 22, 1943; both E291, 1000/K(1), RG85, NARA I.

44. BHF to CO, Attn.: WHW, July 21, 1943; E291, 1000/K(1), RG85, NARA I.

45. LRB to MSL, July 22, 1943.

46. BHF to WFK, December 14, 1943, 2; E291, 1000/K, RG85, NARA I.

47. FMB-AsOICFM, Attn.: WFK, July 13, 1943; E291, 1000/K(1), RG85, NARA I.

48. WCW, KIC, to NDC, no date; [between July 8 and 12, 1943]; E291, 1000/K(1), RG85, NARA I.

49. WCW-AcOICKIC to CINS, Attn.: WFM, July 20, 1943; E291, 1000/K(1), RG85, NARA I.

50. DAR to WFK, November 18, 1943, 2, 4; E291, 1000/K(4), RG85, NARA I.

51. WCW to DAR, September 13, 1943; and BHF to WFK, November 11, 1943; both E291, 1000/K(4), RG85, NARA I.

52. WCW-AcOICKIC to DAR, September 13, 1943; E291, 1000/K(4), RG85, NARA I.

53. Ibid.

54. LRB, personal letter to BHF, undated [probably September 12, 1943]; E291, 1000/K(1), RG85, NARA I.

55. EVA to BHF, September 20, 1943; E291, 1000/K(4), RG85, NARA I.

56. BHF to WFK, November 11, 1943, 2; E291, 1000/K(4), RG85, NARA I.

57. DAR to WFK, November 18, 1943.

58. WFK to DAR, December 2, 1943; E291, 1000/K(4), RG85, NARA I.

59. WFK to BHF, December 3, 1943; E291, 1000/K(4), RG85, NARA I.

60. BHF to WFK, December 14, 1943, 2.

61. "Scott Is New Chief at Japanese Camp," *Clearwater Tribune (Orofino, ID)* 31:40 (December 9, 1943), 6.

62. WFK to DAR, December 2, 1943. For more information on this facility, see Lynda Lin, "Community Groups Work to Place a Mark of History on a Little Known WWII Camp," *Pacific Citizen (Los Angeles, CA)* 144:5 (March 16-April 5, 2007), 1, 12.

63. "Translation of Fred Nomura's Farewell Speech," about April 13, 1942; WFK to LBS, June 20, 1942; MHS-OICTC to WFK-BP, June 9, 1942; Shinosuke Futai, Captain-in-Chief, TC, to MHS-OICTC, March 21, 1942; S. Yoshimura, Captain-in-Chief, TC, to MHS-OICTC, April 8, 1942; Ben Yabuno, Delano JACL, Delano, CA, to MHS-OICTC, April 11, 1942; Former Detainees from Delano and Bakersfield, Santa Fe, NM, by H. C. Okomiya, to MHS-OICTC, April 30, 1942; and "Resume of Mr. Tanejiro Saji's Farewell Message," June 5, 1942; all AN85-58A734, FN56125/27x1, Box 2406, RG85, NARA I.

64. "Remer to Leave Kooskia Internment Camp Soon," *Lewiston (ID) Morning Tribune*, December 5, 1943, 12. Nothing more is known of Remer's subsequent career.

Chapter Six: Finding Freedom in Leisure: Recreation at the Kooskia Internment Camp

1. Yoshito T. Kadotani, KIC, to Sanzo Aso, SFIC, May 28, 1943; E291, 1000/K(2), RG85, NARA I, PSK.

2. Ibid., and WFK to OICSF, April 27, 1943, 1-2; E291, FN56149/443, RG85, NARA I, Fiset. No schedule for movies was yet established for the internees.

3. LBS, "Instruction No. 58, Instructions Concerning the Treatment of Alien Enemy Detainees," April 28, 1942, 5; E291, 1022/X, RG85, NARA I; also available at http://home.comcast.net/~eo9066/1942/42-04/IA119.html (accessed November 9, 2009).

4. MHS to WFK, August 15, 1944, 2; AN85-58A734, FN56125/157, Box 2436, RG85, NARA I; Alfred Keehr and Dorothy Keehr, interview by Ramona Alam Parry, July

12, 1979, transcript, 12, CNFSO; Cecil Boller, interview by author, June 7, 2000, transcript, 10, AACC.

5. PS, July 11 and 12, 1944, 2; AN85-58A734, FN56125/157, Box 2436, RG85, NARA I, and MHS to WFK, August 15, 1944, 2. It was twenty-four by one hundred feet, with a nine-foot ceiling, WFK to JS, Mr. Mangione, Miss Hersey, September 14, 1944; together with CCE to WFK, September 8, 1944, 2; both AN85-58A734, FN56125/157, Box 2436, RG85, NARA I.

6. E. g., Allen H. Eaton, *Beauty behind Barbed Wire: The Arts of the Japanese in Our War Relocation Camps* (New York: Harper & Brothers, 1952), and Delphine Hirasuna, *The Art of Gaman: Arts and Crafts from the Japanese American Internment Camps 1942-1946* (Berkeley: Ten Speed, 2005).

7. BPR, n.d. [1942], 2; E466F, Sumida, Toshio, RG389, NARA II; Kooskia Internment Camp Scrapbook, Historical Photograph Collection, University of Idaho Library, PG 103, formerly owned by Micheal Moshier, son of the late camp guard E. D. (Ed) Moshier.

8. Amelia Jacks, telephone conversation with author, August 20, 1997, and e-mail message to author via Ken Jacks, November 25, 1997. The painter, whom Jacks knew as "Take" [pronounced "Taki"] may be Takeshi Okazaki.

9. Head mechanic Ralph Willhite received two mats. One depicts a rippling, forty-eight-star American flag and the other mat has an embroidered Buddhist swastika, Donald Weseman, letter to author, undated but about November 13, 2006. The mats are now at the Clearwater Historical Museum, Orofino, ID. Bulldozer and grader operator Bill Misner received the pillow cover and two other mats; all are now in the AACC. The pillow cover design is similar to the flag mat except that it has "USA" embroidered above the flag. Of the two mats, one reads "Mother" and the other depicts a sailboat. In explaining why the internee gave these items to Misner, his son, Mike, stated, "My father was very well liked by the internees. He was a kind and thoughtful person and treated them well. Moreover, he was teaching them a skill that could be useful to them when the war was over." Mike Misner also commented, "I have always been struck by the irony of the internees producing the one with the American flag when you consider how they were treated," Mike Misner, letter to author, June 1998.

10. Hozen Seki, [Diary], 1944-1948, December 2, 1944. Tojo was from Washington, DC.

11. Kathleen Warnick, conversation with author, January 20, 2007; Kathleen Warnick and Shirley Nilsson, *Legacy of Lace: Identifying, Collecting, and Preserving American Lace* (New York, Crown, 1988), 116-121. This type of needlework is known as Tenerife lace, sun lace, or wheel lace. The Historical Museum at Fort Missoula, Missoula, MT, owns a photograph of a non-Japanese man working on a hexagonal version of a tabletop loom; skeins of embroidery floss are also visible, Hewitt Memorial Collection, no. 2003.2.9.

12. Keehr and Keehr, interview, 12.

13. Leslie and Steve Weseman, e-mail message to author, October 5, 2006.

14. Donna Wasserstrom and Leslie Piña, *Bakelite Jewelry: Good Better Best* (Atglen, PA: Schiffer, 1997), 29. See Dee Battle and Alayne Lesser, *The Best of Bakelite & other Plastic Jewelry* (Atglen, PA: Schiffer, 1996), 88-89, for a few Bakelite rings, some of which are laminated.

15. Wasserstrom and Piña, *Bakelite Jewelry*, 81.

16. Kadotani to Aso.

17. Louis Fiset, *Imprisoned Apart: The World War II Correspondence of an Issei Couple* (Seattle: University of Washington, 1997), 54-56; Carol Bulger Van Valkenburg, *An Alien Place: The Fort Missoula, Montana, Detention Camp 1941-1944* (Missoula, MT: Pictorial Histories, 1995), 47, 61; Sigrid Arne, "Italians, Japanese at Ft. Missoula Don't Get Along," *Montana Record Herald (Helena, MT)*, approximately August 3, 1942, from Historical Museum at Fort Missoula, Box 8, Research Files, Folder, "Articles of Japanese Internees"; and Angela Cara Pancrazio, "A World of Meaning, Internment Art Stirs Memories: Camp-made Items Tell Vivid Stories of Coping with Desolation," *Oregonian*, February 22, 1999, B1, B8.

18. Boller, interview, 14.

19. Sharon and Mack Hall, e-mail messages to author, November 27 and December 6, 2006.

20. Donald Weseman, letter to author, undated but about October 23, 2006. Employee Bailey Rice may have received a similar piece.

21. DeAnn Scrabeck, e-mail message to author, April 14, 2005.

22. I am grateful to Joan Pills for providing measurements and other information on the chests.

23. "Fugetsu" could be the pen name of the person who made the chest, the name or pen name of the quote's author, or the name or pen name of someone else whose writing the craftsman admired. Yosh Shimoi kindly provided the transliteration, the translation, and the explanation.

24. BPR, April 27, 1942, 2; and IW, OICFM, "Report of Alien Enemy," August 29, 1945; both E466F, Hanamoto, George Hitoshi (Hiroshi), RG389, NARA II. The first document gives his occupation as laborer, whereas the second document calls him a journalist.

25. Amelia Jacks and Edwin Jacks, interview by Dennis Griffith, March 25, 1982, transcript, [5], LDKRS.

26. Hirasuna, *Art of Gaman*, 50-51, 70, 92-93.

27. LBS, "Instruction No. 58," 5.

28. ARM to unknown, "Visit to Japanese Internees, Detainees or Evacuees," July 31, 1944, 10; AN85-58A734, FN56125/157, Box 2436, RG85, NARA I.

29. Jacks and Jacks, interview, [8].

30. MHS to WFK, August 15, 1944, 2.

31. Jacks and Jacks, interview, [8].

32. Keehr and Keehr, interview, 10-11.

33. Seki, [Diary], October 19, 1944.

34. LBS, "Instruction No. 58," 4; WFK to OICFM, June 14, 1943; E291, 1000/K(1), RG85, NARA I.

35. ARM to unknown, "Visit to Japanese Internees," July 31, 1944, 6. Internees whose pay for the road work was less than fifty dollars per month, perhaps because of days they did not work, requested that they also receive the three dollars in canteen credit, but the officer in charge denied it, MHS to WFK, August 15, 1944, 1.

36. LBS, "Instruction No. 58," 4.

37. DA-AsOICKIC [on Federal Prison Camp stationery] to OICFM, June 2, 1943; E291, 1000/K(1), RG85, NARA I.

38. Jacks and Jacks, interview, [9].

39. HVS to OICKIC, February 24, 1944; E291, 1000/K(6), RG85, NARA I. The empty cases, when returned to the brewery, were worth fifty cents each.

40. Amelia Jacks, e-mail message to author via Ken Jacks, November 25, 1997. They went via "the old Van Camp road." The location of this road, its length, and how often it was used as a shortcut from Kooskia to Missoula, is uncertain. The Van Camp Lookout is north (or northeast) of the Lochsa River and west of Bimerick Creek, M. Alfreda Elsensohn, *Pioneer Days in Idaho County*, Vol. 2 (Caldwell, ID: Caxton, 1951), 259, 615.

41. Herman Ronnenberg and Steve Armstrong kindly provided information about Highlander beer. Armstrong further identified the container as a "steinie" or twelve-ounce bottle "typical of those used for beer in the 1930s/early 1940s era," Steve Armstrong, e-mail message to author, September 19, 2005.

42. Although the Kooskia camp is not covered, Minako Waseda, "Extraordinary Circumstances, Exceptional Practices: Music in Japanese American Concentration Camps," *Journal of Asian American Studies* 8:2 (June 2005) is an excellent study of the preservation of Japanese cultural activities in several internment and incarceration camps.

43. Seki, [Diary], September 17, 1944.

44. Ibid., September 18, 1944. In Japanese, *odori* means "dance."

45. Ibid., September 21, 1944.

46. Ibid., September 24 and 28, 1944.

47. Ibid., September 30, 1944.

48. See Waseda, "Extraordinary Circumstances," for musical activities at other camps.

49. BPR, n.d. [1942], 2; E466F, Wazumi, Minoru, RG389, NARA II; Jo Minoru Wazumi, KIC, to Miss Ruth Miller, New York, NY, June 16, 1943; E291, 1000/K(2), RG85, NARA I, PSK. "Meditation" is from the opera *Thais*, written by Jules Massenet (1842-1912) in 1893. The opera is based on a novel by Anatole France. Wazumi did not specify what instrument he played.

50. HVS to MHS, February 29, 1944, together with BHF [by] FLD, USDJ, INS, "Requisition for Supplies" to Supply Officer, October 9, 1943; both AN85-58A734, FN56125/23d, Box 2405, RG85, NARA I.

51. James I. Yano, reply to author's questions dated December 11, 1997, 4.

52. James I. Yano, reply to author's questions dated January 18, 1998, 2. Yano had worked for the Japanese Foreign Trade Bureau in Houston, Texas, and Kawamoto, an architect from New York, was the "brother-in-law of [the] former Ambassador to the U.S."

53. PS, July 11 and 12, 1944, 3.

54. Seki, [Diary], April 3 and 5, 1944.

55. Ibid., May 23, 1944.

56. Kadotani to Aso.

57. James I. Yano, reply to author's questions dated December 11, 1997, 4.

58. Geneva Convention of 1929, Chapter 2, Article 11; see Charles I. Bevans, comp. "Prisoners of War," in *Treaties and Other International Agreements of the United States of America 1776-1949*, vol. 2, Multilateral, 1918-1930, 932-964 (Washington, DC, U.S. Government Printing Office, 1969), 940-941.

59. WRB-AcOICKIC to WFK, March 8, 1945, together with ARM to unknown, "Visit to Japanese Internees, Detainees or Evacuees," March 1, 1945 [*sic*, for March 4], 4; AN85-58A734, FN56125/157, Box 2436, RG85, NARA I.

60. One elderly woman at the WRA's Tule Lake camp "would dig a hole in the dirt floor of the barracks where they lived and bury rice in a pot and let it ferment," The Kitchen Sisters, "Weenie Royale: Food and the Japanese Internment," 3, NPR [National Public Radio], aired December 31, 2007, available at http://www.npr.org/templates/story/story.php?storyId=17335538 (accessed November 12, 2009).

61. Boller, interview, 12.

62. The National Border Patrol Museum in El Paso, TX, owns a copy of the same photograph, captioned "Recreation: Dominos and Beer."

63. ARM to unknown, "Visit to Japanese Internees," July 31, 1944, 8.

64. Ken Adachi, *The Enemy that Never Was: A History of the Japanese Canadians* (Toronto, ON: McClelland and Stewart for the National Japanese Canadian Citizens Association, 1976), 272. One former Japanese Canadian internee said his group played *shogi* "by the light of a kerosene lamp," Takeo Ujo Nakano, *Within the Barbed Wire Fence*, with Leatrice Nakano (Toronto: University of Toronto, 1980), 15.

65. Keehr and Keehr, interview, 11; Jacks and Jacks, interview, [8, 9]. One of the gambling games, called "four, five, six" in English, was played with three dice; the best score was when the dice showed a four, a five, and a six at the same time. Cecil Boller remembered the Japanese pronunciation of this game as *si negu ro*, which he thought meant four, five, six, Boller, interview, 11. Romanized, using the Latin alphabet, the term may be *shigoro*, Peter T. Suzuki, *Linguistic Change in a Unique Cohort: Isseis, Kibeis, and Niseis in the WWII Internment Camps* (Omaha: School of Public Administration, University of Nebraska, 2005), 35; meaning *shi*, four; *go*, five; and *ro*, from *roku*, six. A complicating factor is that the game could also be called *shingoro*, the Japanese pronunciation of the English term "single roll" [of the dice], Suzuki, *Linguistic Change*, 35; this sounds more like what Boller remembered.

66. Keehr and Keehr, interview, 11-12.

67. Boller, interview, 20; Keehr and Keehr, interview, 6.

68. Tish Erb, "Jap Internees Work Hard, Well Treated, at Kooskia Road Camp," *Lewiston (ID) Morning Tribune*, September 26, 1943, sec. 2, p. 1.

69. Bill London, "A Different Kind of Christmas," *Central Idaho Magazine* 1:3 (Winter 1988), 9. There is still an island in the middle of the creek but it is very overgrown, difficult to access, and has not been examined for evidence of introduced plant species.

70. CCE to WFK, September 8, 1944.

71. WCW-AcOICKIC to DAR, September 13, 1943; E291, 1000/K(4), RG85, NARA I.

72. Mike Misner, reply to author's questions dated May 21, 1998.

73. Seki, [Diary], July 6, 1944.

74. Ibid., April 14, 1944. "Too Many Girls" (1940) starred Lucille Ball as Consuelo (Connie) Casey. When spunky Connie entered Pottawatomie College in Stopgap, New Mexico, her father decided to keep her out of trouble by hiring, without Connie's knowledge, four football players as her bodyguards. The film also included Lucy's future husband, Desi Arnaz, and, according to one film critic, this is when they met, Leonard Maltin, ed., *Leonard Maltin's Movie & Video Guide*, 1998 edition (New York: Signet, 1997), 1389.

75. Seki, [Diary], October 1, 1944.

76. Ibid., April 12 and 14, 1945.

77. James I. Yano, reply to author's questions dated January 18, 1998, 1.

78. Erb, "Internees Work Hard."

79. Seki, [Diary], December 11, 1944.

80. Ibid., July 15, 1944. "Mr. Higo" was Seitaro Higo, a laborer from Terminal Island, California, BPR, n.d. [1942], 2; E466F, Higo, Seitaro, RG389, NARA II.

81. Seki, [Diary], July 5, 1944.

82. Yon Shimizu, *The Exiles: An Archival History of the World War II Japanese Road Camps in British Columbia and Ontario* (Wallaceburg, ON: Shimizu Consulting and Publishing, 1993), 329, 373-374.

83. Dennis Griffith, "Internee Housing Area," sketch map drawn from an interview with Amelia and Edwin Jacks, [1982], LDKRS.

84. Boller, interview, 16, 22.

85. Dennis Griffith, "Apgar Cottages," sketch map drawn from an interview with Amelia and Edwin Jacks, [1982], LDKRS.

86. Seki, [Diary], September 7, 1944.

87. BHF to MHS, May 20, 1944; E291, 1000/K(6), RG85, NARA I, and MHS, SFN1036, August 30, 1944; AN85-58A734, FN56125/288, Box 2451, RG85, NARA I.

88. LBS, "Instruction No. 58," 5.

89. FMB-AsOICFM, "Supplemental Inventory of Stores Sold to Immigration & Naturalization Service," June 4, 1943, E291, 1000/S(1), RG85, NARA I; "Inventory of Major Equipment – Purchased Supplement No. 1", May 27, 1943; E291, 1000/S(1), RG85, NARA I.

90. ARM to unknown, "Visit to Japanese Internees," July 31, 1944, 10.

91. CCE to WFK, September 8, 1944.

92. PS, July 11 and 12, 1944, 2.

93. Jacks and Jacks, interview, [8].

94. BHF to T. M. Shiotani, KIC, July 7, 1943; E291, 1000/K(1), RG85, NARA I. Shiotani was actually a chauffeur but may also have had other duties. While at Fort Meade, MD, he renewed his New York chauffeur's license, Tatsuji Mitsu Shiotani, INS, "Alien Enemy Property Receipt," n.d.; E466F, Shiotani, Tatsuji Mitsu, RG389, NARA II.

95. Seki, [Diary], February 17, 1945.

96. James I. Yano, reply to author's questions dated December 11, 1997, 4.

97. PS, July 11 and 12, 1944, 3, and ARM to unknown, "Visit to Japanese Internees," July 31, 1944, 10.

98. PS, July 11 and 12, 1944, 3.

99. Boller, interview, 15. He described it as "just a little folder."

100. Kocho Fukuma, *A Spark of Dharma: The Life of Reverend Hozen Seki*, ed. Hoshin Seki (New York: American Buddhist Study Center, 2001), 79-80.

101. Ibid.

102. Kizaemon Momii, KIC, to Rikito Momii, Topaz Relocation Center, Topaz, UT, June 21, 1943; E291, 1000/K(2), RG85, NARA I, PSK.

103. Kizaemon Momii, KIC, to Rikito Momii, Topaz, UT, June 27, 1943; E291, 1000/K(2), RG85, NARA I, PSK. Rikito Momii did not join the U.S. Army after all. Although he was born in the U.S., his draft board unjustly classified him as an "enemy alien," Rikito Momii, reply to author's questions dated April 30, 1988.

104. Kizaemon Momii, KIC, to Rikito Momii, [Block] 5 - [Barrack] 8 - ["Apartment"] E, Topaz Relocation Center, Topaz, UT, July 28, 1943. It was "not practical" for Rick to keep the urn with him because he was contemplating a transfer to Cleveland, OH. Rick and Yasu Momii kindly provided a photocopy of this letter.

105. Defense stamps, also called war savings stamps, were sold in ten-cent, twenty-five-cent, fifty-cent, and $5 denominations. Stamps worth $18.75 could be exchanged for a $25 defense bond (savings bond, war bond), which also cost $18.75. At maturity, in ten years, the buyer received $25 for the surrendered bond, "Ask Phil - Stamp Collecting Starts Here," No. 147, ["War Savings Stamps"], available at http://www.askphil.org/answers.asp, and Wikipedia: the Free Encyclopedia, "War bond," available at http://en.wikipedia.org/wiki/War_bond (both accessed November 12, 2009).

106. Each individual internee who wished to participate had to obtain a license application form TFE-1, complete it, and then submit it to his nearest Federal Reserve Bank, JWP to LBS, January 15, 1942; and LBS by WFK-BP to NDC, OICFM, January 17, 1942; both AN85-58A734, FN56125/39, Box 2412, RG85, NARA I.

107. James D. Urabe, KIC, to Financial Officer, KIC and FMIC, June 26, 1943; E291, 1000/K(1), RG85, NARA I.

108. James Urabe, KIC, to RH, July 28, 1943; E466F, Urabe, James D., RG389, NARA II.

109. E. g., Seki, [Diary], April 24, 1944.

110. Ibid., December 5, 1944.

111. Hoshin Seki, e-mail message to author, January 31, 2006.

112. Ed and Amelia Jacks, Lewiston, ID, letter to Dennis Griffith, Resource Assistant, LDKRS, April 25, 1982, 1, Fluharty.

113. Erb, "Internees Work Hard."

114. PS, July 11 and 12, 1944, 2.

115. ARM to unknown, "Visit to Japanese Internees," July 31, 1944, 10.

116. Seki, [Diary], April 4 and 16, 1944. Although Buddha's birthday is celebrated in Japan on April 8, Seki did not detail how or when the internees celebrated this event.

117. LBS, "Instruction No. 58," 5-6.

118. NDC-AcACAC to OICKIC, November 20, 1943; E291, 1022/Q, RG85, NARA I.

119. BPR, n.d. [1942], 2; E466F, Sato, Kosaku, RG389, NARA II.

120. Tad Sato, letters to author, November 13 and December 15, 1997.

121. BPR, n.d. [1942], 2; E466F, Asaba, Kinzo, RG389, NARA II.

122. Pauline Asaba, letter to author, January 18, 1998.

123. Yoshi Mamiya, telephone conversation with author, December 13, 1997, and reply to author's questions dated December 18, 1997.

124. Amelia Jacks, e-mail message to author via Ken Jacks, November 25, 1997. There is no indication that this visit might have been conjugal.

125. Keehr and Keehr, interview, 3.

126. LBS, "Instruction No. 58," 3.

127. Ibid., 3, 5.

128. Wallace J. Long, *The Military History of Fort Missoula*, second revision (Missoula, MT: Friends of Historical Museum at Fort Missoula, 2005), 16, has a photograph of Japanese internees golfing, wearing casual clothing and straw Panama hats.

129. FMB-AcOICFM, "Supplemental Inventory," June 4, 1943, 1, and "Inventory of Major Equipment," May 27, 1943. Paddle tennis "... originated ... in 1898 to help

children learn to play tennis," "Paddle Tennis History," http://www.paddle-tennis. com/paddle_tennis_history.htm (accessed November 12, 2009).

130. Kadotani to Aso, and WFK to OICSF, April 27, 1943, 1-2.

131. Kadotani to Aso.

132. BPR, February 27, 1942, 2; E466F, Yoshikawa, Yoshie, RG389, NARA II.

133. Y. Yoshikawa, KIC, to H. Takiguchi, SFIC, May 28, 1943; E291, 1000/K(2), RG85, NARA I, PSK.

134. DA-AsOICKIC to OICFM, June 5, 1943; and BHF to DA-OICKIC, June 8, 1943; both E291, 1000/K(4), RG85, NARA I. Fishing was not allowed in Canyon Creek because it was "restricted"; the reason is unknown.

135. PS, July 11 and 12, 1944, 3.

136. ARM to unknown, "Visit to Japanese Internees," July 31, 1944, 6.

137. Seki, [Diary], June 25, 1944.

138. Chas. Yoshikawa, KIC, to Saima Yokota, SFIC, May 28, 1943; E291, 1000/K(2), RG85, NARA I, PSK.

139. MHS to WFK, August 15, 1944, 1.

140. Shimizu, *Exiles*, 121.

141. FVB to BHF, June 19, 1943, 2; E291, 1000/8, RG85, NARA I.

142. Kadotani to Aso.

143. PS, July 11 and 12, 1944, 3.

144. FMB-AcOICFM, "Supplemental Inventory," June 4, 1943, 1.

145. Keehr and Keehr, interview, 4; Boller, interview, 9, 12.

146. Boller, interview, 7.

147. BPR, March 26, 1942, 1-2; E466F, Tamaki, George, RG389, NARA II.

148. Joseph R. Svinth, *Getting a Grip: Judo in the Nikkei Communities of the Pacific Northwest 1900-1950* (Guelph, Ontario, Canada: EJMAS [Electronic Journals of Martial Arts and Sciences], 2003), 262.

149. Joseph R. Svinth, e-mail messages to author, June 27, 1999, and July 5, 1999, and Svinth, *Getting a Grip*, 121. In the latter work, Mochizuki appears in a group photograph depicting members of the Seattle Dojo [martial arts training hall] about 1927 or 1928, 68.

150. BPR, May 11, 1942, 2; E466F, Mochizuki, Goro, RG389, NARA II.

151. USDJ, INS, "Civilian Alien Enemies In Custody Kooskia Internment Camp, Kooskia, Idaho," February 29, 1944, 2; E271, Box 2, RG85, NARA I.

152. Stacey Hirose, "Kendo," in *Japanese American History: An A-to-Z Reference from 1868 to the Present*, ed. Brian Niiya (New York: Facts on File, 1993), 200. Kendo literally means, "The Way of the Sword." Prior to 1926 the sport was known as *kenjutsu* or *gekken*. Today, most practitioners use bamboo swords rather than steel ones.

153. Ibid., 200.

154. Joseph R. Svinth, e-mail message to author, April 30, 2002.

155. Svinth, e-mail message to author, July 2, 1999.

156. In mid-January 1937, California members of the Hokubei Butoku Kai visited Seattle and gave a kendo demonstration at the Seattle Buddhist Church. Journalist Kizaemon Ikken Momii accompanied the group and subsequently wrote the 1,200 page book, Ikken Momii, *Hokubei Kendo Taiken* (North American Kendo Clubs), (San Francisco: Hokubei Butoku Kai, 1939), Joseph R. Svinth, e-mail to author, March

1, 2004, and his "A Pre-WWII Kendo Helmet from Northern California," *The Iaido Journal*, November 2000, http://ejmas.com/tin/tinart_svinth_1100.htm (accessed November 12, 2009). Momii's book "deals with a brief history of the United States and of Japan and of 'The Way of the Sword' or 'Kendo.'" Written in Japanese, in an edition of one thousand copies, the books cost $5 apiece and were intended for sale only to members of Hokubei Butoku Kai, JLS, "In the Matter of the Detention of Kizaemon Ikken Momii, Report and Recommendation," February 6, 1942, 2; CLCF, Kizaemon Ikken Momii, 146-13-2-11-32; Stack 230/25/2/5, Box 171; RG 60; NARA II.

157. BPR, n.d. [1942], 2; E466F, Uenishi, Kozo, RG389, NARA II. Svinth commented, "the FBI [Federal Bureau of Investigation] liked [Momii's] book a lot because it provided photos and English-language addresses of kendo teachers, which it then used to help its special agents decide who to arrest following the attack on Pearl Harbor," Svinth, e-mail, April 30, 2002. As librarian Thomas Bolling described in his English introduction to a reprint of Momii's book, "The day after Pearl Harbor, most of the owners of this book burned their copies. The reason is that there is a series of portraits of the Emperor, famous generals, patriotic slogans, and so on, in the forematter of the volume. Terrified citizens knew that Kendo could be associated with Japanese militarism in the minds of government authorities. Indeed, the F.B.I. did find this book to be a ready-made directory for the roundup of all Kendo teachers in the days immediately following Pearl Harbor … long before the general Relocation," Thomas E. Bolling, "Introduction," to *Fukkokuban Hokubei Kendo Taikan* (Cyclopedia of the Japanese Kendo Societies in North America, pre-1939), Vol. 1, by Ikken Momii, reprint edition ([Tokyo]: Bunsei Shoin, 2001, available at http://www.bunsei.co.jp/denshi/N_A_preface_e.htm (accessed November 12, 2009).

158. JLS, "In the Matter of the Detention of Kizaemon Ikken Momii," 2.

159. JPO, [Report on] Umajiro Imanishi, April 2, 1942, 1; CLCF, Umajiro Imanishi, 146-13-2-82-531; Stack 230/25/34/3, Box 702, RG60, NARA II.

160. Guy Power, compiler, "FBI Reports on Kendo in Seattle and Portland before World War II," in *Journal of Combative Sport*, November 2003, available at http://ejmas.com/jcs/jcsart_power_1103.htm (accessed November 12, 2009). Joseph R. Svinth kindly provided me with an earlier version of this document.

161. Ibid., 1-3.

162. LW and GT, "Report and Recommendation," November 14, 1943; and EGH, MAEIB, OPMG, In Re: CoS/AE, January 19, 1944; both CLCF, Umajiro Imanishi.

163. Power, "FBI Reports on Kendo," 2, 6.

164. Ibid., 6-7.

165. Ibid., 7.

166. Keehr and Keehr, interview, 8.

167. ARM to unknown, "Visit to Japanese Internees," July 31, 1944, 1, 8.

168. Seki, [Diary], February 25, 1945.

169. Ibid., March 11, 1945.

170. Kadotani to Aso.

171. FMB-AcOICFM, "Supplemental Inventory," June 4, 1943, 1.

172. PS, July 11 and 12, 1944, 3. "Ping-Pong" is a trademark for table tennis.

173. Ibid. Paddle tennis nets are twenty-two feet long by two and one-half feet high, whereas tennis nets are forty-two feet long by three and one-half feet high.

174. PS, July 11 and 12, 1944, 3.

175. Dennis Griffith, "History Lower Canyon Creek Mines/Prison Camp - Oral Interview with Ayden Thomas," Lochsa Ranger District, 2360 - Special Interest Areas, LDKRS, April 26, 1982, 4.

176. FMB-AcOICFM, "Supplemental Inventory," June 4, 1943, 1.

177. PS, July 11 and 12, 1944, 3.

178. Kadotani to Aso.

179. Ibid.; FMB-AcOICFM, "Supplemental Inventory," June 4, 1943, 1. Since the horse-shoes appear on a list of sports equipment, they were for the game rather than for shoeing the camp's horses.

180. Arthur Shinei Yakabi, "My New Beautiful Country," manuscript (Papers of Arthur S. Yakabi, Research Library -- Historical Museum at Ft. Missoula, MT, 1978), 9.

Chapter Seven: Candid and Outspoken: Internee and Employee Perspectives on the Kooskia Internment Camp

1. Several native speakers stated that there is no equivalent term in Japanese for this expression.

2. Hozen Seki, [Diary], 1944-1948, January 1, 1944. The last entry was on April 10, 1947. On the flyleaf of the diary Seki wrote some important dates. These included his arrest on September 23, 1942, and his transfers to Ellis Island, NY; Fort George G. Meade, MD; Fort Missoula, MT; and "Camp Kooskia," ID; the latter on June 15, 1943.

3. LBS, "Instruction No. 58, Instructions Concerning the Treatment of Alien Enemy Detainees," April 28, 1942, 6; E291, 1022/X, RG85, NARA I; also available at http://home.comcast.net/~eo9066/1942/42-04/IA119.html (accessed November 9, 2009).

4. Ibid.

5. ARM to unknown, "Visit to Japanese Internees, Detainees or Evacuees," July 31, 1944; AN85-58A734, FN56125/157, Box 2436, RG85, NARA I.

6. James I. Yano, letters to author, answers to questions dated February 23, 1996, and March 18, 1998, 1; Chiyoko Yano, letter to author, September 16, 1997; James I. Yano, letter to author, October 4, 1997.

7. FB, "In the Matter of Isao Yano alias George Yano, Jimmy Yano Alien Enemy, Order," January 7, 1944; CLCF, Isao Yano, 146-13-2-74-34; Stack 230/25/32/3, Box 659, RG60, NARA II.

8. James I. Yano, letters to author, answers to questions dated October 29, 1997, 2, and November 19, 1997.

9. Seki, [Diary], April 2 and 4, 1944. After Italy surrendered to the Allies on September 8, 1943, most Italian aliens in custody, including Borovicka, subsequently gained parole or release. Borovicka left on February 1, 1944, and Kempski arrived shortly thereafter, LRB to EMS, February 1, 1944; E291, 1000/K(1), RG85, NARA I; USDJ, INS, "Civilian Alien Enemies In Custody - February 29, 1944, Kooskia Internment Camp, Kooskia, Idaho," 1-4; E271, Box 2, RG85, NARA I.

10. ARM to unknown, "Visit to Japanese Internees, Detainees or Evacuees," March 1, 1945 [*sic*, for March 4], 2; AN85-58A734, FN56125/157, Box 2436, RG85, NARA I.

11. ARM to unknown, "Visit to Japanese Internees, Detainees or Evacuees," July 31, 1944, 2.

12. Seki, [Diary], June 30, 1944.

13. Ibid., September 24, 1944. "Watanabe" was probably Ittetsu Watanabe, a salesman from Hawai'i.

14. Ibid., December 1, 1944.

15. Ibid., December 12, 1944.

16. Ibid., December 24, 1944.

17. Ibid., February 11, 1945.

18. ARM to unknown, March 1, 1945, 2. Maeda was a fisherman from California.

19. Seki, [Diary], March 25, 1945.

20. Ibid., March 18, 1945.

21. Ibid., April 21, 1944.

22. Ibid., April 26, 1944.

23. Paul Kashino was a Kibei, meaning a Japanese American who was born in the United States, educated in Japan, and who then returned to the United States, Virginia Kashino Tomita, letter to author, March 25, 1998.

24. Louis Fiset, "Censored!: U.S. Censors and Internment Camp Mail in World War II," in *Guilt by Association: Essays on Japanese Settlement, Internment, and Relocation in the Rocky Mountain West*, ed. Mike Mackey (Powell, WY: Western History Publications, 2001), 76.

25. LBS by WFK-BP, May 5, 1942; E291, 1025A, RG85, NARA I. As many as fifty Koreans may have served as Japanese interpreters, censors, and translators for the INS and other entities, Fiset, "Censored!," 96.

26. PRM to SAAG, Attn. WFK-BP, May 11, 1942; E291, 1025A, RG85, NARA I.

27. PRM to SAAG, May 22, 1942; AN85-58A734, FN56125/27x1, Box 2406, RG85, NARA I.

28. Virginia Tomita, letter to author, March 25, 1998.

29. Seki, [Diary], October 10, 1944.

30. E.g., ibid., February 7 and 22, 1945.

31. Ibid., July 20, 1944. Pauline's trip to Missoula implies that he worked for the INS rather than for the U.S. Bureau of Public Roads.

32. Ibid., July 31 and August 3, 1944.

33. Ibid., August 10, 15, and 18, 1944.

34. Ibid., August 22, 1944.

35. Ibid., August 26, 1944.

36. Ibid., August 27, 1944.

37. Ibid., September 12, 1944.

38. Ibid., September 21, 26, and November 9, 1944, and March 20, 1945.

39. Ibid., October 1 and 20, 1944. Hitoshi Hoshiko was a laborer from Nevada.

40. Ibid., October 7 and 8, 1944.

41. Ibid., January 10, 1945.

42. CCE to WFK, September 8, 1944; FN56125/157, Box 2436, RG85, NARA I.

43. MHS to FdA, August 1, 1944; together with ARM to Spanish Ambassador, Embassy of Spain, Washington, DC, telegram, August 1, 1944; AN85-58A734, FN56125/157, Box 2436, RG85, NARA I.

44. Seki, [Diary], November 11, 1944.

45. Alfred Keehr and Dorothy Keehr, interview by Ramona Alam Parry, July 12, 1979, transcript, 14, CNFSO.

46. Cecil Boller, interview by author, June 7, 2000, transcript, 3, AACC.

47. Shizuko Mishima, "Introduction to Japanese Holidays, Japanese Holidays Calendar," About.com: Japan Travel, available at http://gojapan.about.com/cs/japaneseholidays/a/holidaycalendar.htm (accessed November 15, 2009).

48. Seki, [Diary], July 4, 1944.

49. Although Keehr does not provide a date, Merrill Scott was the superintendent, so the year had to be 1944 because Scott did not arrive at the Kooskia camp until late 1943.

50. Keehr and Keehr, interview, 8, 13.

51. Ibid., 13-14. Keehr's dissatisfaction simmered, culminating in his resignation following another dispute with Scott. When asked if he were still at the camp when it closed, Keehr replied, "No, I and old Scott got into it and I told him what I thought of him." One of Keehr's responsibilities at that time included a daily trip to the village of Kooskia to take the outgoing mail, get the incoming mail, and pick up ten gallons of milk for the internees. Scott expressed his unhappiness with Keehr's reported driving speed and told him that he could not leave camp on his daily trip until 11:00 a.m. Keehr replied, "Well now, that's a smart deal! Leave here at 11:00 and I got 30 miles to go to get [to Kooskia] at 11:30 so that they can get the mail sorted ... to send out." "Well," Scott said, "that's what it's going to be." Then Keehr "blew my top and I told him [what I thought of him]. And he said, 'You're fired!' and I said, 'I quit before I started talking to you,'" ibid., 16-17.

52. Seki, [Diary], November 23, 1944.

53. BHF to OICFM, December 17, 1943; E291, 1000/S(3), RG85, NARA I.

54. Seki, [Diary], December 7, 1944.

55. MHS to WFK, October 12, 1944; AN85-58A734, FN56125/27j, Box 2409, RG85, NARA I.

56. JPL, Memorandum to Gitaro Kozima, Internee Spokesman, December 10, 1945; E306, RG85, NARA I. Although this document postdates the KIC's closure, it describes regulations that were in effect the previous year.

57. Seki, [Diary], December 18, 1944.

58. Ibid., December 20 and 25, 1944.

59. Bill London, "A Different Kind of Christmas," *Central Idaho Magazine* 1:3 (Winter 1988), 8.

60. "Best Wishes for the New Year, The Kooskia Internment Camp, Kooskia, Idaho, U.S.A.," n.d.; AN85-58A734 , FN56125/27j, Box 2409, RG85, NARA I.

61. Asian American Drug Abuse Program, "Events: Mochitsuki," available at http://www.aadapinc.org/events/mochitsuki/ (accessed November 15, 2009).

62. BHF to OICKIC, telegram; December 21, 1943; E291, 1000/K(4), RG85, NARA I.

63. BHF to OICKIC, December 31, 1943; E291, 1000/K(4), RG85, NARA I.

64. Seki, [Diary], December 20 and 30, 1944.

65. Asian American Drug Abuse Program, "Events: Mochitsuki"; "Today the custom of *mochitsuki* is carried on mostly in the temples, shrines, sponsored by the community organizations and continued in the homes of some families. Most of the New Year *mochi* consumed these days, however, is produced by Japanese confectionery stores on *mochi* machines rather than hand pounded."

66. Asian American Drug Abuse Program, "Events: Mochitsuki"; *usu* could also be made from stone or concrete.

67. Mikan Moblog: Everyday Japan through a Lens, "*Shimenawa* and *Gohei*," formerly available at http://www.kamoda.com/moblog/archives/003103.html (accessed May 12, 2005, but gone by August 8, 2007; copy in AACC). I am grateful to Yosh Shimoi for noticing the *shimenawa* decoration. He infers that the photo was taken before they began pounding the *mochi* because it shows the ceremonial *shimenawa*, the men are clean, and their equipment is not wet, Yosh Shimoi, e-mail to author, May 11, 2005.

68. Asian American Drug Abuse Program, "Events: Mochitsuki." Although the bun shape is most traditional, mochi can also be cut into rectangles and fried, grilled, broiled, or lightly boiled, Nijiya Market: Specializing in Imported and Organic Japanese Foods, "Japanese Traditions and Techniques," available at http://www.nijiya.com/www/html/welcme/JapanTechn/Japan%20Traditions.html (accessed November 15, 2009).

69. Guy Urata, "Mochitsuki - A Japanese Custom," formerly available at http://home.att.net/~guyurata/Text/Mochitsuki.html (accessed December 27, 2006, but gone by July 29, 2009; copy in AACC). The mirror, together with the sword and the jewel, comprise the Japanese imperial regalia.

70. Asian American Drug Abuse Program, "Events: Mochitsuki."

71. Urata, "Mochitsuki."

72. Ibid. *Kagami mochi* are often seen as offerings on Japanese graves.

73. Seki, [Diary], December 31, 1944. "Sochu" must be a nickname for one of the internees.

74. Ibid., January 2 and 6, 1945.

75. Yon Shimizu, *The Exiles: An Archival History of the World War II Japanese Road Camps in British Columbia and Ontario* (Wallaceburg, ON: Shimizu Consulting and Publishing, 1993), 303.

76. Seki, [Diary], May 7, 1944. The Works Progress Administration (WPA) camp, closed by the time of Seki's visit, was established in the spring of 1941. Located at Bimerick Creek, about ten miles upriver from the then-prison camp at Canyon Creek, it housed WPA enrollees who were also working on the Lewis-Clark Highway.

77. Ibid., May 28, 1944.

78. Milton (Mickey) Barton, letter to author, March 30, 1998, 1; telephone conversation with author, undated notes (1997?).

79. The photographs are housed at the CNFSO.

80. Seki, [Diary], May 28, 1944.

81. Ibid., July 2 and 3, 1944. Abe was a chauffeur from New York, Hino was a Buddhist priest from Hawai'i, Kono was a waiter from Alaska, and Tamaki ("Big George") was a sawmill worker from Alaska.

82. Ibid., October 14, 1944.

83. Ibid., July 7, 1944. Seitaro Higo was a laborer from California and Keiji Kijima was the camp's dental technician.

84. Ibid., July 29, 1944.

85. Ibid., November 6, 1944.

86. Ibid., March 1 and 10, 1945.

87. Ibid., September 7, 1944.

88. Ibid., April 1, 6, and 10, 1944.

89. Ibid., April 18 and December 14, 1944.

90. Ibid., April 22 and May 3, 1944.

91. Ibid., September 7 and October 16, 1944.

92. Ibid., December 27 and 28, 1944.

93. Ibid., January 20, 1945.

94. Ibid., April 11, 1944. This is stanza four of the Buddhist poem, "At the Grave." For a slightly different version, and the rest of the poem, see Paul Carus, *Buddhist Hymns*, available at http://libweb.uoregon.edu/ec/e-asia/read/budkins.pdf (accessed November 15, 2009).

95. Ibid.

96. Ibid., April 30, May 9, and July 18, 1944.

97. Ibid., July 17, 1944.

98. Ibid., October 22, 28, and November 7, 28, 1944.

99. Ibid., March 30, 1945.

100. Ibid., March 19, 28, 30, and April 1, 1945.

101. Ibid., April 2, 1945.

102. Seki, [Diary], April 4 and 5, 1945.

103. Ibid., April 6, 1945. If this is a Japanese-style bath, it is not so mentioned anywhere, either in Seki's diary or in other documents.

104. Ibid., April 7, 1945. The Stark and Jacks families lived in cottages at Apgar. The phrase, "the kind people of N.Y." implies that the Sekis might have had some help either paying for the trip or looking after things in the family's absence.

105. Ibid., April 8, 1945.

106. Hoshin Seki, e-mail to author, December 28, 2005.

107. Seki, [Diary], April 9, 1945.

108. Seki, e-mail, December 28, 2005.

109. Seki, [Diary], April 10 and 11, 1945.

110. Ibid., April 12, 1945.

111. Ibid., April 24, 1945.

112. Ibid., April 10, 1945.

Chapter Eight: Surviving External Scrutiny: Inspections, Rehearings, and Releases

1. LBS, "Instruction No. 58, Instructions Concerning the Treatment of Alien Enemy Detainees," April 28, 1942; E291, 1022/X, RG85, NARA I; also available at http://home.comcast.net/~eo9066/1942/42-04/IA119.html (accessed November 9, 2009).

2. Ibid., 2.

3. Charles Christopher Eberhardt (1871-1965) of Salina, Kansas, was a career diplomat who served as U.S. Minister to Nicaragua (1925-1929) and to Costa Rica (1930-1933), "The Political Graveyard," "Index to Politicians: Eaton to Eberhardt," available at http://politicalgraveyard.com/bio/eaton-eberhardt.html (accessed November 15, 2009).

4. That visit is mentioned in Eberhardt's report on his and Martin's July 1944 visit; no report from the first visit was located.

5. BHF to WY, June 28, 1943; E291, 1000/K(1), RG85, NARA I.

6. Ibid., 1-2.

7. E.g., Hyung-ju Ahn, "Koreans as Interpreters at Japanese Enemy Alien Detention Centers during World War II," in *Guilt by Association: Essays on Japanese Settlement, Internment, and Relocation in the Rocky Mountain West*, ed. Mike Mackey (Powell, WY: Western History Publications, 2001), 108-109, for beating of future Kooskia internee Otosaburo Sumi at Fort Lincoln, and Louis Fiset, *Imprisoned Apart: The World War II Correspondence of an Issei Couple* (Seattle: University of Washington, 1997), 45, for beatings at Fort Missoula.

8. BHF, "Confidential Memorandum to All Department Heads," Mr. Bayles, LAF, Mr. Harris, Mr. McGee, EMS, Mr. Thomason, December 20, 1943, 1; E291, 1021/Z, RG85, NARA I.

9. Ibid., 1-2, emphasis as in original.

10. ARM to unknown, "Visit to Japanese Internees, Detainees or Evacuees," July 31, 1944, 1-2, 4, 14-15; AN85-58A734, FN56125/157, Box 2436, RG85, NARA I.

11. ARM to WFK, August 9, 1944, 1; AN85-58A734, FN56125/157, Box 2436, RG85, NARA I.

12. Ibid. Because of travel complications, Merrill Scott offered to drive the two men to the WRA's Minidoka, ID, incarceration camp, and from there to the WRA camps at Heart Mountain, WY, and Topaz, UT. For part of the journey they traveled through Yellowstone National Park. Martin commented, off the record, that "in the Yellowstone, I demonstrated my ability to be a real champion, having actually caught more fish than either of my companions - a result happy to contemplate in view of the Missoula fiasco of two years ago," 2.

13. WFK to JS, Mr. Mangione, Miss Hersey, September 14, 1944; together with CCE to WFK, September 8, 1944, 4; both AN85-58A734, FN56125/157, Box 2436, RG85, NARA I. Japanese internees also drove trucks carrying fellow detainees to their various work sites.

14. Ibid.

15. WRB-AcOICKIC to WFK, March 8, 1945; together with ARM to unknown, "Visit to Japanese Internees, Detainees or Evacuees," March 1, 1945 [*sic*, for March 4], 4; both AN85-58A734, FN56125/157, Box 2436, RG85, NARA I.

16. HVS to CO, telegram, March 8, 1944; E291,1000/S(3), RG85, NARA I.

17. Hozen Seki, [Diary], 1944-1948, July 11, 1944.

18. MHS to WFK, August 15, 1944; together with PS to MHS, August 4, 1944; both AN85-58A734, F56125/157, Box 2436, RG85, NARA I.

19. PS, July 11 and 12, 1944, translation dated March 12, 1945, 1, 4; FN56125/157, Box 2436, RG85, NARA I. The delay in the report's availability was due to the time required to translate it into English.

20. BHF to OICKIC, April 19, 1944; E291,1000/S(3), RG85, NARA I.

21. CH to WFK, January 9, 1945; together with WFK to CH, January 12, 1945: together with WFK to OICKIC, January 12, 1945; together with CH to WFK, January 22, 1945; all AN85-58A734, F56125/157, Box 2436, RG85, NARA I.

22. Seki, [Diary], March 2 and 3, 1945.

23. MHS to WFK, August 15, 1944; together with PS to MHS, August 4, 1944.

24. WFK to OICFM, June 3, 1943; E291, FN56149/443, RG85, NARA I, Fiset, and "Japanese at Kooskia Desiring Re-hearing," after June 3, 1943; E291, RG85, NARA I, Fiset. Another list, "Southern District of California Cases Now Detained at Kooskia,

Idaho," June 15, 1943; E291, 1000/K(4), RG85, NARA I, contains forty names; some names are on both lists.

25. EJE to BHF, August 9, 1943; E291, 1036/A, RG85, NARA I.

26. EJE to BHF, September 16, 1943; E291, 1036/A, RG85, NARA I, and BHF to OICKIC, July 5, 1943; E291, 1000/K(4), RG85, NARA I.

27. EJE to BHF, September 10, 1943; E291, 1036/A, RG85, NARA I.

28. GT to BHF, October 25, 1943; E291, 1000/K(4), RG85, NARA I. Turrill enclosed a box of California dates for Fraser "which I hope you and your mother will enjoy." Adele Vanden Heuvel may have been a secretary for di Girolamo, a nanny for Vincent, or a relative of a person in the group.

29. BHF to AdG, telegram, November 1, 1943; E291, 1000/K(4), RG85, NARA I.

30. BHF to WFK, November 11, 1943; E291, 1000/K(4), RG85, NARA I.

31. James I. Yano, letter to author, answers to questions dated December 11, 1997, 2-3.

32. LW and GT, "In the Matter of the Detention of Isao [James] Yano, Internee of the District of Southern Texas, Report and Recommendation," November 14, 1943, 1; CLCF, Isao [James] Yano, 146-13-2-74-34, Stack 230/25/32/3, Box 659, RG60, NARA II.

33. Ibid.

34. Ibid., 2.

35. EGH, MAEIB, OPMG, In Re: CoS/AE, Isao [James] Yano, April 6, 1944; CLCF, Isao [James] Yano.

36. Kosaku Sato, KIC, to OICFM, August 24, 1943; Sato.

37. JCD to EJE, May 18, 1942; Sato.

38. Ibid.

39. LW and GT, "In the Matter of the Detention of Kosaku Sato, Internee of the District of Western Washington, Report and Recommendation," November 13, 1943; Sato.

40. LW and GT, "In the Matter of the Detention of Kosaku Sato."

41. JCD to EJE, December 11, 1943; Sato.

42. DAR to EJE, February 1,1944, FN284/128, Sato.

43. ["Japanese Enemy Alien Card"], 2, Sato.

44. Tad Sato, telephone conversation with author, November 18, 1997.

45. LW and GT, "In the Matter of the Detention of Seiichi Yoshinaka, Internee of the District of Eastern Washington, Report and Recommendation," November 16, 1943; CLCF, Seiichi Yoshinaka, 146-13-2-81-14, RG60, NARA II.

46. RLF, [Report on] Seiichi Yoshinaka, January 16, 1942, 2-3; CLCF, Seiichi Yoshinaka.

47. Mrs. Akiko Yoshinaka, by Takeko Yoshinaka, Moses Lake, WA, to EJE, January 24, 1944, 1; CLCF, Seiichi Yoshinaka.

48. Kazuo Yoshinaka, Moses Lake, WA, to EJE, January 24, 1944; CLCF, Seiichi Yoshinaka.

49. Ibid.

50. A. Yoshinaka by T. Yoshinaka to EJE, January 24, 1944, 1; and Pacific Northwest National Laboratory, "Hanford Townsite, Washington," available at http://ecology.pnl.gov/gallery/landsc/Hanfordtwn.htm?keepThis=true&TB_iframe=true&height=400&width=650 (accessed November 15, 2009), and D. A. Neitzel and others, *Hanford Site National Environmental Policy Act (NEPA) Characterization Report*, PNNL-6415, Revision 17 (Richland, WA: Pacific Northwest National Laboratory for

the U.S. Department of Energy, 2005), available at http://www.pnl.gov/main/publications/external/technical_reports/PNNL-6415Rev17.pdf (accessed November 15, 2009). Ringold, on the Columbia River, was one of several historic settlements, including Hanford and White Bluffs, that were located on the Hanford Site in south central Washington; "The towns and nearly all other structures were razed after the U.S. Government acquired the land for the Hanford Nuclear Reservation in 1943," 4.104, as part of the Manhattan Project which produced plutonium. Portions of the Hanford Site are contaminated with radioactive materials and are now part of the Superfund cleanup process, e.g., Shannon Dininny, "Washington State, DOE Agree on Hanford Cleanup Deadlines," *Moscow-Pullman (ID-WA) Daily News*, August 12, 2009, 4A.

51. LW and GT, Detention of Seiichi Yoshinaka, "Report and Recommendation," November 16, 1943.

52. Ibid.

53. EGH, MAEIB, OPMG, In Re: CoS/DEA, February 14, 1944; CLCF, Seiichi Yoshinaka.

54. EGH, MAEIB, OPMG, In Re: CoS/DEA, March 21, 1944, CLCF, Seiichi Yoshinaka.

55. HVS to MHS, March 9, 1944; together with NDC, FMIC, to OICFM, radiogram, March 9, 1944; E291, 1000/K(4), RG85, NARA I.

56. BPR, April 21, 1942, 2; E466F, Akagi, Henry Kiichi, RG389, NARA II, and "Japanese Aliens on Parole within Immigration District No. 10," June 30, 1944; AN85-58A734, F56125/15, Box 2402, RG85, NARA I.

57. EGH, MAEIB, OPMG, In Re: CoS/DEA, December 21, 1943; and EGH, MAEIB, OPMG, In Re: CoS/AE, April 15, 1944; both E466F, Akagi, Henry Kiichi.

58. Wm. Joe Simonds, "Anderson Ranch Dam," in *The Boise Project*, Bureau of Reclamation History Program, Denver, CO, Research on Historic Reclamation Projects, 1997, available at http://www.usbr.gov/projects//ImageServer?imgName=Doc_1245087693030.pdf (accessed November 15, 2009).

59. GHA, "Shohei Arase," September 6, 1944, 2; CLCF, Shohei Arase, 146-13-2-82-485, Stack 230/25/34/3, Box 701, RG60, NARA II.

60. Betty Arase Okamura, e-mail to author, June 19, 2003.

61. BHF to EJE, Attn.: EJC, December 11, 1943, E291, 1016A, E291, RG85, NARA I.

62. EGH, MAEIB, OPMG, "Report of enemy alien in custody," Chiyeko Yamaguchi, April 6, 1944; and J. L. O'Rourke, USDJ, INS, CCIC, "Report of Alien Enemy," Michihiro Yamaguchi, January 17, 1945; both CLCF, Genji George Yamaguchi, 146-13-2-12-4230, Stack 230/25/10/4, Box 200, RG60, NARA II.

63. Koshio Henry Shima, telephone conversation with author, April 28, 1998. Teruko Shimabukura [*sic*] of the CCIC is listed as the next of kin for both men, DJ, INS, "Civilian Alien Enemies In Custody - Kooskia Internment Camp, Kooskia, Idaho," June 30, 1944, 5; E271, Box 2, RG85, NARA I. With her mother and two siblings in Japan, and her father and other brother interned, she would have been alone in Peru.

64. Koshio Henry Shima, telephone conversation with author, April 13, 1998.

65. Seki, [Diary], e.g., July 11, 1944.

66. Oyobu Watanabe, of the CCIC, is listed as the next of kin for Harukichi Watanabe, DJ, INS, "Civilian Alien Enemies In Custody - Kooskia Internment Camp, Kooskia, Idaho," June 30, 1944, 6; E271, Box 2, RG85, NARA I.

67. Seki, [Diary], July 25, 1944.

68. Seki, [Diary], January 6, 1945.

69. BPR, n.d. [1942], 2; E466F, Kawahara, Tadao, RG389, NARA II, and DAR by WCW to OICFM, July 20, 1943; E291, 1000/K(1), RG85, NARA I.

70. Kazuo Takesaki, KIC, to Sakaye Yoshimura, SFIC, January 14, 1945, AACC. I am grateful to Tim Taira for providing me with a copy of Takesaki's letter, in Japanese, and to June Taira for translating it.

71. In 1940 the United States chartered the *Gripsholm* and turned her into an International Red Cross Exchange Ship. "In May 1942 she made her first repatriation voyage from New York to Goa in order to leave Japanese diplomats and embark American prisoners of war," Daniel Othfors, "Gripsholm (I)/Berlin 1925-1966," available at Daniel Othfors and Henrik Ljungström, "The Great Ocean Liners," http://www. thegreatoceanliners.com/index2.html (accessed November 15, 2009).

72. WFK to OICFM, June 21, 1943; E291, 1000/K(4), RG85, NARA I. Kadotani was a gardener from California and Seike was a shrimp fisherman picked up on a boat in Louisiana.

73. BHF to CO, telegram, June 29, 1943; E291, 1000/K(4), RG85, NARA I.

74. Yoshito Kadotani, KIC, to Miss M. Kadotani, Poston, AZ, July 1, 1943; E291, 1000/K(4), RG85, NARA I, PSK.

75. JDC by JGH to JP(1), April 3, 1944; Gift of Kathleen Kadotani Arima, JANM (97.137.1).

76. DAR to OICFM, July 26, 1943; E291, 1000/K(4), RG85, NARA I.

77. FMB to OICKIC, July 31, 1943; E291, 1000/K(4), RG85, NARA I.

78. Louis Yorikatsu Kakiyama, KIC, to OICFM, July 30, 1943; E291, 1000/K(4), RG85, NARA I. Kakiyama also spelled his first name "Luis."

79. Tokuhei Akena, KIC, to OICFM, August 21, 1943; E291, 1000/K(4), RG85, NARA I.

80. Missoula Mercantile Company, No. 3819-48, for [Tokuhei] Akena, August 26, 1943; and Missoula Mercantile Company, No. 3879-30, for [Louis] Kakiyama, August 26, 1943; both E291, 1000/S(2), RG85, NARA I.

81. FMB-AcOICFM to DAR, August 30, 1943; E291, 1000/K(4), RG85, NARA I.

82. "Sailing List [of] Japanese Embarked for Second Voyage of Gripsholm New York," September 3, 1943, 1-3, 9, 15, 23; E465, Box 2059, RG389, NARA II.

83. Thomas Connell, *America's Japanese Hostages: The World War II Plan for a Japanese Free Latin America* (Westport, CT: Praeger, 2002), 167-168.

Chapter Nine: Friends or Enemies?: Internees Interact with the "Home Front"

1. *Recorder Herald (Salmon, ID)*, "Japs Can Build Road," March 4, 1942, 4. The editor was unaware of Canada's own internment road camp scheme, Barry Broadfoot, *Years of Sorrow, Years of Shame: The Story of Japanese Canadians in World War II* (Toronto: Doubleday Canada, 1977), 143.

2. Chase A. Clark, "Clark Defends Stand on Aliens," *Kamiah (ID) Progress* 37:17 (March 19, 1942), 1.

3. Ibid. Clark overlooked the many Japanese who had already been settled in Idaho for nearly sixty years, particularly in Nampa and Pocatello, Robert C. Sims, "The Japanese American Experience in Idaho," *Idaho Yesterdays* 22:1 (Spring 1978), 2.

4. "Would Work Jap Aliens on Lewis and Clark Highway," *Kamiah (ID) Progress* 37:17 (March 19, 1942), 1. Clark seems to have adopted the suggestion, first proposed in an editorial in a Salmon, ID, newspaper, that Japanese be used for this road construction project, "Can Build Road," *Recorder Herald.*

5. "End to Jap Problem Told By Gov. Clark," *Idaho County Free Press (Grangeville, ID)* 57:3 (May 28, 1942), 10.

6. "Slap That Jap!" [advertisement], *Idaho County Free Press (Grangeville, ID)* 57:13 (August 6, 1942), 5.

7. E.g., Richard H. Minear, *Dr. Seuss Goes to War: The World War II Editorial Cartoons of Theodor Seuss Geisel* (New York: New Press, 1999). An important example of Seuss's anti-Japanese American bias is a cartoon dated February 1942. Titled "Waiting for the Signal From Home … ," it depicts ranks of caricatured Japanese from Washington, Oregon, and California gleefully lining up to receive bricks of "'TNT'" from a booth labeled "Honorable 5th Column," 65.

8. Sandra L. Lee, "Caboose Pulls into Locomotive Park," *Lewiston (ID) Morning Tribune*, September 3, 1997, 5A, 8A; Melba Ashburn, e-mail to author, January 20, 1998. Although no contemporary newspapers referred to this incident, I do not doubt its authenticity.

9. Mrs. C. D. Bretthauer, "Japs Arrive; Housed Locksa [*sic*] Prison Camp," *Idaho County Free Press (Grangeville, ID)* 58:4 (June 3, 1943), 1.

10. Arthur Deschamps, Jr., interview by Susan Buchel, November 20, 1979, transcript, tape 67-1:10-12, Historical Museum at Fort Missoula, Missoula, MT.

11. "Japs to Leave Camp Tomorrow," *Lewiston (ID) Morning Tribune*, May 1, 1945, 10.

12. Milton (Mickey) Barton, letter to author, March 30, 1998, 4.

13. E.g., Frank Bowles, telephone conversation with author, January 19, 1998; Mike Misner, letter to author, answers to questions dated May 21, 1998. Mike remembers getting Milky Ways and Hershey Bars, candy that, during wartime, was "almost impossible to get otherwise."

14. Irene Trenary, telephone conversation with author, February 19, 1998.

15. FdA to Jinjiro Inuzuka, KIC, June 10, 1943; together with Mrs. N. O. Talbot, San Diego, CA, to FdA, June 5, 1943; both E291, 1000/K(2), RG85, NARA I.

16. Talbot to FdA.

17. Ruth Miller, Hartford, CT, to Jo Minoru Wazumi, June 23, 1942; E466F, Wazumi, Minoru, RG389, NARA II.

18. Elizabeth Nesbitt, Philadelphia, PA, to Minoru Wazumi, [June ?, 1942]; E466F, Wazumi, Minoru, RG389, NARA II.

19. Nesbitt to Wazumi, August 18, [1942]; E466F, Wazumi, Minoru.

20. Nesbitt to Wazumi, August 24, 1942; E466F, Wazumi, Minoru.

21. [Conduct report], Fort George G. Meade, MD, March 10, 1943, 2; E466F, Wazumi, Minoru, RG389, NARA II.

22. CLB to PMG, September 24, 1942; E466F, Okazaki, Takeshi, RG389, NARA II.

23. Takeshi Okazaki, SFIC, "Petition for Repatriation," June 21, 1943; E466F, Okazaki, Takeshi, RG389, NARA II. On the petition is the typed and underlined sentence, "I am not wish to be repatrated [*sic*]."

24. Cecil Boller, interview by author, June 7, 2000, transcript, 4, AACC.

25. Cecil Boller, telephone conversation with author, August 20, 1997, and interview, 9.

26. Boller, interview, 8-9. When asked about this cooking method, two informants responded that "since oven cooking is not a tradition in Japan, … this method was something that the Issei developed. [Janet's] guess on the 'blackness' would be that it was either marinated [in soy sauce] or basted with soy sauce while being 'baked.' It could have been a preservation method which was developed by an Issei community which had access to a lot of fish. … there's no standard J[apanese] name from Japan [for this type of blackened fish]," Janet and Seiichi Murai, e-mail to author, May 19, 2005.

27. The trip was probably to the family camp at Crystal City. Dentist Keiji Kijima went there, but Boller does not recall him specifically.

28. Boller, interview, 7-8.

29. Ibid.

30. Alfred Keehr and Dorothy Keehr, interview by Ramona Alam Parry, July 12, 1979, transcript, 7, CNFSO.

31. Bill London, "A Different Kind of Christmas," *Central Idaho Magazine* 1:3 (Winter 1988), 9.

32. Cecil Boller, interview, 11.

33. Jan Boyer, e-mail to author, September 9, 2005.

34. Milton (Mickey) Barton, e-mail to author, September 23, 2004, 2.

35. Milton (Mickey) Barton, telephone conversation with author, 1997?

36. Milton (Mickey) Barton, letter to author, March 30, 1998, 4.

37. EWK to BJF, July 1, 1943; E291, 1000/K(4), RG85, NARA I, and "Misapplied Use of War Prison Labor," *Spokesman-Review (Spokane, WA)* 61:47 (June 30, 1943), 4.

38. BHF to WFK, December 14, 1943; E291, 1000/K, RG85, NARA I.

39. EWK by CSW to BJF, July 28, 1943; together with Mrs. Harvey Gumm, Kooskia, ID, "Japs Get Beer, Rest Get Left"; both E291, 1000/K(1), RG85, NARA I. Kelley misstates the letter's publication date as July 24 for the correct date, July 25, Mrs. Harvey Gumm, letter to the editor, *Spokesman-Review (Spokane, WA)* 61:72 (July 25, 1943), A15.

40. BHF to BJF, August 2, 1943; E291, 1000/K(1), RG85, NARA I, and BHF to WFK, December 14, 1943; E291, 1000/K, RG85, NARA I. A search of the *Spokesman-Review* for that time period failed to locate Gumm's second letter.

41. Boller, interview, 4.

42. TE to BHF, August 1, 1943; E291, 1000/K(4), RG85, NARA I.

43. Ibid.

44. BHF to TE, August 6, 1943; E291, 1000/K(4), RG85, NARA I.

45. TE to BHF, September 3, 1943; E291, 1000/K(4), RG85, NARA I.

46. BHF to TE, September 16, 1943; E291, 1000/K(4), RG85, NARA I.

47. Tish Erb, "Jap Internees Work Hard, Well Treated, at Kooskia Road Camp," *Lewiston (ID) Morning Tribune*, September 26, 1943, sec. 2, pp. 1, 5.

48. Ibid., 1.

49. Ibid.

50. Ibid. Although Erb wrote that the internees had families "from Maine to Mexico," that may have been a slang expression, since Maine was not one of the states mentioned in the records obtained at the National Archives. Former Kooskia camp guard Alfred Keehr remembered that some of the internees were from Florida, Keehr and Keehr, interview, 16, but only one appears on the official lists.

51. Erb, "Internees Work Hard," 1.
52. Ibid.
53. Ibid., 3.
54. Amelia Jacks, telephone conversation with author, August 20, 1997.
55. Irving Kalinoski, telephone conversation with author, August 21, 1997.
56. Helen Thiessen, telephone conversation with author, August 21, 1997. Thiessen was Irving Kalinoski's mother.
57. Ibid. Restaurants, too, needed ration points to procure meat and other rationed commodities during World War II. No information was found to suggest that they received an exemption for feeding internees.
58. Kalinoski, telephone conversation. Because the restaurant only had two stoves, they had to take the hams to Spengler's Bakery, where they cooked them in the bread ovens.
59. EWK by CSW to BHF, July 10, 1943; E291, 1000/K(1), RG85, NARA I.
60. BHF to EWK, July 20, 1943; E291, 1000/K(1), RG85, NARA I.
61. Mae Betty (Piersol) Rainville, letter to author, March 3, 2005.
62. Mae Betty Piersol, St. Joseph's Hospital, Lewiston, ID, to Ed Yoshimura, KIC, August 22, 1944; copy in AACC.
63. Dick Riggs, comment to author, October 20, 2005.
64. Thiessen, telephone conversation.

Chapter Ten: Back to Barbed Wire and Beyond: Closure, and Aftermath, of the Kooskia Internment Camp

1. Hozen Seki, [Diary], 1944-1948, June 23, 1944.
2. Ibid., February 14, 1945.
3. *Monthly Review*, "News of the Month: Kooskia Internment Camp Is Abandoned by Service," 2:2 (May 1945), 148, only 104 internees then remained; Hugh Carter and others, "Administrative History of the Immigration and Naturalization Service during World War II," typescript (General Research Unit, Office of Research and Educational Services, INS, USDJ, INS Library, Washington, DC, 1946), 305.
4. Seki, [Diary], April 20, 1945.
5. Ibid., April 21, 1945.
6. Ibid., April 22, 1945. Although this seems excessive, most of it was probably books. His diary records many such mail-order purchases while he was at the Kooskia camp.
7. "Orofino Sends Group to Lochsa Conclave," *Clearwater Tribune (Orofino, ID)* 33:8 (April 26, 1945), 1; "Work to Be Continued on L-C Highway," *Lewiston (ID) Morning Tribune*, April 28, 1945, 10.
8. Seki, [Diary], April 24, 1945; "Hearing Opens Today On L-C Road Progress," *Lewiston (ID) Morning Tribune*, April 26, 1945, 14; "Public Hearing to Be Held Here Today on L-C Highway Program," *Lewiston (ID) Morning Tribune*, April 27, 1945, 12;
9. Seki, [Diary], April 26, 1945.
10. "Public Hearing," *Lewiston (ID) Morning Tribune*. The article names attendees and the Idaho and Washington communities they represented.

11. Seki, [Diary], April 27, 1945. Seki was then the internees' elected spokesman; Gitaro Kozima was the assistant spokesman; and "Jacks" was employee Ed Jacks, guarding the two internees.

12. "Work to Be Continued," *Lewiston (ID) Morning Tribune.*

13. Seki, [Diary], April 27, 1945.

14. "Work to Be Continued," *Lewiston (ID) Morning Tribune.*

15. Ibid., April 28, 1945.

16. Seki, [Diary], May 1, 1945.

17. Ibid., May 2, 1945.

18. MHS to WFK, February 28, 1945; AN85-58A734, FN56125/157, Box 2436, RG85, NARA I, and Amelia Jacks and Edwin Jacks, interview by Dennis Griffith, March 25, 1982, transcript, [1], LDKRS. Scott transferred to the Fort Stanton, NM, internment camp.

19. WRB-AcOICKIC to CEW, "Collections for miscellaneous salvage articles," May 12, 1945; AN85-58A734, FN56125/288, Box 2451, RG85, NARA I. Beecher left by mid-June 1945 and Emilio J. Morelli became the acting officer in charge, "Japs to Leave Camp Tomorrow," *Lewiston (ID) Morning Tribune*, May 1, 1945; "Jap Internees Leave," *Lewiston (ID) Morning Tribune*, May 3, 1945, 12. For his last official act, Morelli issued an order to discontinue the Kooskia camp's "Farmer Line" telephone service effective June 30, 1945; it had cost $3.00 per year, EJM to PMO, June 11, 1945, with attachments; AN85-58A734, FN56125/289, Box 2451, RG85, NARA I.

20. DJH to IPM, July 17, 1945; AN85-58A734, FN56125/23e, Box 2405, RG85, NARA I.

21. IPM to WFK, July 18, 1945; AN85-58A734, FN56125/23e, Box 2405, RG85, NARA I. A handwritten note on this memo reads, "Mr. Lewis - Ike [McCoy] is huffy. Perhaps you & Ted can offer some suggestions to him."

22. DAR to WFM, August 7, 1943; AN85-58A734, FN56125/23d, Box 2405, RG85, NARA I.

23. Thomas W. Campbell and Ladd Hamilton, "Thousands Witness L-C Highway Dedication," *Lewiston (ID) Morning Tribune*, August 20, 1962, 1. According to Idaho highways historian Cort Conley, "the fact that [the highway] was not completed until 1962 conveys a sense of the convoluted topography," Cort Conley, *Idaho for the Curious* (Cambridge, ID: Backeddy Books, 1982), 107.

24. Wallace G. Lewis, "On the Trail of Lewis and Clark: Building the Lewis-Clark Highway," *Idaho Yesterdays* 43:3 (Fall 1999), 23; Johnny Johnson, "The Time Had Come to Celebrate End of the 'Missing Link,'" *The Golden Age* (Spring/Summer 1996), 15.

25. Campbell and Hamilton, "Thousands Witness L-C Highway Dedication," 3.

26. Exceptions, which do mention the Kooskia Internment Camp, include C. Harvey Gardiner, *Pawns in a Triangle of Hate* (Seattle: University of Washington Press, 1981), 97-99, 126; Brian Niiya, ed., "Internment Camps," in *Japanese American History: An A-to-Z Reference from 1868 to the Present* (New York: Facts on File, 1993), 176; Franklin Ng, ed., "Japanese American Internment," in *The Asian American Encyclopedia* (New York: Marshall Cavendish, 1995), 723; and Patsy Sumie Saiki, *Ganbare! An Example of Japanese Spirit* (Honolulu, HI: Kisaku, 1982), viii. Books published in more recent years generally do mention it, but not always.

27. Bill London, "A Different Kind of Christmas," *Central Idaho Magazine* 1:3 (Winter 1988), 9.

28. E.g., H[oward] Watts and Fred Kuester, "Cultural Site Record [for] 10-IH-870," Oro-fino, ID: CNFSO, 1979. The site number, 10-IH-870, is part of a system devised by the Smithsonian Institution for recording archaeological sites. In an alphabetical list of states, Idaho is tenth; IH stands for Idaho County, and the Canyon Creek Prison Camp/Kooskia Internment Camp site is the 870th archaeological site recorded in Idaho County. See also Alfred Keehr and Dorothy Keehr, interview by Ramona Alam Parry, July 12, 1979, transcript, CNFSO.

29. E.g., Jacks and Jacks, interview, and Dennis Griffith, Reply to: 2360 Special Interest Area. Subject: History of Japanese Internment Period: Canyon Creek Prison Camp Site. Photocopy of handwritten document, LDKRS, [1982]. These materials are now housed at the LDKRS and at the CNFSO.

30. Watts and Kuester, "Cultural Site Record [for] 10-IH-870." For a gripping account of the Carlin Party, see Ladd Hamilton, *Snowbound* (Pullman: Washington State University, 1997).

31. Watts and Kuester, "Cultural Site Record [for] 10-IH-870," 2, and *Asian American Comparative Collection Newsletter*, "Ceramics from the Kooskia Internment Camp, 10-IH-870," 20:2 (June 2003), 3.

32. Micheal Moshier, e-mail message to author, March 27, 2005.

33. National Park Service, *Japanese American Confinement Sites Preservation*, "Public Law 109-441-Dec. 21, 2006, Preservation of Japanese American Confinement Sites," available at http://www.nps.gov/history/hps/HPG/JACS/downloads/Law.pdf (accessed November 16, 2009).

34. Kara Miyagishima, e-mail to author, July 24, 2009; Kathy Hedberg, "UI Prof Goes in Search of the Past," *Lewiston (ID) Tribune*, August 10, 2009, 5A. Assistant professor Stacey Camp of the Department of Sociology/Anthropology will direct the project.

35. Reports that resulted were Priscilla Wegars, "'A Real He-Man's Job:'" Japanese Internees and the Kooskia Internment Camp, Idaho, 1943-1945," for the Civil Liber-ties Public Education Fund (AACC, 1998), and her *Golden State Meets Gem State: Californians at Idaho's Kooskia Internment Camp, 1943-1945* (Moscow, ID: Kooskia Internment Camp Project, 2002), for the California Civil Liberties Public Education Program.

36. National Park Service, *Japanese Americans in World War II*, National Historic Landmark Theme Study, draft, February 2005, available at http://www.cr.nps.gov/nhl/themes/JPNAmericanTS.pdf (accessed November 16, 2009).

37. Ibid., 67, 91. The Kooskia camp is briefly mentioned elsewhere, 37, in that report.

38. Cynthia Reynaud, Kimberly Hirai, and Kjersti Myhre, "An Act of Congress, a Place in History," *Lewiston (ID) Tribune*, January 1, 2007, 1A, 4A, and their "Researcher Says Camp Story is Bigger than Just Idaho," *Lewiston (ID) Tribune*, January 1, 2007, 4A.

39. Carol A. Hennessey, e-mail to author, January 10, 2007.

40. "New 4-Lane Lewiston-Spalding Road, Addition to L-C Highway In Prospect," *Lewiston (ID) Morning Tribune*, May 23, 1952, 12.

41. CCE to WFK, September 8, 1944; AN85-58A734, FN56125/157, Box 2436, RG85, NARA I.

42. James I. Yano, reply to author's questions dated December 11, 1997, 4.

43. American Buddhist Study Center, "The History of the American Buddhist Study Center 1951-2001," available at http://www.americanbuddhiststudycenter.org/abou-tus.html (accessed November 16, 2009).

44. Ibid.

45. Ibid.

46. Kocho Fukuma, *A Spark of Dharma: The Life of Reverend Hozen Seki*, ed. Hoshin Seki (New York: American Buddhist Study Center, 2001).

47. Nao Gunji, "Loyalty Redefined on Day of Remembrance," NCRR, Nikkei for Civil Rights & Redress, formerly National Coalition for Redress/Reparations, http://www.ncrr-la.org/news/3-23-05/2.html (accessed November 16, 2009). The quote is from Harry S Truman, *Proclamation No. 2685, Removal of Alien Enemies*, April 10, 1946, available at John T. Woolley and Gerhard Peters, *The American Presidency Project*, University of California, Santa Barbara, http://www.presidency.ucsb.edu/ws/index.php?pid=58814 (accessed November 16, 2009).

48. Keith Kamisugi, "The Silent Treatment of Toraichi Kono," *AsianWeek (San Francisco, CA)* 27:39 (May 19-25, 2006), 27A, and trailer for Toraichi Kono, "Kono: Living in Silence," available at http://www.myspace.com/toraichikono (accessed November 16, 2009).

49. Wegars, "'A Real He-Man's Job,'" 55-56.

50. EDD, JHT, and EJO, Toraichi Kono (12-1011), "Excerpt of Hearing," December 15, 1945; and Kona [*sic*] Toraichi, Barrack 9, Internment Camp, Santa Fe, New Mexico, To the Honorable Hearing Board, December 6, 1945, 1; both CLCF, Toraichi Kono, 146-13-2-12-1011; Stack 230/25/06/06, Box 124, RG60, NARA II.

51. HMK, Memorandum for Mr. P. E. Foxworth, Re: Itaru Tachibana: Et Al, Espionage (J[apanese]), June 30, 1941; from Toraichi Kono's FBI file, possibly RG65, NARA II, copy in AACC.

52. EGH to AEIB, OPMG, In Re: CoS/DEA, September 25, 1943, and In Re: CoS/DAE (Japanese), May 19, 1944; CLCF, Toraichi Kono.

53. TMC to Toraichi Kono, SFIC, April 8, 1946; CLCF, Toraichi Kono.

54. EDD, JHT, and EJO, Toraichi Kono (12-1011), "Excerpt of Hearing," December 15, 1945; CLCF, Toraichi Kono.

55. Kona [*sic*] Toraichi, Barrack 9, SFIC, To the Honorable Hearing Board, December 6, 1945, 1; CLCF, Toraichi Kono.

56. The letter to Truman, requesting a presidential pardon for Toraichi Kono, is Spencer M. Kono, Chicago, IL, to Mr. Harry S. Truman, President of the United States of America, Washington, DC, May 13, 1946; CLCF, Toraichi Kono. See also Mrs. Yuriko Nadaoka [E. Cleveland, OH] to TCC, [April 4, 1946]; CLCF, Toraichi Kono.

57. TRM, "Report of Alien Enemy," October 1, 1947; and JLO, "Report of Alien Enemy," October 21, 1946; both CLCF, Toraichi Kono.

58. DSL to NNB, March 26, 1947; CLCF, Toraichi Kono.

59. TRM, "Report of Alien Enemy," October 1, 1947.

60. TCC, "In the Matter of Toraichi Kono Alien Enemy, Order," August 25, 1948; CLCF, Toraichi Kono.

61. Social Security Death Index, available at http://ssdi.rootsweb.ancestry.com/cgi-bin/ssdi.cgi (accessed November 16, 2009).

62. Hiroyuki Ono, e-mail to author, March 12, 2006; Philip W. Chung, "The Japanese Heart of the 'Tramp,'" *AsianWeek (San Francisco, CA)* 3:33 (April 6-12, 2007), 14.

63. Jeffery F. Burton and others, *Confinement and Ethnicity: an Overview of World War II Japanese American Relocation Sites*, Publications in Anthropology 74 (Tucson, AZ: Western Archeological and Conservation Center, National Park Service, U.S. Department of the Interior, 1999), 382 (Crystal City), 398 (Santa Fe).

64. For a longer discussion than is possible here, see Thomas Connell, *America's Japanese Hostages: The World War II Plan for a Japanese Free Latin America* (Westport, CT: Praeger, 2002), 188-244.

65. IW to Department of State, Enemy Alien Control Section, Washington, DC, April 11, 1946; AN85-58A734, FN56125/179, Box 2438, RG85, NARA I.

66. Leah Brumer, "Stealing Home," *The East Bay Monthly* 29:2 (November 1998), 25, and Julie Small, "Crystal City Pilgrims Share Memories, Feelings, Desire for Justice," in *Hokubei Mainichi (San Francisco, CA)*, December 17, 1997, reprinted in JPOHP [Japanese Peruvian Oral History Project] *Newsletter* 2 (January 1998), [7-8].

67. Brumer, "Stealing Home," 29, states that about one hundred did eventually return to Peru.

68. Burton and others, *Confinement and Ethnicity*, 382. Some had been there all along, while others were sent to Crystal City from other internment camps that closed.

69. WFK to JS, May 22, 1946; AN85-58A734, FN56125/179, Box 2438, RG85, NARA I.

70. Some 5,620 American citizens of Japanese ancestry renounced their U.S. citizenship to protest their incarceration, W. F. Kelly to Mr. A. Vulliet, World Alliance of Young Men's Christian Associations, 347 Madison Ave., New York 17, N.Y., August 9, 1948, available at http://home.comcast.net/~eo9066/1948/IA102.html (accessed November 16, 2009). Many of these renunciants, as they were called, were forcibly removed to Japan, and others were threatened with removal. Collins and his associates' tireless pursuit of justice enabled their citizenship rights to be restored; see Michi Weglyn, *Years of Infamy: The Untold Story of America's Concentration Camps* (New York: William Morrow, 1976), 253-258, and Tetsuden Kashima, *Judgment without Trial: Japanese American Imprisonment during World War II* (Seattle: University of Washington, 2003), 168-172. Kelly to Vulliet also states that 16,849 persons of Japanese descent were "received by the Immigration and Naturalization Service under the alien enemy program, including those received from outside [the] continental United States and those who were voluntarily interned in order to join the internee-head of the family." That number includes the 5,620 renunciants. The number of U.S.-resident Japanese internees continues to be elusive.

71. E.g., WMC to UC, May 15, 1946; AN85-58A734, FN56125/179, Box 2438, RG85, NARA I.

72. Brumer, "Stealing Home," 29.

73. Koshio Henry Shima graciously provided information on himself. Known at the Kooskia camp as Koshio Shimabukuro, he changed his name when he became a naturalized citizen about March 1961, Koshio Henry Shima, telephone conversations with author, April 13 and 28, 1998, and May 21, 1998.

74. Brumer, "Stealing Home," 29, 45; Commission on Wartime Relocation and Internment of Civilians (CWRIC), *Personal Justice Denied: Report of the Commission on Wartime Relocation and Internment of Civilians*, foreword by Tetsuden Kashima (Washington, DC: Civil Liberties Public Education Fund and Seattle, University of Washington, 1997), 313.

75. Koshio Henry Shima, telephone conversations with author.

76. Ibid.

77. Brumer, "Stealing Home," 29, 45.

78. Ronald Takaki, *Strangers from a Different Shore: A History of Asian Americans* (New York, Penguin, 1990), 413.

79. Noboru Shirai, *Tule Lake: An Issei Memoir* (Sacramento, CA: Muteki, 2001), 207.

80. "Testimony of Mr. Tajitsu [*sic*, for Tatsuji] Shiotani for the Commission on Wartime Relocation and Internment of Civilians, November 23, 1981, New York City," enclosed with ARP to KR, April 14, 1982; LDKRS, Fluharty, photocopy of typescript, AACC. In his testimony, Shiotani described the Kooskia Internment Camp in Idaho but did not name it specifically.

81. CWRIC, *Personal Justice Denied*, 459.

82. Natsu Taylor Saito, *From Chinese Exclusion to Guantánamo Bay: Plenary Power and the Prerogative State* (Boulder: University Press of Colorado, 2007), 68. For information on Italians who were interned, see, for example, Rose D. Scherini, "When Italian Americans Were 'Enemy Aliens,'" in *Una Storia Segreta: The Secret History of Italian American Evacuation and Internment during World War II*, ed. Lawrence DiStasi (Berkeley: Heyday Books, 2001), 10-31. For background to the internment of Germans in general, see Arnold Krammer, *Undue Process: The Untold Story of America's German Alien Internees* (London: Rowman & Littlefield, 1997), 1-81.

83. Ibid., 130. Her examples include the 1882 Chinese Exclusion Act and various states' alien land laws.

84. Frank Iritani and Joanne Iritani, *Ten Visits* (San Mateo, CA: Japanese American Curriculum Project, 1994), 64.

85. Brumer, "Stealing Home," 45.

86. Japanese Peruvian Oral History Project, "What is the JPOHP?," flier (San Francisco: Japanese Peruvian Oral History Project, 1996?). Shimizu's father, now deceased, was a Japanese Peruvian internee. The lawsuit included people who were repatriated to Japan or who had eventually returned to Peru. Another group, the Campaign For Justice, was founded in 1996 by the Japanese American Citizens League (JACL), the ACLU, the NCRR, and the JPOHP, see Campaign For Justice, "Campaign For Justice: Redress Now For Japanese Latin American Internees," leaflet (Gardena, CA: Campaign For Justice, Southern California, 1996?).

87. Brumer, "Stealing Home," 45; Caroline Aoyagi, "Judge Delays Fairness Hearing in *Mochizuki* So Separate JLA Lawsuit Can First Be Heard," *Pacific Citizen (Los Angeles, CA)* 127:10 (November 20-December 17, 1998), 1; Phil Tajitsu Nash, "Amid Impeachment Brouhaha, Some Justice for JLAs," *AsianWeek (San Francisco, CA)* 20:20 (January 14-20, 1999), 10.

88. "U.S. to Pay Japanese Latin Americans," *AsianWeek (San Francisco, CA)* 19:43 (June 18-24, 1998), 8.

89. *Carmen Mochizuki et al. v. The United States*, Case No. 97-294C, Settlement Agreement dated June 10, 1998 (U.S. Court of Federal Claims), Inter-American Commission on Human Rights, available at http://www.cidh.org/annualrep/2006eng/USA.434.03eng.htm (accessed November 16, 2009).

90. "Shima Lawsuit Filed," *JPOHP Newsletter* 3 (September 1998), 1; Brumer, "Stealing Home," 45. Brumer says eighteen refused the settlement.

91. Shima, telephone conversations with author.

92. "Shima Lawsuit," *JPOHP Newsletter*, 1; "Peruvian Sues over Redress Payment," *Oakland Tribune*, August 26, 1998, News-3; "Japanese Latin Americans Seek Redress for Internment in U.S.," *Wall Street Journal*, September 22, 1998, B22.

93. "Japanese Latin Americans Seek Redress," *Wall Street Journal*.

94. "Peruvian Sues," *Oakland (CA) Tribune*.

95. "Judge Postpones Redress Settlement for JLA Internees," *AsianWeek (San Francisco, CA)* 20:33 (November 19-25, 1998), 8.

96. "U.S. to Pay," *AsianWeek (San Francisco, CA)*, 9.

97. "Clinton Signs $15 Billion Bill Allocating $4.3 Million in Redress Payments for JLA [F]ormer WWII Internees," *Pacific Citizen (Los Angeles, CA)* 128:11 (June 4-10, 1999), 1.

98. Campaign For Justice, "Redress Fight Continues in Court, Henry Shima Denied Hearing by Ninth Circuit Court of Appeals," *Campaign For Justice: Redress Now For Japanese Latin Americans!*, (Summer 2001), 3.

99. Social Security Death Index; Shima died on January 14.

100. Saito, *From Chinese Exclusion to Guantánamo Bay*, 110-115, 178, 182. Examples of other U.S. violations of international law include overthrowing the Kingdom of Hawai'i in 1893, annexing Puerto Rico and taking control of Cuba in 1898, seizing the Panama Canal in 1903, occupying Haiti and the Dominican Republic in 1915, and, more recently, backing various coups in Guatemala, Chile, Nicaragua, and Panama, 130, 397n51.

101. Ibid., 115, 129.

102. Ibid., 131, 200; citing several examples, the U.S. "often pressures other [nations] to comply with international law," 130.

103. Teresa Watanabe, "Déjà Vu," *Los Angeles Times Magazine* (June 8, 2003), [17].

104. Ann Koto Hayashi, *Face of the Enemy Heart of a Patriot: Japanese-American Internment Narratives* (New York: Garland, 1995), 127. *Shikata-ga-nai* can also be translated as "acceptance with resignation," Tetsuden Kashima, "Introduction," in Yasutaro Soga, *Life Behind Barbed Wire: The World War II Internment Memoirs of a Hawai'i Issei* (Honolulu: University of Hawai'i, 2008), 11. Other traditional Japanese values, many relevant to surviving the internment and incarceration experience, include "*Kōkō* (filial piety), *On* (debt of gratitude), *Ganbari* (perseverance), *Kansha* (gratitude), *Chūgi* (loyalty), *Sekinin* (responsibility), *Haji/Hokori* (shame/pride), *Meiyo* (honor), ... and *Gisei* (sacrifice), Kashima, "Introduction," 11.

105. Amy Iwasaki Mass, "Psychological Effects of the Camps on Japanese Americans," in *Japanese Americans: From Relocation to Redress*, ed. Roger Daniels, Sandra C. Taylor, and Harry H. L. Kitano (Salt Lake City: University of Utah, 1986), 159.

106. Mass, "Psychological Effects of the Camps," 160-161.

107. Ibid., 161-162.

108. E.g., JA, "Hozen Seki," September 25, 1942; CLCF, Hozen Seki, 146-13-2-51-2146; Stack 230/25/24/3, Box 490, RG 60, NARA II.

109. Watanabe, "Déjà Vu," 20.

110. Ibid., [19].

111. Wikipedia: The Free Encyclopedia, "Geneva Conventions," available at http://en.wikipedia.org/wiki/Geneva_Conventions (accessed November 16, 2009); Joseph Margulies, *Guantánamo and the Abuse of Presidential Power* (New York: Simon and Schuster, 2006), 53. Geneva I was adopted in 1864 and most recently revised in 1949; Geneva II was adopted in 1906; Geneva III was adopted in 1829 and most recently revised in 1949; and Geneva IV was adopted in 1949, Wikipedia, "Geneva Conventions."

112. Charles I. Bevans, compiler, "Prisoners of War," in *Treaties and Other International Agreements of the United States of America 1776-1949*, vol. 2, Multilateral, 1918-1930 (U.S. Government Printing Office, Washington, DC, 1969), 940.

113. Soga, *Life Behind Barbed Wire*, 76.

114. The history of U.S. involvement at Guantánamo illustrates American imperialism at its most imperious. Following the Spanish-American War, the U.S. occupied Cuba in 1901. We agreed to leave provided we obtained certain concessions, among them a long-term lease of Guantánamo for a coaling or naval station. The lease of this forty-five-square-mile property, almost half the size of Washington, DC, "cannot be terminated without the consent of the United States." Thanks to its own water supply, it is completely independent of Cuba. With its own schools, transportation, a McDonald's, and a Starbucks, it is like "a small American city," Margulies, *Guantánamo*, 49-51.

115. Alex Markels, "Will Terrorism Rewrite the Laws of War?" Legal Affairs, National Public Radio, available at http://www.npr.org/templates/story/story.php?storyId=5011464, 1 (accessed November 16, 2009). Markels further traces the history of humane warfare.

116. Margulies, *Guantánamo*, 74-76, 148.

117. Ibid., 74-75.

118. Ibid., 77.

119. Ibid., 76-78, 81. Despite the U.S.'s good intentions, individual soldiers are known to have tortured their North Vietnamese prisoners and committed other well-known atrocities, 82.

120. Ibid., 81. Margulies did not list further U.S. violations.

121. Wikipedia: The Free Encyclopedia, "September 11, 2001 Attacks," available at http://en.wikipedia.org/wiki/September_11,_2001_attacks (accessed November 16, 2009).

122. Robert Looney, "Economic Costs to the United States Stemming From the 9/11 Attacks," *Strategic Insights* 1:6 (August 2002), 1, Center for Contemporary Conflict, Naval Postgraduate School, Monterey, CA, available at http://www.businessandmedia.org/electionomics/2003/election20031110.asp (accessed December 24, 2009).

123. Moustafa Bayoumi, "Choose the Wrong Faith, and Go Directly to Jail," *Lewiston (ID) Tribune*, July 2, 2006, 4F.

124. Ibid. Latinos and Sikhs were mistakenly assulted or killed.

125. Tom Henderson, "Evil Spirits of 1941 Still Hovering over America," *Lewiston (ID) Tribune*, July 10, 2006, 8A. During his presidential campaign, Barack Obama promised to close the Guantánamo Bay facility if he were elected, but by late 2009 some 198 prisoners still remained there, *Moscow-Pullman (ID-WA) Daily News*, "U.S. sends 12 Gitmo Detainees to Their Home Nations," 97:304 (December 21, 2009), 7A.

126. Markels, "Laws of War," 1.

127. "APAs and the Moral Ambiguity of Terrorism," editorial, *AsianWeek (San Francisco, CA)* 27:9 (October 20-26, 2005), 4; the memo, authored by former Justice Department Deputy Assistant Attorney General John Yoo, led to the application of different standards for the Abu Ghraib prison in Iraq and to the U.S.'s detention facility at Guantánamo Bay, Cuba. Markels, "Will Terrorism Rewrite the Laws of War?," 2, has a link to the text of the memo, John Yoo, Memorandum for William J. Haynes II, January 9, 2002, available at http://www.npr.org/documents/2005/nov/torture/tortureyoo.pdf (accessed November 16, 2009).

128. Markels, "Will Terrorism Rewrite the Laws of War?," 1; page 2 has a link to the text of the memo, Alberto R. Gonzales, Memorandum for the President, January 25, 2002, at http://www.npr.org/documents/2005/nov/torture/torturegonzales.pdf, 2 (accessed November 16, 2009).

129. Anne Plummer Flaherty, "Administration Decides All U.S. Detainees Entitled to Geneva Conventions Protections," *Moscow-Pullman (ID-WA) Daily News* 91:162 (July 11, 2006), 1A.

130. David Cole, *Enemy Aliens: Double Standards and Constitutional Freedoms in the War on Terrorism*, (New York: New Press, 2003), 102; the Contingency Plan "specifically identified nationals of Algeria, Libya, Tunisia, Iran, Jordan, Syria, Morocco, and Lebanon as potential targets for such emergency detention"; note that Afghanistan, Iraq, and Saudi Arabia are not on this list.

131. Al Hayward, e-mail to author, September 12, 2005.

132. On September 22, 1988, Canadian Prime Minister Brian Mulroney announced a Redress Settlement for "evacuated" Japanese Canadians. The package included a "formal and sincere apology" from the Prime Minister and a payment of $21,000 Canadian to surviving "evacuees," Canadian Broadcasting Company, CBC Archives, "Clip: Apology and Compensation," September 22, 1988, available at http://archives. cbc.ca/war_conflict/second_world_war/topics/568/ (accessed November 16, 2009).

133. Weglyn, *Years of Infamy*, 267, from a memorandum, Collins to Weglyn, July 21, 1973.

134. Bill Hosokawa, *Nisei: The Quiet Americans*, rev. ed. (Boulder: University Press of Colorado, 2002), 432.

135. Weglyn, *Years of Infamy*, 267-268, from Collins to Weglyn. Indeed, the former Immigration and Naturalization Service is now part of the Department of Homeland Security; on March 1, 2003, the U.S. Immigration and Naturalization Service (INS) transitioned into the Department of Homeland Security (DHS) as the U.S. Citizenship and Immigration Services (USCIS), Wikipedia: The Free Encyclopedia, "Immigration and Naturalization Service," available at http://en.wikipedia.org/wiki/ Immigration_and_Naturalization_Service (accessed November 16, 2009).

136. A Google search for the term "Pearl Harbor of the twenty-first [21st] century" produced over 380,000 instances of its use (accessed February 25, 2010).

137. Saito, *From Chinese Exclusion to Guantánamo Bay*, 155, 207.

138. Ibid., 207.

139. Wikipedia: The Free Encyclopedia, "Martin Niemöller," available at http:// en.wikipedia.org/wiki/Martin_Niem%C3%B6ller (accessed November 16, 2009).

140. Internet Archive Wayback Machine, "Why Is Free Speech So Important?," available at http://web.archive.org/web/20051218122539/http://www.geocities.com/kdelran/ niemoller.html (accessed November 16, 2009).

141. Saito, *From Chinese Exclusion to Guantánamo Bay*, 178, 182.

142. Ibid.; see also her Chapter 3, "Silencing the Constitution," 51-91.

References Cited

Note: Individual documents obtained from the National Archives or from informants are fully cited in the endnotes to the text so do not appear here. Newspaper articles are in order by date; multiple references by the same author are in alphabetical order.

Abraham, Terry, compiler. *A Union List of the Papers of Members of Congress from the Pacific Northwest*. Pullman, WA: Washington State University Library, 1976.

Adachi, Ken. *The Enemy that Never Was: A History of the Japanese Canadians*. Toronto, ON: McClelland and Stewart for the National Japanese Canadian Citizens Association, 1976.

Ahn, Hyung-ju. *Between Two Adversaries: Korean Interpreters at Japanese Alien Enemy Detention Centers during World War II*. Fullerton, CA: California State University, 2002.

———. "Koreans as Interpreters at Japanese Enemy Alien Detention Centers during World War II." In *Guilt by Association: Essays on Japanese Settlement, Internment, and Relocation in the Rocky Mountain West*, ed. Mike Mackey, 101-116. Powell, WY: Western History Publications, 2001.

American Buddhist Study Center. "The History of the American Buddhist Study Center 1951-2001." Available at http://www.americanbuddhist.org/who_we_are/who_we_are.htm.

Amnesty International USA. "Threat and Humiliation: Racial Profiling, National Security, and Human Rights in the United States." Available at http://www.amnestyusa.org/Racial_Profiling/Report__Threat_and_Humiliation/page.do?id=1106664&n1=3&n2=850&n3=1298.

Aoyagi, Caroline. "Judge Delays Fairness Hearing in *Mochizuki* So Separate JLA Lawsuit Can First Be Heard." *Pacific Citizen* 127, no. 10 (November 20-December 17, 1998): 1, 12.

Arne, Sigrid. "Italians, Japanese at Ft. Missoula Don't Get Along." *Montana Record Herald (Helena, MT)*, approximately August 3, 1942. From Historical Museum at Fort Missoula, Box 8, Research Files, Folder, "Articles of Japanese Internees."

Asian American Comparative Collection. Available at http://www.uiweb.uidaho.edu/LS/AACC/.

———. The Kooskia Internment Camp Project. "Justice Department and U.S. Army Internment Camps and Detention Stations in the U.S. during World War II." Available at http://www.uiweb.uidaho.edu/LS/AACC/JusticeCampsWWII.htm.

——. The Kooskia Internment Camp Project. "Obtaining Department of Justice (DOJ) Closed Legal Case Files (CLCF) from the National Archives and Records Administration (NARA)." Available at http://www.uiweb.uidaho.edu/LS/AACC/CLCF.htm.

——. The Kooskia Internment Camp Project. "Tables Related to Food and Clothing." Available at http://www.uiweb.uidaho.edu/LS/AACC/FoodClothing.htm.

Asian American Comparative Collection Newsletter. "Ceramics from the Kooskia Internment Camp, 10-IH-870." 20, no. 2 (June 2003): 3.

Asian American Drug Abuse Program. "Events: Mochitsuki." Available at http://www.aadapinc.org/events/mochitsuki/.

AsianWeek (San Francisco, CA). "U.S. to Pay Japanese Latin Americans." 19, no. 43 (June 18-24, 1998): 8-9.

——. "Judge Postpones Redress Settlement for JLA Internees." 20, no. 33 (November 19-25, 1998): 8.

——. "APAs and the Moral Ambiguity of Terrorism." Editorial. 27, no. 9 (October 20-26, 2005): 4.

"Ask Phil - Stamp Collecting Starts Here." No. 147, ["War Savings Stamps"]. Available at http://www.askphil.org/answers.asp.

Baker, Lillian. *American and Japanese Relocation in World War II: Fact, Fiction, & Fallacy.* Medford, OR: Webb Research Group, 1990.

Barnhart, Edward N. "Japanese Internees from Peru." *Pacific Historical Review* 31, no. 2 (May 1962): 169-178.

Battle, Dee, and Alayne Lesser. *The Best of Bakelite & other Plastic Jewelry.* Atglen, PA: Schiffer, 1996.

Bayoumi, Moustafa. "Choose the Wrong Faith, and Go Directly to Jail." *Lewiston (ID) Tribune.* July 2, 2006, 4F.

Bevans, Charles I., comp. "Prisoners of War." In *Treaties and Other International Agreements of the United States of America 1776-1949,* vol. 2, *Multilateral, 1918-1930,* 932-964. Washington, DC, U.S. Government Printing Office, 1969.

Boller, Cecil. Interview by author, June 7, 2000. Transcription of tape recording. Asian American Comparative Collection, University of Idaho, Moscow.

Bolling, Thomas E. "Introduction." In *Fukkokuban Hokubei Kendo Taikan* [Taiken] (Cyclopedia of the Japanese Kendo Societies in North America, pre-1939), Vol. 1, by Ikken Momii. Reprint edition. [Tokyo]: Bunsei Shoin, 2001. Formerly available at http://www.bunsei.co.jp/denshi/N_A_preface_e.htm. Copy in Asian American Comparative Collection, University of Idaho, Moscow.

Boone, Lalia. *Idaho Place Names: A Geographical Dictionary.* Moscow: University of Idaho, 1988.

Bretthauer, Mrs. C. D. "Japs Arrive; Housed Locksa [*sic*] Prison Camp." *Idaho County Free Press (Grangeville, ID)* 58, no. 4 (June 3, 1943): 1.

Broadfoot, Barry. *Years of Sorrow, Years of Shame: The Story of Japanese Canadians in World War II.* Toronto: Doubleday Canada, 1977.

Brumer, Leah. "Stealing Home." *The East Bay Monthly* 29, no. 2 (November 1998): 25-27, 29, 45.

Burton, Jeffery F., Mary M. Farrell, Florence B. Lord, and Richard W. Lord. *Confinement and Ethnicity: an Overview of World War II Japanese American Relocation Sites.* Publications in Anthropology, no. 74. Tucson, AZ: Western Archeological and Conservation Center, National Park Service, U. S. Department of the Interior, 1999.

Also available at National Park Service, http://www.nps.gov/history/history/on-line_books/anthropology74/index.htm.

Campaign For Justice. "Campaign For Justice: Redress Now For Japanese Latin American Internees." Leaflet. Gardena, CA: Campaign For Justice, Southern California, 1996?

——. "Redress Fight Continues in Court, Henry Shima Denied Hearing by Ninth Circuit Court of Appeals." *Campaign For Justice: Redress Now For Japanese Latin Americans!* (Summer 2001): 3.

Campbell, Thomas W., and Ladd Hamilton. "Thousands Witness L-C Highway Dedication." *Lewiston (ID) Morning Tribune,* August 20, 1962, 1, 3.

Canadian Broadcasting Company. CBC Archives. "Clip: Apology and Compensation." September 22, 1988. Available at http://archives.cbc.ca/war_conflict/second_world_war/topics/568/.

Carmen Mochizuki et al. v. The United States, Case No. 97-294C. Settlement Agreement dated June 10, 1998 (U.S. Court of Federal Claims). Inter-American Commission on Human Rights. Available at http://www.cidh.org/annualrep/2006eng/USA.434.03eng.htm.

Carter, Hugh, LeRoy B. DePuy, Ernest Rubin, and Marguerite Milan. "Administrative History of the Immigration and Naturalization Service during World War II." Typescript, in General Research Unit, Office of Research and Educational Services, U.S. Department of Homeland Security. Immigration and Naturalization Service Library, Washington, DC, 1946.

Carus, Paul. *Buddhist Hymns.* Available at http://libweb.uoregon.edu/ec/e-asia/read/budkins.pdf.

Christgau, John. *"Enemies:" World War II Alien Internment.* Ames: Iowa State University, 1985.

Chung, Philip W. "The Japanese Heart of the 'Tramp.'" *AsianWeek (San Francisco, CA)* 3, no. 33 (April 6-12, 2007): 14.

Clark, Chase A. "Clark Defends Stand on Aliens." *Kamiah (ID) Progress* 37, no. 17 (March 19, 1942): 1.

Clark, Paul Frederick. "Those Other Camps: An Oral History Analysis of Japanese Alien Enemy Internment during World War II." Master's thesis, California State University, Fullerton, 1980.

Clearwater Tribune (Orofino, ID). "Jap Contingent Goes to Lochsa Road Job." 31, no. 12 (May 27, 1943): 1.

——. "Lochsa Prison Camp Holds 134 Japanese." 31, no. 14 (June 10, 1943): 8.

——. "Scott Is New Chief at Japanese Camp." 31, no. 40 (December 9, 1943): 6.

——. "Orofino Sends Group to Lochsa Conclave." 33, no. 8 (April 26, 1945): 1.

Cole, David. *Enemy Aliens: Double Standards and Constitutional Freedoms in the War on Terrorism.* New York: New Press, 2003.

Commission on Wartime Relocation and Internment of Civilians. *Personal Justice Denied: Report of the Commission on Wartime Relocation and Internment of Civilians.* Foreword by Tetsuden Kashima. Washington, DC: Civil Liberties Public Education Fund and Seattle, University of Washington, 1997. Originally published in two vols., Washington, DC: U.S. Government Printing Office, 1982, 1983.

Conley, Cort. *Idaho for the Curious.* Cambridge, ID: Backeddy Books, 1982.

Connell, Thomas, III. *America's Japanese Hostages: The World War II Plan for a Japanese*

Free Latin America. Westport, CT: Praeger, 2002.

———. "The Internment of Latin American Japanese in the United States during World War Two: The Peruvian Japanese Experience." Ph.D. diss., Florida State University, Tallahassee, 1995.

Culley, John J[oel]. "Enemy Alien Control in the United States during World War II: A Survey." In *Alien Justice: Wartime Internment in Australia and North America,* ed. Kay Saunders and Roger Daniels, 138-151. St. Lucia, Queensland, Australia: University of Queensland, 2000.

———. "The Santa Fe Internment Camp and the Justice Department Program for Enemy Aliens." In *Japanese Americans: From Relocation to Redress,* ed. Roger Daniels, Sandra C. Taylor, and Harry H. L. Kitano, 57-71. Salt Lake City: University of Utah, 1986.

CWRIC, see Commission on Wartime Relocation and Internment of Civilians.

Daniels, Roger. *Asian America: Chinese and Japanese in the United States since 1850.* Seattle: University of Washington, 1988.

———. "The Conference Keynote Address: Relocation, Redress, and the Report, A Historical Appraisal." In *Japanese Americans: From Relocation to Redress,* ed. Roger Daniels, Sandra C. Taylor, and Harry H. L. Kitano, 3-9. Salt Lake City: University of Utah, 1986.

———. "The Internment of Japanese Nationals in the United States during World War II." *Halcyon* 17 (1995): 65-75.

———. "Words Do Matter: A Note on Inappropriate Terminology and the Incarceration of the Japanese Americans." In *Nikkei in the Pacific Northwest: Japanese Americans and Japanese Canadians in the Twentieth Century,* ed. Louis Fiset and Gail M. Nomura, 190-214. Seattle: Center for the Study of the Pacific Northwest in association with University of Washington, 2005.

Densho: The Japanese American Legacy Project. Available at http://www.densho.org/.

———. "A Note on Terminology." Available at http://www.densho.org/default.asp?path=/ assets/sharedpages/glossary.asp?section=home.

———. *2006 Annual Report.* Seattle: Densho, 2006.

Deschamps, Arthur, Jr. Interview by Susan Buchel, November 20, 1979. Transcript, tapes 67-1, 67-2. Historical Museum at Fort Missoula, Missoula, MT.

Dininny, Shannon. "Washington State, DOE Agree on Hanford Cleanup Deadlines." *Moscow-Pullman (ID-WA) Daily News,* August 12, 2009, 4A.

Donald, Heidi Gurcke. *We Were Not the Enemy: Remembering the United States' Latin-American Civilian Internment Program of World War II.* New York, iUniversie, 2006.

"[Duties of] Financial Officer." N.d. Copy in Asian American Comparative Collection, University of Idaho, Moscow.

Eaton, Allen H. *Beauty behind Barbed Wire: The Arts of the Japanese in Our War Relocation Camps.* New York: Harper & Brothers, 1952.

Elsensohn, M. Alfreda. *Pioneer Days in Idaho County.* Vol. 2. Caldwell, ID: Caxton, 1951.

Erb, Tish. "Jap Internees Work Hard, Well Treated, at Kooskia Road Camp." *Lewiston (ID) Morning Tribune,* September 26, 1943, sec. 2, pp. 1, 5.

Fiset, Louis. *Camp Harmony: Seattle's Japanese Americans and the Puyallup Assembly Center.* Champaign, IL: University of Illinois, 2009.

———. "Censored!: U.S. Censors and Internment Camp Mail in World War II." In *Guilt by Association: Essays on Japanese Settlement, Internment, and Relocation in the Rocky Mountain West*, ed. Mike Mackey, 69-100. Powell, WY: Western History Publications, 2001.

———. *Imprisoned Apart: The World War II Correspondence of an Issei Couple*. Seattle: University of Washington, 1997.

———. "Return to Sender: U.S. Censorship of Enemy Alien Mail in World War II." *Prologue* 33, no. 1 (Spring 2001): 21-35.

Flaherty, Anne Plummer. "Administration Decides All U.S. Detainees Entitled to Geneva Conventions Protections." *Moscow-Pullman (ID-WA) Daily News* 91, no. 162 (July 11, 2006): 1A, 10A.

Ford, Gerald R. *Presidential Proclamation 4417*. Available at http://www.ford.utexas.edu/LIBRARY/SPEECHES/760111p.htm.

Freier, Ludwig (Lud). "Bitter-Loot [*sic*; possibly a pun] Trail." *Lochsa (ID) Pioneer* 1, no. 8 (June 1940): 30. Reprinted as "Bitter-Root Trail" in *The Golden Age* 26, no. 1 (Spring and Summer 2006): 15-18.

Friedman, Max Paul. *Nazis and Good Neighbors: The United States Campaign against the Germans of Latin America in World War II*. New York: Cambridge University Press, 2003.

Fugita, Stephen S., and Marilyn Fernandez. "Religion and Japanese Americans' View of Their World War II Incarceration." *Journal of Asian American Studies* 5, no. 2 (June 2002): 113-137.

Fujita, Frank. *Foo, A Japanese-American Prisoner of the Rising Sun: The Secret Prison Diary of Frank "Foo" Fujita*. Denton, TX: University of North Texas, 1993.

Fukuma, Kocho. *A Spark of Dharma: The Life of Reverend Hozen Seki*, ed. Hoshin Seki. New York: American Buddhist Study Center, 2001.

Gardiner, C. Harvey. *The Japanese and Peru 1873-1973*. Albuquerque: University of New Mexico, 1975.

———. *Pawns in a Triangle of Hate*. Seattle: University of Washington, 1981.

Geneva Convention. Available at http://www.icrc.org/IHL.nsf/52d68d14de6160e0c12563da005fdb1b/eb1571b00daec90ec125641e00402aa6?OpenDocument.

George, Marilyn. "Petersburg's Oldest Citizen Looks Back on a Happy Life." *Alaskan Southeaster*, 1996?: 10-11.

———. "Tom Kito Looks Back: A Cannery Worker and Then Some." *Alaska Fisherman's Journal* (November 1996): sec. 2, pp. 29?, 30-32.

George, Marilyn, and Pamela Cravez. "Forced from Their Homes … Petersburg's Kitos Remember Prison Camps." *Senior Voice* (February 1990): 9.

Gonzales, Alberto R. Memorandum for the President. January 25, 2002. Available at http://www.npr.org/documents/2005/nov/torture/torturegonzales.pdf.

Griffith, Dennis. "Apgar Cottages." Sketch map based on drawing by Amelia and Edwin Jacks. Lochsa District, Kooskia Ranger Station, Kooskia, ID [1982].

———. "History Lower Canyon Creek Mines/Prison Camp - Oral Interview with Ayden Thomas." April 26, 1982. Lochsa Ranger District, 2360 - Special Interest Areas. Lochsa District, Kooskia Ranger Station, Kooskia, ID.

———. "Internee Housing Area." Sketch map based on drawing by Amelia and Edwin

Jacks. Lochsa District, Kooskia Ranger Station, Kooskia, ID [1982].

———. "Reply to: 2360 Special Interest Area. Subject: History of Japanese Internment Period: Canyon Creek Prison Camp Site." Photocopy of handwritten document, Lochsa District, Kooskia Ranger Station, Kooskia, Idaho, [1982].

Gumm, Mrs. Harvey. Letter to the editor. *Spokesman-Review (Spokane, WA)* 61, no. 72 (July 25, 1943): A15.

Gunji, Nao. "Loyalty Redefined on Day of Remembrance." NCRR, Nikkei for Civil Rights & Redress, formerly National Coalition for Redress/Reparations. Available at http://www.ncrr-la.org/news/3-23-05/2.html.

Hamilton, Ladd. *Snowbound*. Pullman: Washington State University, 1997.

Hayashi, Ann Koto. *Face of the Enemy Heart of a Patriot: Japanese-American Internment Narratives*. New York: Garland, 1995.

Hedberg, Kathy. "UI Prof Goes in Search of the Past." *Lewiston (ID) Tribune*, August 10, 2009, 5A.

Henderson, Tom. "Evil Spirits of 1941 Still Hovering over America." *Lewiston (ID) Tribune*, July 10, 2006, 8A.

Higashide, Seiichi. *Adios to Tears: The Memoirs of a Japanese-Peruvian Internee in U.S. Concentration Camps*. Honolulu: E&E Kudo, 1993.

Hirabayashi, James. "'Concentration Camp' or 'Relocation Center:' What's in a Name?" *Japanese American National Museum Quarterly* 9, no. 3 (Fall 1994): 5-10.

Hirasuna, Delphine. *The Art of Gaman: Arts and Crafts from the Japanese American Internment Camps 1942-1946*. Berkeley: Ten Speed, 2005.

Hirose, Stacey. "Kendo." In *Japanese American History: An A-to-Z Reference from 1868 to the Present*, ed. Brian Niiya, 200. New York: Facts on File, 1993.

Honda, Harry K. "A Personal Search of the Public Archives Uncovers Lives of WWII Japanese Canadians." Draft typescript, April 22, 2000; prepared for the U.S. Nisei visiting Canada. Copy in Asian American Comparative Collection, University of Idaho, Moscow.

Hosokawa, Bill. *Nisei: The Quiet Americans*. Rev. ed. Boulder: University Press of Colorado, 1992.

Hutchinson, E. P., and Ernest Rubin. "Estimating the Resident Alien Population of the United States." *Journal of the American Statistical Association* 42, no. 239 (September 1947): 385-400.

Idaho County Free Press (Grangeville, ID). "End to Jap Problem Told By Gov. Clark." 57, no. 3 (May 28, 1942): 10.

———. "Slap That Jap!" Advertisement. 57, no. 13 (August 6, 1942): 5.

Internet Archive Wayback Machine. "Why Is Free Speech So Important?" Available at http://web.archive.org/web/20051218122539/http://www.geocities.com/kdelran/niemoller.html.

Iritani, Frank, and Joanne Iritani. *Ten Visits*. San Mateo, CA: Japanese American Curriculum Project, 1994.

Irons, Peter. *Justice at War*. Berkeley: University of California, 1993.

Ishizuka, Karen L. *Lost and Found: Reclaiming the Japanese American Incarceration*. Urbana, University of Illinois, 2006.

Islamic Cultural Center of Fresno. Media Coverage about ICCF. "JACL Director Honored by Islamic Cultural Center." From Hokubei.com, May 8, 2008. Available at http://www.icfresno.org/multimedia/04e.htm.

Jacks, Amelia, and Edwin Jacks. Interview by Dennis Griffith, March 25, 1982. Transcript, Lochsa District, Kooskia Ranger Station, Kooskia, ID.

Jacobs, Arthur D. "Chronology - Suspicion, Arrest, and Internment: The War Years," December 8, 1941. *The Freedom of Information Times*. Available at http://www.foitimes.com/internment/chrono.htm.

———. *The Prison Called Hohenasperg*. N.p.: Universal Publishers, 1999.

Japanese Peruvian Oral History Project. "What is the JPOHP?" San Francisco: Japanese Peruvian Oral History Project, 1996?

Johnson, Johnny. "The Time Had Come to Celebrate End of the 'Missing Link.'" *The Golden Age* (Spring/Summer 1996): 10-15. Lewiston, ID: Nez Perce County Historical Society.

JPOHP Newsletter. "Shima Lawsuit Filed." 3 (September 1998): 1. San Francisco.

Kamiah (ID) Progress. Articles, not individually cited, on CCC camps. 1933.

———. "Interest Shown in Lewis-Clark Route." 33, no. 28 (May 26, 1938): 1.

———. "L-C Highway Gets Important Boost." 35(14):1. February 22, 1940.

———. "Would Work Jap Aliens on Lewis and Clark Highway." 37, no. 17 (March 19, 1942): 1.

Kamisugi, Keith. "The Silent Treatment of Toraichi Kono." *AsianWeek (San Francisco, CA)* 27, no. 39 (May 19-25, 2006): 27A.

Kashima, Tetsuden. "American Mistreatment of Internees during World War II: Enemy Alien Japanese." In *Japanese Americans: From Relocation to Redress*, ed. Roger Daniels, Sandra C. Taylor, and Harry H. L. Kitano, 52-56. Salt Lake City: University of Utah, 1986.

———. "Introduction." In Yasutaro Soga, *Life Behind Barbed Wire: The World War II Internment Memoirs of a Hawai'i Issei*, 1-16. Honolulu: University of Hawai'i, 2008.

———. *Judgment without Trial: Japanese American Imprisonment during World War II*. Seattle: University of Washington, 2003.

Keehr, Alfred, and Dorothy Keehr. Interview by Ramona Alam Parry, July 12, 1979. Transcript, Clearwater National Forest Supervisor's Office, Orofino, ID.

Kelly, W. F., Assistant Commissioner, Immigration and Naturalization Service, to Mr. A. Vulliet, World Alliance of Young Men's Christian Associations. Letter, August 9, 1948. Available at http://home.comcast.net/~eo9066/1948/IA102.html.

Kitchen Sisters. "Weenie Royale: Food and the Japanese Internment." NPR [National Public Radio], aired December 31, 2007. Available at http://www.npr.org/templates/story/story.php?storyId=17335538.

Kono, Toraichi. "Kono: Living in Silence." Trailer available at http://www.myspace.com/toraichikono.

Kooskia (ID) Mountaineer. Articles, not individually cited, on CCC camps. 1933.

Kooskia Internment Camp Scrapbook. Historical Photograph Collection. University of Idaho Library, PG 103. See also "Kooskia Internment Camp Scrapbook." University of Idaho Library Digital Collections. Available at http://contentdm.lib.uidaho.edu/cdm4/browse.php?CISOROOT=/spec_kic.

Krammer, Arnold. *Undue Process: The Untold Story of America's German Alien Internees*. London: Rowman & Littlefield, 1997.

Kumamoto, Bob. "The Search for Spies: American Counterintelligence and the Japanese

American Community 1931-1942." *Amerasia Journal* 6, no. 2 (1979): 45-75.

Lee, Sandra L. "Caboose Pulls into Locomotive Park." *Lewiston (ID) Morning Tribune,* September 3, 1997, 5A, 8A.

Levie, Howard S., ed. 'United States and Others v. Sadao Araki and Others (International Military Tribunal for the Far East (IMTFE)[)], (4-12 November 1948).' In "Documents on Prisoners of War," *International Law Studies* 60 (1979): 437-476. Newport, RI: Naval War College.

Lewis, Wallace G. "On the Trail of Lewis and Clark: Building the Lewis-Clark Highway." *Idaho Yesterdays* 43, no. 3 (Fall 1999): 13-24.

Lewiston (ID) Morning Tribune. "Curious Crowd Watches Arrival of 104 Japs under Armed Guard." May 28, 1943, 14.

———. "16 Japs, Under Guard of Army, to Prison Camp." May 29, 1943, 10.

———. "Jap Camp Gets 14 More Men." June 8, 1943, 10.

———. "More Japs at Kooskia Camp." September 22, 1943, 12.

———. "Remer to Leave Kooskia Internment Camp Soon." December 5, 1943, 12.

———. "Hearing Opens Today On L-C Road Progress." April 26, 1945, 12.

———. "Public Hearing to Be Held Here Today on L-C Highway Program." April 27, 1945, 12.

———. "Work to Be Continued on L-C Highway." April 28, 1945, 10.

———. "Japs to Leave Camp Tomorrow." May 1, 1945, 10.

———. "Jap Internees Leave." May 3, 1945, 12.

———. "New 4-Lane Lewiston-Spalding Road, Addition to L-C Highway In Prospect." May 23, 1952, 12.

———. 'Prison Labor Helped Open Canyon Route.' In "Lewis & Clark Highway Edition," August 19, 1962, sec. 2, p. 22.

Library of Congress. "A Century of Lawmaking for a New Nation: U.S. Congressional Documents and Debates, 1774 - 1875." Statutes at Large, 41st Congress, 2nd Session, 103-104. 'An Act to establish an [*sic*] uniform Rule of Naturalization.' Available at http://memory.loc.gov/cgi-bin/ampage?collId=llsl&fileName=001/llsl001. db&recNum=226.

———. "A Century of Lawmaking for a New Nation: U.S. Congressional Documents and Debates, 1774 - 1875," Statutes at Large, 41st Congress, 2nd Session, 254-256. 'An Act to amend the Naturalization Laws and to punish Crimes against the same, and for other Purposes.' Available at http://memory.loc.gov/cgi-bin/ampage?collId=llsl& fileName=016/llsl016.db&recNum=289.

Lin, Lynda. "Community Groups Work to Place a Mark of History on a Little Known WWII Camp." *Pacific Citizen (Los Angeles, CA)* 144, no. 5 (March 16-April 5, 2007): 1, 12.

Lochsa (ID) Pioneer. Newsletter of the Canyon Creek Prison Camp, Kooskia, ID. Various issues available at Nez Perce County Historical Society, Lewiston, ID; at University of Idaho Library Special Collections, Moscow; and at Yale University Library, New Haven, CT.

London, Bill. "A Different Kind of Christmas." *Central Idaho Magazine* 1, no. 3 (Winter 1988): 8-9.

Long, Wallace J. *The Military History of Fort Missoula,* second revision. Missoula: Friends of Historical Museum at Fort Missoula, 2005.

Looney, Robert. "Economic Costs to the United States Stemming From the 9/11 Attacks."

Strategic Insights 1, no. 6 (August 2002): 1. Center for Contemporary Conflict, Naval Postgraduate School, Monterey, California. Available at http://www.businessandmedia.org/electionomics/2003/election20031110.asp.

Malkin, Michelle. *In Defense of Internment: The Case for 'Racial Profiling' in World War II and the War on Terror.* Washington, DC: Regnery, 2004.

Maltin, Leonard, ed. *Leonard Maltin's Movie & Video Guide.* 1998 edition. New York: Signet, 1997.

Mangione, Jerre. *An Ethnic at Large: A Memoir of America in the Thirties and Forties.* New York: G. P. Putnam's Sons, 1978.

Margulies, Joseph. *Guantánamo and the Abuse of Presidential Power.* New York: Simon and Schuster, 2006.

Markels, Alex. "Will Terrorism Rewrite the Laws of War?" Legal Affairs, National Public Radio. Available at http://www.npr.org/templates/story/story.php?storyId=5011464.

Mass, Amy Iwasaki. "Psychological Effects of the Camps on Japanese Americans." In *Japanese Americans: From Relocation to Redress*, ed. Roger Daniels, Sandra C. Taylor, and Harry H. L. Kitano, 159-162. Salt Lake City: University of Utah, 1986.

Matsuda, Diane, Director, California Civil Liberties Public Education Program, Sacramento, CA. Letter to Tim Fought, ed., *Herald and News (Klamath Falls, OR)*, May 15, 2003, 2. Copy in Asian American Comparative Collection, University of Idaho, Moscow.

Mikan Moblog: Everyday Japan through a Lens. "*Shimenawa* and *Gohei.*" Formerly available at http://www.kamoda.com/moblog/archives/003103.html. Copy in Asian American Comparative Collection, University of Idaho, Moscow.

Minear, Richard H. *Dr. Seuss Goes to War: The World War II Editorial Cartoons of Theodor Seuss Geisel.* New York: New Press, 1999.

Mishima, Shizuko. "Introduction to Japanese Holidays, Japanese Holidays Calendar." About.com: Japan Travel. Available at http://gojapan.about.com/cs/japaneseholidays/a/holidaycalendar.htm.

Mitsui, James Masao. *Crossing the Phantom River.* Port Townsend, WA: Graywolf, 1978.

Mochizuki, Ken. "Bainbridge Island Memorial: Let It Not Happen Again." *International Examiner (Seattle, WA)* 33, no. 7 (April 5-18, 2006): 4.

Momii, Ikken. *Hokubei Kendo Taiken* (North American Kendo Clubs). San Francisco: Hokubei Butoku Kai, 1939.

Monthly Review. "News of the Month: Kooskia Internment Camp is Abandoned by Service." 2, no. 2 (May 1945): 148. Washington, DC: Department of Justice, Immigration and Naturalization Service.

Moscow-Pullman (ID-WA) Daily News. "U.S. sends 12 Gitmo Detainees to Their Home Nations." 97, no. 304 (December 21, 2009): 7A.

Nakano, Takeo Jo. *Within the Barbed Wire Fence.* With Laetrile Nakano. Toronto, ON: University of Toronto, 1980.

Nash, Phil Tajitsu. "Amid Impeachment Brouhaha, Some Justice for JLAs." *AsianWeek (San Francisco, CA)* 20, no. 20 (January 14-20, 1999): 10.

National Archives and Records Administration (NARA). Japanese Americans during WWII: Relocation & Internment. "Check Military Records Related to the Relocation and Internment of Japanese-Americans during World War II." Available at http://www.archives.gov/research/japanese-americans/military.html.

———. Record Group 60. General Records of the Department of Justice, National

Archives at College Park, College Park, MD.

———. Record Group 65. Records of the Federal Bureau of Investigation. National Archives at College Park, College Park, MD.

———. Record Group 85. Records of the Immigration and Naturalization Service. National Archives Building, Washington, DC.

———. Record Group 389. Office of the Provost Marshal General. National Archives at College Park, College Park, MD.

National Park Service. *Japanese Americans in World War II*. National Historic Landmark Theme Study, draft. February 2005. Available at http://www.cr.nps.gov/nhl/themes/JPNAmericanTS.pdf.

———. *Japanese American Confinement Sites Preservation*. "Public Law 109-441-Dec. 21, 2006, Preservation of Japanese American Confinement Sites." Available at http://www.nps.gov/history/hps/HPG/JACS/downloads/Law.pdf.

Naturalization Act of 1790. Available at http://www.historicaldocuments.com/ImmigrationActof1790.htm.

Neitzel, D. A., and others. *Hanford Site National Environmental Policy Act (NEPA) Characterization Report*, PNNL-6415, Revision 17. Richland, WA: Pacific Northwest National Laboratory for the U.S. Department of Energy, 2005. Available at http://www.pnl.gov/main/publications/external/technical_reports/PNNL-6415Rev17.pdf.

New York Times. "Help Wanted - Male." July 21, 1944, 30.

Ng, Franklin, ed. "Japanese American Internment." In *The Asian American Encyclopedia*, 716-727. New York: Marshall Cavendish, 1995.

Niiya, Brian, ed. "Internment Camps." in *Japanese American History: An A-to-Z Reference from 1868 to the Present*, 175-176. New York: Facts on File, 1993.

———. "Inu." in *Japanese American History: An A-to-Z Reference from 1868 to the Present*, 177-178. New York: Facts on File, 1993.

Nijiya Market: Specializing in Imported and Organic Japanese Foods. "Japanese Traditions and Techniques." Formerly available at http://www.nijiya.com/www/html/welcme/JapanTechn/Japan%20Traditions.html. Copy in Asian American Comparative Collection, University of Idaho, Moscow.

Oakland (CA) Tribune. "Peruvian Sues over Redress Payment." August 26, 1998, News-3.

Othfors, Daniel. "Gripsholm (I)/Berlin 1925-1966." In Daniel Othfors and Henrik Ljungström, "The Great Ocean Liners." Available at http://www.greatoceanliners.net/gripsholm1.html.

Pacific Citizen (Los Angeles, CA). "Clinton Signs $15 Billion Bill Allocating $4.3 Million in Redress Payments for JLA [F]ormer WWII Internees." 128, no. 11 (June 4-10, 1999): 1.

———. "APAs in the News," 'JACL to be Honored with Spirit Award.' 146, no. 5 (September 7-20, 2007): 5.

Pacific Northwest National Laboratory. "Hanford Townsite, Washington." Available at http://www.pnl.gov/ecology/Gallery/Landsc/Hanfordtwn.htm.

"Paddle Tennis History." Available at http://www.paddle-tennis.com/paddle_tennis_history.htm.

Pancrazio, Angela Cara. "A World of Meaning, Internment Art Stirs Memories: Camp-made Items Tell Vivid Stories of Coping with Desolation." *Oregonian*, February 22,

1999, B1, B8.

"The Political Graveyard: Index to Politicians: Eaton to Eberhardt." Available at http://politicalgraveyard.com/bio/eaton-eberhardt.html.

Potlatch Corporation. Pres-to-log Division. Records, 1933-1989. University of Idaho Library Special Collections, Moscow, ID. Manuscript Groups 135, 139, 192, and 388.

Power, Guy, compiler. "FBI Reports on Kendo in Seattle and Portland before World War II." *Journal of Combative Sport*, November 2003. Available at http://ejmas.com/jcs/jcsart_power_1103.htm.

Recorder Herald (Salmon, ID). "Japs Can Build Road." March 4, 1942, 4.

Reynaud, Cynthia, Kimberly Hirai, and Kjersti Myhre. "An Act of Congress, a Place in History." *Lewiston (ID) Tribune*, January 1, 2007, 1A, 4A.

———. "Researcher Says Camp Story is Bigger than Just Idaho." *Lewiston (ID) Tribune*, January 1, 2007, 4A.

Robinson, Greg. *By Order of the President: FDR and the Internment of Japanese Americans*. Cambridge, MA: Harvard University, 2001.

———. *A Tragedy of Democracy: Japanese Confinement in North America*. New York: Columbia University, 2009.

Roosevelt, Franklin D. *Executive Order 9066*. Available at http://www.foitimes.com/internment/EO9066.html.

———. *Executive Order 9102*. Available at http://www.nps.gov/manz/eo9102.htm.

———. *Presidential Proclamation No. 2525, Alien Enemies - Japanese*. Available at http://www.foitimes.com/internment/Proc2525.html.

Saiki, Patsy Sumie. *Ganbare! An Example of Japanese Spirit*. Honolulu: Kisaku, 1982.

Saito, Natsu Taylor. *From Chinese Exclusion to Guantánamo Bay: Plenary Power and the Prerogative State*. Boulder: University Press of Colorado, 2007.

Scherini, Rose D. "When Italian Americans Were 'Enemy Aliens.'" In *Una Storia Segreta: The Secret History of Italian American Evacuation and Internment during World War II*, ed. Lawrence DiStasi, 10-31. Berkeley: Heyday Books, 2001.

Schofield, Lemuel B. "Instruction No. 58: Instructions Concerning the Treatment of Alien Enemy Detainees," April 28, 1942. U.S. Department of Justice, Immigration and Naturalization Service, Philadelphia, PA. Available at http://home.comcast.net/~eo9066/1942/42-04/IA119.html.

Scrapbook, see Kooskia Internment Camp Scrapbook.

Seki, Hozen. [Diary]. 1944-1948. Copy in Asian American Comparative Collection, University of Idaho, Moscow.

Shimizu, Yon. *The Exiles: An Archival History of the World War II Japanese Road Camps in British Columbia and Ontario*. Wallaceburg, ON: Shimizu Consulting and Publishing, 1993.

Shiotani, Tatsuji. "Testimony of Mr. Tajitsu [*sic*] Shiotani for the Commission on Wartime Relocation and Internment of Civilians, November 23, 1981, New York City." Copy in Asian American Comparative Collection, University of Idaho, Moscow.

Shirai, Noboru. *Tule Lake: An Issei Memoir*. Sacramento, CA: Muteki, 2001.

Simonds, Wm. [*sic*] Joe. "Anderson Ranch Dam." In *The Boise Project* (Second Draft). Bureau of Reclamation, "Dams, Projects & Powerplants." Denver: Bureau of

Reclamation History Program, Research on Historic Reclamation Projects, 1997. Available at http://www.usbr.gov/dataweb/projects/idaho/boise/history. html#Anderson.

Sims, Robert C. "The Japanese American Experience in Idaho," *Idaho Yesterdays* 22, no. 1 (Spring 1978): 2-10.

———. "The 'Free Zone' Nikkei: Japanese Americans in Idaho and Eastern Oregon in World War II." In *Nikkei in the Pacific Northwest: Japanese Americans and Japanese Canadians in the Twentieth Century*, ed. Louis Fiset and Gail M. Nomura, 236-253. Seattle: Center for the Study of the Pacific Northwest in association with University of Washington, 2005.

Small, Julie. "Crystal City Pilgrims Share Memories, Feelings, Desire for Justice." Originally published in *Hokubei Mainichi (San Francisco, CA)*, December 17, 1997, page number unknown. Reprinted in *JPOHP [Japanese Peruvian Oral History Project] Newsletter* 2 (January 1998): [7-8].

Smith, Christopher. "Park Service Asks to Cut 'Internment' from WWII Prison Camp Name." *Moscow-Pullman (ID-WA) Daily News.* 91, no. 148 (June 24-25, 2007): 7A.

Social Security Death Index. Available at http://ancestry.com/ssdi/advanced.htm.

Soga, Yasutaro. *Life Behind Barbed Wire: The World War II Internment Memoirs of a Hawai'i Issei.* Translated by Kihei Hirai and with an introduction by Tetsuden Kashima. Honolulu: University of Hawai'i, 2008. Originally published in Japanese, 1948.

Space, Ralph S. *The Clearwater Story: A History of the Clearwater National Forest.* [Missoula, MT]: U.S.D.A. Forest Service, Northern Region, 1979.

Spokesman-Review (Spokane, WA). "Misapplied Use of War Prison Labor." 61, no. 47 (June 30, 1943): 4.

Suzuki, Peter T. *Linguistic Change in a Unique Cohort: Isseis, Kibeis, and Niseis in the WWII Internment Camps.* Omaha: School of Public Administration, University of Nebraska, 2005.

Svinth, Joseph R. *Getting a Grip: Judo in the Nikkei Communities of the Pacific Northwest 1900-1950.* Guelph, ON: EJMAS [Electronic Journals of Martial Arts and Sciences], 2003.

———. "A Pre-WWII Kendo Helmet from Northern California." In *The Iaido Journal*, November 2000. Available at http://ejmas.com/tin/tinart_svinth_1100.htm.

Takaki, Ronald. *Strangers from a Different Shore: A History of Asian Americans.* New York: Penguin, 1990.

Tillitt, Malvern Hall. "Army-Navy Pay Tops Most Civilians': Unmarried Private's Income Equivalent to $3,600 Salary." *Barron's National Business and Financial Weekly*, April 24, 1944. Available at http://www.usmm.org/barrons.html.

Topaz (UT) Times/Weekly Saturday Times. "Death - Momii." 2, no. 13 (January 16, 1943): 4.

Tree Troopers' Tattler. District Headquarters, Civilian Conservation Corps, Lewiston, ID. Copies at Idaho State Historical Society Library and Archives, Boise.

Truman, Harry S. *Proclamation No. 2685, Removal of Alien Enemies,* April 10, 1946. In *The American Presidency Project*, ed. John T. Woolley and Gerhard Peters, University of California, Santa Barbara. Available at http://www.presidency.ucsb. edu/ws/index.php?pid=58814.

Urata, Guy. "Mochitsuki - A Japanese Custom." Formerly available at http://home.att. net/~guyurata/Text/Mochitsuki.html. Copy in Asian American Comparative

Collection, University of Idaho, Moscow.

U.S. Army. *Public Proclamation No. 2*. San Francisco: Headquarters Western Defense Command and Fourth Army, March 16, 1942. Copy in Japanese American National Library, San Francisco.

U.S. Citizenship and Immigration Services (USCIS). Available at uscis.gov.

U.S. Code. Section 21, Title 50. "An Act Respecting Alien Enemies." Section 1, approved July 6, 1798. United States Statutes at Large. Available from The Avalon Project at http://avalon.law.yale.edu/18th_century/alien.asp.

U.S. Department of Labor. *Dictionary of Occupational Titles. Part II. Group Arrangement of Occupational Titles and Codes*. Prepared by the Job Analysis and Information Section, Division of Standards and Research. Washington, DC: U.S. Government Printing Office, 1939.

Uyeda, Clifford. "Japanese Peruvians and the U.S. Internment Camps." *Nikkei Heritage* 5, no. 3 (Summer 1993): 4-8, 10.

Van Valkenburg, Carol Bulger. *An Alien Place: The Fort Missoula, Montana, Detention Camp 1941-1944*. Missoula, MT: Pictorial Histories, 1995.

Waiser, Bill. *Park Prisoners: The Untold Story of Western Canada's National Parks, 1915-1946*. Saskatoon, SK: Fifth House, 1995.

Wall Street Journal. "Japanese Latin Americans Seek Redress for Internment in U.S." September 22, 1998, B22.

Warnick, Kathleen, and Shirley Nilsson. *Legacy of Lace: Identifying, Collecting, and Preserving American Lace*. New York: Crown, 1988.

Waseda, Minako. "Extraordinary Circumstances, Exceptional Practices: Music in Japanese American Concentration Camps." *Journal of Asian American Studies* 8, no. 2 (June 2005): 171-209.

Wasserstrom, Donna, and Leslie Piña. *Bakelite Jewelry: Good Better Best*. Atglen, PA: Schiffer, 1997.

Watanabe, Teresa. "Déjà Vu." *Los Angeles Times Magazine* (June 8, 2003): 17-20, 46.

Watts, H[oward], and Fred Kuester. "Cultural Site Record [for] 10-IH-870." Clearwater National Forest Supervisor's Office, Orofino, ID, 1979.

Webster, Eddie. "Peep at a Camera-Shy Jap." Photograph. *Lewiston (ID) Morning Tribune*. May 29, 1943, 10.

Wegars, Priscilla. *Golden State Meets Gem State: Californians at Idaho's Kooskia Internment Camp, 1943-1945*. Moscow, ID: Kooskia Internment Camp Project, 2002.

———. "Japanese Internees and Idaho's Kooskia Internment Camp, 1943-1945." For the Idaho Humanities Council, 2000.

———. *Polly Bemis: A Chinese American Pioneer*. Cambridge, ID: Backeddy, 2003.

———. "'A Real He-Man's Job': Japanese Internees and the Kooskia Internment Camp, Idaho, 1943-1945." For the Civil Liberties Public Education Fund, 1998.

Wegars, Priscilla, ed. *Hidden Heritage: Historical Archaeology of the Overseas Chinese*. Amityville, NY: Baywood. 1993.

Weglyn, Michi. *Years of Infamy: The Untold Story of America's Concentration Camps*. New York: William Morrow, 1976.

Whitehead, Don. *The FBI Story: A Report to the People*. New York: Random House, 1956.

Wikipedia: The Free Encyclopedia. "Fourteenth Amendment to the United States Constitution." Available at http://en.wikipedia.org/wiki/

Fourteenth_Amendment_to_the_United_States_Constitution.

———. "Geneva Conventions." Available at http://en.wikipedia.org/wiki/ Geneva_Conventions.

———. "Immigration and Naturalization Service." Available at http://en.wikipedia.org/ wiki/Immigration_and_Naturalization_Service.

———. "Martin Niemöller." Available at http://en.wikipedia.org/wiki/ Martin_Niem%C3%B6ller.

———. "September 11, 2001 Attacks." Available at http://en.wikipedia.org/wiki/ September_11,_2001_attacks.

———. "War bond." Available at http://en.wikipedia.org/wiki/War_bond.

Williams, Duncan Ryūken. "Camp Dharma: Japanese-American Buddhist Identity and the Internment Experience of World War II." In *Westward Dharma: Buddhism beyond Asia*, ed. Charles S. Prebish and Martin Baumann, 191-200. Berkeley: University of California, 2002.

———. "Complex Loyalties: Issei Buddhist Ministers during the Wartime Incarceration." *Pacific World: Journal of the Institute of Buddhist Studies*, Third Series (5, 2003): 255-274.

"Work Roster-Daily Time Report." May. Canyon Creek Internment Camp [*sic*]. Clearwater National Forest Supervisor's Office, Orofino, ID, 1944.

Yakabi, Arthur Shinei. "My New Beautiful Country." Manuscript. Papers of Arthur S. Yakabi, Research Library -- Historical Museum at Ft. Missoula, MT, 1978.

Yamashita, Kanshi Stanley. "The Saga of the Japanese Americans: 1870-1942." *American Baptist Quarterly* 13, no. 1 (March 1994): 4-47.

Yoo, John. Memorandum for William J. Haynes II. January 9, 2002. Available at http://www.npr.org/documents/2005/nov/torture/tortureyoo.pdf.

Index

For names of all internees, including those not listed here, and for their pre-internment hometowns and occupations, *see* Appendix, 201-213. A number in **boldface** indicates an illustration.